W9-AUY-235

HIGH SCHOOL LIBRARY
SUNNYSIDE, WASHINGTON

CAREER OPPORTUNITIES IN LAW AND THE LEGAL INDUSTRY

Second Edition

SUSAN ECHAORE-MCDAVID

Ferguson

An imprint of Infobase Publishing

To Jennifer Ergina Ereno and Franchesca Mae Cadelina.
Strength, wisdom, love, and joy. That's what you two are all about!

Career Opportunities in Law and the Legal Industry, Second Edition

Copyright © 2007, 2002 by Susan Echaore-McDavid

All rights reserved. No part of this book may be reproduced or utilized in any form or by any means, electronic or mechanical, including photocopying, recording, or by any information storage or retrieval systems, without permission in writing from the publisher. For information contact:

Ferguson
An imprint of Infobase Publishing
132 West 31st Street
New York NY 10001

ISBN-10: 0-8160-6716-3
ISBN-13: 978-0-8160-6716-9

Library of Congress Cataloging-in-Publication Data

Echaore-McDavid, Susan.
    Career opportunities in law and the legal industry / Susan Echaore-McDavid.—2nd ed.
        p. cm.
    Includes bibliographical references and index.
    ISBN 0-8160-6716-3 (hc : alk. paper)
    1. Law—Vocational guidance—United States. 2. Lawyers—Employment—United States. 3. Practice of law—United States. I. Title.
    KF297.E245 2007
    340.023'73—dc22   2006021357

Ferguson books are available at special discounts when purchased in bulk quantities for businesses, associations, institutions, or sales promotions. Please call our Special Sales Department in New York at (212) 967-8800 or (800) 322-8755.

You can find Ferguson on the World Wide Web at http://www.fergpubco.com

Cover design by Nora Wertz/Salvatore Luongo

Printed in the United States of America

VB Hermitage 10 9 8 7 6 5 4 3 2 1

This book is printed on acid-free paper.

CONTENTS

INDUSTRY OUTLOOK

What professions come to mind when you think of the field of law? What kind of career options do you think are available in the legal industry?

Lawyers and judges: those are the two occupations—and career options—that people usually think of when it comes to law or the legal industry. Indeed, lawyers and judges are the major players, but they would not be able to perform their jobs without legal, office, and administrative assistance from paralegals, legal clerks, secretaries, document processors, administrators, technology specialists, and other professionals. All those support professionals in the law office and courtroom are part of the legal industry. You will learn about some of them in this book, as well as about lawyers and judges. In addition, you will discover that there are many other legal-related professions, some of which may surprise you. For instance, did you know that labor arbitrators, ethics officers, juvenile counselors, lobbyists, title examiners, process servers, legal reporters, law professors, and law library technicians are also part of the legal industry?

Traditionally, the legal industry covers professions in the areas of law, courts, law enforcement, and corrections and rehabilitation. However, this industry also includes a wide range of legal-related occupations that are found in other fields and industries. Many of these professions offer different litigation services to attorneys, such as trial consulting, expert witness services, or private investigation. Some professionals perform legal-related work in such areas as compliance, conflict resolution, contract administration, patent prosecution, or human resource management. Other legal-related occupations are found in the areas of politics, publishing, education, career services, and library services.

So, as you can see, a variety of occupations and career options are available in the field of law and the legal industry. In this book, you will learn about 107 of them.

What's New in the Second Edition?

Twenty new job profiles, a new appendix, "Professional Certification Programs," and a glossary have been added to the second edition of *Career Opportunities in Law and the Legal Industry*. In addition, all the original profiles have been updated with information about salaries, employment prospects, job requirements, and job duties. Furthermore, contact information and Web site addresses have been updated in the appendixes.

Your Options in the Field of Law

Anyone who is considering a career in law should know that there are many options. Attorneys usually narrow their practice of law to a few, or even one, substantive area—such as criminal law, elder law, or environmental law—depending on their interests. Attorneys also have a choice of different settings in which to work. They can work in the private sector as solo practitioners, as associates and partners in law firms, or as in-house counsel in private corporations. Opportunities are also available in the public sector, where attorneys work in government agencies, public-interest groups, and nonprofit organizations.

Alternative law careers are also available for those who do not want to become attorneys. You can combine your interest in law with your other interests and ambitions. For example, you might become a journalist who writes about the law; an educator who designs training programs for judges; a forensic psychologist who provides expert witness services; a legal administrator who runs a public-interest organization; a compliance officer who works for a health care provider; a technology specialist who provides consulting services specifically to law offices; or an administrative judge who rules on regulatory cases for a government agency such as the Environmental Protection Agency.

For many of these alternative careers, employers require that candidates possess law degrees and have some legal experience. In addition, employers may require that candidates hold a bachelor's or advanced degree in a field that is related to a particular profession. If you are interested in pursuing a career that involves law, you might consider enrolling in a joint JD (juris doctor) program as well as a graduate degree program in another field. Various law schools offer a variety of programs that award a JD as well as a master's degree in psychology, environmental science, business administration, nonprofit management, public administration, library science, or another discipline.

Growing Industries

Many of the occupations were chosen for this book because of the increasing need for qualified persons to fill positions. Since the 1990s, for example, there has been a particular demand for attorneys who specialize in such practice areas as intellectual property law, environmental law, elder law, health care, and litigation. Among the legal support positions that law offices seek to fill are qualified paralegals, legal secretaries, receptionists, and legal technology support staff.

Some of the professions described in this book have grown in recent years. For example, many legal-related occupations in the workplace, such as compliance officers, ethics officers, and contract administrators, have emerged due to the increasing number of complex employment and labor laws and regulations. Conflict resolution is another growth field because of the increasing number of disputing parties who are looking for quicker and less expensive alternatives to litigation.

The growing acceptance of technology in the law office and courtroom has also given rise to a number of new professions. These include electronic resources librarians, knowledge managers, legal technology consultants, and legal support technicians. They also include such litigation support specialists as legal videographers and demonstrative evidence specialists.

Job Outlook

The employment growth varies for the different occupations that are discussed in this book. For example, the Bureau of Labor Statistics, which is part of the U.S. Department of Labor, predicts that employment during the period 2004 to 2014 should increase from 9 to 17 percent for attorneys, judges, legal secretaries, court reporters, legal secretaries, law enforcement officers, and insurance claims adjusters and examiners. The job growth for paralegals, library technicians, postsecondary teachers, marketing managers, human resources managers, actuaries, real estate appraisers, and management analysts is anticipated to increase by 18 to 26 percent.

Computer scientists and database administrators are expected to be among the fastest growing occupations through 2014. On the other hand, the BLS reports that employment for librarians should be increasing slowly, between 0 and 8 percent; however, job opportunities should be strong because a large number of librarians are becoming eligible for retirement in these coming years.

In addition to job growth, workers in all occupations will be needed to replace those who advance to higher positions, transfer to other jobs, retire, or leave the workforce for various reasons.

Keep in mind that the job market fluctuates with the health of the nation's economy. When the economy is in a downturn, many employers lay workers off and hire fewer employees.

Salary Information

The salary information provided in this book consists of estimated figures. The figures can give you an idea of what professionals may earn. As you read about salaries, be aware that they vary from region to region. An individual's salary is also dependent on such factors as the individual's experience and education, the job responsibilities and duties for a position, and the size and type of an employer.

Salary information for many of the occupations in this book comes from the U.S. Bureau of Labor Statistics. Each year it conducts an *Occupational Employment Statistics* (OES) survey to obtain estimates of occupational employment and wages across all industries for the United States, individual states, and selected metropolitan areas. As this book was being written, the national occupational employment and wage estimates for 2005 were available. For current information, visit the OES home page at http://www.bls.gov/oes.

Explore Your Career Options

The purpose of *Career Opportunities in Law and the Legal Industry* is to provide you with a useful tool for your career exploration. As you come across professions that interest you, take the time to learn more about them. Read books that explore a profession in more depth and read professional newspapers, magazines, and journals. If possible, talk with professionals about their jobs, and, perhaps, observe them at work.

The World Wide Web is also a valuable resource for career exploration. Visit Web sites for professional associations and other organizations that are related to the occupations in which you're interested. Also go to Web sites of employers—law firms, businesses, government agencies, and so forth—to get an idea of what it may be like to work in such a setting. At many Web sites, you will find articles posted about occupations and the industry along with links that lead to other related Web sites or Web pages. Many employers and organizations also include career information and job listings on their Web sites.

In addition, take advantage of the career center at your school or library. If there is a law school near you, visit its career services department and browse through its available resources. While you're at the law school, talk with career counselors and even law instructors.

Get hands-on experience working in the fields and settings in which you're interested. If you are a high school student, find out if there is a work experience program for which you qualify. Talk about your interests with the program coordinator and see if you can be placed in a law firm, court office, social service agency, or other appropriate setting. If you are a college student, find out about available internships (or part-time jobs) in the fields and settings that interest you. If you are interested in a public interest career, learn about volunteer opportunities with nonprofit associations related to the areas (such as environmental law, legal assistance, or criminal justice social services) in which you are interested.

As you explore different career possibilities, you will discover the kind of careers you might like—and don't like. Furthermore, you will also be gaining valuable experience and building a network of contacts for future references.

Good luck—and have fun—with your career exploration!

ACKNOWLEDGMENTS

The second edition of this book could not have been completed without the help of many people. I especially want to express my gratitude to the following people for taking the time out of their busy schedules to answer my questions about their professions:

Andrew Adkins, Director, Legal Technology Institute, Levin College of Law, University of Florida; Paul L. Biderman, Director, Institute of Public Law, University of New Mexico School of Law; Ken Broda-Bahm, Ph.D., Senior Litigation Consultant; Nancy Byerly Jones, Law and Mediation Offices of Nancy Byerly Jones, PLLC; Jennifer Ergina Ereno, Esquire; Debbie Ginsberg, Electronic Resources Librarian; Douglas A. Green, Ph.D., Douglas Green Associates, Inc., Past-President American Society of Trial Consultants; Cathy Hankins, Certified PP, PLS, NALS . . . the association for legal professionals; International Legal Technology Association; Paul A. Lange, Esquire, Law Offices of Paul A. Lange; and Allen Max Luger, Esquire.

Randi Mayes, Executive Director, International Legal Technology; Sam Matlick, Director of Membership and Communications, National Association of Enrolled Agents; Michele G. Miles, Esquire, Executive Director, Institute of Business Appraisers; Barbara Jacobs Rielly; Rosemary Shiels, Esquire, Editor-in-Chief, *ALA Management Encyclopedia*, Association of Legal Administrators; Marina Sirras, President, Board of Directors, National Association of Legal Search Consultants; Sharon C. Taggart-Preiser, CAM; and Susan Zuber, CAE, Executive Vice President, National Association of Enrolled Agents.

In addition, I wish to thank Richard A. McDavid, my personal editor and husband extraordinaire, who willingly checked my manuscript before it headed over to the brilliant group at Facts On File, Inc. I especially want to thank Sarah Fogarty and Vanessa Nittoli. And, most of all, thank you, James Chambers, for being such an understanding and patient editor.

Furthermore, I wish to again express my gratitude to the following people who helped me learn about the various occupations in this book while I was writing the first edition:

Andrew Adkins; Sally Andress, RP; Ted Baker; Steve Bernheim, Litigation Specialist; Paul L. Biderman; Bill Brandt; Gina Viola Brown; Christopher W. Bruce; Mary E. Burns, PLS.

Maureen E. Conner; Dan Copfer; Alan Crowe; Peter Davis; Kevin Donahue; Marge Dover; Professor Robert J. Goldstein; Carol O'Brien English, Ph.D., ASA; Jennifer Ergina Ereno; Jaime Fatás; James R. Gripp; Bruce F. Hamm, J.D.; Andrea Healy; John Horn; Marshall Jorpeland; Joseph A. Marasco; Gayle Marquette; Amy K. McDavid, J.D.

Patricia McEvoy, Ph.D.; John L. Mellitz; Russell Gene Newman; Patricia A. Pap; Mae Pittman; Oliva Poole; Pat Prudhomme; Joyce A. Pratt; Lisa Shanholtzer Quirk; Barbara Rielly; Melissa Rosen.

Mary T. Sammon, Director; Andrew Sheldon, J.D., Ph.D., Kathy Shimpock, Esquire; Dwayne Smith; Sergeant Mark Stallo; Judith A. Stein, Esquire; Ralph Thomas; and Richard P. Zicari Jr.

HOW TO USE THIS BOOK

Career Opportunities in Law and the Legal Industry covers 107 legal and legal-related occupations that you may enter with or without law school training. You'll learn about various types of:

- attorneys in the private and public sectors
- judges
- alternative dispute resolution practitioners
- legal, office, and administrative support personnel found in legal settings
- professionals who provide litigation support to attorneys
- counselors and social workers
- legal-related professionals in compliance, education, publishing, insurance, and other fields and industries

For each of the 107 occupations, you will learn what the job is like. You will learn what basic requirements are needed to enter the profession. You will also learn what the salary, job market, and advancement prospects are like for each profession. Perhaps after reading about some, or all, of the professions in this book, you will find one that is right for you.

Sources of Information

The information presented in *Career Opportunities in Law and the Legal Industry* comes from a variety of sources. Many professionals (attorneys, law professors, legal recruiters, legal support personnel), professional associations, and other organizations were contacted for information. The research process also involved reading books, newspapers, journals, and other periodicals relating to the occupations in this book. Other sources of information included brochures, pamphlets, and other written materials from professional associations, federal agencies, businesses, and other organizations. Job descriptions, work guidelines, and other work-related materials for the different professions were also studied.

The World Wide Web was also a valuable source. A wide range of Web sites were visited to learn about the 107 professions that are described in this book. These Web sites include professional societies, trade associations, law schools, universities, government agencies, social service agencies, law firms, businesses, and online professional periodicals, among others.

How This Book Is Organized

Career Opportunities in Law and the Legal Industry is designed to be easy to use and read. The 107 jobs are divided into 15 sections. A section may have as few as three profiles to as many as 12 profiles. The profiles are usually two or three pages long. They follow the same format so that you may read the job profiles or sections in any order that you prefer.

The first two sections describe opportunities for attorneys in a variety of settings and in several practice areas. The third section discusses some judge positions, while the fourth section contains different types of alternative dispute resolution practitioners. The job profiles in sections five through nine deal with office, administrative, legal, and other professions that provide support to attorneys and courts of law. Alternative career options for individuals who may or may not hold law degrees are covered in the last six sections. These include opportunities in education, publishing, librarianship, management, compliance, and politics.

The Job Profiles

The job profiles give you basic information about 107 legal and legal-related careers. Each job profile starts with a *Career Profile,* a summary of the position's major duties, salary, job outlook, and promotion possibilities. It also sums up general requirements and special skills needed for a job, as well as any characteristics that successful professionals may share. The *Career Ladder* section is a visual presentation of a typical career path.

The rest of the occupational profile is divided into the following parts:

- The *Position Description* details a profession's major responsibilities and provides information about working conditions.
- *Salaries* presents a general idea of the wages that professionals may earn.
- *Employment Prospects* provides a general idea of the job market for an occupation.
- *Advancement Prospects* discusses possible ways that professionals may advance in their careers.
- *Education and Training* describes the type of education and training that may be required to enter a profession.
- *Special Requirements* covers any professional license, certification, or registration that may be required.
- *Experience, Skills, and Personality Traits* generally covers the job requirements needed for entry-level positions. It also describes some basic employability qualities that employers expect job candidates to have. In addition, this

section describes some personality traits that successful professionals have in common.

- *Unions and Associations* provides the names of some professional associations and other organizations that professionals are eligible to join.
- *Tips for Entry* offers general advice for gaining work experience, finding jobs, and improving employability. It also suggests ways to find more information on the World Wide Web.

Additional Resources

At the end of the book are six appendixes that provide additional resources for the occupations described in *Career Opportunities in Law and the Legal Industry*. Appendix I provides Web resources to learn about educational and training programs for some of the professions described in this book, while Appendix II gives a list of professional certification programs. In Appendix III, you can find contact information for state bar admission offices that grant licenses to attorneys, and in Appendix IV, a listing of state bar associations. Appendix V presents contact information for professional unions and associations. In Appendix VI, you can learn about resources on the World Wide Web, which can help you learn more about the various legal and legal-related professions in this book.

At the back of the book is also a glossary that contains some of the terms used in this book. In addition, there is a bibliography that provides titles of periodicals and books, which may help you learn more about the professions that interest you.

The World Wide Web

Throughout *Career Opportunities in Law and the Legal Industry,* Web site addresses for various professional organizations and other resources are provided so that you can learn more on your own. All the Web sites were accessible as the book was being written. Keep in mind that the Web site owners may change URLs, remove the Web pages to which you have been referred, or shut down their Web sites completely. Should you come across a URL that does not work, try to find the new address by entering the name of the organization or person in a search engine.

This Books Is Yours

Career Opportunities in Law and the Legal Industry is your reference book. Use it to read about jobs in which you are interested. Use it to learn about professions that you never knew existed. Use it to start your search for the career of your dreams.

Good luck!

ATTORNEYS

ATTORNEY (PRIVATE PRACTICE)

CAREER PROFILE

Duties: Provide legal advice and services to clients; prepare legal documents, conduct legal research, and perform other legal duties; perform other general duties as required

Alternate Title(s): Associate, Partner; Employment Lawyer, Appellate Lawyer, Criminal Lawyer, or other title that reflects a specific area of practice

Salary Range: $49,000 to $146,000+

Employment Prospects: Good

Advancement Prospects: Good

Prerequisites:

　Education or Training—A law (J.D.) degree; a bachelor's degree in any field

　Experience—Completion of a law clerkship is preferred by many employers

　Special Skills and Personality Traits—Research, writing, communication, interpersonal, and self-management skills; analytical, responsible, creative, persistent, flexible

　Special Requirements—States require lawyers to be admitted to their state bar; federal courts require registration to practice

CAREER LADDER

```
┌─────────────────────────────────────┐
│     Partner or Solo Practitioner     │
└─────────────────────────────────────┘

┌─────────────────────────────────────┐
│ Senior Associate or Solo Practitioner│
└─────────────────────────────────────┘

┌─────────────────────────────────────┐
│          Junior Associate            │
└─────────────────────────────────────┘

┌─────────────────────────────────────┐
│            Law Student               │
└─────────────────────────────────────┘
```

Position Description

The majority of Attorneys, or lawyers, in the United States work in private practice. That is, they offer their legal services for profit. Many of them are associates or partners in law firms, which range in size from small offices of two lawyers to large firms with 300 or more lawyers. Many other private Attorneys are solo practitioners.

Private Attorneys practice in many areas of law including criminal, appellate, real estate, family, elder, tort, bankruptcy, tax, insurance, health care, immigration, and intellectual property law, among others. These lawyers may handle personal or business legal matters for their clients who may be individuals as well as small businesses, multinational corporations, nonprofit organizations, government agencies, and other organizations. They advise clients with legal transactions, such as estate planning, insurance claims, labor contracts, and corporate mergers. They perform litigation, or trial work, for clients, in which they prepare civil lawsuits or defense criminal cases for court trials. Private Attorneys also perform various other legal services for clients such as conducting alternative dispute resolution sessions, representing clients before administrative bodies of governmental agencies, lobbying elected officials, or drafting laws, policies, or procedures.

Attorneys establish a special relationship with each client and are obligated to put each client's interest above their own. Their job involves interviewing clients to learn about their legal needs, and determining the legal issues and facts relating to their clients' legal problems. Attorneys then perform legal research to identify what laws apply to their clients' cases, and develop appropriate legal solutions. They advise clients of their legal rights and obligations, and execute legal tasks accordingly, such as setting up a trust fund, preparing a business contract, or filing a complaint in the proper trial court.

In addition to their paid work, many Attorneys sometimes perform pro bono services. That is, they provide free legal services to economically disadvantaged individuals.

Many private Attorneys specialize their practice in a number of ways. Many become specialists in one or a few areas of law. Some concentrate on providing services to a particular clientele, such as financial institutions, health care providers, artists, or the sports industry. Many Attorneys specialize by doing only litigation or transactional work.

Some solo practitioners and law firms choose to engage in general practice in which they offer a variety of transactional and litigation services in a number of practice areas. For example, a general practice firm might offer legal services in the areas of family law, estate planning, tax law, personal injury, and criminal law. The lawyers in such a firm would perform such diverse services as drafting wills, representing clients before tax collection authorities, negotiating settlements for personal injury cases, dealing with divorce cases, and handling criminal cases.

In law firms, entry-level Attorneys typically begin their careers by performing routine legal tasks, while working under the guidance and supervision of senior lawyers. As Attorneys gain experience, they are assigned to increasingly more complicated cases. They work on projects alone or in teams, and sometimes are assigned to projects in other practice areas. In many law firms, Attorneys are under pressure to fulfill a minimum of billable hours—the number of working hours for which the law firm can bill a client.

Solo practitioners have more flexible schedules than Attorneys in law firms. They can determine their own work hours, the types of cases they will take, and the size of their caseload. In addition to practicing law, solo practitioners are responsible for their own office management. They supervise legal support staff, hire and train staff, pay bills and taxes, and perform other managerial and administrative duties.

Attorneys perform a variety of legal duties every day. They conduct legal research that involves many hours working in law libraries as well as on electronic and Internet databases. They also maintain contact with their clients in person, on the phone, and through e-mail. Additionally, Attorneys review and analyze legal documents, write legal correspondence, and draft briefs, contracts, and other legal documents.

Attorneys are responsible for performing non-legal duties as well. For example, Attorneys may supervise junior associates as well as paralegals, legal secretaries, and other legal support staff. Solo practitioners as well as Attorneys in law firms are responsible for generating new business for their office.

Private Attorneys work long and irregular hours to meet deadlines, and often work more than 60 hours per week.

Salaries

Salaries for Attorneys vary, depending on such factors as their experience, job duties, employer, and geographical location. Attorneys who work in large law firms in large metropolitan areas—such as New York, San Francisco, and Chicago—usually earn the highest wages.

The U.S. Bureau of Labor Statistics (BLS) reports, in its May 2005 *Occupational Employment Statistics* (OES) survey, that the estimated annual salary for most Attorneys ranged between $49,180 and $145,600. According to the *2005 Associate Salary Survey* by NALP, the median salaries for law associates ranged from $67,500 (in firms with two to 25 lawyers) to $125,000 (in firms of more than 500 lawyers); and for eighth-year associates, from $109,000 to $181,500.

Attorneys in law firms generally receive annual bonuses in addition to their salaries.

Employment Prospects

The BLS reported in its May 2005 OES survey that about 529,190 lawyers were employed in the United States. In general, the overall employment for Attorneys is expected to increase by 9 to 17 percent through 2014.

Job competition is strong for both entry-level and experienced positions. Entry-level candidates who have graduated from the top law schools with excellent academic records typically have the best job prospects.

Law firms are generally categorized as small firms (less than 10 attorneys), medium firms, and large firms (usually more than 50 attorneys). Small firms (and solo practices) are found throughout the country, while medium and large firms are mostly located in urban areas. According to the BLS, opportunities should be strongest for lawyers who practice in the areas of intellectual property, health care, elder, environmental, energy, and antitrust law.

Advancement Prospects

In most law firms, Attorneys start as junior associates. After five to 10 years, they may become partners, which gives them a share in the profits of their law firms.

Some Attorneys move from one firm to another to pursue positions with higher pay, more prestige, or more complex responsibilities. Others seek lawyer positions in corporations, government agencies, or public-interest organizations. For many Attorneys, their top career goal is to become successful solo practitioners.

Furthermore, Attorneys can pursue other careers; for example, they can become judges, law professors, law librarians, FBI special agents, lobbyists, politicians, and corporate executives.

Education and Training

To become an Attorney, individuals must earn a juris doctor (J.D.) degree. Most state bar associations require that law students graduate from law schools accredited by the American Bar Association or by the proper state authority.

Admission requirements vary among law schools, but all schools require that applicants hold at least a bachelor's degree (in any field) as well as submit their Law School Admission Test (LSAT) scores. The competition to get into law school is strong, especially for the top schools such as Columbia University School of Law, Harvard Law School, Northwestern University School of Law, Stanford Law School, University of Chicago Law School, and Yale Law School. Law schools consider applicants' LSAT scores, undergraduate work, work experience, and other factors to determine their aptitude for the study of law.

Full-time law students usually complete their studies in three years, while part-time students take four years. The first year in law school generally focuses on such basic courses as contracts, torts, civil procedure, constitutional law, criminal law, and legal research. During the other years, students choose elective courses in different areas of law as well as gain practical lawyering experience through legal clinics, moot court competitions, and practice trials.

Most law firms provide their employees with in-house training and education programs. Many law firms have mentor programs that team new associates with senior members.

Special Requirements

To practice law in a state (or a U.S. territory or Washington, D.C.), lawyers must first gain admission to that state's bar association. Every jurisdiction has its own eligibility requirements, which usually involves passing a bar examination. For specific information, contact the state bar admission office where you wish to practice. See Appendix III for a list of offices.

Once individuals are admitted to a state bar, they receive a certificate or license to practice law in that state. Many states require Attorneys to complete continuing legal education courses to maintain their license to practice.

To practice before a federal court, Attorneys must be registered with that court. Each federal court has its own qualifications for admission.

Experience, Skills, and Personality Traits

Law firms generally prefer to hire first-year associates who have completed law clerkships in law firms, court systems, government agencies, or corporate legal departments.

To succeed in their profession, Attorneys need excellent research, writing, and communication skills. Interpersonal skills are also essential, as lawyers must work well with colleagues, clients, judges, and others. In addition, Attorneys need strong self-management skills—the ability to prioritize and organize tasks, meet deadlines, work well under stress, and so forth. Being analytical, responsible, creative, persistent, and flexible are a few personality traits that successful Attorneys share.

Unions and Associations

Most Attorneys are members of local and state bar associations. In some states, membership in the state bar association is mandatory. For a list of state bar associations, see Appendix IV.

Many Attorneys also join a national bar association such as the American Bar Association or the National Lawyers Association. In addition, many Attorneys belong to various special-interest bar associations such as the Association of Trial Lawyers of America, the American Intellectual Property Law Association, the National Asian Pacific American Bar Association, or the National Association of Women Lawyers. For contact information for these organizations, see Appendix V.

Tips for Entry

1. While in middle school and high school, you can start preparing for a career in law by developing good study habits.
2. Some Attorneys gain work experience by signing up with temporary agencies that place lawyers in short-term or temporary positions with law firms.
3. Learn as much as you can about a prospective employer and key people (such as partners) before going to a job interview. If the law firm has a Web site, be sure to check out all the links that are accessible.
4. Use the Internet to learn more about lawyers and how to become one. Some Web sites you might visit are: American Bar Association Career Counsel, http://www.abanet.org/careercounsel, and HG.org, http://www.hg.org. To learn about other links, see Appendix VI.

CORPORATE COUNSEL

CAREER PROFILE

Duties: Provide legal advice and services to corporations; may provide business advice; perform legal duties as required

Alternate Title(s): In-House Counsel, Staff Attorney; a title that reflects a position such as Deputy General Counsel

Salary Range: $68,000 to $180,000

Employment Prospects: Good

Advancement Prospects: Good

Prerequisites:

    Education or Training—A law (J.D) degree

    Experience—Corporate law experience; knowledge of and general experience in business as well as in the corporation's particular industry

    Special Skills and Personality Traits—Administrative, management, writing, communication, negotiating, interpersonal, and teamwork skills; be self-starter, analytical, collaborative, flexible

    Special Requirements—States require lawyers to be admitted to their state bar; federal courts require registration to practice

CAREER LADDER

```
┌─────────────────────────────┐
│      Managing Counsel        │
└─────────────────────────────┘

┌─────────────────────────────┐
│   Senior Corporate Counsel   │
└─────────────────────────────┘

┌─────────────────────────────┐
│      Corporate Counsel       │
└─────────────────────────────┘
```

Position Description

Many corporations—from small start-up firms to huge multinational companies—have internal legal departments to address a wide array of legal and business issues. The lawyers who staff these law departments are generally known as Corporate Counsels. In addition to corporate law, they might practice intellectual property, securities, tax, employment, real estate, and international commercial law, among others.

Unlike private lawyers, Corporate Counsels represent only one client—their employer, who is the corporation. Corporate Counsels serve the legal interests of the corporations, not the people who own the businesses nor those who run them.

Corporate Counsels typically work in a fast-paced environment. They meet with corporate board members and chief executive officers as well as with management and supervisory staff. They perform a wide range of legal duties, which vary from one employer to the next. The following are some legal duties that Corporate Counsels perform:

- review new business agreements for vendors and subcontractors
- negotiate employee contracts
- draft legal documents
- advise managers on regulatory and compliance matters
- prepare and file government reports
- conduct training workshops on compliance matters for managers and supervisors
- write employee handbooks
- review promotional materials
- identify legal issues relating to proposed products or offerings
- assist in the structuring of joint ventures with other organizations
- counsel managers and supervisors about employee disciplinary matters
- represent their clients before administrative boards and court trials

- supervise outside lawyers who are hired to provide specific legal services such as litigation

Many Corporate Counsels are also part of the management teams that provide strategy and planning advice for corporations. In providing business advice, Corporate Counsels must carefully watch that their business advice and legal advice do not mix.

Corporate Counsels may work alone or with other in-house lawyers. Small or new corporations usually have one or two lawyers on staff, while large corporations may have various lawyers, each specializing in one or more practice areas.

Corporate Counsels work a regular 40-hour work schedule. They put in additional hours as needed to complete projects.

Salary

Salaries for Corporate Counsels vary, depending on factors such as their experience, employer, and geographical location. Attorneys at the management level typically earn higher wages than nonmanagement counsels. According to the *Altman Weil Law Department Compensation Benchmarking Survey, 2005 Edition,* the average annual salary for nonmanagement lawyers were as follows: recent law graduates, $67,500; staff attorneys, $93,300; senior attorneys, $156,300; high-level specialists, $179,500.

Employment Prospects

Opportunities generally become available as Corporate Counsels transfer to other jobs, advance to higher positions, or retire. Employers will create additional positions to fit growing needs.

Since the 1990s, the demand for Corporate Counsels has continually increased partly due to the growing number of businesses that recognize the benefits of having in-house counsels. Entry-level positions are mostly found in large corporate legal departments that have the time and resources to train inexperienced lawyers.

Advancement Prospects

Corporate Counsels who are interested in administrative and management positions can advance to become supervisory attorneys, managing attorneys, deputy chiefs (second in command), and eventually to general counsels or chief legal officers. Many Corporate Counsels move from one corporation to the next in pursuit of the top positions.

Education and Training

Employers require that Corporate Counsels have a juris doctor (J.D.) degree, preferably from a law school accredited by the American Bar Association.

Throughout their careers, Corporate Counsels enroll in training programs and continuing education programs to strengthen and build their legal skills and knowledge of substantial areas.

Special Requirements

Corporate Counsels must be admitted to the state bar where they practice, and must maintain their license to practice by fulfilling any bar requirements. To represent clients in any federal court or administrative office (such as the U.S. Patents and Trademarks Offices), attorneys must first register for admission.

Experience, Skills, and Personality Traits

Requirements vary from one employer to the next. In general, employers seek candidates who have experience in corporate law as well as in the particular areas of law (such as trademark law) they will be practicing. Additionally, candidates have general experience in business as well as in the industry (such as technology) in which they will be working.

Corporate Counsels must have strong administrative and management skills. In addition they need excellent writing, communication, and negotiating skills, as well as interpersonal and teamwork skills. Being a self-starter, analytical, collaborative, and flexible are some personality traits that successful Corporate Counsels share.

Unions and Associations

Many Corporate Counsels belong to local, state, or national bar associations to take advantage of networking opportunities, professional services, and professional resources. Many legal bars, such as the American Bar Association, have corporate counsel sections. In addition, there are bar associations devoted to in-house counsels such as the Association of Corporate Counsel and the Minority Corporate Counsel Association. For contact information, see Appendix V.

Tips for Entry

1. To enhance your employability, enroll in a few business administration courses.
2. Network with legal peers as well as other professionals in your chosen industry, as many Corporate Counsels have found jobs informally through their contacts.
3. Contact the corporate law departments where you would like to work. If vacancies are not available, you might ask for an informational interview with the general counsel or other key person in the department. This type of interview gives you a chance to learn more about a company as well as to let the company know about your skills.
4. You can learn more about the Corporate Counsel profession on the Internet. One place to start is at the Association of Corporate Counsel Web site at http://www.acca.com. For more links, see Appendix VI.

PUBLIC INTEREST LAWYER

CAREER PROFILE

Duties: Provide legal counsel and services to underrepresented individuals as well as to nonprofit organizations and other public interest groups; perform legal duties as required

Alternate Title(s): Staff Attorney; a title, such as Environmental Attorney, that reflects a particular practice area

Salary Range: $34,000 to $50,000, for entry-level positions

Employment Prospects: Fair

Advancement Prospects: Fair

Prerequisites:

Education or Training—A law (J.D.) degree; on-the-job training

Experience—Previous work experience in public interest law is required or strongly preferred

Special Skills and Personality Traits—Legal research, legal writing, communication, interpersonal, and self-management skills; be enthusiastic, energetic, dedicated, compassionate, creative, flexible

Special Requirements—States require lawyers to be admitted to their state bar; federal courts require registration for lawyers to practice

CAREER LADDER

```
┌─────────────────────────────────┐
│      Senior Staff Attorney      │
└─────────────────────────────────┘

┌─────────────────────────────────┐
│         Staff Attorney          │
└─────────────────────────────────┘

┌─────────────────────────────────┐
│ Lawyer, Law Clerk, or Law Student │
└─────────────────────────────────┘
```

Position Description

Public Interest Lawyers provide legal advice and services to nonprofit organizations as well as to individuals on limited incomes. They practice in all areas of law, including environmental, civil rights, consumer protection, health, family law, and environmental law, among others.

Public Interest Lawyers are employed in a wide variety of settings. Many work for public-interest law centers which advocate for legal reforms on behalf of the general public. These organizations work on social issues such as human rights, civil rights, women's issues, education, voting rights, and the environment. Public Interest Lawyers review proposed laws in legislation and advise organizations on how the laws may affect their particular cause. They also draft legislation, as well as lobby legislators. In addition, these attorneys handle litigation. They take on civil action suits that affect the legal rights of a large group of people.

Some Public Interest Lawyers work for citizen action groups, special-interest organizations, lobbying groups, or other nonprofit organizations that advocate specific social concerns. These lawyers work as part of a team of scientists, policy analysts, and others to promote the particular goals of their organizations. The attorneys perform a variety of legal activities that include litigating, lobbying legislators, and organizing.

Many Public Interest Lawyers provide direct legal services to people. They mostly work for legal assistance programs that offer legal counsel and representation to those who cannot afford private counsel. These attorneys mostly handle civil cases, practicing in such areas as social security and disability benefits, health care issues, domestic relations, employment law, landlord-tenant relations, and consumer protection rights. Attorneys who work for legal aid programs sometimes handle criminal cases as well.

Some Public Interest Lawyers work in private or non-profit law firms. Many of these lawyers do law reform litigation for nonprofit organizations. They might also provide low-fee legal services to people on limited incomes.

Salaries

Public Interest Lawyers typically earn lower wages than attorneys who work in private, corporate, and governmental settings. Their salaries vary, depending on such factors as their experience, job duties, employer, and geographical location. Salaries for entry-level attorneys generally range from $20,000 to $50,000 per year. Lawyers working in public-interest law firms usually earn more than those working in nonprofit organizations.

Employment Prospects

Opportunities for Public Interest Lawyers are available throughout the United States in urban, suburban, and rural settings. However, job openings usually become available when attorneys transfer to other positions or retire.

In nonprofit organizations, the hiring of new attorneys and the capacity to maintain staff levels is subject to the organizations' ability to raise sufficient funds through grants and other development activities.

Advancement Prospects

Public Interest Attorneys generally measure success by winning cases for their clients and effecting social changes. For those who desire administrative or management responsibilities, opportunities are available but limited. The top goal for some lawyers is to start their own public interest law firm.

Other career paths lead to becoming lobbyists, elected officials, and executive directors of public interest organizations.

Education and Training

Public Interest Lawyers earn a juris doctor (J.D.) degree, usually from a law school accredited by the American Bar Association.

Many law schools offer clinics in which students can gain public-interest work experience. Students receive assignments to work with legal services offices, public defender's offices, and other public interest groups.

Special Requirements

To practice law in a state (or in Washington, D.C., or a U.S. territory), attorneys must first gain admission to that state's bar. For specific eligibility requirements, contact the state bar admission office where you wish to practice. See Appendix III for a list of offices.

To practice before any federal court, Public Interest Lawyers must first apply for admission.

Experience, Skills, and Personality Traits

Employers look for candidates who are dedicated to their causes, which are demonstrated through their volunteer work. Because of their limited budgets, employers hire lawyers who do not need extensive training. Candidates may have gained their lawyering experience through law clerkships, summer internships, law school clinics, and volunteer work.

Public Interest Lawyers need excellent legal research and legal writing skills. Having strong communication and interpersonal skills is also important, as they must be able to work with many people from various backgrounds. In addition, they need strong self-management skills—such as the ability to work independently, prioritize and organize tasks, solve problems, and work well under stress. Being enthusiastic, energetic, dedicated, compassionate, creative, and flexible are a few personality traits that successful Public Interest Lawyers share.

Unions and Associations

Public Interest Lawyers join various bar associations to take advantage of professional services and resources as well as networking opportunities. Most are members of local and state bar associations. In some states, membership in the state bar is mandatory.

Many also belong to the American Bar Association, the National Lawyers Guild, or another national bar association. In addition, many of them join special-interest associations such as the National Legal Aid and Defender Association, the American Immigration Lawyers Association, or the National Employment Lawyers Association. For contact information, see Appendix V.

Tips for Entry

1. While in high school or college, find out if a public interest career is right for you. Volunteer your services at a nonprofit organization, community group, or other public interest group that interests you.
2. Participate in conferences sponsored by public interest organizations that interest you. Meet lawyers, directors, organizers, and others to begin building a network of contacts whom you can call when you are ready to do your job search.
3. Many public interest employers do not have the budget to advertise widely for job openings. Thus, take the initiative and contact employers for whom you would like to work.
4. Check out your law school's career center. Many public interest groups and legal services agencies send job vacancy information to these offices. Most, if not all law school career centers serve alumni as well as students.
5. Learn more about public interest law on the Internet. You might start by visiting the Equal Justice Works Web site at http://www.equaljusticeworks.org. For more links, see Appendix VI.

GOVERNMENT LAWYER

<table>
<tr><td>

CAREER PROFILE

</td><td>

CAREER LADDER

</td></tr>
<tr><td>

Duties: Provide legal services and advice to government agencies; perform duties as required

Alternate Title(s): A title that reflects a certain occupation, such as U.S. Attorney, Staff Attorney, City Attorney

Salary Range: $49,000 to $146,000

Employment Prospects: Good

Advancement Prospects: Good

Prerequisites:

  Education or Training—A law (J.D.) degree; a specific undergraduate or graduate degree may be required

  Experience—One or more years practicing law

  Special Skills and Personality Traits—Legal research, writing, analytical, organizational, communication, interpersonal, and teamwork skills; be intelligent, responsible, creative, dedicated, flexible

  Special Requirements—States require lawyers to be admitted to their state bar; federal courts registration for lawyers to practice

</td><td>

```
┌─────────────────────────────────┐
│  Senior or Supervising Attorney │
└─────────────────────────────────┘

┌─────────────────────────────────┐
│           Attorney              │
└─────────────────────────────────┘

┌─────────────────────────────────┐
│      Attorney (Entry-level)     │
└─────────────────────────────────┘
```

</td></tr>
</table>

Position Description

In the United States, thousands of attorneys practice law as government employees. These lawyers serve only one client—their employer—that may be the federal government or a state or local government. As public-service employees, Government Lawyers are charged with providing legal counsel and advocacy in the public interest.

Government Lawyers practice in all areas of law, including criminal, immigration, tax, intellectual property, consumer protection, environmental, labor, military, Indian, and worker's compensation law, among others. They perform a number of legal tasks. For example, they may be involved in counseling government officials or employees about legal matters; developing governmental policies and procedures; drafting laws, regulations, or ordinances; or preparing for civil or criminal trials.

Government Lawyers serve in the executive, legislative, and judicial branches of government. Staff attorneys are employed in the wide range of government agencies—such as planning, tax, social services, transportation, and environmental departments—that are responsible for executing and enforcing governmental laws, regulations, and codes. Many attorneys specifically provide legal assistance to city councils, state officials, Congress members, or other executive and legislative leaders.

In the state and federal court systems, Government Lawyers work as staff attorneys and law clerks to provide legal support and advice to judges and court staff. Many Government Lawyers are hired as trial attorneys at the local, state, and federal levels. They might defend their employers in civil lawsuits or act as prosecutors in criminal cases. Some trial attorneys work as public defenders, who serve as criminal lawyers for impoverished defendants.

Like all attorneys, Government Lawyers perform the same general legal tasks. They review legal documents; conduct legal research; draft legal correspondence, documents, and other materials; and so on. They also perform various other duties that are specific to their positions.

Government Lawyers have a 40-hour work schedule; but many put in additional hours at night and on weekends to complete their assignments.

Salaries

Salaries for Government Lawyers vary, depending on such factors as their experience, position, employer, and geographical location. According to the May 2005 *Occupational Employment Statistics* (OES) survey, by the U.S. Bureau of Labor Statistics (BLS), the estimated annual salary for most lawyers ranged between $49,180 and $145,600. The estimated annual mean wage for local Government Lawyers was $80,840; for state lawyers, $73,970; and for federal lawyers, $112,210.

Employment Prospects

The BLS reports in its May 2005 OES survey that an estimated 105,810 Government Lawyers were employed in the United States. About 46 percent worked at the local government level.

The largest employer of Government Lawyers is the U.S. Department of Justice. Other large federal employers are the military and the U.S. Department of Treasury. At the state level, Attorney Generals' offices are typically the largest state government employers of attorneys. At the local level, most lawyer positions are found with the offices of the city attorney, district attorney, county counsel, and public defender.

In general, job opportunities for any government agency depend on staffing needs, turnover rates, and the agency's budget. Most opportunities become available as attorneys retire, resign, or transfer to other positions. New positions may be created when funding is available.

Advancement Prospects

Government Lawyers can advance to supervisory and administrative positions, based on their experience, abilities, and job availability. Government Lawyers who seek leadership positions are usually appointed for limited terms by executive or legislative officials. In some state and local governments, they are elected for limited terms by voters.

Many former Government Lawyers have used their positions as stepping stones to careers as private lawyers, in-house counsel, and public interest lawyers.

Education and Training

Government Lawyers have juris doctor (J.D.) degrees. (Most employers prefer graduates from law schools accredited by the American Bar Association.) Government agencies that serve particular interests may require or strongly prefer candidates with specific undergraduate or graduate degrees. For example, an environmental regulatory agency usually prefers lawyers with science or engineering training.

Government agencies usually provide initial and ongoing training programs for their attorneys. In addition, Government Lawyers enroll in outside training and continuing education programs throughout their careers to develop and improve their legal skills and knowledge.

Special Requirements

Government Lawyers are required to be licensed attorneys. In addition, they must apply for admission to practice before a federal court.

Experience, Skills, and Personality Traits

Qualifications vary and depend on the position that is being offered. Many positions, including entry-level ones, require one or more years of experience practicing law.

Like all attorneys, Government Lawyers need excellent legal research, writing, and analytical skills, as well as strong organizational and communication skills. Having effective interpersonal and teamwork skills is also important. Being intelligent, responsible, creative, dedicated, and flexible are a few personality traits that successful Government Lawyers share. Furthermore, they have a deep commitment to serve the best interests of the public welfare.

Unions and Associations

Government Lawyers join professional bar associations to take advantage of networking opportunities, training programs, and other professional services and resources. Most Government Lawyers are members of local and state bar associations. (In some states, membership in the state bar association is mandatory.) Many Attorneys belong to a national trade association such as the American Bar Association. In addition, many join special-interest organizations such as the National Association of Women Lawyers, the Federal Bar Association, the International Municipal Lawyers Association, or the National District Attorneys Association. For contact information, see Appendix V.

Tips for Entry

1. You can gain experience working in the government as a law student or undergraduate. Many agencies offer internship and student work experience programs.
2. The U.S. Office of Personnel Management (OPM) posts jobs listings for all federal agencies. For information, visit its jobs Web site, USAJOBS, at http://www.usajobs.opm.gov.
3. Contact each government agency, division, and bureau where you wish to work. Ask for information about job vacancies and hiring procedures.
4. Use the Internet to learn more about a particular government agency or a state or local government. To find relevant Web sites, enter the name of the agency (example: *U.S. Department of Justice* or the type of government (example: *New York government, or Chicago government*) in a search engine.

PROSECUTOR

CAREER PROFILE

Duties: Conduct criminal proceedings on behalf of the government; enforce laws; may handle civil litigation

Alternate Title(s): Prosecuting Attorney; a title that reflects a specific job such as District Attorney, County Prosecutor, or Assistant U.S. Attorney

Salary Range: $46,000 to $119,000, for federal prosecutors

Employment Prospects: Good

Advancement Prospects: Good

Prerequisites:

Education or Training—A law (J.D.) degree

Experience—One or more years of experience as a practicing lawyer; previous litigation experience preferred

Special Skills and Personality Traits—Research, writing, communication, interpersonal, self-management skills; be enthusiastic, intelligent, responsible, creative, persistent, flexible

Special Requirements—States require lawyers to be admitted to their state bar; federal courts require registration for lawyers to practice

CAREER LADDER

```
┌─────────────────────────────────────┐
│   Senior or Supervisory Prosecutor   │
└─────────────────────────────────────┘

┌─────────────────────────────────────┐
│             Prosecutor               │
└─────────────────────────────────────┘

┌─────────────────────────────────────┐
│  Law Student, Law Clerk, or Attorney │
└─────────────────────────────────────┘
```

Position Description

Prosecutors are government lawyers who take legal action against individuals or groups on behalf of governmental bodies. They engage in both criminal and civil litigation. Some also handle appeals cases in appellate courts. In the United States, Prosecutors are employed at the local, state, and federal levels of government.

Most Prosecutors are involved in enforcing criminal laws. They are responsible for proving that criminal defendants, whether charged with felony or misdemeanor offenses, are guilty of committing crimes. Their job includes issuing criminal charges against suspects. In some jurisdictions, criminal Prosecutors present the information to grand juries, which decide whether there is sufficient proof to charge suspects.

Some Prosecutors are assigned to the civil unit in prosecuting offices. These lawyers are responsible for defending governmental bodies, whether as plaintiffs or defendants, in civil law suits. Their cases involve a wide range of disputes, including environmental, employment, property, tax, contracts, and personal injury matters, among others. Civil Prosecutors may also be assigned to provide general legal advice to governmental officials or agencies. They perform such duties as reviewing legal documents for officials or helping officials draft proposed laws or ordinances.

The job of Prosecutors is complex and demanding. They carry a heavy caseload, and must make sure that the legal process is followed for every case. They might work on a case alone or with other Prosecutors.

Prosecutors perform various tasks while preparing for criminal or civil litigation. For example, they gather information about the facts and issues by reviewing legal documents and records related to their cases and by conducting legal research. They collect physical evidence and interview witnesses and others that may support their cases. They prepare pretrial motions and briefs, meet necessary court deadlines, and attend required pretrial hearings and conferences. Prosecutors also develop strategies to build up the best case against the other party, as well as ready all legal documents and demonstrative evidence for the trials.

Either judges or juries may hear criminal or civil cases. All judges have their own specific set of procedures that attorneys are expected to follow. The trial process is generally the same for both civil and criminal trials. In a jury trial, attorneys of both parties participate in selecting the jurors as well as make suggestion for jury instructions.

The trial starts with opening statements by the Prosecutor and the defense attorney, in which each side describes what each expects to prove in the trial. Both sides present their case through direct examination of their witnesses and introduction of physical evidence. Each side may cross-examine the other side's witnesses, as well as make appropriate objections to testimony, evidence, and other matters. After presenting their sides, the Prosecutor and the defense attorney make their closing statements.

Generally most cases do not reach the trial stage. Civil Prosecutors are often able to negotiate settlements with the other parties. Plea bargains are usually made between criminal Prosecutors and the defense lawyers. Prosecutors offer to issue a lesser charge, if a defendant agrees to plead guilty to that charge. The defendant then receives a lesser form of punishment, such as a shorter jail or prison sentence.

Federal prosecution is done by the assistant U.S. attorneys of the U.S. Attorneys' Office (USAO), a division of the U.S. Department of Justice. These prosecuting attorneys handle both civil and criminal litigation for the federal government. Criminal Prosecutors handle cases that involve violations of the U.S. Criminal Code, such as bank robberies, counterfeiting, civil rights violations, interstate child support cases, immigration violations, and certain violent crimes.

Prosecutors at the state government level are known as assistant state attorneys. These Prosecutors are employed by their state Attorney General's office. At the county level, Prosecutors are part of the District Attorney (or County Prosecuting Attorney) offices. These offices prosecute defendants who have committed state offenses within their jurisdiction; they also provide legal counsel and representation to county officers and departments. County Prosecutors are known as assistant district attorneys (or assistant prosecuting attorneys).

Many city governments employ Prosecutors, also known as assistant city attorneys. These government lawyers handle civil matters as well as criminal misdemeanors and violations against city ordinances.

Chief prosecutors are either appointed by an executive body or elected by the people. For example, U.S. attorneys, the heads of district USAO offices, are appointed by the president of the United States; district attorneys, county officials, are usually elected by the voters in their counties. The heads usually receive a limited term appointment, which may be renewed through reappointment or re-election.

Staff prosecuting attorneys in all government offices are selected through regular hiring processes. Their jobs are not affected when new head Prosecutors are appointed or elected to office.

Prosecutors often put in more than 40 hours a week to perform their various duties. Some Prosecutors are hired on a part-time basis or to temporary positions.

Salaries

Salaries for Prosecutors vary, depending on such factors as their experience, job duties, employer, and geographical location. According to the *2006 Public Sector and Public Interest Attorney Salary Report* by NALP, the median salaries for local prosecuting attorneys ranged from $43,915 (for entry-level lawyers) to $72,970 (for lawyers with 11 to 15 years experience). For state prosecuting attorneys, the median salaries ranged from $46,374 (for entry-level lawyers) to $67,712 (for lawyers with 11 to 15 years experience).

U.S. assistant attorneys earn salaries based on the Administratively Determined pay scale. Information about this pay scale is unavailable, but it is about equivalent to the General Schedule (GS) scale, another federal pay schedule. Prosecuting attorneys earn salaries similar to the GS-11 to GS-15 levels. In 2006, the basic pay for these levels ranged from $46,189 to $118,957. Federal employees also receive locality pay that is based on the geographical location where they work. Those living in areas with higher living costs typically earn higher wages.

Employment Prospects

Most job openings become available as Prosecutors retire, resign, or transfer to other positions. An agency may create new positions when funding is available. More opportunities are available at the local level, where the turnover rate is higher.

Employers usually require candidates to be U.S. citizens. Candidates must also submit to a selection process that may include written exams, oral interviews, drug testing, background checks, and polygraph examinations.

Advancement Prospects

Prosecutors can advance to supervisory and administrative positions, depending on the size and needs of the office.

Many Prosecutors seek advancement in terms of being assigned more complex cases, earning higher pay, and receiving recognition from peers and the public. This may involve obtaining positions in other government offices.

Prosecutors can also pursue careers in private law firms, corporate law departments, or with other government agencies. In addition, they can pursue other legal-related career paths by becoming judges, law librarians, FBI special agents, and politicians.

Education and Training

Employers require that Prosecutors have a juris doctor (J.D.) degree from a law school accredited by the American Bar Association.

All new Prosecutors receive orientation training as well as learn on the job. Employers provide in-house or other training programs.

Special Requirements

To practice law in a state (or U.S. territory or Washington, D.C.), lawyers must first gain admission to that state's bar. For specific eligibility information, contact the bar admission office for the jurisdiction where you wish to practice. See Appendix III for a list of offices.

To practice in federal courts, attorneys must apply for admission. Each court has its own set of requirements.

Experience, Skills, and Personality Traits

Requirements vary with the different employers. In general, most employers prefer to hire candidates who have one or more years of experience after graduation from law school. They also look for candidates with previous litigation experience. In addition, they show an interest in public service.

To succeed in their profession, Prosecutors need excellent research, writing, and communication skills. Interpersonal skills are also essential, as lawyers must work well with colleagues, clients, judges, and others. In addition, they need strong self-management skills—such as the ability to prioritize and organize tasks, and work well under stress. Being enthusiastic, intelligent, responsible, creative, persistent, and flexible are a few personality traits that successful Prosecutors share.

Unions and Associations

Prosecutors belong to various bar associations to take advantage of networking opportunities and other professional services and resources. In some states, attorneys are required to be members of the state bar association. Many Prosecutors join national bar associations such as the American Bar Association. They also join special-interest groups such as the Federal Bar Association, the National District Attorneys Association, the National Criminal Justice Association, or the American Association fo Justice. For contact information for these organizations, see Appendix V.

Tips for Entry

1. To begin exploring a career as a Prosecutor, contact the city or county Prosecutor's office in your area. Some offices sponsor education programs for high school and middle school students.
2. Gain experience by interning or volunteering in a Prosecutor's office. Contact local, state, and federal Prosecutor offices for internship possibilities and how to apply.
3. To learn more about the U.S. Attorneys' Office, visit its Web site at http://www.usdoj.gov/usao. For information about employment, go to the U.S. Department of Justice's Office of Attorney Recruitment and Management Web site at http://www.usdoj.gov/oarm.
4. Many local and state Prosecutor offices have Web pages on the Internet. To find some Web pages, use such keywords as *prosecuting attorney, city prosecutor, county prosecutor, district attorney,* or *state attorney general.*

PUBLIC DEFENDER

CAREER PROFILE

Duties: Provide legal counsel and representation for indigent defendants; prepare for court trials; perform legal tasks as required

Alternate Title(s): A title that reflects a specific job such as Federal Defender or Juvenile Defender

Salary Range: $43,000 to $66,000

Employment Prospects: Good

Advancement Prospects: Poor

Prerequisites:

Education or Training—A law (J.D.) degree

Experience—One or more years as a practicing lawyer; criminal trial experience preferred

Special Skills and Personality Traits—Legal writing, advocacy, communication, presentation, and self-management skills; be optimistic, determined, aggressive, independent, creative, sympathetic

Special Requirements—States require lawyers to be admitted to their state bar; federal courts require registration for lawyers to practice

CAREER LADDER

```
┌─────────────────────────────┐
│  Supervising or Managing     │
│  Public Defender             │
└─────────────────────────────┘

┌─────────────────────────────┐
│  Assistant Public Defender   │
└─────────────────────────────┘

┌─────────────────────────────┐
│  Law Student or Lawyer       │
└─────────────────────────────┘
```

Position Description

Public Defenders are criminal lawyers employed by the government to represent indigent (or poor) defendants. In the United States, persons who are accused of committing a crime that is punishable by prison or jail have the constitutional right to be defended by a lawyer. If they cannot afford to hire a private lawyer, the judge may appoint a lawyer—a Public Defender—to represent them.

Public Defenders carry heavy caseloads that include clients charged with misdemeanor and felony crimes. They may be appointed to serve adult or juvenile offenders. In some jurisdictions, Public Defenders are also assigned to represent the mentally ill and the developmentally disabled in civil commitment proceedings. For example, a Public Defender might represent a developmentally disabled woman who was involuntarily placed in a residential facility and wishes to be released.

Like private criminal lawyers, Public Defenders are obligated to provide each of their clients with the best legal defense that they can. They also ensure that their clients' constitutional rights are not being compromised.

Throughout their workdays, they handle various cases that are at different stages of the criminal process. For example, Public Defenders:

- assess newly assigned cases
- attend arraignments and hearings
- negotiate plea bargains with the prosecuting attorneys
- prepare for trials, which includes tasks such as interviewing clients and witnesses, visiting crime scenes, preparing exhibits, developing defense strategies, and so on
- perform legal research
- participate in the selection of jury members for trials
- try court cases

In large offices, Public Defenders may be assigned to handle different stages of the criminal procedure for all cases. For example, new Public Defenders may be responsible for arraignment hearings or assessing cases, while experienced appellate lawyers handle appeals cases.

Public defender programs are established at local, state, and federal levels. In large metropolitan areas, the public defender office may be part of the city or county government. In rural areas and small counties, solo practitioners or private law firms are contracted to provide public defender services.

The head of public defender programs is actually called the Public Defender. They oversee the day-to-day administration and management of their programs. They also educate the public about the role of the Public Defender. Depending on their staffing needs, they may or may not represent indigents. Chief Public Defenders are either appointed or elected into office. They serve a limited term upon which they may be reappointed or reelected.

Serving under the chief Public Defender are the staff attorneys, often known as assistant Public Defenders or deputy Public Defenders. Their positions are rarely in jeopardy when new Public Defenders are appointed or elected.

Salaries

Salaries for Public Defenders vary, depending on their education, geographical location, and other factors. According to the *2006 Public Sector and Public Interest Attorney Salary Report* by NALP, the median salaries for Public Defenders ranged from $43,300 (for entry-level lawyers) to $65,500 (for lawyers with 11 to 15 years experience).

Employment Prospects

Most opportunities become available as Public Defenders resign, transfer to other positions, or retire. Employers create additional positions to meet growing needs as long as funding is available.

Advancement Prospects

Public Defenders can advance to a limited number of supervisory and administrative positions. Those in top positions typically spend less time in litigation. Many career Public Defenders pursue advancement by seeking more complex assignments, earning higher wages, and receiving professional recognition.

The Public Defender position has been the starting point of many lawyers' careers. After working in a Public Defender's office for a few years, many lawyers seek employment with law firms, corporate legal departments, or other government agencies. Some start practices in criminal law as solo practitioners or as heads of small law firms.

Education and Training

Employers require that Public Defenders have a juris doctor (J.D.) degree, preferably from a law school accredited by the American Bar Association. New Public Defenders receive initial training on the job. Many employers also have ongoing training programs.

Special Requirements

To practice law in a state (or U.S. territory or Washington, D.C.), lawyers must first gain admission to that state's bar. For specific eligibility information, contact the bar admission office for the jurisdiction where you wish to practice. See Appendix III for a list of offices.

To practice in federal courts, attorneys must apply for admission. Each court has its own set of requirements.

Experience, Skills, and Personality Traits

Many employers require or strongly prefer candidates with one or more years of experience in the practice of law. They particularly look for lawyers with criminal trial experience. In addition, good candidates demonstrate a commitment to public service.

Public Defenders have excellent legal writing and advocacy skills, as well as superior communication and presentation skills. In addition, they have strong self-management skills—the ability to manage heavy caseloads, prioritize and organize tasks, work well under stress, and so forth.

Being optimistic, determined, aggressive, independent, creative, and sympathetic are a few personality traits that successful Public Defenders share. Furthermore, they are dedicated to the concept of the right to counsel for all people.

Unions and Associations

Public Defenders are typically members of their local and state bar associations as well as national bars such as the American Bar Association. Many belong to bar associations that specifically serve the interests of criminal defense lawyers or Public Defenders, such as the National Association of Criminal Defense Lawyers, the National Legal Aid and Defender Association, or the Association of Federal Defense Attorneys. (For contact information, see Appendix V.) By joining professional associations, Public Defenders take advantage of professional services, professional resources, and networking opportunities.

Tips for Entry

1. To gain experience as an undergraduate or a law student, obtain internship or volunteer positions in a Public Defender office.
2. Attend conferences and meetings for Public Defenders and network with participants.
3. Contact Public Defender offices directly for information about vacancies and hiring procedures.
4. Use the Internet to learn more about a Public Defender career. To get a list of relevant Web sites, enter the keywords *public defender or federal defender* in any search engine. For some links, see Appendix VI.

JUDICIAL LAW CLERK

CAREER PROFILE

Duties: Provide legal support to a judge; conduct legal research; provide legal analysis; draft opinions and other legal documents; perform other duties as required

Alternate Title(s): None

Salary Range: $38,000 to $101,000, for federal clerks

Employment Prospects: Good

Advancement Prospects: Poor

Prerequisites:

Education or Training—A law (J.D.) degree; on-the-job training

Experience—May require one year of legal experience; for career law clerks, experience as law clerks or practicing attorneys may be required

Special Skills and Personality Traits—Legal research, legal writing, computer, communication, analytical, interpersonal, and teamwork skills; be mature, detail-oriented, discreet, impartial, honest, flexible

Special Requirements—Be admitted to a state bar association

CAREER LADDER

```
┌─────────────────────────────────────┐
│   Attorney (in any work setting)     │
│   or Other Law-Related Profession    │
└─────────────────────────────────────┘

┌─────────────────────────────────────┐
│         Judicial Law Clerk           │
└─────────────────────────────────────┘

┌─────────────────────────────────────┐
│            Law Student               │
└─────────────────────────────────────┘
```

Position Description

Judicial Law Clerks provide legal support services to judges in local, state, and federal courts. They work closely with judges in trial, appellate, and special courts (such as family courts) as well as in governmental administrative offices. Most clerks are recent law school graduates who have been personally selected to a one- to two-year term appointment by the judges they serve. Under the judges' supervision and guidance, these law clerks perform a broad range of duties.

One major duty is conducting independent legal research. When judges require additional information to help them rule on a case, they assign Judicial Law Clerks to research the issues. These clerks conduct their search for relevant laws, court decisions, briefs, and opinions in law libraries as well as on computer and Internet databases.

Judicial Law Clerks are also responsible for providing judges with legal analysis. For example, clerks prepare bench memorandums to help judges decide on the proper disposition of cases. A bench memorandum sums up each party's position in a case and the issues. Additionally, it offers recommendations about how to handle the case.

Judicial Law Clerks are also involved with drafting opinions, orders, and other legal documents. Judges review and edit these first drafts into their final documents. The Law Clerks follow specific guidelines and formats for composing the various documents. They make sure that they use formal and precise language and that all citations are correct.

Judicial Law Clerks perform other duties which vary from court to court. For example, they might:

- review drafts of judges' works for errors of fact and law
- proofread legal documents and correct grammar, spelling, punctuation, and typographical errors
- maintain law libraries
- review professional journals and recent opinions to keep themselves and judges up to date on current legal issues
- serve as the judge's contact person for attorneys
- perform clerical and administrative tasks

Judicial Law Clerks are expected to work on different legal issues, handle various legal tasks simultaneously, and meet deadlines. Their job requires them to work closely with court attorneys and other staff members.

Law Clerks may be assigned to individual judges or work for several judges. Sometimes Judicial Law Clerks are hired to temporary appointments for one year or less for emergency reasons. Some federal appointments are for career positions of four years or longer.

Salaries

Salaries for Judicial Law Clerks vary, depending on factors such as their employer, experience, and geographical location. Federal courts typically pay higher salaries than state and municipal courts.

Judicial Law Clerks in the federal court system earn salaries based on the Judicial Salary Plan. Information about this pay scale is unavailable, but it is roughly equivalent to the General Schedule (GS) scale, another federal pay schedule. Depending on their qualifications, new appointees earn salaries similar to the GS-9 to GS-14 levels. In 2006, the basic pay for these levels ranged from $38,175 to $101,130. Federal employees also receive locality pay that is based on the geographical location where they work. Those living in areas with higher levels of income typically earn higher wages.

Employment Prospects

Judicial Law Clerks are employed by state and federal courts as well as by administrative hearing offices in government agencies. Opportunities are available yearly to replace Law Clerks whose terms are ending. However, the competition for judicial clerkships is keen.

Judicial clerkships are typically temporary positions. On occasion, judges hire Law Clerks on a permanent basis.

Advancement Prospects

In general, Judicial Law Clerks use their experience as the beginning step leading to their attorney careers. Their next step may be in positions as law firm associates, solo practitioners, government lawyers, prosecutors, public defenders, corporate lawyers, or public interest attorneys. Judicial Law Clerks can also pursue other legal-related careers such as becoming legal researchers, legal reporters, or law professors.

Education and Training

Applicants for law clerkships must possess a juris doctor (J.D.) degree. Judges usually hire candidates who have recently graduated from a law school that is accredited by the American Bar Association or by the proper state authority.

Judicial Law Clerks receive on-the-job training.

Special Requirements

Judges may require that Judicial Law Clerks hold membership in a state bar association.

Every state (as well as U.S. territory and the District of Columbia) requires that lawyers must gain admission to the state bar in order to practice law in that state. For eligibility information, contact the state bar admission office where you wish to practice. See Appendix III for a list of offices.

Experience, Skills, and Personality Traits

Qualifications vary with the different judges. Generally, candidates must be knowledgeable about legal principles, statutory and case law, court rules, and court procedures. Some judges prefer to hire candidates who have at least one year of legal experience. For career clerk positions, some judges hire only experienced law clerks or practicing attorneys.

Judicial Law Clerks need excellent legal research skills, including the use of Internet databases. They also must have superior writing and analytical skills. In addition they need strong communication, interpersonal, and teamwork skills. Being mature, detail-oriented, discreet, impartial, honest, and flexible are some personality traits that successful Judicial Law Clerks share.

Unions and Associations

Judicial Law Clerks join local, state, and national legal associations to take advantage of networking opportunities and other professional services and resources. In many states, membership in the state bar association is mandatory. Some special-interest bar associations that Judicial Law Clerks might join include the American Bar Association, the National Lawyers Association, the Federal Bar Association, or the National Bar Association. For contact information, see Appendix V.

Tips for Entry

1. Many judges prefer candidates who have moot court experience, worked on their school's law review, or have published legal articles.
2. Contact the judges for whom you would like to work to learn about their specific requirements and application process.
3. Start your research into judicial clerkships in your first year of law school. Some judges offer clerkships to second-year law students. The clerkships would begin after graduation.
4. Learn more about judicial clerkships on the Internet. You might start by visiting these Web sites: Judicial Clerkships, http://www.judicialclerkships.com, and The Federal Law Clerk Information System, http://lawclerks.ao.uscourts.gov. For more links, see Appendix VI.

STAFF ATTORNEY, COURT

CAREER PROFILE

Duties: Provide legal advice and analysis to whole courts or panels of judges; conduct legal research, prepare legal documents, and perform other legal tasks as required

Alternate Title(s): Court Counsel; a title that reflects a particular job such as Court Research Lawyer or Trial Court Staff Attorney

Salary Range: $49,000 to $146,000+

Employment Prospects: Fair

Advancement Prospects: Poor

Prerequisites:

Education or Training—A law (J.D.) degree

Experience—One or more years of previous lawyering experience

Special Skills and Personality Traits—Analytical, research, writing, computer, interpersonal, and communication skills; be detail-oriented, collegial, flexible, respectful, and trustworthy

Special Requirements—States require lawyers to be admitted to their state bar; federal courts require registration for lawyers to practice

CAREER LADDER

```
┌─────────────────────────────┐
│    Senior Staff Attorney     │
└─────────────────────────────┘

┌─────────────────────────────┐
│       Staff Attorney         │
└─────────────────────────────┘

┌─────────────────────────────┐
│    Law Clerk or Attorney     │
└─────────────────────────────┘
```

Position Description

Court Staff Attorneys are responsible for providing judges with legal support, including complex legal analysis, legal research, and legal advice. Unlike judicial law clerks who serve individual judges, Staff Attorneys assist entire courts or panels of judges. These court lawyers work at the local, state, or federal level. Many of them work in appellate courts, and some work in general jurisdiction courts or special jurisdiction courts such as family courts and bankruptcy courts. They may report directly to a senior Staff Attorney, a chief judge, or a committee of judges.

Much of their work involves conducting legal research for judges about substantive or procedural issues or questions that pertain to the cases before the judges. Staff Attorneys gather information from legal resources in law libraries, as well as on electronic and Internet databases. They sometimes confer with attorneys, judges, court administrators, and others who are experts in a particular subject matter. Staff Attorneys carefully examine, analyze, and interpret the data and then give their written summaries and analyses to the judges.

At the request of judges, Staff Attorneys also:

- review legal documents (such as motions, briefs, and trial records) and evaluate the issues as well as offer recommendations for properly settling a legal matter
- draft orders, briefs, opinions, or other legal documents for judges to review and approve
- advise judges about proper judicial action for a case, either in written form or verbally
- attend and assist at hearings or hearings

The work of Staff Attorneys also varies, depending on the type of court they serve. For example, Staff Attorneys in appellate courts may be involved in reviewing appeals that are filed in their court, processing habeas corpus petitions, or cataloging legal issues that are relevant to the types of appeals cases that a court reviews.

Staff Attorneys are also assigned other responsibilities that support judges, court administrators, and other court personnel. They may take on special legal research projects, assist with developing a court's legal programs, update law libraries, serve on court committees, supervise law interns or mentor law clerks, or present legal seminars, for example.

Entry-level court Staff Attorneys typically work under close supervision of senior attorneys as well as judges. As lawyers gain experience, they are given increasingly more difficult assignments that require less supervision. Senior attorneys may be appointed to supervisory positions in which they have the additional responsibility of directing and guiding the work of staff attorneys as well as administrative and clerical support staff. Judges sometimes assign senior Staff Attorneys to serve as temporary judges (or judges pro tem) in cases that they are qualified to handle.

All Staff Attorneys are expected to perform work that conforms to their court's standards for quality. Their work is oftentimes stressful, as they are required to handle tight deadlines on a continual basis.

Court Staff Attorneys work full time. Most of these positions are for one- or two-year terms, while some positions are appointed for an indefinite time period. A term position may be renewed, depending on the lawyer's job performance, the court's workload, and available funding.

Salaries

Salaries for court Staff Attorneys vary, depending on such factors as their experience, job duties, employer, and geographical location. The estimated annual salary for most attorneys, overall, ranged between $49,180 and $145,600, according to the May 2005 *Occupational Employment Statistics* survey by the U.S. Bureau of Labor Statistics.

Employment Prospects

Opportunities generally become available as lawyers transfer to other jobs or advance to higher positions. Courts may create additional positions to meet growing demands, if funding is available. During times when budgets are tight, courts may find it difficult to maintain current staffing or to hire new staff for openings.

Job competition is strong for both entry-level and experienced positions. Entry-level candidates who have graduated from the top law schools with excellent academic records typically have the best job prospects.

Advancement Prospects

Advancement opportunities are limited to few senior or supervisory Staff Attorney positions.

Most lawyers hold several jobs in various work settings throughout their law careers. After serving several years as court Staff Attorneys, individuals may pursue opportunities in law firms, corporate law departments, government agencies, prosecuting attorney's offices, or public interest organizations. Some of them pursue legal-related careers by becoming law professors, law librarians, legal researchers, or legal writers.

Education and Training

Employers generally hire lawyers who have earned a juris doctor (J.D.) degree from a law school accredited by the American Bar Association or by a proper state authority.

New employees usually receive training under the supervision of experienced Staff Attorneys.

Special Requirements

Most employers require that candidates be active members of a state bar association. They may hire qualified candidates without a bar membership on the condition that they obtain it within a certain time period.

Every state (as well as the District of Columbia and U.S. territories) has its own eligibility requirements for admission. For specific information, contact the state bar admission office where you wish to practice. See Appendix III for a list of offices.

Experience, Special Skills, and Personality Traits

Requirements vary with the individual courts. Many courts prefer to hire candidates who have a few years of experience as a practicing attorney. Sometimes employers will hire recent law graduates who demonstrate exceptional legal writing and research skills, as well as have qualifying experience, which they may have gained through internships, employment, or volunteer work.

Court Staff Attorneys must have superior analytical, research, and writing skills to be effective at their work. Strong computer skills are also important for them to have. In addition, they need excellent interpersonal and communication skills, as they must be able to work well with judges, court staff, and others. Being detail-oriented, collegial, flexible, respectful, and trustworthy are some personality traits that successful Staff Attorneys share.

Unions and Associations

Most court Staff Attorneys are members of local, state, or national bar associations. In some states, membership in the state bar association is mandatory. (For a list of state bar associations, see Appendix IV.) By joining associations, lawyers can take advantage of networking opportunities and other professional services and resources.

Tips for Entry

1. As a law student, you might gain experience by obtaining a judicial internship or externship.

2. Talk with current or former court Staff Attorneys about their experience as well as for suggestions about finding a position. If you don't know anyone personally, contact colleagues, professors, or your law school career center for help.

3. Apply separately to each federal court for which you are interested in working, as each court does its own hiring of court personnel.

4. Use the Internet to learn more about the court system in which you would like to work. For information about the federal courts, visit the Federal Judiciary Web site, http://www.uscourts.gov. To find a specific state or local court, enter its name into a search engine.

JUDGE ADVOCATE

CAREER PROFILE

Duties: Serve as a military officer; provide legal services and counsel to military officers and enlisted personnel; perform duties as required

Alternate Title(s): None

Salary Range: $33,000 for newly commissioned officers

Employment Prospects: Good

Advancement Prospects: Good

Prerequisites:

Education or Training—A law (J.D.) degree; completion of officer training and military legal programs

Experience—Previous lawyering experience preferred

Special Skills and Personality Traits—Writing, communication, interpersonal, teamwork, organizational, and self-management skills; be courageous, honest, respectful, flexible, resourceful, disciplined

Special Requirements—Be admitted to practice before the highest court in a state or in a federal court

CAREER LADDER

```
┌─────────────────────────────┐
│   Senior Judge Advocate     │
└─────────────────────────────┘

┌─────────────────────────────┐
│      Judge Advocate         │
└─────────────────────────────┘

┌─────────────────────────────┐
│         Recruit             │
└─────────────────────────────┘
```

Position Description

Judge Advocates are military lawyers who serve in the U.S. Armed Forces. Their job is to provide legal assistance and counsel to military officers and enlisted personnel. Within the army, air force, navy, and marines, these military lawyers are part of their branch's Judge Advocate General's Corps, or JAG Corps. In the coast guard, Judge Advocates are part of the branch's legal program.

Judge Advocates perform a wide range of legal activities. Their assignments may involve performing legal transactions; providing legal assistance to military personnel and their families; advising base commanders on administrative or operational matters; engaging in civil litigation; or prosecuting or defending criminal cases. On occasion, they may be assigned as special assistant U.S. Attorneys to prosecute criminal cases in federal courts.

Throughout their careers, Judge Advocates practice in various areas of law. Some of these areas include:

- military justice, or criminal law—which involves advising commanders about disciplinary matters as well as prosecuting or defending court-martial cases

- estate planning, housing disputes, or family problems
- appellate litigation—drafting briefs and preparing oral arguments for civil and criminal appellate cases
- contract law—advising base officers on contracts for major construction, acquisition, and procurements
- tort claims—processing personal property claims made by military personnel as well as civilians
- administrative law—advising officers of the legal aspects related to operating installations
- international law—advising overseas commanders on agreements governing U.S. military forces
- operational law—providing legal counsel to commanders during military operations

All Judge Advocates are commissioned as officers, whose first duty is to serve as military leaders. The army, air force, navy, and marines are all part of the U.S. Department of Defense. The coast guard is part of the U.S. Department of Homeland Security, except for during times of war when it becomes part of the navy.

Judge Advocates are obligated to serve at least eight years, which may be a combination of active and reserve duty. Their initial tour of active duty is three or four years, depending on their branch. They may be assigned to any location in the world.

Salaries

Judge Advocates earn a base pay, which varies according to their pay grade (or rank), length of service, and geographical location. Those living in areas with a higher cost of living usually earn higher pay. In 2006, the annual base pay for newly commissioned Judge Advocates started at about $33,000.

Along with their salaries, military lawyers receive non-taxable allowances for housing and food (or subsistence). They are also given allowances for military uniforms and for performing certain types of duty such as foreign duty. In addition, they receive health benefits, vacation leave, military base shopping privileges, and other benefits. After completing 20 years of service, military lawyers are eligible for retirement benefits.

Employment Prospects

The U.S. Armed Forces hire new attorneys each year. The number of opportunities for directly commissioned Judge Advocates varies with each branch. For example, the air force selects between 100 to 120 attorneys. Other branches have fewer opportunities. However, keep in mind that the military also has recruitment programs for law school students and military personnel.

The competition for Judge Advocate positions in all five branches is keen.

Advancement Prospects

In the army, air force, and marines, Judge Advocates begin their career as first lieutenants, while those in the navy and coast guard start as lieutenants-junior grade. Career officers are promoted to higher ranks based on their job performance and experience as well as the availability of positions. Other advancement prospects include being assigned to supervisory, teaching, or military judge positions.

Education and Training

Judge Advocates must possess a juris doctor (J.D.) degree, granted by a law school accredited by the American Bar Association.

All recruits complete several weeks of an officers training program, in which they learn the basic responsibilities and skills of being officers in their particular branch, as well as receive physical fitness training. Upon completion of this program, they go through several more weeks of their branch's legal training program. They receive instruction in military law, military justice (criminal) procedure, and other areas of law as they pertain to the armed forces.

Special Requirements

To qualify for a Judge Advocate position, applicants must be admitted to practice before the highest court of a state, a territory, or Washington, D.C., or before any federal court. In addition, they must be U.S. citizens and meet the age requirements specified by the branch in which they are seeking a commission. They must also pass a physical exam and a background investigation.

Experience, Skills, and Personality Traits

Employers usually prefer applicants who have previous lawyering experience. They may have gained their experience through employment, internships, law clerkships, law school clinics, or volunteer work.

To perform well at their job, Judge Advocates need excellent writing, communication, interpersonal, teamwork, organizational, and self-management skills. Being courageous, honest, respectful, flexible, resourceful, and disciplined are some personality traits that successful Judge Advocates share.

Unions and Associations

Many Judge Advocates join bar associations, such as the American Bar Association or the Federal Bar Association, as well as professional societies, such as the Judge Advocates Association, that serve their particular areas of interest. (For contact information, see Appendix V.) As members of such organizations, they can take advantage of networking opportunities and other professional services and resources.

Tips for Entry

1. Get an idea if a military lawyer career may be for you. As a law student, obtain an internship with the military branch in which you are interested.
2. Each branch has different Judge Advocate recruitment programs for law school students, attorneys, and military personnel. To learn about the programs for a specific branch, contact your local recruiter.
3. Learn more about Judge Advocates on the Internet. The Web sites for the different military programs are: U.S. Air Force JAG, http://www.jagusaf.hq.af.mil; U.S. Army JAG, http://www.jagcnet.army.mil; U.S. Navy JAG, http://www.jag.navy.mil; U.S. Marine Corps JAG, http://sja.hqmc.usmc.mil; and U.S. Coast Guard Legal Program, http://www.uscg.mil/legal.

ATTORNEYS—
PRACTICE AREAS

APPELLATE ATTORNEY

CAREER PROFILE

Duties: Provide legal advice and services related to criminal or civil appeals; prepare legal briefs; present oral arguments; and perform other legal tasks as required

Alternate Title(s): Federal Appellate Defender or other title that reflects a particular job

Salary Range: $49,000 to $146,000

Employment Prospects: Good

Advancement Prospects: Good

Prerequisites:

    Education or Training—A law (J.D.) degree

    Experience—Appellate law and trial experience preferred

    Special Skills and Personality Traits—Legal writing, legal research, legal analysis, organizational, communication, presentation, teamwork, and interpersonal skills; be intelligent, adaptable, persuasive, and confident

    Special Requirements—States require lawyers to be admitted to their state bar; federal courts require registration for lawyers to practice

CAREER LADDER

```
┌─────────────────────────────┐
│   Senior Associate, Partner, │
│     or Solo Practitioner     │
└─────────────────────────────┘

┌─────────────────────────────┐
│      Appellate Attorney      │
└─────────────────────────────┘

┌─────────────────────────────┐
│     Attorney or Law Clerk    │
└─────────────────────────────┘
```

Position Description

Appellate Attorneys are litigation lawyers who specialize by appealing cases in state and federal higher courts called appellate courts. These courts may overturn decisions that are made in the trial courts if they find that errors had occurred in the trial procedure or in the application of the law, and such errors affected the decisions.

Appellate Attorneys handle appeals for criminal or civil cases. They may represent the appellant (the party petitioning for a appeal) or the respondent (the other party). These attorneys do not retry cases, nor do they introduce new evidence at appellate hearings. Their job is to present arguments either for or against appealing the decision of trial cases.

The appellate process begins after a court trial is ended. The Appellate Attorneys obtain and review all court transcripts and court records that have been filed in a trial to determine whether a case can be appealed. An appeal can only be made on issues that have been brought up and challenged at the trial. After a thorough review, Appellate Attorneys advise clients of their chances for filing an appeal, as well as give them an idea of how long the appeal can take and the estimated cost of the total appeals procedure. Throughout the appeals process, they inform their clients of the status of their cases. Appellate Attorneys also represent their clients in settlement negotiations.

Appellate Attorneys are responsible for following the appellate procedures of each state or federal appellate court precisely. For example, they file motions and briefs by the established deadlines, attach the appropriate statements and forms, and follow the required formats for writing legal statements. Unlike trial judges, judges in appellate courts make their decisions based on legal briefs, or written legal statements. Thus, Appellate Attorneys have the challenge of writing clear and concise legal arguments that address only the particular issues and include appropriate case precedents that support their appeal or response.

Appellate Attorneys may have the opportunity to also present oral arguments before a panel of appellate judges. But they are usually given a time limit of 10 to 30 minutes.

Often the time is used to answer questions from the judges or to clarify points in their written briefs.

If a party is unhappy with the results of an appeal, Appellate Attorneys can petition to a higher appellate court to review the case. In most states, the state supreme court is the highest appeals court. In the federal judicial system, the highest court of appeals is the U.S. Supreme Court. Appellate Attorneys can appeal a state case all the way to the U.S. Supreme Court if the case involves a constitutional or federal issue.

Appellate Attorneys work long and irregular hours, often more than 40 hours per week.

Salaries

Salaries for Appellate Attorneys vary, depending on factors such as their experience, employer, and geographical location. Lawyers in private practice typically earn higher salaries than government or public interest lawyers. Also, lawyers who live in metropolitan areas usually earn higher wages.

The U.S. Bureau of Labor Statistics reports, in its May 2005 *Occupational Employment Statistics* survey, that the estimated annual salary for most attorneys overall ranged between $49,180 and $145,600.

Employment Prospects

The U.S. Attorneys' Office (USAO), in the U.S. Department of Justice, is one of the larger employers of Appellate Attorneys. Other employers include state justice departments, state and federal appellate defenders, and state and federal commissions. Appellate lawyers are also employed as staff attorneys for appellate judges in the state and federal court systems. In addition, Appellate Attorneys work for public interest organizations and private law firms. Some Appellate Attorneys are solo practitioners.

Competition is usually high for available positions. Most opportunities become available as lawyers resign, retire, or transfer to other positions. Employers will create additional positions to fit growing demands for more appellate specialists.

Advancement Prospects

Administrative and management positions are available, but limited. Many Appellate Attorneys pursue advancement in terms of earning higher pay, being assigned to more complex cases, or receiving professional recognition.

Appellate Attorneys might pursue other career paths such as becoming judges, law professors, or elected officials.

Education and Training

Appellate Attorneys hold a juris doctor (J.D.) degree. Most state bars require that students graduate from law schools accredited by the American Bar Association or by the proper state authority.

Throughout their careers, Appellate Attorneys enroll in continuing education and training programs to strengthen their legal skills and expertise.

Special Requirements

To practice law in a state (or a U.S. territory or Washington, D.C.), lawyers must first gain admission to that state's bar. For specific eligibility requirements, contact the state bar admission office where you wish to practice. See Appendix III for a list of offices.

Appellate Attorneys must register for admission in each federal court in which they plan to practice.

Experience, Skills, and Personality Traits

Employers generally look for candidates who have appellate law experience, which may have been gained through a law clerkship with an appellate judge. In addition, candidates have trial experience.

Appellate Lawyers must have superior legal writing skills, being able to explain complex ideas clearly and succinctly. In addition, they need excellent legal research and legal analysis skills. Furthermore, they must have strong organizational, communication, presentation, teamwork, and interpersonal skills. Some personality traits that successful Appellate Lawyers share are being intelligent, adaptable, persuasive, and confident.

Unions and Associations

Appellate Attorneys join professional organizations to take advantage of networking opportunities, training, and other professional services and resources. Most lawyers belong to their local and state bar associations. In some states, membership in the state bar association is mandatory. In addition they join national associations such as the American Bar Association and the National Lawyers Association. Experienced Appellate Attorneys are eligible to join the American Academy of Appellate Lawyers. For contact information, see Appendix V.

Tips for Entry

1. Some experts in the field suggest that law students who are interested in appellate practice try to obtain an appellate clerkship as well as participate on their school's law review or other law journal.
2. Gain appellate experience by taking pro bono cases.
3. Continually improve your writing and reasoning skills.
4. Some state bars grant board certification to Appellate Attorneys who meet a particular level of expertise. Some lawyers obtain this specialist certification to enhance their professional credibility.
5. Learn more about appellate law on the Internet. To get a list of relevant Web sites, enter the keywords *appellate law* or *appellate attorney* in a search engine. For some links, see Appendix VI.

CRIMINAL LAWYER

CAREER PROFILE

Duties: Provide legal counsel and services to criminal defendants; perform duties as required

Alternate Title(s): Criminal Defense Lawyer

Salary Range: $49,000 to $146,000

Employment Prospects: Fair

Advancement Prospects: Fair

Prerequisites:

Education or Training—A law (J.D.) degree

Experience—Experience in the practice of criminal law

Special Skills and Personality Traits—Research, writing, analytical, presentation, communication, and self-management skills; be aggressive, smart, brave, flexible, organized, creative, and persuasive

Special Requirements—States require lawyers to be admitted to their state bar; federal courts require registration for lawyers to practice

CAREER LADDER

```
┌─────────────────────────────────────┐
│     Partner or Solo Practitioner     │
└─────────────────────────────────────┘

┌─────────────────────────────────────┐
│  Senior Associate or Solo Practitioner │
└─────────────────────────────────────┘

┌─────────────────────────────────────┐
│          Junior Associate            │
└─────────────────────────────────────┘
```

Position Description

Criminal Lawyers are experts in the practice of criminal law and criminal court procedures. They are engaged with cases in local, state, or federal court systems that may involve juveniles or adults who are suspected of committing misdemeanor or felony crimes. These attorneys handle a wide range of criminal cases, including vandalism, burglary, driving under the influence of alcohol, drug possession, armed robbery, assault, rape, kidnapping, manslaughter, murder, fraud, embezzlement, and treason, among others.

Under the U.S. Constitution, accused criminals have the right to hire a lawyer to defend them in court. Hence, many criminal defendants hire private criminal defense attorneys to represent them at arraignments, pretrial hearings, settlement conferences, trials, and sentence hearings.

Private Criminal Lawyers are obligated to provide their clients with legal counsel that is in their best interest. It is also their duty to ensure that defendants' constitutional rights are not being compromised. All final decisions on any matter, however, are made by the defendants. For example,

a defendant may choose to plead guilty at the arraignment or to waive the right to a jury trial.

When defendants cannot afford to hire a private lawyer, courts are required to appoint a Criminal Lawyer known as a public defender to represent them. Public defenders are employed by the government to represent indigent (or poor) criminal defendants. Like private Criminal Lawyers, public defenders must provide their clients with the best legal defense that they can.

The prosecutors who enforce criminal laws are also Criminal Lawyers. These lawyers are employed by governmental bodies, and work on their behalf. They are responsible for issuing criminal charges against suspects, and proving without a doubt that the defendants are guilty of their crimes.

Criminal Lawyers typically manage several cases at a time, each at different stages of the criminal process. They may work on cases alone or with other lawyers.

Preparing for criminal litigation involves many complex tasks, and Criminal Lawyers typically use the services of paralegals, investigators, litigation consultants, and others to help them prepare the best defense or prosecution for each of their cases. Some of the tasks they perform for each case include:

- collecting police reports, evidence, and all other relevant information
- examining the crime scene
- interviewing witnesses
- conducting legal research
- analyzing the facts and issues of a case
- locating expert witnesses who can testify on issues that support the defense or prosecution
- preparing demonstrative exhibits
- developing defense or prosecution strategies

Criminal Lawyers also participate in negotiations to settle cases before they reach the trial stage. Criminal defense attorneys and prosecutors are often able to agree on plea bargains in which the defendants receive lesser sentencing by pleading guilty to lesser criminal charges.

Cases that go to trial may be presented before either judges or juries. All criminal trials follow the same procedure, but every court has its own specific set of rules which attorneys are expected to follow. In a jury trial, the criminal defense and prosecutor are involved with selecting the jurors as well as making suggestion for jury instructions.

The trial starts with opening statements from the prosecutor and criminal defense attorney. Each side describes what each expects to prove in the trial. Both sides present their case through direct examination of their witnesses and introduction of physical evidence. Each side may cross-examine the other side's witnesses, as well as make appropriate objections to testimony, evidence, and other matters. After presenting their sides, the prosecutor and defense attorney make their closing statements, in which they explain why the defendant is guilty or innocent of his or her charges.

The judge or jury deliberates on all the facts presented to them and decides on the verdict. If a verdict is guilty, the defendant may petition for appeals in state or federal appellate courts. Unless they are experts in appellate law, Criminal Lawyers do not handle appeals.

Criminal Lawyers work long and irregular hours, often working more than 40 hours per week.

Salaries

Salaries for Criminal Lawyers vary, depending on such factors as their experience, employer, and geographical location. According to the U.S. Bureau of Labor Statistics, in its May 2005 *Occupational Employment Statistics* survey, the majority of lawyers earned an estimated annual salary between $49,180 and $145,600.

Employment Prospects

Criminal defense lawyers work in law firms of all sizes, but most are solo practitioners or part of small firms.

These lawyers also find employment as public defenders at the local, state, and federal levels of government, as well as with public interest organizations that serve individuals on limited incomes. Prosecutors are employed by prosecuting attorney's offices at all three levels of government.

Competition for jobs is keen. Opportunities generally become available as Criminal Lawyers transfer to other jobs, advance to higher positions, or retire. Employers will create additional positions to meet growing needs. In government agencies and public interest organizations, the ability to hire new attorneys or maintain current levels of staffing is dependent on funding.

Advancement Prospects

Most Criminal Lawyers realize success by earning higher wages, being recognized for their work, and being assigned more complex cases.

Criminal Lawyers might pursue other careers by becoming law professors, criminal investigators, FBI special agents, or judges.

Education and Training

Criminal Lawyers, like all lawyers, hold a juris doctor (J.D.) degree. Throughout their careers, many enroll in training and continuing education programs to build and strengthen their legal skills.

Special Requirements

To practice law in a state (or a U.S. territory or Washington, D.C.), lawyers must first gain admission to that state's bar. Every jurisdiction has its own eligibility requirements. For specific information, contact the state bar admission office where you wish to practice. See Appendix III for a list of offices.

Attorneys must apply for admission to practice in a federal court. All federal courts have their own requirements for admission.

Experience, Skills, and Personality Traits

Employers (and clients) typically choose candidates who have experience in the practice of criminal law. A recent law graduate with significant clinical experience may be considered.

Criminal Lawyers have excellent research, writing, and analytical skills. They also have superior presentation and communication skills, being able to think quickly and to clearly articulate complex ideas off the top of their heads. In addition, they have strong self-management skills—such as the ability to prioritize and organize multiple tasks, meet deadlines, and work well under stress. Being aggressive, smart, brave, flexible, organized, creative, and persuasive are a few personality traits that successful Criminal Lawyers share.

Unions and Associations

Most Criminal Lawyers are members of local and state bar associations. (In some states, membership in the state bar association is mandatory.) Many lawyers also join a national bar association such as the American Bar Association or the National Lawyers Association.

In addition, many belong to various special-interest associations such as the National Association of Criminal Defense Lawyers, the American Association for Justice, the National District Attorneys Association, or the Association of Federal Defense Attorneys. (For contact information, see Appendix V.) By joining attorney associations, lawyers can take advantage of networking opportunities and other professional services and resources.

Tips for Entry

1. Talk to Criminal Lawyers who work in different settings to get an idea of what their work is like. Also read books about crime and criminal cases, as well as attend criminal trials.

2. As a law student, gain criminal law experience by obtaining an internship, part-time job, or volunteer position with a law firm, public defender's office, or prosecutor's office.

3. Many private Criminal Lawyers started their careers as prosecuting attorneys and public defenders.

4. You can learn more about criminal law on the Internet. Enter the keyword *criminal law* or *criminal lawyer* in any search engine to get a list of relevant Web sites. For some links, see Appendix VI.

ELDER LAW ATTORNEY

CAREER PROFILE	CAREER LADDER

CAREER PROFILE

Duties: Provide counsel and legal services to senior citizens; assess nonlegal needs of clients and refer them to appropriate service providers; perform duties as required

Alternate Title(s): None

Salary Range: $49,000 to $146,000

Employment Prospects: Good

Advancement Prospects: Good

Prerequisites:

Education or Training—A law (J.D.) degree

Experience—Experience working with the elderly; familiarity with the various government programs in which the elderly participate

Special Skills and Personality Traits—Legal research, writing, communication, interpersonal, and teamwork skills; be patient, calm, trusting, respectful, empathetic, and compassionate

Special Requirements—States require lawyers to be admitted to their state bar; federal courts require registration for lawyers to practice

CAREER LADDER

```
┌─────────────────────────────────────┐
│     Partner or Solo Practitioner     │
└─────────────────────────────────────┘

┌─────────────────────────────────────┐
│  Senior Associate or Solo Practitioner │
└─────────────────────────────────────┘

┌─────────────────────────────────────┐
│           Junior Associate           │
└─────────────────────────────────────┘
```

Position Description

Elder Law Attorneys specialize in a practice that serves the legal needs of the older population, usually categorized as senior citizens or the elderly. They counsel elderly clients and their family members on a wide range of issues related to aging and death. Some of these issues include:

- estate planning—how clients wish to have their property and assets distributed to family members and others after their death.
- guardianships and conservatorships—who shall make financial and other decisions for clients in the event they become mentally or physically unable to make those decisions
- claims for public benefits such as Social Security, Medicare, veterans' benefits, and disability
- retirement benefits
- insurance claims against nursing homes or other service providers

- housing matters, such as home equity conversions or landlord-tenant problems
- financial planning for possible long-term care needs in nursing homes, as well as the transfer of assets so that a spouse would not become impoverished in the event the other must enter a nursing home
- tax planning
- civil rights matters, including age discrimination in the workplace
- consumer protection issues, including elder fraud
- elder abuse
- nursing home issues, including patients' rights and quality care

Much of these lawyers' work involves legal transactions. They draft legal documents such as wills, trusts, and durable powers of attorney. They review contracts in such areas as insurance, finance, and nursing homes, and advise clients on their content and legal rights. They complete applications for claims, benefits, or appeals with government agencies, insurance companies, nursing homes, and other institutions. They also represent clients in administrative hearings before government agencies, as well as talk on their clients' behalf to nursing homes, employers, insurance companies, and others.

In addition, Elder Law Attorneys are trained to assess clients' nonlegal needs. For example, a client may be in need of affordable housing, another client could use financial assistance with utility bills, another client may be experiencing elder abuse, and still another client may be in need of mental health counseling. Elder Law Attorneys are typically part of a formal or informal network of social workers, psychologists, health care providers, financial advisors, clergy, and others who work with the elderly. Thus, Elder Law Attorneys can refer clients to the appropriate professionals for assistance.

Most Elder Law Attorneys are solo practitioners or work in small private firms.

Elder Law Attorneys often work more than 40 hours a week to complete their various duties as well as to meet with clients at times that are convenient for them.

Salaries

Salaries for Elder Law Attorneys vary, depending on such factors as their experience and geographical location.

Specific salary information for these lawyers is unavailable. However the estimated annual salary for most attorneys ranged between $49,180 and $145,600, according to the May 2005 *Occupational Employment Statistics* survey by the U.S. Bureau of Labor Statistics.

Employment Prospects

Elder law is one of the fastest growing specialty practices in the United States, according to some experts in the field. The demand for qualified Elder Law Attorneys is expected to continue for years to come, because of the many individuals who are reaching retirement age each year and need legal help addressing the various issues that they must face.

Advancement Prospects

In law firms, Elder Law Attorneys may advance to supervisory, administrative, or management positions, depending on the size of the firm. For many Elder Law Attorneys, their career goal is to become successful solo practitioners or partners in elder law practices.

Education and Training

Elder Law Attorneys are required to earn a juris doctor (J.D.) degree. Most state bar associations require that students graduate from law schools accredited by the American Bar Association or by the proper state authority.

Throughout their careers, Elder Law Attorneys enroll in continuing education and training programs to build up and strengthen their legal skills and expertise.

Special Requirements

To practice law in a state—or U.S. territory or Washington, D.C.—individuals must first gain admission to that state's bar. For information about eligibility requirements, contact the state bar admission office where you wish to practice. See Appendix III for a list of offices.

To practice before federal courts, lawyers must apply for admission. Separate registration is required for the different federal courts.

Experience, Skills, and Personality Traits

Employers generally look for candidates who have practical experience and knowledge about the social, health, and economic needs of the elderly. In addition, candidates should be familiar with the various government programs in which the elderly may participate.

Elder Law Attorneys must have superb legal research and writing skills. Having excellent communication, interpersonal, and teamwork skills is also important, as they must be able to work well with their clients as well as relatives, social workers, and others involved with their clients' needs. Being patient, calm, trusting, respectful, empathetic, and compassionate are a few personality traits common to successful Elder Law Attorneys.

Unions and Associations

Elder Law Attorneys belong to local and state bar associations, as well as national associations such as the American Bar Association. In some states, membership in the state bar association is mandatory. In addition, many join special-interest organizations, such as the National Academy of Elder Law Attorneys and the American College of Trust and Estate Counsel. (For contact information, see Appendix V.) By joining professional organizations, Attorneys can take advantage of networking opportunities and other professional services and resources.

Tips for Entry

1. To get an idea if you might be interested in an elder law practice, volunteer at a senior center, nursing home, or agency such as the Alzheimer's Association or the American Association of Retired Persons (AARP) that serves the needs of older citizens.
2. To enhance their employability, many Elder Law Attorneys became certified by the National Elder Law Foundation (NELF) when they become eligible. For information, visit the NELF Web site at http://www.nelf.org.
3. While in law school, obtain a summer associate or law clerkship position in a law firm that practices elder law.
4. You can learn more about the elder law practice on the Internet. You might start by visiting Elder Law Answers.com, http://www.elderlawanswers.com. For more links, see Appendix VI.

EMPLOYMENT LAWYER

CAREER PROFILE

Duties: Provide legal counsel and services to clients regarding workplace issues and problems; perform duties as required

Alternate Title(s): A title, such as Employment Benefits Lawyer, that reflects a specialty

Salary Range: $49,000 to $146,000

Employment Prospects: Good

Advancement Prospects: Good

Prerequisites:

Education or Training—A law (J.D.) degree

Experience—One or more years practicing employment law

Special Skills and Personality Traits—Research, writing, communication, interpersonal, and self-management skills; analytical, responsible, creative, persistent, flexible

Special Requirements—States require lawyers to be admitted to their state bar; federal courts require registration for lawyers to practice

CAREER LADDER

```
┌─────────────────────────────────────┐
│      Partner or Solo Practitioner     │
└─────────────────────────────────────┘

┌─────────────────────────────────────┐
│  Senior Associate or Solo Practitioner │
└─────────────────────────────────────┘

┌─────────────────────────────────────┐
│           Junior Associate            │
└─────────────────────────────────────┘
```

Position Description

Employment Lawyers specialize in the practice of law which covers a wide variety of problems and issues that may arise in the workplace. These attorneys are knowledgeable about federal, state, and local employment laws that cover such areas as:

- wage and overtime standards
- termination of employment
- employee benefits
- workers' compensation
- workplace safety
- discrimination against employees based on ancestry, color, creed, disability, marital status, medical condition, national origin, race, religion, sex, sexual orientation, or age
- sexual harassment
- privacy rights that employees may or may not have—for example, employers may request that their employees submit to random drug testing

Most Employment Lawyers focus their practice in a few areas of employment law. Some Employment Lawyers also handle legal matters that involve labor law, which covers the area of collective bargaining between management and employees.

Many Employment Lawyers specialize in providing legal services to either employers (also referred to as management) or employees. Attorneys who work with employers generally provide preventative lawyering. That is, they help clients create workplace policies and procedures that comply with employment laws. In doing so, employers may lessen the risk of lawsuits by their employees.

As counsel to employers, Employment Lawyers perform a variety of legal tasks. For example, they review contracts with vendors and independent contractors. They advise on personnel matters such as employee disciplinary actions or harassment claims. They also represent their clients before government administrative boards relating to issues such as wage issues, discrimination claims, or workplace safety violations. Many Employment Lawyers perform litigation work, defending their clients in state and federal courts.

Employment Lawyers whose clients are employees perform a variety of transaction or litigation services. For example: They review employment contracts for clients. They advise clients of their legal rights regarding specific issues and suggest different legal actions that they could take to resolve the issues. They counsel clients on disciplinary matters. They mediate agreements between clients and their employers. They also represent individuals in civil lawsuits against employers.

Employment Lawyers work in various settings. Many are private lawyers. Some work in private law firms as associates or partners, while others are solo practitioners. Other Employment Lawyers work in law departments of corporations as in-house counsel. Still others are employed by public interest organizations that offer legal services to employees, especially those on limited incomes.

Like all attorneys, Employment Lawyers typically put in more than 40 hours a week to complete their various duties.

Salaries

Salaries for Employment Lawyers vary, depending on factors such as their experience, job responsibilities, employer, and geographical location.

Specific salary information for Employment Lawyers is unavailable. However the estimated annual salary for most attorneys ranged between $49,180 and $145,600, according to the May 2005 *Occupational Employment Statistics* survey by the U.S. Bureau of Labor Statistics.

Employment Prospects

Because of the wide range of complex employment laws, there will continually be a need for attorneys who specialize in this area. Most opportunities become available to replace lawyers who retire, resign, or transfer to other positions. The creation of new positions depend on staffing needs as well as budgets.

Advancement Prospects

Many Employment Lawyers move from one law firm to another to pursue positions with higher pay, more prestige, or with more complex responsibilities. For many Employment Lawyers, their top career goal is to become successful law firm partners or solo practitioners.

Education and Training

Employment Lawyers earn bachelor's degrees in any field prior to earning a juris doctor degree. Most employers prefer to hire lawyers who have graduated from a law school accredited by the American Bar Association.

Many employers provide their employees with in-house training and education programs. In addition, many Employment Lawyers voluntarily enroll in training and education programs sponsored by legal associations to improve their legal skills and knowledge.

Special Requirements

To practice law in any state (as well as in a U.S. territory or Washington, D.C.), lawyers must be admitted to that state's bar. For eligibility information, contact the state bar admission office where you wish to practice. See Appendix III for a list of offices.

To practice before federal courts, lawyers must apply for admission. Separate registration is required for the different federal courts.

Experience, Skills, and Personality Traits

Most employers require that candidates have one or more years experience as practicing lawyers, particularly in the area of employment law.

Employment Lawyers need excellent research, writing, and communication skills. Interpersonal skills are also essential, as lawyers must work well with colleagues, clients, judges, and others. In addition, attorneys need strong self-management skills—the ability to prioritize and organize tasks, meet deadlines, work well under stress, and so forth. Being analytical, responsible, creative, persistent, and flexible are a few personality traits that successful Employment Lawyers share.

Unions and Associations

Most Employment Lawyers are members of local and state bar associations. (In some states, memberships in the state bar association is mandatory.) In addition, many Employment Lawyers join a national bar association such as the American Bar Association or the National Lawyers Guild. Those who counsel employees are eligible to join the National Employment Lawyers Association. By joining professional organizations, lawyers can take advantage of networking opportunities, education programs, job listings, and other professional services and resources. (For contact information for the above organizations, see Appendix VI.)

Tips for Entry

1. Having experience working in human resources or personnel departments may enhance your employability with many employers.
2. Take courses in employment law while in law school.
3. Contact your professors of employment law courses for leads to summer associate and law clerkship positions, as well as for full-time positions.
4. Learn more about the practice of employment law on the Internet. You might start by visiting the Employment Law Information Network Web site at http://www.elinfonet.com. For more links, see Appendix VI.

ENVIRONMENTAL LAWYER

CAREER PROFILE

Duties: Provide legal counsel and services to clients regarding environmental issues; perform duties as required

Alternate Title(s): None

Salary Range: $49,000 to $146,000

Employment Prospects: Good

Advancement Prospects: Good

Prerequisites:

Education or Training—A law (J.D.) degree; a college degree in environmental studies, environmental science, or environmental engineering preferred

Experience—Knowledge and skills in science or engineering; environmental law experience preferred

Special Skills and Personality Traits—Research, writing, communication, problem-solving, negotiation, interpersonal, teamwork skills; be intelligent, diplomatic, creative, flexible

Special Requirements—States require lawyers to be admitted to their state bar; federal courts require registration for lawyers to practice

CAREER LADDER

```
┌─────────────────────────┐
│        Partner          │
└─────────────────────────┘

┌─────────────────────────┐
│    Senior Associate     │
└─────────────────────────┘

┌─────────────────────────┐
│    Junior Associate     │
└─────────────────────────┘
```

Position Description

Environmental law is a relatively young practice in the United States. It emerged in the 1970s when laws were passed to protect the environment from contamination. Today there are many complex federal, state, and local environmental laws and regulations in which Environmental Lawyers are experts, including in such areas as air pollution, water pollution, hazardous waste management, and wilderness and wildlife protection. Some of these lawyers also handle legal matters that extend into the areas of energy law and the conservation of natural resources.

Environmental Lawyers work in different settings. Many private lawyers are employed by private or nonprofit law firms, while some are solo practitioners. Some Environmental Lawyers are employed as staff attorneys in public interest organizations, and others work as in-house counsel for law departments in corporations. In general, Environmental Lawyers do three types of legal activities for their clients: transactions, environmental litigation, and the enforcement of environmental statutes and regulations.

Some Environmental Lawyers specialize in providing legal services to clients in the private sector, such as small business owners, manufacturers, real estate developers, agricultural growers, and logging companies. They advise clients of environmental laws with which they must comply. They also review prospective environmental legislation and explain how it can affect their clients' business. In addition, they complete applications for regulatory approvals from government agencies, as well as represent their clients before government administrative boards. Environmental Lawyers may also handle litigation for civil lawsuits.

Other Environmental Lawyers specialize in providing legal counsel to individuals, citizen action groups, and environmental conservation groups. Their work generally involves environmental litigation, representing clients in civil lawsuits against the government or private sector. Some Environmental Lawyers also perform lobbying services and assist in the drafting of proposed legislation.

Many Environmental Lawyers are employed by environmental regulatory agencies at the local, state, or federal level. Their duties include advising government agencies of their legal obligations to the public; drafting proposed laws and regulations; counseling staff on legal matters related to new policy that is being made; and preparing civil lawsuits.

Environmental Lawyers work long and irregular hours, often working more than 40 hours per week.

Salaries

Salaries for Environmental Lawyers vary, depending on such factors as their experience, employer, and geographical location. Specific salary information for these lawyers is unavailable. However the estimated annual salary for most attorneys ranged between $49,180 and $145,600, according to the U.S. Bureau of Labor Statistics (BLS) May 2005 *Occupational Employment Statistics* survey.

Employment Prospects

According to the BLS, the overall employment for attorneys is predicted to increase by 9 to 17 percent through 2014. Environmental practice is among the areas of law that are expected to have an increased demand for legal services.

Jobs are highly competitive in all work settings—law firms, public interest groups, corporate law departments, and government. Opportunities for entry-level positions are more favorable in the public sector, especially at the local and state levels.

Advancement Prospects

Many Environmental Lawyers start their careers working with a government agency or public interest group, then transfer to private law firms. In any work setting, Environmental Lawyers can advance to administrative and management positions.

Environmental Lawyers can also pursue other related careers, such as law professors, corporate environmental compliance managers, environmental organizers, lobbyists, or environmental policy advisers to government agencies.

Education and Training

Environmental Lawyers have juris doctor (J.D.) degrees. Most employers prefer to hire candidates who have graduated from a law school accredited by the American Bar Association. In addition, they look for candidates who hold a college degree in environmental studies, science, or engineering.

Throughout their careers, Environmental Lawyers enroll in training and continuing education programs to increase their legal skills and knowledge in environmental law.

Special Requirements

To practice law in a state (or a U.S. territory or Washington, D.C.), lawyers must first gain admission to that state's bar.

Every jurisdiction has its own eligibility requirements. For specific information, contact the state bar admission office where you wish to practice. See Appendix III for a list of offices.

Attorneys must be registered to practice law in federal courts. They need to register separately for each court in which they plan to practice.

Experience, Skills, and Personality Traits

Employers prefer to hire candidates who have experience in the particular areas of environmental law in which they will work. They may have gained their experience through law clerkships, internships, employment, or volunteer work. In addition, many employers seek candidates who have knowledge and experience in science or engineering.

To succeed in their profession, Attorneys need excellent research, writing, communication, problem-solving, and negotiation skills. Interpersonal and teamwork skills are also essential, as lawyers must work well with colleagues, clients, and others. Being intelligent, diplomatic, creative, and flexible are a few personality traits that successful Environmental Lawyers share.

Unions and Associations

Many Environmental Lawyers join bar associations to take advantage of networking opportunities, education programs, and other professional services and resources. They join local and state bar associations, as well as national bar associations such as the American Bar Association and the National Lawyers Guild. (For contact information, see Appendix V.) Some bar associations have environmental divisions or sections.

Tips for Entry

1. You can start gaining valuable experience in middle school or high school by getting involved with an environmental group.
2. To gain environmental law experience, obtain an internship, part-time job, or volunteer position with an environmental law firm or public interest organization.
3. Contact local and state environmental regulatory agencies for available job openings. Law enforcement agencies and natural resources departments may also have opportunities for Environmental Lawyers. At the federal level, two agencies you might check are the U.S. Department of Justice (http://www.usdoj.gov) and the Environmental Protection Agency (http://www.epa.gov).
4. Learn more about environmental law on the Internet. Using any of these keywords in a search engine can bring up relevant Web sites: *environmental law, environmental law careers,* or *environmental lawyer.* For some links, see Appendix VI.

HEALTH LAWYER

CAREER PROFILE

Duties: Provide legal counsel and services to patients or health-care providers or other organizations in the health-care industry; perform duties as required

Alternate Title(s): Health Law Attorney, Health Care Lawyer, Hospital Attorney

Salary Range: $49,000 to $146,000

Employment Prospects: Good

Advancement Prospects: Good

Prerequisites:

Education or Training—A law (J.D.) degree

Experience—Prior practice in health law preferred

Special Skills and Personality Traits—Research, writing, analytical, teamwork, interpersonal, and communication skills; be accurate, energetic, enthusiastic, self-motivated, quick-witted, and dedicated

Special Requirements—States require lawyers to be admitted to their state bar; federal courts require registration for lawyers to practice

CAREER LADDER

```
┌─────────────────────────────────────┐
│     Partner or Managing Attorney     │
└─────────────────────────────────────┘

┌─────────────────────────────────────┐
│          Senior Associate            │
│       or Senior Staff Attorney       │
└─────────────────────────────────────┘

┌─────────────────────────────────────┐
│   Junior Associate or Staff Attorney │
└─────────────────────────────────────┘
```

Position Description

Health Lawyers specialize in the practice of complicated local, state, and federal laws that regulate the health-care industry in the United States. These attorneys engage in legal matters related to personal healthcare, medical practice, the financing of health-care delivery systems, professional credentialing, and conducting medical research, among other areas.

Health Attorneys perform transactional or litigation work, depending on the legal needs of their clients. Their clients may include:

- patients
- health-care providers; for example, medical doctors, nurses, and other health-care professionals as well as hospitals, nursing homes, rehabilitation centers, and other health-care facilities
- health-care payers, such as insurance companies and health maintenance organizations (HMOs)
- health-care suppliers, such as pharmaceutical, medical equipment, and health-care supplies companies
- teaching hospitals as well as academic medical centers, which conduct medical research
- health-care and medical professional and trade associations
- groups that perform lobbying work for health-care organizations
- accrediting organizations that evaluate and accredit health-care organizations and programs that have met standard requirements for quality and safety

Health Lawyers advise their clients on a wide range of health-care issues, such as medical malpractice, health insurance disputes, fraud and abuse, Medicare reimbursement claims, long term care, professional licensure, medical staff discipline, employee health benefits, compliance programs, antitrust, ethics, medical research, and bioterrorism. In addition, Health Lawyers handle legal cases for many clients involving other areas of law such as corporate, administrative, criminal, tax, employment, and intellectual property laws. For example, health-care facilities, providers, or payers may seek advice from Health Lawyers about mergers or acquisitions, labor or employment issues, or taxation problems that are special to the health-care industry.

Health Lawyers are employed in various settings. Many of them work in private practice as solo practitioners, or as associates or partners in law firms that have health law sections. Some private lawyers practice in small firms that offer law services exclusively to health-care providers. It is not uncommon for many Health Lawyers to represent clients in different states.

Many Health Lawyers are employed by the legal departments within health-care providers, payers, suppliers, and other organizations that are involved in the health-care industry. As in-house counsels, these attorneys provide legal services and advise their employers on legal matters that are concerned with the day-to-day operations.

Many other Health Lawyers work in government settings. At the federal level, many Health Lawyers are hired by the different agencies that have federal jurisdiction over health matters, such as the U.S. Department of Health and Human Services, the Occupational Safety and Health Administration, the Public Health Service, and the Centers for Disease Control and Prevention. In addition, Health Lawyers are employed by other agencies such as the Internal Revenue Service, the U.S. Department of Defense, the U.S. Department of Justice, or the Federal Trade Commission that are also involved in health-care issues.

At the state level, attorneys with health-care law expertise are employed in various agencies, such as the health department that regulates health-care providers, the insurance department that controls health insurance companies, and the labor department that handles cases regarding workplace conditions in health-care facilities and other health-related employers. Health Lawyers also work in state attorney general offices where they are involved in prosecuting cases regarding physician licensing, Medicaid fraud, and other health-related issues.

At both the state and federal government levels, Health Lawyers assist legislators and executive officers to develop laws, regulations, and policies that affect the delivery and financing of health-care services.

Health Lawyers are also employed by city government agencies to handle health-care matters at the local level. Furthermore, Health Lawyers work with legal aid societies and other public interest groups. In the public service setting, these attorneys might assist clients on limited incomes or work with nonprofit organizations that advocate for legal reforms on behalf of the general public.

Health Lawyers establish a special relationship with each of their clients, and are obligated to put each client's interests above their own. Regardless of their work setting, Health Lawyers perform many similar tasks. They conduct research on legal and health-care issues, review and analyze legal documents, and negotiate contracts. They prepare legal correspondence and documents as well as assist cli-

ents in the preparation of required medical or legal forms and reports for government agencies. They keep up with new and pending health-care legislation and regulations and counsel their clients accordingly. Health Lawyers also represent their clients in business meetings, administrative law hearings, depositions, and court trials.

Health Lawyers perform other duties that vary according to their experience, work setting, and clientele. For example, in-house counsels and private lawyers with corporate clients help their clients meet federal and state laws, regulations, procedures, and requirements by assisting them in the design of appropriate corporate compliance programs.

As they gain experience, Health Lawyers might choose to specialize in any number of ways. They might perform only certain types of litigation or transactional work; for example, litigation lawyers might do only insurance defense work. Health Lawyers, in any work setting, might specialize in the practice of specific health-care issues or laws. Private lawyers might specialize in providing services to particular clients, such as patients, physician groups, or pharmaceutical companies.

Health Lawyers work long and irregular hours, and often work evenings and on weekends to complete their tasks or to meet deadlines.

Salaries

Salaries for Health Lawyers vary, depending on such factors as their experience, employer, and geographical location. The estimated annual salary for most lawyers overall ranged between $49,180 and $145,600, according to the May 2005 *Occupational Employment Statistics survey* by the U.S. Bureau of Labor Statistics.

Employment Prospects

In general, job openings become available as Health Lawyer transfer to other jobs, advance to higher positions, or retire. Employers will create new staff positions to meet growing demands for the services of Health Lawyers.

Some experts in the field say that the need for qualified Health Lawyers shall always be favorable, because the health-care industry is such a regulated, complex, and sophisticated industry.

Advancement Prospects

Health Lawyers may advance in various ways, depending on their ambitions and interests. They might specialize in particular areas of health law or pursue positions in desired work settings. They can also follow other career paths by becoming law school professors, health-care lobbyists, policy analysts, or executive officers of health-care establishments.

In law firms, lawyers begin as associates and after several years become partners or move on to other interests.

In corporate and government settings, lawyers can advance to supervisory and management positions. Entrepreneurial lawyers may become solo practitioners or start their own law firms.

Education and Training

Health Lawyers possess a juris doctor (J.D.) degree. Most employers prefer that candidates earned their degree from a law school accredited by the American Bar Association.

Some law schools offer health law programs, in which students can receive instruction in such health-care issues as antitrust, insurance law, disability, bioethics, health-care financing, and elder law. Students also gain practical experience in health law clinics.

Special Requirements

Some employers require that Health Lawyers be licensed to practice in more than one state. To practice law in a state (or U.S. territory or Washington D.C.), individuals must first gain admission to that state's bar. Every jurisdiction has its own eligibility requirements. For specific information, contact the state bar admission office where you wish to practice. See Appendix III for a list of offices.

To practice before a federal court, Health Lawyers must apply for admission. Separate registration is required for each federal court.

Experience, Special Skills, and Personality Traits

Requirements vary with the different types of employers. In general, employers prefer to hire candidates who have prior experience practicing health law in a law firm or within an appropriate health-care provider setting. Employers also look for candidates who are knowledgeable about the particular issues (such as Medicare issues) and health-care laws with which they would work.

Health Lawyers must have excellent research, writing, analytical, and teamwork skills. They also need strong inter-personal and communication skills, as they must be able to work effectively with co-workers, clients, and others who come from diverse backgrounds. Being accurate, energetic, enthusiastic, self-motivated, quick-witted, and dedicated are some personality traits that successful Health Lawyers have in common.

Unions and Associations

Most Health Lawyers join professional organizations to take advantage of professional resources and services such as networking opportunities, continuing education programs, and professional publications. Many of these lawyers are members of local and state bar associations. (In some states, membership in a state bar is mandatory to practice law in that state.) Many also join associations that serve the particular interests of health-care attorneys such as the American Health Lawyers Association, the American Association of Nurse Attorneys, and the American Bar Association Health Law Section. For contact information for these organizations, see Appendix V.

Tips for Entry

1. Obtain a law clerkship in a firm or organization that practices health-care law to gain experience as well as to make sure it is an area that fits your interests.
2. Many Health Lawyers had previous careers as nurses, physicians, or other health-care practitioners or administrators.
3. Employers typically seek candidates who have strong academic records.
4. Many law firms, hospitals, and other employers post job listings for Health Lawyers on their Web sites.
5. Use the Internet to learn more about health-care law. You might start by visiting this Web site by William L. Manning: The Health Law Resource, http://www.netreach.net/~wmanning. For more links, see Appendix VI.

INDIAN LAW ATTORNEY

CAREER PROFILE

Duties: Provide legal counsel and services to clients on legal matters related to issues that concern American Indian and Alaska Native tribes; perform duties as required

Alternate Title(s): Tribal Law Attorney; a title that reflects a particular job such as Tribal Prosecutor

Salary Range: $49,000 to $146,000

Employment Prospects: Good

Advancement Prospects: Good

Prerequisites:

Education or Training—A law (J.D.) degree

Experience—Previous lawyering experience preferred

Special Skills and Personality Traits—Research, analytical, writing, communication, problem-solving, negotiation, interpersonal, and teamwork skills; be organized, dependable, trustworthy, and dedicated

Special Requirements—States require lawyers to be admitted to their state bar; federal courts require registration for lawyers to practice

CAREER LADDER

```
┌─────────────────────────────────┐
│   Partner or Managing Attorney   │
└─────────────────────────────────┘

┌─────────────────────────────────┐
│        Senior Associate          │
│    or Senior Staff Attorney      │
└─────────────────────────────────┘

┌─────────────────────────────────┐
│  Junior Associate or Staff Attorney  │
└─────────────────────────────────┘
```

Position Description

In the United States, over 550 American Indian and Alaska Native tribes are federally recognized as sovereign nations. Each tribe has its own system of government, and can engage in government-to-government relations with the United States and with the individual states, as well as be eligible for federal services. Although federally recognized tribes are self-governing, the activities that take place on tribal lands are regulated by three jurisdictions—the tribal, federal, and state governments.

Indian Law Attorneys are experts in the complex practice of tribal, federal, and state laws that affect the affairs of individuals and tribes on and near tribal lands. Their clients may include tribal governments, tribal business enterprises, and government agencies, as well as non-native companies that seek to do business on or near tribal lands.

These lawyers advise clients on a wide range of diverse issues relating to tribal sovereignty, treaty rights, trust lands, criminal jurisdiction, child welfare, taxation, zoning, water rights, gaming, hunting and fishing rights, and environmental protection, among other matters. Depending on the needs of their clients, Indian Law Attorneys may be involved with transactional, negotiation, or regulatory work.

They perform litigation work as well, and may represent tribal governments or non-native clients. They litigate criminal or civil cases before tribal, federal, and state courts. Some of them handle appellate cases. They also represent clients on matters before administrative agencies, such as the Bureau of Indian Affairs, the Federal Energy Regulatory Commission, and the Environmental Protection Agency. In addition, they may represent tribal clients in disputes with other tribes.

Indian Law Attorneys also assist clients—both natives and non-natives—with business and economic ventures on or near tribal lands, such as the development of casinos, hotels, restaurants, golf courses, convention centers, affordable housing, shopping centers, and gas stations. Attorneys advise on the structuring and financing of development projects, as well as draft and negotiate commercial leases, construction contracts, mortgages, development agreements, and other types of contracts.

Many of these attorneys advise tribal leaders on governmental issues and assist them with developing and implementing governmental policies and strategies. Additionally, they help leaders draft appropriate legislation and codes regarding tribal membership, taxation, game and fish management, traffic issues, and other matters. Further, Indian Law Attorneys counsel tribal clients on ways to protect archaeological and cultural resources on their lands.

Some Indian Law Attorneys perform lobbying work in state and federal capitols. On behalf of their clients, they might seek funding or favorable legislation. Other Indian Law Attorneys help executive bodies and legislatures to develop policies and legislation regarding Indian affairs.

Because there are so many aspects of Indian law, attorneys specialize in one or several areas. For example, some attorneys become specialists in Indian gaming laws and regulations. Many lawyers also specialize by performing certain types of legal work or by serving certain clientele.

Indian Law Attorneys work in different settings. Many of them work in private law firms as staff attorneys, associates, or partners. Others are solo practitioners. Some law firms offer services exclusively to American Indian and Alaska Native tribes.

Many Indian Law Attorneys are hired by tribes as in-house counsels. A tribe's legal staff may consist of one or more lawyers who provide legal counsel and services on matters related to the tribe. Some attorneys also handle the prosecution of traffic and criminal law violations before tribal courts.

Indian Law Attorneys also work in various government agencies, such as state Indian affairs departments, the U.S. Bureau of Indian Affairs, the U.S. Environmental Protection Agency, the U.S. Department of the Interior, the Federal Bureau of Investigation, and the U.S. Congress. Still other Indian Law Attorneys work for public interest organizations that provide free legal services to low-income tribal members. Along with handling a caseload, many of these lawyers perform outreach and community education.

Regardless of their work setting, Indian Law Attorneys are involved with various routine legal tasks each day. They meet with clients; they conduct legal research; they review and analyze legal documents; they prepare legal documents, reports, and correspondence; and they keep up the latest court decisions, proposed legislation, and other issues that affect their clients. These attorneys typically put in more than 40 hour a week to complete their duties and meet necessary deadlines.

Salaries

Salaries for Indian Law Attorneys vary, depending on such factors as their experience, employer, and geographical location. Specific salary information for these attorneys is unavailable. However, the estimated annual salary for most lawyers ranged between $49,180 and $145,600, according to the May 2005 *Occupational Employment Statistics survey* by the U.S. Bureau of Labor Statistics.

Employment Prospects

Opportunities generally become available as attorneys transfer to other jobs, retire, or advance to higher positions. Employers create additional positions to meet their growing needs, as long as funding is available.

The Indian law practice is a small field, but in recent years has been growing. Much of this is due to the increase in the number of Indian casino operations that has created a multi-billion dollar industry. Increasingly more tribes are establishing internal law departments as well as hiring private law firms to help them with legal issues related to running businesses, starting new enterprises, developing housing, and other business, cultural, and political matters. Additionally, this should create a demand for Indian Law Attorneys to assist clients who wish to do business with Native American tribes.

Advancement Prospects

Indian Law Attorneys may advance in various ways, depending on their ambitions, interests, and work settings. In law firms, lawyers begin as associates and after several years become partners or move on to other interests. In corporate and government settings, lawyers can advance to supervisory and management positions. Entrepreneurial lawyers may become solo practitioners or start their own law firms.

Indian Law Attorneys can also follow other law-related career paths. For example, they can become judges, lobbyists, law school professors, or executive directors of public interest organizations.

Education and Training

Indian Law Attorneys earn a juris doctor (J.D.) degree, after completing three or four years of law school. Most employers prefer to hire candidates who have graduated from a school accredited by the American Bar Association or a proper state authority.

Along with offering Indian law courses, some law schools conduct clinics to give students practical experience in working with tribes and individuals.

Many employers provide their employees with training and education programs. For example, some law firms have mentor programs that team new associates with senior members.

Special Requirements

To practice law in a state (or the District of Columbia or a U.S. territory), attorneys must first gain admission to that state's bar. For specific eligibility information, contact the state bar admission office where you wish to practice. See Appendix III for a list of offices.

To practice before a federal court, lawyers must apply for admission. Separate registration is required for each federal court.

Experience, Special Skills, and Personality Traits

Requirements vary with the different types of employers. In general, employers prefer to hire candidates who have prior experience in the practice of Indian law. Recent law school graduates may have gained their experience through law clerkships, internships, volunteer work, or employment. Employers also seek candidates who have an understanding of the history, culture, religion, and values of the American Indian or Alaska Native tribes with whom they will work.

To work effectively, Indian Law Attorneys need research, analytical, writing, communication, problem solving, negotiation, interpersonal, and teamwork skills. Being organized, dependable, trustworthy, and dedicated are some personality traits that successful Indian Law Attorneys share.

Unions and Associations

Indian Law Attorneys join local and state bar associations to take advantage of networking opportunities and other professional services and resources. (In some states, state bar membership is mandatory.) These attorneys also become members of national associations such as the American Bar Association or the National Lawyers Association. In addition, many Indian Law Attorneys belong to various special-interest associations such as the Federal Bar Association, the American Association for Justice, or the National Legal Aid and Defender Association. For contact information for all of the above organizations, see Appendix V.

Tips for Entry

1. While in high school or college, get an idea if a career in Indian law interests you. Learn about tribal governments and courts, as well as about the various issues that affect Native Americans.
2. In law school, take one or more courses in Indian law. You also might gain practical experience by participating in an Indian law clinic, or interning in a law firm with an Indian law practice, a legal service, or a public interest organization that serves the Native American population.
3. When doing a job search, remember to contact colleagues as well as former professors, classmates, supervisors, and co-workers about job leads.
4. Use the Internet to learn more about Indian law practice. You might start by visiting these Web sites: National Tribal Justice Resource Center, http://www.tribalresourcecenter.org, and Wisconsin Judicare's Indian Law Office, http://www.judicare.org/ilo.htm. For more links, see Appendix VI.

INTELLECTUAL PROPERTY (IP) ATTORNEY

CAREER PROFILE

Duties: Provide legal counsel and services to owners of intellectual property; perform duties as required

Alternate Title(s): Patent Lawyer, or other title that reflects a specific intellectual property area

Salary Range: $49,000 to $146,000

Employment Prospects: Good

Advancement Prospects: Good

Prerequisites:

Education or Training—A law (J.D.) degree; for patent lawyers, a college degree in engineering, physics, or science preferred

Experience—Previous lawyering experience; be knowledgeable about or experienced in the IP discipline in which they'll work; business experience preferred

Special Skills and Personality Traits—Legal research, writing, communication, and negotiation skills; be analytical, responsible, creative, persistent, flexible

Special Requirements—States require lawyers to be admitted to their state bar; federal courts require registration for lawyers to practice

CAREER LADDER

```
┌─────────────────────────────────┐
│   Partner or Solo Practitioner  │
└─────────────────────────────────┘

┌─────────────────────────────────┐
│        Senior Associate         │
└─────────────────────────────────┘

┌─────────────────────────────────┐
│        Junior Associate         │
└─────────────────────────────────┘
```

Position Description

Intellectual Property (IP) Attorneys practice in areas of law that protect the exclusive rights of clients who own property that has been created by the human mind. Intellectual property includes artistic and scientific work such as poetry, stories, plays, music, paintings, sculptures, cartoons, software, inventions, chemical formulations, manufacturing processes, and trade secrets. All forms of intellectual property are assets that can be sold, licensed, exchanged, or given away like real and personal property. Therefore, intellectual property laws have been created to prevent the sale or use of such property without the authorization of the owners. To ensure that their rights are protected in the United States, the owners must register their property with the appropriate federal agency, such as the U.S. Patent and Trademark Office.

Intellectual property law is divided into several areas. Typically, IP Attorneys specialize in one of those areas. Many specialize in patent law, which protects inventions as well as scientific and medical discoveries. (These lawyers are sometimes known as patent lawyers.) Some IP Attorneys specialize in copyright law, which protects the authorship of books, drawings, sound recordings, movies, maps, choreographic works, and computer programs, among others.

Some lawyers are involved in trademark law, which protects brand names and symbols that stand for a particular good or service. Other IP Attorneys specialize in trade secret law. This body of laws protects formulas, patterns, devices, strategies, and any other confidential information that a business develops to have an advantage over its competitors. IP Attorneys also practice in licensing laws, unfair competition laws, as well as statutes that regulate against counterfeiting and piracy of intellectual property. Further, some IP Attorneys are engaged in computer law, which concentrates on the protection of software and hardware that their clients have created.

IP Attorneys counsel individuals (such as authors, musicians, artists, inventors, and scientists) as well as small-business owners, corporations, and other organizations. They may handle transactional or litigation work, depending on the needs of their clients. For example, they might:

- advise clients of their rights and procedures for legally protecting their property
- counsel clients on whether they may be infringing on the intellectual property rights of another party
- draft legal documents such as licensing agreements
- prepare and file applications with the appropriate government agencies
- review business agreements and other legal contracts
- negotiate sales of rights for their clients
- represent clients before administrative agencies or courts regarding clients' rights of copyright, patent, or trademark
- defend or prosecute in civil suit trials

IP Attorneys work in private law firms, government agencies, and universities. Many are also employed as in-house counsels by businesses and companies in all industries.

IP Attorneys usually work more than 40 hours a week to complete their legal tasks and meet deadlines.

Salaries
Salaries for IP Attorneys vary, depending on such factors as their experience, employer, and geographical location. The U.S. Bureau of Labor Statistics reports, in its May 2005 *Occupational Employment Statistics* survey, that the estimated annual salary for most attorneys ranged between $49,180 and $145,600.

Employment Prospects
Intellectual property law practice has been one of the fastest-growing areas, and some experts in the field see no end to the nationwide demand for IP Attorneys. Particularly in demand are IP Attorneys (especially patent lawyers) with engineering or science backgrounds.

Advancement Prospects
IP Attorneys can advance to administrative and management positions in any work setting. Many IP Attorneys pursue positions with different employers to earn higher pay and receive more complex responsibilities. Private lawyers also pursue advancement by becoming law partners, which gives them a share in the profits of their law firms.

Education and Training
Employers prefer to hire candidates who possess a juris doctor (J.D.) degree from a law school accredited by the American Bar Association. Undergraduate degrees may be in any field. However, employers usually seek candidates for patent lawyer positions who hold a college degree or have a strong academic background in engineering, physics, or natural sciences.

Many employers provide entry-level lawyers with on-the-job training.

Special Requirements
IP Attorneys must be admitted to a state's bar association in order to practice law in that state. All states, as well as the District of Columbia and the U.S. territories have their own eligibility requirements. For specific information, contact the state bar admission office where you wish to practice. See Appendix III for a list of offices.

IP Attorneys must also register in each federal court before they are able to practice there. Additionally, if they want to practice patent law before the U.S. Patent and Trademark office, they must first pass a patent bar exam in order to be admitted.

Experience, Skills, and Personality Traits
Employers seek candidates who have lawyering experience, which may have been gained through internships, law clerkships, volunteer work, or employment. They also prefer to hire candidates who have general knowledge or experience in the art, technology, or science discipline in which they would be working. In addition, candidates should have basic knowledge of business and economics. Like all lawyers, IP Attorneys need excellent legal research and writing skills, as well as communication and negotiation skills. Being analytical, responsible, creative, persistent, and flexible are a few personality traits that successful IP Attorneys share.

Unions and Associations
IP Attorneys join local, state, and national bar associations to take advantage of education programs and other professional services and resources, as well as networking opportunities. Many also become members of organizations that serve their particular interests such as the American Intellectual Property Law Association, the International Trademark Association, the Copyright Society of the USA, and the Licensing Executive Society. For contact information, see Appendix V.

Tips for Entry
1. To gain knowledge of the IP field, you might take one or more courses in IP law.
2. Join a student organization that addresses IP issues. Participate in the group's activities, attend conferences, and start networking.
3. Obtain a summer associate or law clerk position with a law firm that has an IP practice.
4. Many law schools, bar associations, legal publications, and employers post job listings on their Web sites.
5. Learn more about IP law on the Internet. You might start by visiting these Web sites: American Intellectual Property Law Association, http://www.aipla.org, and U.S. Patent and Trademark Office, http://www.uspto.gov. For more links see Appendix VI.

LITIGATION ATTORNEY, CIVIL

CAREER PROFILE

Duties: Handle civil lawsuits for clients; prepare and file legal documents, collect facts and evidence, negotiate settlements, try cases, and perform other litigation tasks; perform other duties as required

Alternate Title(s): Trial Lawyer, Litigator

Salary Range: $49,000 to $146,000+

Employment Prospects: Good

Advancement Prospects: Good

Prerequisites:

  Education or Training—A law (J.D.) degree

  Experience—Some experience desirable

  Special Skills and Personality Traits—Negotiation, presentation, communication, writing, organizational, interpersonal, and self-management skills; be detail-oriented, quick-witted, creative, persuasive, and focused

  Special Requirements—States require lawyers to be admitted to their state bar; federal courts require registration for lawyers to practice

CAREER LADDER

```
┌─────────────────────────────┐
│  Senior Associate or Partner │
└─────────────────────────────┘

┌─────────────────────────────┐
│          Associate          │
└─────────────────────────────┘

┌─────────────────────────────┐
│       Junior Associate      │
└─────────────────────────────┘
```

Position Description

Litigation is the complex process of resolving disputes between two parties in a court of law, which can take several months or years to complete. Lawyers who specialize in the practice of trying cases in court are known as trial lawyers or Litigation Attorneys. They are experienced in handling jury selection, examining and cross-examining witnesses, analyzing evidence, presenting arguments before a judge or jury, and other essential skills.

Civil Litigation Attorneys handle lawsuits for clients who may be individuals, citizen's groups, professionals, small business owners, corporations, manufacturers, government agencies, community organizations, schools, nonprofit organizations, or other organizations or institutions. On behalf of their clients, these lawyers prosecute for them or defend them in court about disputes that may involve personal injury, business transactions, business torts, insurance contracts, bankruptcy, professional malpractice, contractor claims, products liability, collections, employment matters, landlord issues, family law, or probate, to name just a few areas.

The party who files a lawsuit is called the plaintiff, and the other party is known as the defendant. In a civil lawsuit, it is the job of the plaintiff's lawyer to prove that the plaintiff's complaint against the defendant is true and that the defendant should be ordered by the court to either do or stop a particular action. The defendant may also be ordered to pay the plaintiff for damages they may have suffered because of the defendant's actions.

Litigation Attorneys try civil cases in state or federal courts. Some of them also handle administrative claims or disputes for clients before administrative bodies of government agencies, such as local planning commissions, state environmental agencies, the U.S. Federal Aviation Administration, or the U.S. Social Security Administration.

Lawsuits formally start when attorneys for the plaintiff file a legal document known as a complaint in a court of law that has the jurisdiction to hear a particular dispute. This document describes the plaintiff's allegations and the evidence that supports their claims, as well as the relief that the plaintiff seeks from the court. Attorneys also serve a summons and the complaint to the defendant. The defendant's lawyers prepare and file an answer (a legal document) in court within a given time frame. This document describes the defendant's objections to the plaintiff's complaint. The lawyers may also file a complaint against the plaintiff or other third parties whom the defendant believes is responsible for the situation in question.

The next stage in litigation is known as discovery, which is usually the longest phase in the process. Attorneys collect and evaluate facts and evidence that are relevant to their client's case, as well as support their client's claims. They follow specific court procedures to gather essential information. They may ask the other party to complete a set of written questions called interrogatories, which must be answered under oath. Lawyers may also request documents from the other party that may be related to their claims, such as correspondence, employments records, medical records, company policies, bank statements, or police records. In addition, Litigation Attorneys hold depositions, in which they obtain sworn testimony from the other party or from witnesses. Lawyers ask questions about the facts, events, and people that are involved or related to the case.

Because most lawsuits involve technical subjects that are beyond their knowledge or expertise, Litigation Attorneys hire the consulting services of subject matter experts. These litigation consultants help lawyers understand issues in medicine, psychology, finance, engineering, science, or other areas, so that they can prepare their case for trial. Attorneys also use subject matter experts to review their case and provide expert witness testimony that supports their case at depositions or trials.

Throughout the discovery phase, Litigation Attorneys are continually negotiating a settlement for their client. Negotiations can continue up to the moment that a judge or jury makes a verdict. The majority of litigation cases are settled before a case even goes to trial.

If a case goes to trial, a judge or a jury may hear it. The attorneys follow a certain protocol as well as comply with rules of the court, which differs with each judge. In a jury trial, Litigation Attorneys participate in the selection of jury members. Before a trial begins, Litigation Attorneys prepare and submit a brief to the judge that details the arguments and evidence that they will present.

The trial starts with opening statements from the attorneys, in which each side describes what each expects to prove in the trial. The attorneys then take turns presenting evidence before the court through witness testimony. Each side may cross-examine the other party's witnesses, as well as make appropriate objections to testimony, evidence, and other matters. When both parties have presented all of their evidence, the attorneys take turns making their closing arguments. Then the judge or jury deliberates on the evidence and makes a verdict.

Once a settlement is made or a judge or jury has made its verdict, the litigation process is done. However, when a plaintiff or defendant does not agree with the verdict, the party may file an appeal in a higher court (an appellate court) to review the trial court proceeding and determine if errors were made in trying the case. Civil Litigation Attorneys usually refer their clients to appellate lawyers unless they are experienced in practicing appellate law.

Litigation can take several years to complete. Many attorneys handle more than one case at a time. They may work on a case alone or as part of a team.

Litigation Attorneys perform various legal tasks each day. They conduct legal research, review and analyze legal documents, write legal correspondence, and prepare legal documents such as motions, briefs, and contracts. They keep clients up-to-date with their cases, whether in person, by phone, or through e-mails or correspondence. These lawyers also direct and guide paralegals, legal secretaries, and other staff members, who provide them with essential legal, administrative, or clerical support.

Most Litigation Attorneys work in private practice. They may be solo practitioners, members of small law firms that specialize in a few areas of law, or members of large firms. Some private attorneys and law firms focus their practice by serving either plaintiffs or defendants, or for certain types of clientele such as health-care providers, insurance companies, or public interest organizations. Litigation Attorneys are also employed by law departments of corporations, government agencies, and public interest organizations.

Civil Litigation Attorneys work long and irregular hours. They often put in more than 60 hours a week to complete legal tasks and meet deadlines.

Salaries

Salaries for civil Litigation Attorneys vary, depending on such factors as their experience, employer, and geographical location. The U.S. Bureau of Labor Statistics (BLS) reports, in its May 2005 *Occupational Employment Statistics* survey, that the estimated annual salary for most attorneys ranged between $49,180 and $145,600. According to the *2005 Associate Salary Survey* by NALP, the median salaries for law associates ranged from $67,500 (in firms with two to 25 lawyers) to $125,000 (in firms of more than 500 lawyers); and for eighth-year associates, from $109,000 to $181,500.

Employment Prospects

Competition is keen for job openings. In general, overall employment for attorneys is expected to increase by 9 to 17 percent through 2014, according to the BLS. In addition to job growth, opportunities will become available as lawyers retire, advance to hire positions, or transfer to other jobs.

The BLS reports an increasing demand for lawyers who practice in the areas of antitrust, elder, energy, environmental, health care, and intellectual property law.

Advancement Prospects

Like all other lawyers, Litigation Attorneys can advance in any number of ways according to their interests and ambitions. Some attorneys move from one firm to the next to pursue positions with higher pay, more prestige, or more complex responsibilities. Some attorneys seek litigator positions in corporate law departments, government agencies, or public interest organizations.

In law firms, attorneys can advance from associates to partners, which give them a share in their firm's profits. Lawyers with entrepreneurial ambitions become solo practitioners or start their own law firms. Some attorneys pursue other legal-related careers by becoming judges, law professors, law librarians, or politicians.

Education and Training

Most employers prefer to hire lawyers who have earned a juris doctor (J.D.) degree from law schools accredited by the American Bar Association or by a proper state authority.

Most law firms provide their employees with in-house training and education programs. Many law firms have mentor programs that team new associates with senior members.

Throughout their careers, Litigation Attorneys enroll in courses, workshops, and seminars to update their skills and knowledge.

Special Requirements

Litigation Lawyers must hold active membership in the state bar that governs the jurisdiction where they practice. Every state (as well as U.S. territory or Washington, D.C.) has its own eligibility requirements. For specific information, contact the state bar admission office where you wish to practice. See Appendix III for a list of offices.

To practice before a federal court, attorneys must apply for admission. Separate registration is required for each federal court.

Experience, Special Skills, and Personality Traits

Many employers hire recent law school graduates for positions in their litigation practice. For entry-level positions they generally seek candidates who express a strong interest in litigation and have some litigation experience that they may have gained through internships, volunteer work, or employment.

Litigation Attorneys must have excellent negotiation, presentation, communication, writing, organizational, and interpersonal skills to perform well at their job. In addition they need superior self-management skills, including the ability to prioritize multiple tasks, work independently, handle stressful situations, and meet tight deadlines. Being detail-oriented, quick-witted, creative, persuasive, and focused are some personality traits that successful Litigation Attorneys share.

Unions and Associations

Litigation Attorneys join bar associations to take advantage of networking opportunities, professional publications, and other professional resources and services. Bar associations are available at the local, state, and national levels. In some states, membership in the state bar association is mandatory. (For a list of state bar associations, see Appendix IV.) Nationally, these lawyers might join such special-interest associations as the American Association for Justice, the American Bar Association Section of Litigation, or DRI (a national association for defense trial lawyers). For contact information for these organizations, see Appendix V.

Tips for Entry

1. As a high school or college student, observe a few trials to get an idea if civil litigation may interest you.
2. Some experts suggest taking an acting course to help you develop narrative skills as well as a confident presence before groups.
3. A willingness to relocate may enhance your chances of employment. However, keep in mind that if you move to another state, you will need to gain admittance to that state's bar.
4. Use the Internet to learn more about Litigation Attorneys. You might start by visiting the American Association for Justice Web site at http://www.atla.org. For more links, see Appendix VI.

PERSONAL INJURY LAWYER

CAREER PROFILE

Duties: Provide legal advice and services to clients with personal injury claims; prepare and file insurance claims; perform litigation work; negotiate settlements; perform legal duties as required

Alternate Title(s): Tort Attorney

Salary Range: $49,000 to $146,000

Employment Prospects: Good

Advancement Prospects: Good

Prerequisites:

Education or Training—A law (J.D.) degree

Experience—Some experience desirable

Special Skills and Personality Traits—Writing, communication, organizational, time management, and interpersonal skills; be friendly, assertive, analytical, and dedicated

Special Requirements—States require lawyers to be admitted to their state bar; federal courts require registration for lawyers to practice

CAREER LADDER

```
┌─────────────────────────────┐
│  Senior Associate or Partner │
└─────────────────────────────┘

┌─────────────────────────────┐
│         Associate           │
└─────────────────────────────┘

┌─────────────────────────────┐
│      Junior Associate       │
└─────────────────────────────┘
```

Position Description

Personal Injury Lawyers offer legal assistance to individuals who have suffered harm, injury, or loss due to the fault of others. These attorneys are experts in the practice of tort law, which is a body of civil laws that regulates acts of wrongdoing (or torts) by individuals or groups, such as businesses, manufacturers, and institutions. Tort law allows for injured parties to recover the cost of medical expenses, lost income, pain, emotional distress, and other damages that they have endured, as well to prevent the party at fault from repeating their wrongful behavior.

Personal Injury Lawyers take on clients who have experienced much pain and suffering. Some clients may have permanent injuries or disabilities. Their clients' physical or psychological injuries may have been the result of dog bites, slips or falls, automobile accidents, road defects, workplace accidents, medical malpractice, intentional misconduct, false arrest, defective consumer products, environmental contamination, or some other negligent act. Personal Injury Lawyers also handle cases that involve the wrongful death of their clients' family members.

On behalf of their clients, Personal Injury Lawyers seek to recover financial compensation, usually from the negligent party's insurance company. To do that, these attorneys must prove two issues. One is that the negligent party is liable, or responsible for paying damages. The other is that the negligent party must compensate their clients with an appropriate amount of money, which could be as much as hundreds of thousands of dollars or more.

Most Personal Injury Lawyers offer a free consultation to potential clients. They review individuals' claims and advise them on whether or not they have a legitimate case. When Personal Injury lawyers are hired for a case, they usually work on a contingency basis. Clients do not pay any attorneys' fees. Instead, attorneys receive a percentage of the total amount that clients recover for their damages.

Most personal injury cases begin as insurance claims. Attorneys prepare and file paperwork to establish a claim with the negligent party's insurance company. They gather evidence of the party's responsibility and present such materials as expert reports, medical records, and medical bills to the company. These attorneys also submit settlement demands, as well as past court verdicts or settlements that are comparable to their client's claim.

When settlements cannot be agreed upon in a timely matter, Personal Injury Lawyers begin the litigation process for clients. Lawyers prepare a court document known as a pleading that describes the plaintiff's (their client) complaint against the defendant (the negligent party). Lawyers file this document in a state or federal court, as well as have it served to the defendant.

Preparing for a trial takes several months. Attorneys for both sides are given time to collect facts through exchange of documents, interrogatories, and depositions. They also develop strategies to build up the best case for their clients.

Most personal injury cases are settled before they reach the trial stage. If lawsuits do go to trial, Personal Injury Lawyers are responsible for trying the case before either a jury or a judge. They present their case through direct examination of their witnesses and the introduction of physical evidence. They cross-examine the other side's witnesses, as well as make appropriate objections to testimony, evidence, and other matters.

Throughout the litigation process, Personal Injury Lawyers continue settlement negotiations. An offer may be accepted any time before a verdict has been made.

Attorneys maintain close contact with their clients, and provide them with regular updates on and realistic assessments of the status of their case. Although Personal Injury Lawyers have the legal expertise, clients make the decisions on how their case should proceed and whether to accept a settlement offer.

Attorneys typically assemble a legal support team to help them with various aspects of their cases. They employ paralegals and legal secretaries to perform routine legal and administrative tasks, under their supervision and guidance. Lawyers also hire the services of private investigators to seek evidence and witnesses, as well as consult with experts in such subject matter as medicine or engineering that is related to their clients' cases.

Like all attorneys, Personal Injury Lawyers perform a variety of legal tasks each day. They update clients on their cases, they conduct legal research, they review and analyze legal documents, they prepare motions, briefs, contracts, and other legal documents, and they keep up with the current developments in personal injury law, for example.

Personal Injury Attorneys work long and irregular hours. They often put in more than 60 hours a week to complete legal tasks.

Salaries

Salaries for Personal Injury Lawyers vary, depending on such factors as their experience, employer, and geographical location. The estimated annual salary for most lawyers overall ranged between $49,180 and $145,600, according to the May 2005 *Occupational Employment Statistics* survey by the U.S. Bureau of Labor Statistics.

Employment Prospects

Most Personal Injury Lawyers are solo practitioners or members of small law firms. Opportunities in law firms generally become available when attorneys retire, transfer to other jobs, or advance to higher positions. Employers may create additional positions to meet growing needs.

Personal Injury Lawyers can also seek employment as insurance defense attorneys with law firms that specialize in insurance defense work. Law departments within insurance companies and corporations also hire tort attorneys.

Advancement Prospects

In law firms, lawyers begin as associates and, after several years, become partners or move on to other interests. Lawyers with entrepreneurial ambitions become solo practitioners or start their own law firms.

Many Personal Injury Attorneys advance by gaining a professional reputation, earning a higher income, and winning complex cases.

Education and Training

Personal Injury Lawyers complete three or four years of law school to earn a juris doctor (J.D.) degree. Most employers prefer to hire candidates who have earned their J.D. from a school accredited by the American Bar Association.

Throughout their careers, Personal Injury Lawyers enroll in continuing education and training programs to update their skills and knowledge.

Special Requirements

Personal Injury Lawyers must be admitted to the state bar in each state where they practice. All states, as well as the District of Columbia and the U.S. territories, have their own eligibility requirements for admission. For specific information, contact the state bar admission office where you wish to practice. See Appendix III for a list of offices.

To practice before a federal court, attorneys must apply for admission. Separate registration is required for each federal court.

Experience, Special Skills, and Personality Traits

Many law firms hire recent law school graduates for entry-level positions. Employers desire candidates who have practical experience in tort law.

To perform well at their work, Personal Injury Lawyers need effective writing, communication, organizational, time management, and interpersonal skills. Being friendly, assertive, analytical, and dedicated are some personality traits that successful Personal Injury Lawyers share.

Unions and Associations

Personal Injury Lawyers join local and state bar associations to take advantage of networking opportunities and other professional services and resources. (In some states, state bar membership is mandatory.) They also join a national association such as the National Lawyers Association, as well as special-interest organizations such as the National Association of Personal Injury Lawyers. For contact information, see Appendix V.

Tips for Entry

1. Being able to communicate well and clearly to clients, judges, and others is important. Hence, continue improving your writing, oral, and, in particular, your listening skills.

2. As a law student, gain practical experience by obtaining a law clerkship or summer associate position with a personal injury firm.

3. Contact employers for whom you want to work about job openings. Be prepared to complete job applications and to provide résumés, as well as to talk about yourself and what you have to offer their firm.

4. Use the Internet to learn more about personal injury law. You might start by visiting Personal Injury Lawyer.com, http://www.personalinjurylawyer.com, and Injury Board.com, http://www.injuryboard.com. For more links, see Appendix VI.

REAL ESTATE ATTORNEY

CAREER PROFILE	CAREER LADDER

Duties: Provide legal advice and services to clients regarding real estate transactions or litigation; perform duties as required

Alternate Title(s): Property Attorney

Salary Range: $49,000 to $146,000

Employment Prospects: Good

Advancement Prospects: Good

Prerequisites:

Education or Training—A law (J.D.) degree

Experience—Previous experience in real estate law preferred

Special Skills and Personality Traits—Negotiation, organizational, communication, and interpersonal skills; be cooperative, honest, trustworthy, detail-oriented, and creative

Special Requirements—States require lawyers to be admitted to their state bar; federal courts require registration for lawyers to practice

```
┌─────────────────────────────────┐
│  Partner or Managing Attorney   │
└─────────────────────────────────┘

┌─────────────────────────────────┐
│     Senior Associate or         │
│    Senior Staff Attorney        │
└─────────────────────────────────┘

┌─────────────────────────────────┐
│ Junior Associate or Staff Attorney │
└─────────────────────────────────┘
```

Position Description

Real Estate Attorneys offer legal advice and services to individuals and groups who need help with their residential, commercial, or industrial real estate transactions or investments. Their clients may include individuals and small business owners, as well as corporations, public housing authorities and other government agencies, nonprofit organizations, and other institutions. Many Real Estate Attorneys also advise and represent real estate brokers, developers, construction firms, financial institutions, and other service companies within the real estate industry.

Real Estate Attorneys address a wide range of legal issues involved in the sale, purchase, development, finance, or operation of real property such as houses, apartment complexes, schools, hospitals, retail centers, resorts, office buildings, parking garages, industrial sites, and agricultural land. For example, these lawyers might assist:

- individuals to buy or sell houses, condominiums, or other residential units
- tenants to resolve landlord disputes
- condominium associations to handle tax issues
- property owners to convert their real estate for income-producing purposes
- small business owners to lease offices or other types of commercial space
- farmers to obtain easement to neighboring properties
- educational institutions to acquire land for future expansion
- corporations to comply with local, state, and federal environmental regulations in order to obtain approval for building new commercial facilities
- hotel owners to restructure debt for troubled properties
- developers to obtain loans to finance the construction of multifamily housing developments
- industrial developers to seek changes in zoning regulations for vacant land for new projects
- real estate offices to establish property management sections

Real Estate Attorneys establish a special relationship with each client and are obligated to put each client's interest above their own. They help their clients make the best deals, and ensure that their real estate transactions run smoothly.

These attorneys perform various legal tasks. They evaluate the financing options that are available to clients, and advise them about the advantages and disadvantages of each option. Attorneys inform their clients about any laws or regulations that may affect their transactions, as well as describe any restrictions that may apply to property that their clients wish to purchase or lease.

Attorneys examine all contracts involved in a transaction, such as purchase agreements, financial documents, leases, or land contracts, and explain the details to their clients, making sure they understand and agree to all contractual terms before signing a legal document. These lawyers also negotiate the terms of contracts, mortgages, and other matters that are more favorable for their clients.

In purchase transactions, attorneys investigate the title to the property to verify that the seller is the legal property owner and that the title is free and clear to be transferred to new owners.

Furthermore, Real Estate Attorneys may represent their clients before local planning commissions, city councils, or community organizations, where they answer questions about legal issues related to real estate projects that their clients wish to develop or construct. Some Real Estate Attorneys also handle litigation regarding contractual or regulatory issues. These attorneys might represent their clients before the administrative boards of regulatory agencies or before state or federal courts.

Because real estate law is so broad, many attorneys specialize. For example, some Real Estate Attorneys focus their work on the needs of clients seeking to buy or purchase homes, while other lawyers concentrate on working with corporate clients.

Real Estate Attorneys work in different settings. Private lawyers who work with individuals and small business owners are usually solo practitioners or lawyers in general practice firms. Attorneys in large real estate firms typically serve the interests of corporations, schools, government agencies, and other large institutions as well as real estate agencies, developers, property management firms, financial institutions, and organizations within the real estate industry.

Many real estate specialists work in law departments of corporations, insurance companies, financial institutions, title companies, and real estate offices. These lawyers also find employment with nonprofit organizations, as well as government agencies such as local public housing authorities, state development agencies, or the U.S. Department of Housing and Urban Development.

Real Estate Attorneys typically work long hours to complete their various duties as well as to meet deadlines. It is not uncommon for them to work more than 60 hours per week. Some Real Estate Attorneys are involved with projects that require them to travel to other cities, states, and even other countries.

Salaries

Salaries for Real Estate Attorneys vary, depending on such factors as their experience, employer, and geographical location. Specific salary information for these lawyers is unavailable. However, according to the U.S. Bureau of Labor Statistics, in its May 2005 *Occupational Employment Statistics* survey the estimated annual salary for most lawyers ranged between $49,180 and $145,600.

Employment Prospects

In general, job openings become available when Real Estate Attorneys transfer to other jobs, advance to higher positions, or retire. Employers create additional positions to meet their growing needs. When the real estate market is strong, the demand for Real Estate Attorneys increases.

Advancement Prospects

Real Estate Attorneys may advance in various ways, depending on their ambitions and interests. In law firms, lawyers begin as associates and after several years become partners or move on to other interests. Lawyers can also advance to supervisory and management positions. Entrepreneurial lawyers may become solo practitioners or start their own law firms.

Education and Training

Real Estate Attorneys possess a juris doctor (J.D.) degree, which they have earned after completing three or four years of law school. Employers usually prefer to hire candidates who have graduated from a school accredited by the American Bar Association or a proper state authority.

Novice attorneys typically receive supervision and guidance from experienced lawyers. For example, some law firms have mentor programs that team new associates with senior members. Some employers provide their employees with formal training programs.

Special Requirements

To practice law in a state—as well as a U.S. territory or the District of Columbia—individuals must first gain admission to that state's bar. For information about eligibility requirements, contact the state bar admission office where you wish to practice. See Appendix III for a list of offices.

To practice before a federal court, Real Estate Attorneys must apply for admission. Separate registration is required for each federal court.

Experience, Special Skills, and Personality Traits

Requirements vary with the different types of employers. In general, employers prefer to hire candidates who have prior experience in the practice of real estate law. Recent law school graduates may have gained their experience through law clerkships, internships, volunteer work, or employment.

Real Estate Attorneys need strong negotiation and organizational skills for their work. Communication and interpersonal skills are also important, as these lawyers need to be able to work effectively and closely with clients, real estate agents, financial officers, and others.

Some personality traits that Real Estate Attorneys have in common include being cooperative, honest, trustworthy, detail-oriented, and creative.

Unions and Associations

Real Estate Attorneys may join local, state, and national bar associations to take advantage of education programs, networking opportunities, and other professional services and resources. (In some states, state bar membership is mandatory.) Many attorney associations, such as the American Bar Association, have a real estate law section.

Tips for Entry

1. While in law school, find out if real estate law is the right field for you by taking one or more real estate law courses.
2. Gain practical experience by obtaining a law clerkship or summer associate position in a law firm with a real estate practice.
3. As a junior associate, let senior associates and partners in your firm know that you are interested in doing real estate work. You might offer to handle simple real estate closings for clients, for example.
4. Use the Internet to learn more about real estate law as well as the real estate industry. You might start by visiting these Web sites: Illinois Real Estate Lawyers Association, http://www.reallaw.org, and Real Estate ABC.com, http://www.realestateabc.com. For more links, see Appendix VI.

TAX ATTORNEY

CAREER PROFILE

Duties: Provide legal advice and services pertaining to tax matters; perform legal duties as required

Alternate Title(s): None

Salary Range: $49,000 to $146,000

Employment Prospects: Good

Advancement Prospects: Good

Prerequisites:

Education or Training—A juris doctor (J.D.) degree; master of law degree in taxation usually preferred

Experience—One or more years of practice in tax law

Special Skills and Personality Traits—Research, writing, analytical, problem-solving, communication, interpersonal, negotiation, and conflict resolution skills; be organized, detail-oriented, persuasive, articulate, self-assured, and dedicated

Special Requirements—States require lawyers to be admitted to their state bar; federal courts require registration for lawyers to practice

CAREER LADDER

```
┌─────────────────────────────────┐
│   Senior Associate or Partner   │
└─────────────────────────────────┘

┌─────────────────────────────────┐
│           Associate             │
└─────────────────────────────────┘

┌─────────────────────────────────┐
│        Junior Associate         │
└─────────────────────────────────┘
```

Position Description

In the United States, taxes are levied on individuals and businesses at the local, state, and federal levels of government to raise money for the cost of running governmental operations as well as for providing essential services, such as education, social services, law enforcement, national defense, public works, and transportation systems. Individuals and businesses must pay various taxes on the different types of activities in which they are engaged. Some of these taxes may include personal income, social security, business income, payroll, sales, property, gift, and excise taxes, among others. Because taxation laws are complicated—and continually changing—many individuals and businesses seek legal assistance from Tax Attorneys before making important personal decisions or business transactions.

Tax Attorneys are experts in the practice of tax laws, regulations, and codes that are established by the different levels of government in the United States. Many of them also specialize in the tax laws of other nations. Tax Attorneys offer their legal services and counsel to individuals, as well as to small business owners, large companies, and multinational corporations.

Tax Attorneys are probably best known for helping clients resolve their tax problems with local and state tax authorities as well as with the Internal Revenue Service (IRS), the federal tax collection agency. These attorneys defend their clients who have tax returns that are being challenged by tax authorities. Tax Attorneys represent their clients at required meetings, audits, and hearings with the IRS or a local or state tax authority. They may also defend their clients in litigation issues before the U.S. tax court or in a state or federal trial court.

Tax Attorneys also perform various types of transaction work. Many of these lawyers specialize in tax planning. They devise strategies to reduce the taxation obligation on clients' income and investments. For example, individuals might reduce their tax burden by putting some of their money in trusts, or giving some of their money away as gifts to family members.

Some Tax Attorneys provide legal assistance to individuals in the area of estate planning. They advise clients on ways that they might lessen the taxes on their assets when they are distributed to their beneficiaries before or upon their death.

Many Tax Attorneys focus on providing assistance to corporations with business transactions. They counsel corporate clients on the tax consequences of business transactions, such as internal reorganizations, mergers, or acquisitions. They also help clients structure their transactions so that they meet their financial goals as well as cut their tax liabilities. In addition, Tax Attorneys give legal and tax advice on issues regarding payroll, employee benefit plans, capital gains and losses, and the distribution of profits, among other issues.

Some Tax Attorneys assist non-profit organizations—such as charities, churches, private foundations, and community-based organizations—that are exempt from paying taxes. They help these organizations comply with the appropriate requirements and procedures to maintain their tax-exempt status.

Tax Attorneys work in different settings. Many work in private practice. They may work as solo practitioners, or as associates or partners in small tax law firms or in law firms with tax law sections. Most private lawyers specialize in doing either transactional work or tax litigation, also known as tax controversy work.

Some Tax Attorneys are employed by large accounting firms. Others work as in-house counsel in law departments of large corporations. Other Tax Attorneys are employed in the different levels of government. In addition to being employed by government agencies that administer tax laws, Tax Attorneys hold legal and policy positions with legislative bodies. The Office of Chief Counsel, a federal agency, is the top employer of Tax Attorneys in the United States. They employ about 1,500 lawyers to provide legal advice and representation to the IRS as well as to litigate tax cases against individuals, companies, and foreign bodies.

Like all other lawyers, Tax Attorneys establish a special relationship with each of their clients, and are obligated to put each client's interests above their own. They are also obliged to be fair, unbiased, and impartial, while interpreting tax laws that favor neither the government nor the taxpayer.

Tax Attorneys perform a variety of duties, many of which are specific to their work setting and position. They also perform various legal tasks that are the same in any work setting. They conduct legal research, analyze and evaluate legal documents, write legal correspondence, draft legal documents, and meet with clients. These lawyers are also responsible for keeping up with changes in tax laws, regulations, and codes, as well as for evaluating how these changes may affect their clients. They advise their clients accordingly.

Tax Attorneys often work more than 40 hours a week to complete their tasks and meet deadlines.

Salaries

Salaries for Tax Attorneys vary, depending on such factors as their education, experience, employer, and geographical location. According to the May 2005 *Occupational Employment Statistics* survey by the U.S. Bureau of Labor Statistics, the estimated annual salary for most lawyers overall ranged between $49,180 and $145,600.

Employment Prospects

Job openings usually become available as lawyers retire, advance to other positions, or transfer to other jobs. Employers will create additional positions to meet their growing needs.

Opportunities are continually favorable for qualified Tax Attorneys in private law firms, corporate law departments, and government agencies.

Advancement Prospects

Tax Attorneys may advance in various ways, depending on their ambitions and interests. For example, they might choose to specialize in litigation or practice in real estate law, corporate law, or other related areas.

In law firms, lawyers begin as associates and, after several years, become partners or move on to other interests. In corporate and government settings, lawyers can advance to supervisory and management positions. Entrepreneurial lawyers may become solo practitioners or start their own law firms.

Education and Training

Employers typically prefer to hire candidates who have earned their juris doctor (J.D.) degree from a law school accredited by the American Bar Association. Many employers also seek candidates, for both entry-level and experienced positions, who possess the master of laws (LL.M) degree in taxation. Some employers expect Tax Attorneys in their employ to eventually obtain the LL.M degree.

Employers usually provide lawyers with in-house training programs. In addition, Tax Attorneys enroll in continuing education programs and training programs to update their skills and knowledge.

Special Requirements

To practice law in a state (or U.S. territory or Washington, D.C.), individuals must first gain admission to that state's bar. Every jurisdiction has its own eligibility requirements. For specific information, contact the state bar admission office where you wish to practice. See Appendix III for a list of offices.

To practice before the U.S. Tax Court or any other federal court, Tax Attorneys must apply for admission. Separate registration is required for each federal court.

Experience, Special Skills, and Personality Traits
Employers usually prefer to hire candidates for junior positions who have one or more years of experience in practicing tax law. They may have gained their experience through law school clinics, employment, law clerkships, or pro bono work.

Tax Attorneys need excellent research, writing, analytical, and problem-solving skills for their work. They must also have strong communication, interpersonal, negotiation, and conflict resolution skills. Being organized, detail-oriented, persuasive, articulate, self-assured, and dedicated are some personality traits that successful Tax Attorneys have in common.

Unions and Associations
Many Tax Attorneys join professional organizations to take advantage of networking opportunities and other professional services and resources. They join bar associations that serve their diverse interests such as the American Bar Association (ABA) Section of Taxation, Federal Bar Association, or the American Association for Justice. Tax Attorneys may be required to be members of the state bar that governs the jurisdiction where they practice.

Tax Attorneys are also eligible to join societies for tax professionals, such as the Institute for Professionals in Tax-ation, the Tax Executives Institute, or the National Association of Tax Professionals.

For contact information for the above organizations, see Appendix V.

Tips for Entry
1. Some employers prefer candidates who have an undergraduate degree in accounting or who have taken some accounting courses.
2. In law school, take one or more courses on tax law to determine if it is an area in which you might like to practice.
3. As a law student, seek a summer position with a law firm that practices tax law. Let your interviewers know about your interest in that practice area.
4. The IRS Office of Chief Counsel is the largest employer of Tax Attorneys. It has vacancies for entry-level and experienced positions. For information about jobs, as well as internships and law clerkships, visit the IRS webpage at http://jobs.irs.gov/car_opp_atty.html.
5. Learn more about Tax Attorneys and tax law on the Internet. You might start by visiting the ABA Tax Section Web site, http://www.abanet.org/tax/home.html. For more links, see Appendix VI.

JUDGES

TRIAL JUDGE
(GENERAL JURISDICTION)

CAREER PROFILE

Duties: Preside over court trials, conduct hearings, research law, review court documents, supervise staff, and perform other judicial duties

Alternate Title(s): District Court Judge or other title that reflects a specific position

Salary Range: $94,000 to $165,000 for state judges; $165,200 for federal judges (in 2006)

Employment Prospects: Poor

Advancement Prospects: Poor

Prerequisites:

Education or Training—A law (J.D.) degree

Experience—Previous experience as a lawyer

Special Skills and Personality Traits—Case management, interpersonal, and communication skills; be patient, courteous, fair, objective, and hardworking

CAREER LADDER

```
┌─────────────────────────────────┐
│  Presiding Judge or Judge in a   │
│    higher state or federal court │
└─────────────────────────────────┘

┌─────────────────────────────────┐
│  Trial Court Judge (state or     │
│   federal, general jurisdiction) │
└─────────────────────────────────┘

┌─────────────────────────────────┐
│  Attorney or Judge (in a lower   │
│             court)               │
└─────────────────────────────────┘
```

Position Description

The United States has two separate levels of court systems—the federal court system and the individual state court systems. Trial Judges are responsible for ensuring that the law is being applied fairly and without bias throughout court proceedings. They also have the duty to make sure that court trials run smoothly and efficiently.

Trial Judges preside in either limited or general jurisdiction trial courts. Judges in limited jurisdiction courts, such as the federal tax court and the county family court, can only hear cases that are pertinent to their type of court. Trial Judges in general jurisdiction courts can hear a wide range of civil and criminal cases.

At the state level, general jurisdiction Trial Judges preside in superior courts, which might also be called district courts or circuit courts. State Trial Judges hear cases that involve the laws of their particular states. At the federal level, general jurisdiction Trial Judges preside in U.S. district courts. They hear cases that involve the federal government, constitutional issues, federal law violations, or lawsuits between citizens of different states.

Trial Judges are responsible for overseeing court proceedings, which may take a few days, several weeks, or months to complete. Judges make sure that lawyers, witnesses, and jurors follow court procedures, and that both sides of a dispute or criminal case have the opportunity to be heard. Trial Judges determine the facts surrounding a case, and rule on the admissibility of physical evidence and witness testimony that is submitted in court. Judges must stay objective throughout court proceedings. They cannot in any way influence the outcome of a trial.

A trial may be decided by a Trial Judge or by a jury. Either a Trial Judge or the jury determines if an accused party is guilty or not guilty, or who is the wronged party in a civil dispute. A Trial Judge has the power to overrule a jury's verdict, but such instances are rare.

In a jury trial, a Trial Judge oversees the selection process of jury members. The lawyers generally do most of the interviewing and choosing of potential jurors. The judge may also question potential jurors, as well as dismiss them from the jury. When the trial begins, the Trial Judge instructs jurors about applicable laws and about their duty to deduce the facts from the evidence that is presented before the bench. During the jury's deliberation, the judge clarifies any legal questions that the jury may ask.

In federal courts and most state courts, Trial Judges are responsible for making the formal judgment of punishment in criminal cases. Judges may grant probation or a prison sentence. In some states, Trial Judges can hand down a capital punishment sentence.

Trial Judges also preside over other hearings, such as pretrial hearings, sentence hearings, and settlement conferences. In addition, they perform other tasks. For example, they research legal issues, review pleadings and motions, and supervise law clerks, secretaries, and other court support staff.

Each court has its own system for assigning Trial Judges to cases. Some courts, for example, make assignments by a random drawing of names; other courts assign judges according to their expertise in certain areas of law.

Trial Judges are either appointed or elected to serve. Federal judges are appointed by the president, with confirmation by the U.S. Senate. They serve a life term. State judges serve limited terms that may be renewed. In some states, judges are appointed by the governor or state legislature for one term, and then are elected by the voters for additional terms. In other states, judges run for office on either a partisan or nonpartisan ballot.

Judges usually work 40 hours a week, and work additional hours when needed.

Salaries

Salaries for Trial Judges vary, depending on such factors as their employer and geographical location. The annual salary for state Trial Judges in general jurisdiction trial courts ranged from $94,093 to $165,200, according to the January 2006 *Survey of Judicial Salaries,* by the National Center for State Courts. The annual salary in 2006 for federal (district court) Trial Judges was $165,200.

Employment Prospects

The number of judgeships at the state level are established by state legislatures, and at the federal level, by Congress. Creation of new positions is limited by the availability of state or federal funds. Most opportunities become available as judges retire or resign. The competition for available positions is keen and intense, as it involves being nominated for candidacy, and then being appointed to the bench or elected by the voters.

Advancement Prospects

Advancement opportunities are limited. Judges may serve as supervisory or presiding judges for their courts, but for limited terms. Trial Judges might seek appointments to higher state and federal courts.

At both the state and federal levels, retired Trial Court Judges may continue as senior judges, assisting with court caseloads when needed.

Education and Training

Judges typically have law (juris doctor) degrees.

Newly elected or appointed Trial Judges receive orientation training. Many states require that judges complete continuing education courses throughout their careers.

Experience, Skills, and Personality Traits

Most states require that candidates for Trial Judges be practicing lawyers or have practiced for a minimum number of years. At the federal level, Trial Judges are not required to be attorneys, but most judges were attorneys prior to their nomination. Judges should have strong case management skills, as well as excellent interpersonal and communication skills. They should be able to work well under stress and handle political pressure. Being patient, courteous, fair, objective, and hardworking are a few personality traits that successful Trial Judges share.

Unions and Associations

Many Trial Judges join professional associations such as the American Judges Association to take advantage of professional services and resources, such as networking opportunities. Judges are also eligible to join the American Bar Association; federal judges can join the Federal Bar Association. For contact information, see Appendix V.

Tips for Entry

1. Lawyers can contact the courts in which they would like to preside to learn about the application process for judicial positions.
2. Network with judges, lawyers, and others to learn about current or upcoming vacancies.
3. Learn more about the U.S. court systems on the Internet. You might start by visiting these Web sites: the American Judicature Society, http://www.ajs.org, and U.S. District Courts, http://www.uscourts.gov/districtcourts.html. For more links, see Appendix VI.

MUNICIPAL JUDGE

CAREER PROFILE

Duties: Preside over criminal and civil trials in limited jurisdiction courts; perform judicial duties as required

Alternate Title(s): City Judge, Town Judge, Village Judge, Police Court Judge

Salary Range: $26,000 to $145,000

Employment Prospects: Poor

Advancement Prospects: Poor

Prerequisites:

Education or Training—J.D. (law degree) may be required; orientation training

Experience—Several years of experience as a practicing lawyer

Special Skills and Personality Traits—Case management, interpersonal, and communication skills; be patient, courteous, fair, objective, hardworking

CAREER LADDER

```
┌─────────────────────────────────────┐
│ Presiding Judge or Judge in a higher │
│      state or federal court          │
└─────────────────────────────────────┘

┌─────────────────────────────────────┐
│         Municipal Judge              │
└─────────────────────────────────────┘

┌─────────────────────────────────────┐
│            Attorney                  │
└─────────────────────────────────────┘
```

Position Description

Municipal Judges are trial judges in limited jurisdiction courts called municipal, or city, courts. The municipal courts are the lowest level of state courts. They are sometimes known as police courts, city courts, township courts, or village courts. The jurisdiction of these courts extends to the boundaries of the municipalities—cities, towns, boroughs, or villages.

Municipal judges preside over both civil and criminal trials. The types of cases vary from court to court. In general, Municipal Judges have the authority to hear any or all of these types of cases:

- civil lawsuits that involve monetary values ranging between $3,000 and $25,000 in property or cash, depending on the municipality
- violations of municipal codes such as in landlord-tenant cases or in cases involving building infractions
- criminal misdemeanors such as disorderly conduct, shoplifting, simple assault, and lewdness
- domestic violence cases
- violations of motor vehicle and traffic laws, including parking tickets, speeding, reckless driving, and driving under the influence of alcohol or drugs

In some courts, Municipal Judges may conduct preliminary hearings for defendants accused of committing felonies.

Municipal Judges conduct jury and nonjury trials as well as pretrial conferences and other hearings. Their duties also include reading motions and pleadings, researching legal issues, and supervising their court staff. Municipal Judges may also handle the issuing of court processes, such as summons, subpoenas, and warrants.

Depending on the municipality, Municipal Judges may be appointed by mayors or city councils or elected by city voters. They serve limited terms, usually four to 10 years.

Municipal Judges may serve on a part-time or full-time basis.

Salaries

Salaries for Municipal Judges vary, depending on factors such as their employer and geographical location. Specific salary information for Municipal Judges is unavailable. The estimated annual salary for most judges overall ranged from $26,250 to $145,290, according to the May 2005 *Occupational Employment Statistics* survey by the U.S. Bureau of Labor Statistics. The estimated annual mean wage for judges at the local government level was $74,860.

Employment Prospects

Opportunities are limited, and usually become available as Municipal Judges retire or resign. Competition for positions is typically intense due to the political nature of obtaining appointments or being elected by voters in a municipality.

Advancement Prospects

Although many Municipal Judges possess a juris doctor (J.D.) degree, the law degree may not be a formal requirement to become a judge. Municipal Judges can be selected to serve as supervisory or presiding judges in their courts, but these are for limited terms. Many Municipal Judges seek appointments to district courts, other state courts, or federal courts.

Education and Training

Newly elected or appointed Municipal Judges receive orientation training. Some municipal courts require their judges to complete a minimum of continuing education units each year.

Experience, Skills, and Personality Traits

Most Municipal Judges are experienced lawyers who have been practicing in their communities for several years. Some municipalities require judicial candidates to have been practicing lawyers for a minimum number of years. In some municipalities, candidates are not required to be lawyers, but must meet special training requirements.

Municipal Judges, like all judges, need excellent case management skills, as well as superior interpersonal and communication skills. They should be able to work well under stress and to handle political pressure. Being patient, courteous, fair, objective, and hardworking are a few personality traits that successful Municipal Judges share.

Unions and Associations

Municipal Judges join professional associations to take advantage of training programs, professional resources, and other professional services. Their membership also provides them with various opportunities to network with judges, lawyers, and other professionals. Many Municipal Judges are members of local or state municipal court associations and attorney bar associations.

Some national professional associations that Municipal Judges might join are the American Judges Association, the American Judicature Society, and the American Bar Association. For contact information, see Appendix V.

Tips for Entry

1. Observe the proceedings in a municipal court room to get an idea of what Municipal Judges do.
2. Some family courts require candidates to possess membership in their state's bar association.
3. You will need to build up a support base in your community to become a Municipal Judge. To start, get involved in community service and social activities. Also network with elected officials, lawyers, and judges, as well as local business people and citizens.
4. Learn more about municipal courts and judges on the Internet. Many municipal courts have web pages. To get a list of web pages, enter the keywords *municipal court* in a search engine. For other links to resources about Municipal Judges, see Appendix VI.

FAMILY COURT JUDGE

CAREER PROFILE

Duties: Hear cases that involve children and family issues such as divorce, child abuse, domestic violence, and juvenile delinquency; perform judicial duties as required

Alternate Title(s): Family Judge, Municipal Judge, District Judge

Salary Range: $26,000 to $145,000

Employment Prospects: Poor

Advancement Prospects: Poor

Prerequisites:

    Education or Training—J.D. (law degree) may be required; orientation training

    Experience—Experience as attorneys in family law practice; knowledgeable about psychology, child development and related disciplines

    Special Skills and Personality Traits—Case management, writing, analytical, interpersonal, and communication skills; be patient, respectful, fair, impartial, decisive, dedicated

CAREER LADDER

```
┌─────────────────────────────┐
│      Presiding Judge         │
│ or Judge in a higher court   │
└─────────────────────────────┘

┌─────────────────────────────┐
│      Family Court Judge      │
└─────────────────────────────┘

┌─────────────────────────────┐
│          Attorney            │
└─────────────────────────────┘
```

Position Description

Family Court Judges are trial judges in special limited-jurisdiction courts. They conduct legal proceedings that focus solely on problems and issues concerning families and children. Family members or social agencies may submit petitions to have their cases heard in family courts.

Family courts are established at the local and state government levels. Their main purpose is to help and protect families whose unity is being threatened and to help families find ways to stay together. These courts also make sure that children are receiving care, guidance, and discipline that is in their best interest. Thus, to achieve their objectives, family courts work closely with social service agencies and other resources in their communities.

Family Court Judges preside over a wide range of family law cases. These can vary from one court to the next. Some family law cases that a Family Court Judge may have the authority to hear are:

- divorce, legal separation, and annulment
- alimony and child support
- child custody and visitation
- child abuse and neglect
- legal guardianships of children and disabled persons
- paternity
- adoption
- termination of parental rights
- child protection cases, which involves removing children from families and placing them in foster care
- juvenile delinquency, including law violations and status offenses
- domestic violence and other criminal offenses that happen within a family
- commitment of mentally ill family members to hospitals or other health care facilities

In family courts, cases are tried only before the Family Court Judges. In other words, the judges hear the testimony and make the final decision. The legal proceedings are called hearings, and are less formal than trials. Family Court Judges conduct unbiased and impartial hearings in an orderly procedure. The opposing parties each have the opportunity to present evidence that supports their case.

After hearing the testimony, Family Court Judges decide if the facts of the case have been proved. If they have not, the case is dismissed. If the facts have been proved as true, then the judges decide what should happen to the parties. For example, in a child custody case, a judge may decide which parent has physical custody of the child. Or, in a juvenile crime case, a judge may decide to send the child to a prison for juveniles or place the child on probation on the condition that the child and family attend weekly counseling sessions.

Generally, family court hearings are open to the public. But on occasion, judges close the courtroom to the public to protect the privacy of the parties. They may also exclude certain people from the courtroom if they feel children are at risk of being harmed.

Family Court Judges also conduct other types of hearings and conferences, such as status hearings and emergency hearings. Their duties also include reviewing motions and pleadings, reading legal documents, researching legal issues, and writing orders and opinions. In addition, they supervise law clerks, judicial assistants, and other court support staff.

Family Court Judges serve terms that vary from court to court. These judges are selected in one of two ways. They may be appointed initially by state or local executives and then run in a retention election after serving their first term. Or they may be elected by popular vote in partisan or nonpartisan elections. In some localities, judges are elected or appointed as trial judges and then assigned to positions in family court.

Family Court Judges work 40 hours a week, putting in additional hours when needed.

Salaries

Salaries for Family Court Judges vary, depending on their geographical location and other factors. According to the May 2005 *Occupational Employment Statistics* survey, by the U.S. Bureau of Labor Statistics, the estimated annual salary for most judges overall ranged between $26,250 and $145,290.

Employment Prospects

Most positions become available when judges complete their terms or when they resign, retire, or leave for other reasons before their terms end. A court may create new positions to meet the demands of increasing caseloads if funds are available.

Advancement Prospects

Family Court Judges may be selected to serve as supervisory or presiding judges for limited terms. Many Family Court Judges pursue appointments for judgeships in higher state courts as well as in federal courts.

Education and Training

There are no standard educational requirements to become a Family Court Judge. However, many jurisdictions prefer to select candidates who have a legal background and possess a juris doctor (J.D.) degree.

New Family Court Judges receive orientation training. Many states require that judges complete annual legal and judicial training and continuing education programs.

Throughout their careers, Family Court Judges participate in training and education programs related to juvenile justice, child development, and family issues.

Experience, Skills, and Personality Traits

Many Family Court Judges are lawyers who have practiced for several years in the area of family law. In addition, they are knowledgeable about psychology, child development, and related disciplines.

Family Court Judges need excellent case management, writing, and analytical skills, as well as strong interpersonal and communication skills. Being patient, respectful, fair, impartial, decisive, and dedicated are a few personality traits that successful Family Court Judges share.

Unions and Associations

Many Family Court Judges join professional associations to take advantage of professional services and resources as well as networking opportunities with their colleagues. One organization that specifically serves their profession is the National Council of Juvenile and Family Court Judges. Some other national associations are the American Judges Association and the American Bar Association. (For contact information, see Appendix V.) Many Family Court Judges also join local and state attorney bars.

Tips for Entry

1. Volunteer with community agencies that serve the different social needs of children, youth, or families. Find out if the area of family law is right for you.
2. Some family courts require candidates to possess membership in their state's bar association.
3. Read about different family issues. Observe family courts in action. Visit community and social agencies that work with children, youth, or families. You might also volunteer or obtain jobs or internships with a social or community agency.
4. You can learn more about family courts and family law on the Internet. To find relevant web pages, enter any of these keywords in a search engine: *family court, family court judge,* or *family law.* For some links, see Appendix VI.

BANKRUPTCY JUDGE

CAREER PROFILE

Duties: Oversee the administration of bankruptcy cases; conduct conferences, hearings, and trials; make final decisions on cases; perform duties as required

Alternate Title(s): Chief Bankruptcy Judge

Salary: $151,984

Employment Prospects: Poor

Advancement Prospects: Poor

Prerequisites:

Education or Training—J.D. (law degree) usually required; orientation training

Experience—Minimum of five years in active law practice or other acceptable qualifying experience

Special Skills and Personality Traits—Case management, interpersonal, and communication skills; be patient, courteous, fair, objective, and hardworking

Special Requirements—Be admitted to a state bar association

CAREER LADDER

```
┌─────────────────────────────┐
│   Chief Bankruptcy Judge    │
└─────────────────────────────┘

┌─────────────────────────────┐
│     Bankruptcy Judge        │
└─────────────────────────────┘

┌─────────────────────────────┐
│         Attorney            │
└─────────────────────────────┘
```

Position Description

In the United States, debtors who are experiencing such deep financial difficulties that they cannot pay their creditors may file for bankruptcy in federal courts. Bankruptcy is a legal procedure that protects debtors so that they can reorganize their finances in order to pay off some or all of their debts. The federal district courts have exclusive jurisdiction over bankruptcy cases. Bankruptcy Judges are in charge of overseeing the administration of these cases. They are also responsible for deciding disputes that creditors may have with bankruptcy cases.

Debtors may be persons, businesses, corporations, municipalities, government agencies, and institutions. When debtors file their petitions, the courts automatically place an order, called a stay, on their debts. This order prevents creditors from taking any kind of collections action while the stay is in effect.

There are generally two types of bankruptcy proceedings. In one proceeding, the bankruptcy court sells most of a debtor's property and distributes the cash among the creditors. In the other proceeding, a debtor proposes a financial plan for paying back some or all of his or her debts to the creditors. Bankruptcy Judges do not handle the day-to-day management of individual cases. Instead, they appoint trustees to administer individual cases.

Bankruptcy Judges hold conferences and hearings with debtors and trustees in person or by telephone. They have the authority to make final decisions on bankruptcy cases. For example, they approve or disapprove the petitions that debtors initially file. They approve or disapprove repayment plans. They can also discharge some or all debts in a case. That means a debtor does not have to repay creditors for those debts that a Bankruptcy Judge discharges.

Bankruptcy Judges also conduct trials that involve disputes between the debtors and their creditors. Litigation in bankruptcy courts is conducted the same way as in trial courts. There are pretrial proceedings, settlement conferences, and so on. Cases may be heard before judges or juries.

Bankruptcy Judges handle various tasks in their work. For example, they:

- schedule weekly or monthly calendars
- review motions
- research the law for legal precedents
- write orders and opinions, following specific formats

Bankruptcy judges are appointed for 14-year terms by the Judges of the U.S. Court of Appeals. They may be reappointed for unlimited terms.

On occasion, Bankruptcy Judges are temporarily assigned to other bankruptcy courts where judges are handling heavy caseloads.

Salaries

All U.S. Bankruptcy Judges earn the same pay, which is set by the U.S. Congress. In 2006, their annual salary was $151,984.

Employment Prospects

As of 2006, there are 90 bankruptcy courts and 350 bankruptcy judgeships. The U.S. Congress sets the number of bankruptcy judgeships based on the recommendations of the Judicial Conference of the United States.

Opportunities typically become available as terms end for Bankruptcy Judges or when they are not reappointed. Vacancies also open up when judges die, retire, or resign before their terms are over. Additional bankruptcy judgeships—temporary or permanent—may be created to meet increasing caseloads.

Advancement Prospects

Advancement opportunities are limited. Bankruptcy Judges may serve as supervisory or presiding judges for their courts, but for limited terms. Retired judges may continue as senior judges, assisting with court caseloads when needed.

Education and Training

There are no formal educational requirements to become a Bankruptcy Judge. However, these judges must be members of a state bar association when they are appointed to the bench. To be a member of any state bar, individuals must possess a juris doctor (J.D.) degree.

Newly appointed Bankruptcy Judges receive orientation training. They also complete training and education programs throughout their careers.

Special Requirements

To qualify for a bankruptcy judgeship, applicants must be licensed attorneys. They must be in good standing of the highest court of at least one state, the District of Columbia, or the Commonwealth of Puerto Rico.

Experience, Skills, and Personality Traits

Candidates must have actively practiced law for at least five years. They may also qualify by having had experience as:

- a judge of a state court of record or other state judicial officer
- a U.S. magistrate judge, bankruptcy referee, or other federal judicial officer
- an attorney for a state of federal government agency
- a judicial law clerk

Bankruptcy Judges need strong case management skills, as well as excellent interpersonal and communication skills. Some personality traits that successful Bankruptcy Judges share are being patient, courteous, fair, objective, and hardworking.

Unions and Associations

Many Bankruptcy Judges join professional associations to take advantage of professional services and resources as well as networking opportunities with their colleagues. One organization that serves their profession is the National Conference of Bankruptcy Judges. Some other organizations that they might join are the American Bankruptcy Institute, the American Judges Association, the American Bar Association, and the Federal Bar Association. For contact information, see Appendix V.

Tips for Entry

1. While in law school, get an idea if bankruptcy law might be an area that suits you. For example, you might obtain an internship with a bankruptcy court or a law firm that specializes in bankruptcy law.
2. Nominees for bankruptcy judgeships must be a member in good standing of every bar association to which they belong.
3. Use the Internet to learn more about bankruptcy courts as well as bankruptcy in general. You might start by visiting these Web sites: U.S. Bankruptcy Courts, http://www.uscourts.gov/bankruptcycourts.html, and American Bankruptcy Institute, http://www.abiworld.org. For more links, see Appendix VI.

APPELLATE JUDGE

CAREER PROFILE

Duties: Review petitions to appeal the court decisions made in trial courts; examine briefs; conduct legal research; write opinions; and perform other judicial duties

Alternate Title(s): Justice

Salary Range: $101,000 to $212,000

Employment Prospects: Poor

Advancement Prospects: Poor

Prerequisites:

Education or Training—J.D. (law degree) usually required; orientation training

Experience—Previous experience as a lawyer or judge usually preferred

Special Skills and Personality Traits—Case management, interpersonal, and communication skills; be calm, respectful, fair, analytical, hardworking

Special Requirements—Admission to a state bar association may be required

CAREER LADDER

```
┌─────────────────────────────────────┐
│  Presiding Judge or Judge in a higher │
│       state or federal court          │
└─────────────────────────────────────┘

┌─────────────────────────────────────┐
│      Appellate Court Judge            │
│     (state or federal court)          │
└─────────────────────────────────────┘

┌─────────────────────────────────────┐
│  Attorney or Judge (in a lower court) │
└─────────────────────────────────────┘
```

Position Description

The U.S. court system has two types of courts, each serving a different function. Trial courts determine the facts of criminal and civil cases and make judgments based on the testimony and evidence presented in court. If litigants disagree with the decisions, they can file petitions with the appellate courts. These petitions are reviewed by Appellate Judges. They do not retry cases nor hear new evidence. Their duty is to determine if errors have been made during the trial process which resulted in a miscarriage of justice.

Appellate courts are part of both the federal and state court systems. The federal system has two levels of appellate courts—the courts of appeals, one each in the 13 judicial circuits, and the Supreme Court, which is the highest court in the country. Most states have two levels of appeals courts. In these states, litigants first file their appeals with a court of appeal, or an intermediate appellate court. If they are unhappy with the decision, they may appeal their case to the state supreme court. A few states have only one appeals court, the state supreme court, also known as the court of last resort.

Appellate cases are reviewed by a panel of Appellate Judges. They review lawyers' arguments in the form of legal briefs (written legal statements). They may also listen to oral arguments from the lawyers, but limit their time to between 10 and 30 minutes.

The judges make one of three decisions. They may agree with the decision made by a trial judge. They may reverse a trial court's decision. Or they may send a case back to the trial court for a retrial. If a litigant disagrees with the appellate court's decision, the party can appeal to a higher court.

Appellate Judges spend most of their time in chambers and law libraries, reviewing briefs and motions, researching the law, and writing and editing opinions (decisions). They spend only a few hours each week in the courtroom hearing oral arguments.

In addition to their judiciary duties, many Appellate Judges teach courses at law schools, colleges, and universities, as well as lead workshops and seminars sponsored by professional associations. Many write articles and books about the legal and judicial systems. Some also give presentations to professional associations, schools, community groups, and so on.

Appellate Judges are selected in various ways. Federal Appellate Judges are appointed by the president with the approval of the U.S. Senate. They serve a lifetime term. They can only be removed from office through impeachment.

At the state level, the selection process varies from state to state. Some states choose their Appellate Judges in either partisan or nonpartisan elections. (Partisan elections mean that judges run for office as members of a political party.) In other states, the governor appoints Appellate Judges who have been nominated by a state judicial nominating committee. These state appointments may require confirmation by the state senate. After completing their first term, governor-appointed judges usually face a retention election, in which voters decide whether to keep those judges in office.

In many states, Appellate Judges serve fixed renewable terms, which may range from six to 14 years. A few states allow judges to hold lifetime terms.

Judges usually work 40 hours a week, and often work additional hours when needed.

Salaries

Salaries for Appellate Judges vary, depending on factors such as their experience and geographical location. According to the January 2006 *Survey of Judicial Salaries,* by the National Center for State Courts, salaries for state Appellate Judges ranged as follows: $101,612 to $170,694 for judges in intermediate appellate courts; $100,884 to $182,071 for associate justices in courts of last resort; and $102,466 to $198,567 for chief justices in the highest state court.

Salaries for federal appellate judges in 2006 were $175,100 for circuit judges, $203,000 for Supreme Court associate justices, and $212,100 for the chief justice of the Supreme Court.

Employment Prospects

The number of federal judgeships are established by the U.S.Congress, and at the state level, by state legislatures.

The competition for judgeships is keen and intense, as it involves being nominated for candidacy and then being appointed to the bench or elected by the voters. Most vacancies become available as Appellate Judges retire or resign.

Advancement Prospects

Appellate Judges may be selected as chief judges of their courts, which are administrative positions for limited terms. At both the state and federal levels, retired Appellate Judges may continue as senior judges, assisting with court caseloads when needed.

Education and Training

Appellate Judges in the state courts are required to possess a juris doctor (J.D.) degree. There are no formal educational requirements for Appellate Judges in the federal courts; however, most of these judges have extensive backgrounds as lawyers.

New Appellate Judges in federal and state courts complete orientation training. Many states require that judges complete continuing education courses throughout their careers on the bench.

Special Requirements

A state may require that its Appellate Judges be members of its state attorney bar association. Some states require that candidates be a bar association member for a minimum number of years.

Experience, Skills, and Personality Traits

At the federal level, Appellate Judges are not required to be attorneys. However, most federal judges held positions as government lawyers, attorneys in private practice, law professors, or judges in state or federal courts prior to their nomination.

Most states require that candidates for Appellate Judges be practicing lawyers or have practiced for a minimum number of years.

Appellate Judges need strong case management skills, as well as excellent interpersonal and communication skills. Successful Appellate Judges share several personality traits, such as being calm, respectful, fair, analytical, and hardworking.

Unions and Associations

Appellate Judges join professional associations such as the American Judges Association and the American Bar Association to take advantage of professional resources, professional services, and networking opportunities. Many federal judges join the Federal Bar Association. For contact information for these groups, see Appendix V.

Tips for Entry

1. Read biographies about Appellate Judges to get an idea of the various career paths that have lead different individuals to their judgeships.
2. To gain experience in appellate courts, you might obtain internships while in law school. You might also apply for law clerk positions with Appellate Judges.
3. You can learn more about appellate courts on the Internet. Many state and federal appellate courts have web pages. To get a list of web pages, enter any of these keywords in a search engine: *appellate court, state appellate court,* or *federal appellate court.* For some links, see Appendix VI.

ADMINISTRATIVE LAW JUDGE

CAREER PROFILE

Duties: Preside over legal proceedings for government agencies; perform judicial duties such as reviewing motions, researching law, and writing opinions

Alternate Title(s): Hearing Officer, Hearing Examiner, Appeals Referee, Magistrate

Salary Range: $36,000 to $128,000

Employment Prospects: Fair

Advancement Prospects: Poor

Prerequisites:

Education or Training—J.D. (law degree) may be required; orientation training

Experience—Experience as a trial lawyer or other qualifying work experience

Special Skills and Personality Traits—Analytical, organizational; legal writing, communication, and interpersonal skills; objective, decisive, unbiased, calm, respectful

CAREER LADDER

```
┌─────────────────────────────────────┐
│   Chief Administrative Law Judge     │
└─────────────────────────────────────┘

┌─────────────────────────────────────┐
│     Administrative Law Judge         │
└─────────────────────────────────────┘

┌─────────────────────────────────────┐
│            Attorney                  │
└─────────────────────────────────────┘
```

Position Description

In the United States, federal, state, and local government agencies are responsible for administering laws in such areas as health, welfare, tax, environment, labor, professional licensure, workplace safety, and public utilities regulations. Government agencies create and enforce the regulations that govern the activities of businesses and industries, as well as the issuance of government benefits (such as Social Security or unemployment benefits). They also establish the regulations for the enforcement of laws, such as environmental, civil rights, and employment laws.

Administrative Law Judges (ALJs) conduct legal proceedings, or administrative hearings, for government agencies. They have the authority to make rulings on disputes and complaints that individuals, businesses, or others may have with government agencies. They preside over various type of cases. For example:

- An individual disputes an agency's decision to deny, limit, or end his or her government benefits.
- A business or corporation disputes an agency's ruling on how it can run its activities or services.
- A government agency claims that an individual, business, or organization has violated a government law or regulation—such as a workplace safety regulation, civil rights law, environmental law, building code, or tax rule.
- An individual claims that a business, licensed by a government agency, has violated the agency's regulations.

Although ALJs are employed by government agencies, they are ethically bound to conduct fair and impartial legal proceedings. They do not discuss cases with the involved parties, including the government agencies.

Administrative hearings are informal, but follow specific procedures. The length of a hearing may be as short as 15 minutes or as long as several weeks. Unlike court trials, administrative hearings do not involve juries. Also, individuals may represent themselves or choose to be represented by lawyers. ALJs do not have the authority to appoint or select attorneys for individuals. Nor can they order the losing party to pay the other party's legal costs.

ALJs might work alone or as members of a hearing board. They may conduct hearings in person as well as by telephone or videoconference. Some ALJs travel to other locations to conduct hearings.

At the hearings, ALJs listen to the arguments of the opposing parties who may present evidence to support their cases. When the hearings are complete, ALJs review the testimony and evidence and make their decisions. They may make either a final decision or a recommended decision. Final decisions are issued to the parties involved in the case while recommended decisions are sent to the proper officials who make the final decisions.

Administrative Law Judges handle a large number of cases each year. In addition to conducting hearings, they perform other duties. They also conduct prehearings and settlement conferences. They review motions, research legal precedents, write decisions, advise agency officials on matters of law, and develop procedural rules.

State Administrative Law Judges work full time or part time. Some state agencies hire ALJs on a contractual basis, paying them an hourly or daily rate.

Salaries

Salaries for ALJs vary, depending on their experience, employer, and geographical location. According to the May 2005 *Occupational Employment Statistics* (OES) survey, by the U.S. Bureau of Labor Statistics (BLS), the estimated annual salary for most ALJs ranged between $36,060 and $127,650.

Employment Prospects

The BLS reports in its November 2004 OES survey that about 15,510 administrative law judges, adjudicators, and hearing officers were employed in the United States. More than half worked for state government agencies.

The competition is high for available positions. Generally most opportunities become available as ALJs resign or retire. The creation of new positions is limited to the availability of funding.

Advancement Prospects

Advancement opportunities are limited to such positions as supervisory or chief ALJs. Many pursue ALJ positions with other federal or state agencies, which may result in an increase in pay.

Education and Training

Depending on their employers, ALJs may be required to possess a juris doctor (J.D.) degree. Federal agencies typically appoint ALJs who are lawyers, while some state agencies select ALJs who have non-lawyer backgrounds.

New ALJs receive orientation training. Throughout their careers, most ALJs complete mandatory—as well as voluntary—training and continuing education programs. Along with building up their legal and judiciary skills, they continue to learn more about the topics of the various cases that they handle each day.

Experience, Skills, and Personality Traits

Requirements vary with the different employers. For example, many administrative agencies seek candidates who have several years of experience as a practicing lawyer including trial experience. Agencies may substitute other work experience for candidates who have served in such positions as a judge of a court of record or a hearing officer of an administrative agency. Most agencies prefer candidates who are knowledgeable about administrative law and procedures, and who are familiar with the area of concern (such as social security) in which they will be working.

ALJs must have excellent analytical, organizational, and legal writing skills. They also need communication and interpersonal skills to work effectively with the general public, attorneys, and agencies.

Some personality traits that successful ALJs share are being objective, decisive, unbiased, calm, and respectful.

Unions and Associations

Many ALJs join professional associations to take advantage of professional resources, professional services, and networking opportunities. Two national organizations are the National Association of Administrative Law Judges and the National Conference of Administrative Law Judiciary. The Federal Administrative Law Judges Conference and the Association of Administrative Law Judges, a collective bargaining unit, serve the interests of federal ALJs. For contact information for these organizations, see Appendix V.

Tips for Entry

1. Contact administrative hearing offices for which you would like to work. Ask about their requirements and selection process for ALJs.
2. Although federal ALJs work in different agencies, they are hired under a program administered by the Office of Personnel Management (OPM). To check for ALJ openings, visit the OPM's job Web site at http://www. usajobs.opm.gov.
3. You can learn more about administrative law and ALJs on the Internet. Enter any of these keywords in a search engine to find pertinent web pages: *administrative law, administrative law judge, administrative law office,* or *administrative law division.* For some links, see Appendix VI.

ALTERNATIVE DISPUTE RESOLUTION (ADR) PRACTITIONERS

NEUTRAL

CAREER PROFILE

Duties: Provide mediation, arbitration, or other type of dispute resolution; perform duties as required

Alternate Title(s): Mediator, Arbitrator, Facilitator, Conciliator, Ombudsperson, Referee, Alternative Dispute Resolution (ADR) Specialist, Conflict Resolution Specialist

Salary Range: $27,000 to $97,000+

Employment Prospects: Good

Advancement Prospects: Fair

Prerequisites:

Education or Training—Dispute resolution training required

Experience—Prior alternative dispute resolution experience

Special Skills and Personality Traits—Negotiation, interpersonal, communication, and listening skills; assimilate and synthesize information and data quickly; be impartial, unbiased, patient, courteous, sincere, trustworthy, flexible

Special Requirements—Professional certification or registration may be required

CAREER LADDER

```
┌─────────────────────────────────────┐
│  Alternative Dispute Resolution Trainer  │
│     or ADR Program Director          │
└─────────────────────────────────────┘

┌─────────────────────────────────────┐
│              Neutral                 │
└─────────────────────────────────────┘

┌─────────────────────────────────────┐
│              Trainee                 │
└─────────────────────────────────────┘
```

Position Description

Neutrals are trained professionals in alternative dispute resolution (ADR), or conflict resolution, processes. They help opposing parties settle their problems without going through litigation or administrative procedures. Neutrals are engaged in various types of disputes, involving family, personal injury, workplace, business, consumer, community, medical, and public policy issues, among others. They work in such settings as courts, government agencies, communities, corporations, and educational institutions.

Opposing parties agree to ADR sessions on a voluntary basis. These sessions are informal, but confidential. The Neutrals' role is to help the opposing parties define the issues and focus their discussion only on those issues. Neutrals meet with opposing parties both together and separately. Most sessions usually last a few hours. More complex issues may require several sessions over several days.

There are several types of ADR, in which Neutrals may specialize. Arbitration and mediation are probably the two most familiar forms of ADR. In arbitration, Neutrals decide the outcome for the disputing parties. The neutral (or arbitrator) listens to the evidence and argument offered by each party, and then issues a decision which, in most cases, is enforceable by the courts.

In mediation, Neutrals do not make outcome decisions. The Neutral (or mediator) helps the opposing parties discuss their problems and explore alternatives for resolving them. With a mediator's guidance, the parties decide on the solution that is most agreeable to both parties.

The following are some other forms of ADR.

• Facilitation: Neutrals keep the discussion between opposing parties on a positive track.
• Conciliation: Neutrals help conflicting parties restore their relationship to a previous level of trust, so that they can work on reaching agreements to their problems.
• Neutral evaluation: Neutrals listen to the summaries of opposing parties and offer an opinion on what may hap-

pen to their case if it is brought before a trial court or administrative agency.

- Fact-finding: Neutrals gather information to determine the facts of a dispute in connection with a court case, a corporate internal investigation, or other situation.
- Mini-trial: Neutrals listen to a summary of the evidence and arguments that opposing parties would present at a trial.

Depending on the nature of a dispute, a Neutral might combine mediation, arbitration, and other ADR forms.

Individuals, groups, courts, and others usually choose Neutrals from panels, or rosters, established by professional associations, local attorney bars, community mediation centers, government agencies, universities, private ADR referral services, and other groups. Many Neutrals are part of several panels or rosters. Depending on the organization, Neutrals are nominated to a panel or receive an exclusive invitation from the organization. With some groups, Neutrals may apply for inclusion on a panel if they meet the panel's requirements.

Many Neutrals are employed on a part-time or full-time basis by courts, law firms, government agencies, academic institutions, corporations, nonprofit organizations, and community mediation centers. Neutrals in staff positions may also perform non-ADR duties. For example, family court mediators may also have counseling duties. Many staff Neutrals, usually called Dispute Resolution Specialists, mostly manage cases. In other words, they review cases to decide if ADR is appropriate and, if so, which form of ADR would work best. They also find appropriate Neutrals for cases, and monitor the cases throughout the process.

Many Neutrals in private practice are associates or partners in ADR firms. Most others are self-employed as independent contractors. Some independent contractors offer ADR services on a part-time basis while working as lawyers, judges, social workers, counselors, teachers, executives, or other occupations. Independent contractors are responsible for managing such office tasks as invoicing clients, paying bills and taxes, marketing their services, and maintaining their offices.

Many other Neutrals are volunteers and offer ADR services on a pro bono basis.

Neutrals sometimes are required to travel to ADR sessions, which may be held in distant cities or states.

Salaries

Salaries for Neutrals vary, depending on their employer, experience, geographical location, and other factors. According to the May 2005 *Occupational Employment Statistics* survey, by the U.S. Bureau of Labor Statistics, the estimated annual salary for most arbitrators, mediators, and conciliators ranged between $27,270 and $96,640.

Many Neutrals are volunteers and provide services for free. Independent Neutrals earn an hourly or per-session fee. Their rates vary, depending on such factors as their experi-

ence, reputation, and the complexity of their cases. Top Neutrals can earn salaries up to six figures or more.

Employment Prospects

Opportunities are favorable for Neutrals, especially for volunteers. The job market is expected to steadily grow in the coming years, as increasingly more employers in the private, public, and nonprofit sectors are using mediation and other types of dispute resolution to settle both internal and external problems. In addition, the growing awareness of the public about dispute resolution services should also contribute to the demand for professional Neutrals.

Advancement Prospects

Neutrals may advance in any number of ways, depending on their ambitions and interests. With additional experience and training, Neutrals may become dispute resolution trainers or consultants. They can also pursue administrative opportunities as dispute resolution program managers or directors in government agencies, corporations, nonprofit organizations, or dispute resolution firms. Some Neutrals start their own firms that offer ADR services.

Education and Training

Training requirements for Neutrals vary among employers as well as organizations that sponsor a roster of ADR professionals. Many professional associations also set their own training requirements for their memberships.

In general, many individuals begin by completing a basic 40-hour training program through a community ADR program, private ADR firm, or another recognized program. After completing these programs, many individuals obtain apprenticeships under experienced Neutrals for further training.

Neutrals are expected to enroll in continuing education and training programs throughout their careers to increase their knowledge and skills. Some Neutrals earn a professional certificate or an advanced degree in ADR.

Special Requirements

All ADR referral services, associations, courts, and others have their own set of certification and registration requirements for Neutrals who wish to be on their rosters or panels. For example, a state court system may require that Neutrals be certified by a court-approved training program, as well as be registered with the state and local court systems.

Experience, Skills, and Personality Traits

Neutrals come from various backgrounds—law, social work, psychology, theology, counseling, education, human resources, medicine, business, policy, and other fields.

Employers and organizations that refer Neutrals generally look for individuals who have several years of ADR experience. Neutrals also have the appropriate experience and knowledge in the practice areas (such as family, business, or workplace disputes) in which they wish to handle cases.

Neutrals must have excellent negotiation skills and interpersonal skills as well as superior communication and listening skills. They are able to assimilate and synthesize information and data quickly. In addition, Neutrals can relate to people from various backgrounds and with diverse points of view.

Some personality traits that successful Neutrals share are being impartial, unbiased, patient, courteous, sincere, trusting, and flexible.

Unions and Associations

Many Neutrals join local, state, and national associations to take advantage of professional resources and services, such as training programs, publications, job referrals, and opportunities to network with peers. Some national organizations that represent Neutrals are:

- American Arbitration Association
- American Bar Association Dispute Resolution Section

- American College of Civil Trial Mediators
- Association for Conflict Resolution
- Association of Attorney-Mediators
- National Association for Community Mediation

For contact information, see Appendix V.

Tips for Entry

1. Join a professional association and actively participate in its programs.
2. Many Neutrals begin their careers as volunteers in order to gain experience and professional exposure.
3. Contact professional associations, courts, local bar associations, and ADR referral services that have panels of Neutrals. Ask about their requirements and application process.
4. Use the Internet to learn more about Neutrals and the ADR field. You might start by visiting these Web sites: Association for Conflict Resolution, http://www.acrnet.org, and Mediate.com, http://www.mediate.com. For more links, see Appendix VI.

COURT MEDIATOR

CAREER PROFILE

Duties: Use the mediation process to settle issues between opposing parties; perform duties as required

Alternate Title(s): Family Court Mediator

Salary Range: $27,000 to $97,000

Employment Prospects: Good

Advancement Prospects: Fair

Prerequisites:

Education or Training—J.D. (law degree) may be required; complete court-approved training programs

Experience—Requirements vary with each court

Special Skills and Personality Traits—Interpersonal, listening, communication, and interviewing skills; able to handle people of diverse backgrounds and views as well as manage emotional individuals; be objective, unbiased, composed, trustworthy, courteous, flexible, creative

Special Requirements—Court certification and/or registration may be required

CAREER LADDER

```
┌─────────────────────────────┐
│   Court Mediator/Trainer     │
│    or Program Director       │
└─────────────────────────────┘

┌─────────────────────────────┐
│      Court Mediator          │
└─────────────────────────────┘

┌─────────────────────────────┐
│        Trainee               │
└─────────────────────────────┘
```

Position Description

In many state and federal courts, the alternative dispute resolution (ADR) process known as mediation is used to resolve court cases. Through this process, trained Court Mediators help opposing parties reach mutual agreements to settle their disputes. Court Mediators are engaged in various types of cases, involving divorce, child custody, small claims, personal injury, employment, environmental, bankruptcy, and appellate issues, among others.

Court mediation does not take the place of litigation. A judge may recommend that a case go into mediation on a voluntary basis. Some courts require certain cases to go through the mediation process before a hearing or trial date is set. Court Mediators do not act as judges nor as arbitrators. They do not hear testimony, make rulings, or render decisions or awards. Any decisions made in a mediation process are by the involved parties.

The mediation sessions are usually conducted in a neutral place, such as at a meeting room in a courthouse. Most mediation sessions last a few hours, but complex cases sometimes continue for a few days.

Court Mediators meet with the parties in joint sessions, as well as with each party in separate private caucuses. They are trained to help both sides identify and analyze the issues of their cases, as well as to get them to generate options for settlement. The mediation process is informal, but confidential.

The opposing parties are required to participate fully in the mediation session until a settlement has been reached. When the parties cannot come to any agreement, Court Mediators may declare an impasse to end the session. These mediators may also end the process at any time if they determine that the parties are unwilling to cooperate or to achieve a reasonable agreement. Either party may terminate the mediation process at any time as well.

When opposing parties have achieved a settlement, an agreement is written and signed by the participants. The written agreement is like a contract and therefore is enforceable in court. If the parties cannot reach an agreement, the case goes back to the court for litigation.

Some Court Mediators are employed as staff members of the courts, and usually perform additional duties. For example, a Family Court Mediator may also perform counseling duties. Some courts refer mediation cases to ADR programs run by bar associations, nonprofit corporations, or private services. Many courts maintain a roster of eligible Court Mediators to whom cases are referred. Some courts use only qualified volunteers as Court Mediators, while others use independent contractors.

Many Court Mediators offer other ADR services such as arbitration, facilitation, case evaluation, and mini-trials. Independent contractors may offer their services to government agencies, corporations, community groups, and other organizations.

Salaries

Salaries for Court Mediators vary, depending on such factors as their education, experience, and geographical location. According to the May 2005 *Occupational Employment Statistics* survey, by the U.S. Bureau of Labor Statistics, the estimated annual salary for most mediators overall ranged between $27,270 and $96,640.

Some Court Mediators are volunteers and provide services for free. Independent contractors earn an hourly or per-session fee.

Employment Prospects

The demand for Court Mediators is expected to increase in the coming years due to the growing number of court mediation programs being established in state and federal courts. Some programs are authorized by legal mandate, court rule, or administrative order. Other programs are set up to reduce the number of trial cases, decrease the cost of litigation, speed the resolution of cases, and for other reasons.

Advancement Prospects

Court Mediators generally realize advancement in terms of their professional reputation, by being sought out to handle complex cases, and by earning higher incomes.

Court Mediators can also become ADR program coordinators or directors, trainers, or consultants.

Education and Training

In many jurisdictions, Court Mediators must possess a juris doctor (J.D.) degree. In courts that use nonlawyers for family court mediation services, candidates must have either a bachelor's or master's degree in psychology, social work, or other related field.

Most courts require that entry-level mediators complete court-approved mediation training programs, which include classroom instruction as well as supervised mediations and observations. Some courts require additional training in the practice areas, such as family disputes, in which the mediators will work.

Throughout their careers, Court Mediators enroll in education and training programs to maintain and build their mediation skills.

Special Requirements

Courts usually require that Court Mediators be court-certified. In addition, they must be registered in each court where they wish to work.

Experience, Skills, and Personality Traits

State and federal courts each have their own set of eligibility requirements for Court Mediators. Most courts require that Court Mediators be lawyers who have been in practice for several years. Many courts use nonlawyer mediators who have extensive professional experience in their subject matter (such as children and family issues) and are knowledgeable about court procedures.

Court Mediators need excellent interpersonal, listening, communication, and interviewing skills. They are able to handle people from diverse backgrounds and with different views. Additionally, they can manage individuals who become upset, angry, or otherwise emotional. Being objective, unbiased, composed, trustworthy, courteous, flexible, and creative are some personality traits that successful Court Mediators share.

Unions and Associations

Many Court Mediators belong to professional associations to take advantage of networking opportunities and other professional services and resources. Some national societies that they might join are the Association for Conflict Resolution, the American College of Civil Trial Mediators, the Alternate Dispute Resolution Section of the American Bar Association, and the Association of Family and Conciliation Courts. For contact information, see Appendix V.

Tips for Entry

1. Talk with Court Mediators to learn more about their work.
2. Contact the individual state and federal courts in which you would like to work for information about their mediation programs.
3. Learn more about court mediation programs on the Internet. To find pertinent Web sites, enter the keywords *court mediators* or *court ADR programs* in a search engine. For some links, see Appendix VI.

FAMILY LAW MEDIATOR

CAREER PROFILE

Duties: Facilitate mediation between opposing parties in family law cases; perform duties as required

Alternate Title(s): Family Court Counselor, Family Counselor-Mediator, Custody/Visitation Mediator, and Conciliation Court Counselor/Mediator

Salary Range: $27,000 to $97,000

Employment Prospects: Good

Advancement Prospects: Fair

Prerequisites:

　Education or Training—Educational requirements vary; completion of court-approved training programs

　Experience—Requirements vary with each court

　Special Skills and Personality Traits—Analytical, organizational, computer, writing, communication, interpersonal, and human relations skills; be creative, courteous, fair, objective, trustworthy, and respectful

　Special Requirements—Court certification and/or registration may be required

CAREER LADDER

```
┌─────────────────────────────────┐
│   Senior Family Law Mediator    │
└─────────────────────────────────┘

┌─────────────────────────────────┐
│      Family Law Mediator        │
└─────────────────────────────────┘

┌─────────────────────────────────┐
│            Trainee              │
└─────────────────────────────────┘
```

Position Description

Today in the United States, many family courts encourage people to try to settle their disputes in mediation, a form of alternative dispute resolution. This is an informal process in which Family Law Mediators help opposing parties work together to find agreeable solutions to the issues that they have. These mediators handle a wide range of issues involved in such cases as child custody, child visitation, divorce, adoption, paternity, emancipation, underage marriage, and adult guardianship cases, among other family law cases. For example, mediators might help divorced parents come up with an agreeable schedule for their children to visit with each of them.

Mediation for a family law case can take place at any time, even before a case is filed in court. In certain cases, such as child custody or child visitation cases, judges may require that disputants try to resolve their differences in mediation first.

Family Law Mediators lead sessions alone or in teams of two. They meet with opposing parties in joint sessions, and if necessary with each party separately. All mediation sessions, or meetings, are private and confidential. They usually last two to three hours. Many parties are able to resolve some or all of their issues within two to six sessions.

Mediators begin the mediation process by explaining the mediation process and making sure that all parties understand it. Either party as well as the mediator may terminate the mediation process at any time. For example, mediators may stop the process if they determine that the parties are uncooperative, or if one party is using fear, threats, or intimidation to get his or her way.

Family Law Mediators and the involved parties determine what issues need to be resolved. Mediators ask questions as well as review any legal documents that the parties provide to develop an understanding of the family history. Mediators facilitate discussion on each issue, and try to get the opposing parties to come up with solutions on which they can both agree. In cases that involve children or other family members, Mediators ensure that the opposing parties consider the other family members' best interests as well.

Mediators can present legal information for parties to consider, but they cannot give any legal advice. Family Law Mediators remain impartial; they do not offer any personal opinions; they do not judge who is right or wrong; they do not make decisions.

When the opposing parties reach an agreement to some or all of their issues, mediators then prepare a document that clearly describes their settlement. The parties can choose to take the written agreement to their lawyers for review. After both parties sign the agreement, the document is submitted to the court. If the court approves, it becomes a legal document that is enforceable in court. Any issues that could not be resolved in mediation are worked out in court.

Family Law Mediators are trained neutrals. Along with being experienced in family mediation procedures, they are knowledgeable about family law, family development, child welfare, and the types of issues that are brought up in family mediation cases. They also establish close working relationships with judges, court staff, lawyers, mental health professionals, community agencies, and the general public.

Some Family Law Mediators are employees of family court systems. Others are independent contractors who may be private practitioners or members of nonprofit mediation groups. Many independent contractors offer their services for free to individuals who are on limited incomes.

Court-employed mediators are assigned other responsibilities that may include case development, outreach activities, and administrative duties. They may perform such duties as investigating child custody allegations; providing counseling and referral services to cases referred by the court; working with mental health and community agencies to develop activities and programs for their clientele; conducting court studies about child custody and other family law issues; or attending professional conferences on behalf of their programs.

Family Law Mediators may work full time or part time.

Salaries

Salaries for Family Law Mediators vary, depending on such factors as their education, experience, and geographical location. According to the May 2005 *Occupational Employment Statistics* survey, by the U.S. Bureau of Labor Statistics (BLS), the estimated annual salary for most mediators ranged between $27,270 and $96,640.

Some Court Mediators are volunteers and provide services for free. Independent contractors earn an hourly or per-session fee.

Employment Prospects

In general, opportunities for mediators are favorable. According to the BLS, the employment for mediators overall is expected to increase by 9 to 17 percent through 2014.

Staff openings for Family Law Mediators typically become available as individuals transfer to other jobs or advance to higher positions. Employers will create additional staff positions to meet growing demands if funding is available.

Advancement Prospects

Family Law Mediators may advance to supervisory and managerial positions, which are limited. They can also become mediation trainers and consultants.

Many mediators realize advancement through job satisfaction, by earning higher incomes, and by being sought out to handle complex cases.

Education and Training

Educational requirements vary with the different employers. For example, many family court programs prefer to hire candidates who possess a master's degree in social work, psychology, family counseling, or another related field.

Entry-level mediators are expected to complete court-approved mediation training programs, which include classroom instruction as well as supervised mediations and observations. Mediators must complete a minimum number of hours of continuing education every year or two years.

Throughout their careers, Family Law Mediators enroll in courses, workshops, and seminars to update their skills and knowledge.

Special Requirements

Family courts usually require that mediators be court-certified. In addition, they must be registered in the courts where they practice.

Family Law Mediators must possess a current license for their profession as a lawyer or mental health professional.

Experience, Special Skills, and Personality Traits

All family courts have their own set of requirements for Family Law Mediators. In general, they seek experienced mediators who have experience in or are knowledgeable about family law cases.

To perform well at their work, Family Law Mediators must have excellent analytical, organizational, computer, writing, and communication skills. They also need superior interpersonal and human relations skills, as they must work well with people of different backgrounds. Being creative, courteous, fair, objective, trustworthy, and respectful are some personality traits that successful Family Law Mediators have in common.

Unions and Associations

By joining professional associations, Family Law Mediators can take advantage of networking opportunities, professional publications, and other professional resources and services. Two national societies are the Association of Family and Conciliation Courts and the Association for Conflict Resolution. For contact information, see Appendix V.

Tips for Entry

1. Employers sometimes consider recent graduates of a master's degree program in social work or another related field, if they have qualifying work experience. Many employers prefer candidates who have clinical experience involving children and families.

2. Being proficient in Spanish or another language may enhance your employability, especially in areas that need mediators with your particular foreign language skills.

3. Contact family courts, private mediation firms, and nonprofit mediation groups directly about job openings.

4. Use the Internet to learn more about family court mediation. To get a list of Web sites, enter the keywords *family court mediation* or *family court mediators* into a search engine. To learn about some links, see Appendix VI.

ARBITRATOR, LABOR OR EMPLOYMENT

CAREER PROFILE

Duties: Facilitate arbitration cases for either labor-management or employment disputes; make final decisions or awards; perform other duties as required

Alternate Title(s): Labor Arbitrator, Employment Arbitrator

Salary Range: $27,000 to $97,000

Employment Prospects: Fair

Advancement Prospects: Poor

Prerequisites:

Education or Training—Complete arbitration training

Experience—Employment Arbitrators need experience in employment law; labor Arbitrators need experience in collective bargaining, labor management relations, and labor law

Special Skills and Personality Traits—Negotiation, problem-solving, interpersonal, communication, and listening skills; be impartial, fair, unbiased, patient, courteous, trustworthy, flexible

CAREER LADDER

```
┌─────────────────────────────────┐
│      Full-time Arbitrator       │
└─────────────────────────────────┘

┌─────────────────────────────────┐
│      Part-time Arbitrator       │
└─────────────────────────────────┘

┌─────────────────────────────────┐
│     Lawyer, Law Professor,      │
│  Business Executive, Labor Union│
│ Representative, or Other Profession│
└─────────────────────────────────┘
```

Position Description

Arbitrators help opposing parties in a dispute to resolve their problems or issues without going through litigation or administrative hearings. These professional neutrals are trained in the alternative dispute resolution (ADR) process known as arbitration.

The arbitration process allows opposing parties to present their cases in a less formal setting than the courtroom. The Arbitrators have the authority to make the final decisions or awards. In most arbitration cases, the Arbitrators' decisions are final and binding in courts of law.

Many Arbitrators specialize in settling labor-management or employment disputes. Labor Arbitrators handle cases that involve collective bargaining negotiations about wages, benefits, working conditions, and other issues between groups of employees (or labor) and their employers (or management). Employment Arbitrators handle employment cases that involve various workplace grievances between employees and employers, such as discrimination, breach of employment contracts, or wrongful termination.

With some arbitration cases, opposing parties voluntarily agree to use this form of ADR to settle their differences. Other cases go into arbitration because of legal mandates, court rule, or contractual agreements.

In arbitration, the opposing parties together select one or more Arbitrators. (Either disputant may be represented by a legal counsel or other authorized representative.) Arbitrators are usually selected from rosters maintained by an administrative agency (such as the Federal Mediation and Conciliation Service) or a private nonprofit arbitration administration agency (such as the National Academy of Arbitrators).

Arbitrators conduct prehearing meetings with the disputants to determine when and where the hearing shall take place and how long it will last. Arbitrators also discuss other matters that may help make the proceedings move quickly, including defining the issues to be arbitrated; outlining the laws and rules that will apply to the proceeding; explaining the use of witnesses; and determining whether arguments will be summed up orally or in writing.

Arbitrators have the authority to establish the rules of conduct for the hearings. For example, they can decide whether nonwitnesses may attend a hearing. Arbitrators also have the duty of safeguarding the confidentiality of arbitration hearings.

During the proceedings, the disputants present their case before the Arbitrators. Each side has the equal burden of proof, and so produces physical evidence and witnesses to prove their case. If necessary, Arbitrators may subpoena witnesses or documents that are relevant to a case, as well as conduct any necessary inspections or investigations.

After all the evidence has been submitted and testimony heard, the Arbitrators close the hearings. They may take several days or weeks to make their final decisions. When a board of Arbitrators presides, the majority of Arbitrators must agree on a decision unless the law or court requires an unanimous agreement.

Many Arbitrators use other forms of ADR, such as mediation, case evaluation, and mini-trials, to settle labor-management or employment disputes.

Arbitrators provide their services on a part-time or full-time basis. Part-time Arbitrators usually work full time in their principal occupation as a lawyer, professor, judge, or other profession.

Salaries

Salaries for Arbitrators vary, depending on their employer, experience, geographical location, and other factors. According to the May 2005 *Occupational Employment Statistics* survey, by the U.S. Bureau of Labor Statistics (BLS), the estimated annual salary for most arbitrators, ranged between $27,270 and $96,640.

Independent Arbitrators generally earn hourly or per diem fees. Their rates vary, depending on their experience, reputation, and other factors.

Employment Prospects

Opportunities for neutrals who specialize in labor and employment arbitration are expected to grow, as most companies prefer to resolve labor-management disputes outside of court. The BLS predicts that employment for Arbitrators overall should increase by 9 to 17 percent through 2014.

Advancement Prospects

Most arbitrators realize advancement in terms of their professional reputation, by earning higher incomes, or by being sought out to handle complex cases.

With additional experience and training, Arbitrators may become dispute resolution trainers or consultants. They can also pursue administrative opportunities as dispute resolution program managers or directors in government agencies, corporations, nonprofit organizations, or dispute resolution firms. Some Arbitrators start their own firms that offer various ADR services.

Education and Training

Arbitrators are generally required to complete arbitration training programs. In addition, they are expected to enroll in education and training programs throughout their careers to maintain and develop their skills and knowledge in ADR as well as practice areas.

Experience, Skills, and Personality Traits

Labor and employment Arbitrators come from different backgrounds. Some are lawyers, former judges, and law professors. Others are former labor union representatives or employee relations specialists and directors.

Employment Arbitrators should be experienced in the field of employment law. Labor Arbitrators should have extensive experience in collective bargaining, labor management relations, and labor law.

Arbitrators must have excellent negotiation, problem-solving, and interpersonal skills. Superior communication and listening skills are also needed. Being impartial, fair, unbiased, patient, courteous, trustworthy, and flexible are some personality traits that successful Labor and Employment Arbitrators share.

Unions and Associations

Labor and employment Arbitrators join local, state, and national associations to take advantage of professional resources and services, such as training programs, publications, job referrals, and opportunities to network with peers. Some national organizations are the National Academy of Arbitrators, American Arbitration Association, Association for Conflict Resolution, and American Bar Association Dispute Resolution Section. For contact information, see Appendix V.

Tips for Entry

1. Learn as much as you can about the arbitration process, as well as other forms of alternative dispute resolution.
2. To gain practical experience, you might volunteer in a community mediation center, a court ADR program, or another mediation program.
3. Use the Internet to learn more about arbitration. To find relevant Web sites enter any of these keywords in a search engine: *arbitration, labor arbitration,* or *employment arbitration.* For some links, see Appendix VI.

LEGAL SUPPORT PROFESSIONALS

LEGAL SUPPORT PROFESSIONAL

CAREER PROFILE

Duties: Provide general office, administrative, and/or legal support; perform duties as assigned

Alternate Title(s): Legal Clerk, Legal Secretary, Paralegal, Case Clerk, Bookkeeping Clerk, Legal Word Processor, or other title that reflects a specific occupation

Salary Range: $15,000 to $113,000

Employment Prospects: Good

Advancement Prospects: Good

Prerequisites:

Education or Training—Educational requirements vary with the different occupations; on-the-job training

Experience—Previous experience in legal settings preferred

Special Skills and Personality Traits—Communication, interpersonal, teamwork, self-management, writing, and computer skills; ability to operate office equipment; be enthusiastic, positive, dependable, hardworking, organized, detail-oriented

CAREER LADDER

```
┌─────────────────────────────────┐
│   Assistant Law Office Manager  │
│     or Supervising Paralegal    │
└─────────────────────────────────┘

┌─────────────────────────────────┐
│  Legal Secretary, Paralegal, or │
│  Legal Specialist (such as      │
│  Records Clerk)                 │
└─────────────────────────────────┘

┌─────────────────────────────────┐
│    Legal Receptionist, Legal    │
│  Word Processor, or Legal       │
│  Assistant Clerk                │
└─────────────────────────────────┘

┌─────────────────────────────────┐
│  General Office Clerk (Law      │
│  Office)                        │
└─────────────────────────────────┘
```

Position Description

Various types of Legal Support Professionals help lawyers run their offices efficiently and effectively. In general, Legal Support Professionals perform duties in one or more of these areas—office, administrative, technological, or legal support. The following are some of the more common occupations found in law firms and law departments in corporations, government agencies, and other organizations.

File clerks place correspondence, documents, invoices, and other records in appropriate file folders. They also find and retrieve records that are requested by lawyers, paralegals, and others. They may also perform a variety of routine office tasks such as distribute mail, photocopy papers, and run errands.

Legal receptionists greet clients and visitors to the office and direct them to appropriate staff members. Most of these Legal Support Professionals also handle incoming telephone calls.

Legal word processors produce legal documents, correspondence, and other materials on word processors or com-

puter systems. They make sure that the finished products are correct, accurate, and have been properly formatted.

Records clerks or records specialists set up and maintain clients' case files for lawyers. They prepare new files, index legal documents, track files in computer databases, update files, access files for information as requested by lawyers, and perform other duties.

Information technology specialists provide law offices with various types of technical support. Their duties include maintaining and upgrading hardware, software, databases, and networks. They also analyze specific legal and nonlegal needs, and troubleshoot technical problems.

Case clerks or case assistants provide litigation support to paralegals and attorneys. Case clerks are responsible for maintaining and organizing files for assigned criminal or civil cases. They perform such tasks as coding legal documents, keeping documents in alphabetical and chronological order, and preparing indexes for documents and pleadings.

Calendar clerks maintain the court calendar that shows the court dates (court filings, hearings, and trials) for all lawyers in their offices. These clerks also keep the office up to date with new court rules and procedures, and provide lawyers with regular calendar reports. In addition, the clerks make sure that legal documents being filed are in compliance with court procedure and rules.

Docket clerks maintain the patent, trademark, and other intellectual property logs for which their law firm or department is responsible. Their tasks include updating databases, preparing progress reports, monitoring attorney deadlines, opening and sorting mail, and processing invoices.

Legal secretaries provide support directly to one or more lawyers. Their primary duties are preparing legal correspondence and documents, and maintaining lawyers' schedules and legal files. Many also conduct legal research.

Litigation secretaries provide administrative support to litigation attorneys. These legal secretaries may be involved in civil or criminal litigation.

Paralegals or legal assistants are specially trained to assist lawyers with a variety of substantial legal tasks. Under the direction and supervision of attorneys, they interview clients, prepare legal documents, conduct legal research, draft documents, and prepare clients for trials.

Legal administrators oversee the daily nonlawyer operations of the law office. They are in charge of all management functions, including administrative policies and procedures, human resources, marketing, financial management, information systems, and facilities management.

Legal Support Professionals may be permanent or temporary employees. They may work full time or part time. In large firms, some staff members, such as legal word processors work different shifts.

Salaries

Salaries for Legal Support Professionals vary, depending on such factors as their occupation, education, experience, employer, and geographical location. The U.S. Bureau of Labor Statistics reported, in its May 2005 *Occupational Employment Statistics* survey, the following estimated annual salary ranges for most employees working in these occupations:

- file clerks—$14,690 to $33,600
- word processors—$19,200 to $43,550
- receptionists and information clerks—$15,200 to $33,030
- general office clerks—$14,530 to $36,460
- computer support specialists—$24,230 to $67,460
- legal secretaries—$23,380 to $57,510
- paralegals and legal assistants—$26,270 to $65,330
- office managers—$25,950 to $69,730
- administrative services managers—$32,770 to $113,150

Employment Prospects

Opportunities are readily available for qualified Legal Support Professionals. According to experts in the field, the job market is particularly favorable for legal secretaries, paralegals, and information technology personnel. Most job openings will become available as individuals advance to higher positions, transfer to other occupations, retire, or leave the workforce for various reasons. Employers will create additional positions as their companies grow as well as to fit their staffing needs.

Advancement Prospects

Legal Support Professionals can advance in any number of ways, depending on their interests and ambitions. With additional experience and training, entry-level workers, such as file clerks, receptionists, and word processors, can pursue higher-level positions as office clerks, legal assistant clerks, secretaries, legal assistants, and paralegals.

Those who are interested in pursuing legal administrative and management careers can become department coordinators (such as records coordinators) and legal administrators (such as human resource managers and office managers). Still another option for many is to earn a college degree and then continue on to law school to eventually become lawyers.

Education and Training

Educational requirements vary from employer to employer. Minimally, Legal Support Professionals must possess a high school diploma or general equivalency diploma. Many employers prefer to hire candidates who have an associate degree or some college training for the higher office and administrative positions. Many employers prefer candidates for information technology, paralegal, and some legal assistant positions to possess a bachelor's degree in an appropriate field.

Entry-level support staff typically receive on-the-job training, and work under the guidance of experienced Legal Support Professionals. Many employers provide their staff with ongoing training programs to help them update their skills and increase their knowledge about legal terms and procedures.

Experience, Skills, and Personality Traits

Specific requirements for the different positions vary. In general, employers prefer to hire candidates with previous experience working in legal settings or who have general knowledge of legal terminology and procedures. Entry-level candidates may have gained their experience or knowledge through coursework, work-study programs, employment, or volunteer work.

Legal Support Professionals, regardless of their position, should have excellent communication, interpersonal, and teamwork skills. Additionally, they need strong self-management skills—the ability to perform several tasks at a time, be punctual, handle stressful situations, and so on.

Legal Support Professionals also need strong writing and computer skills, and should be able to operate office equipment such as fax machines and copiers.

Being enthusiastic, positive, dependable, hardworking, organized, and detail-oriented are some personality traits that successful Legal Support Professionals share.

Unions and Associations

Various professional associations are available to Legal Support Professionals at the local, state, and national levels. By joining one or more societies, they can take advantage of networking opportunities, training programs, professional certification, and other professional services and resources.

Some national societies that serve the interests of different Legal Support Professionals include:

- American Bar Association
- Association of Legal Administrators
- International Association of Administrative Professionals
- International Legal Technology Association
- Legal Secretaries International, Inc.
- NALS
- National Association of Legal Assistants
- National Paralegal Association

For contact information for the above organizations, see Appendix V.

Tips for Entry

1. Such high school courses as English, speech, math, typing or keyboarding, computer, and business can help you prepare for a career as a Legal Support Professional.
2. Many community colleges have certification or degree programs in legal studies that prepare graduates for various Legal Support Professional positions. Graduation from such a program, or at least completion of several courses, may enhance your employability.
3. To gain experience, you might sign up with temporary agencies that recruit legal support personnel for law firms and legal departments.
4. Contact law firms and legal departments in corporations, government agencies, and other institutions directly about current and future vacancies.
5. You can learn more about the various legal support occupations on the Internet. Use a job title, such as *paralegal* or *legal records clerk,* as the keyword to enter in any search engine. For some links, see Appendix VI.

LEGAL RECEPTIONIST

CAREER PROFILE

Duties: Greet visitors to law offices; answer phones; perform other duties as required

Alternate Title(s): None

Salary Range: $15,000 to $33,000

Employment Prospects: Good

Advancement Prospects: Good

Prerequisites:

Education or Training—High school diploma; on-the-job training

Experience—Previous office or customer service experience is preferred

Special Skills and Personality Traits—Interpersonal, teamwork, communication, self-management skills; typing or keyboarding skills and familiarity with office machines; be friendly, tactful, composed, organized, reliable, flexible

CAREER LADDER

```
┌─────────────────────────────────────────┐
│        Legal Secretary, Paralegal,       │
│   or Other Legal Support Professional    │
└─────────────────────────────────────────┘

┌─────────────────────────────────────────┐
│           Legal Receptionist             │
└─────────────────────────────────────────┘

┌─────────────────────────────────────────┐
│        Legal Receptionist Trainee        │
└─────────────────────────────────────────┘
```

Position Description

Legal Receptionists are often the first employees that clients and visitors meet when they come to a law office. Hence, these legal support professionals are expected to make a good first impression for law firms and legal departments.

Legal Receptionists usually sit at desks in lobbies or front offices. They are responsible for greeting visitors and determining the purpose of their visits. Receptionists inform appropriate staff members about their visitors, as well as direct visitors to their destinations. If visitors must wait for their appointments, receptionists invite them to sit until lawyers or other staff members are ready to see them.

Legal Receptionists help provide their offices with security, as they monitor who enters the offices. In some offices, Legal Receptionists request that visitors sign in and sign out on visitor logs. Many Legal Receptionists also oversee the receipt and distribution of legal documents from delivery services.

Many Legal Receptionists are responsible for answering incoming calls, often handling multiline phones or switchboards. They direct calls to the appropriate personnel in the offices. They take phone messages for staff who are absent or unable to answer the phone, and make sure the staff members receive messages.

Some Legal Receptionists are also responsible for answering questions from the public, as well as for providing general information about their law firm or legal department.

In some law offices, Legal Receptionists keep track of conference room assignments, as well as prepare conference rooms for meetings and order food for meetings. Some maintain the office kitchen.

Legal Receptionists may also be assigned clerical tasks. For example, they may complete fax transmissions, do filing, photocopy documents, type correspondence, open and sort mail, update appointment calendars, and purchase office supplies.

In some offices, Legal Receptionists are hired to perform additional roles, such as those of an office clerk, legal word processor, or legal secretary.

Legal Receptionists work full time or part time. In some offices, Legal Receptionists work evening shifts.

Salaries

Salaries for Legal Receptionists vary, depending on their experience, education, job duties, employer, and other factors. According to the May 2005 *Occupational Employment Statistics* (OES) survey, by the U.S. Bureau of Labor Statistics (BLS), the estimated annual salary for most receptionists overall ranged between $15,200 and $33,030.

Employment Prospects

Over one million receptionists are employed throughout the different industries in the United States, according to the BLS' May 2005 OES survey. This federal agency further reported that employment for receptionists (and other information clerks) overall is expected to increase by 18 to 26 percent through 2014. This is partly due to the rapid growth in service industries, including the legal services industry. In addition to job growth, opportunities for Legal Receptionists will become available as they transfer to other jobs or leave the workforce for various reasons.

Experienced Legal Receptionists are generally sought by large law firms, while smaller and midsize law firms usually look for Legal Receptionists who are willing to perform the duties of legal secretaries.

Advancement Prospects

Legal Receptionists can advance in any number of ways, depending on their interests and ambitions. With further training and experience, they can become legal word processors, legal secretaries, legal assistant clerks, paralegals, and law office managers. Another path is to continue their education to earn their law degree and become lawyers.

Education and Training

Employers typically require that Legal Receptionists have at least a high school diploma or general equivalency diploma. Some employers prefer candidates who have some college or postsecondary training, particularly in business or office skills. Employers provide new employees with on-the-job training.

Experience, Skills, and Personality Traits

Work experience requirements vary from employer to employer. Many employers prefer applicants who have previous receptionist or customer service work experience, or who have general office experience in law settings. They look for candidates who have a clear speaking voice and a professional appearance.

Legal Receptionists need excellent interpersonal, teamwork, and communication skills, as they are constantly interacting with visitors, clients, attorneys, and other legal staff. They also need strong self-management skills—such as the ability to be punctual, handle several tasks at the same time, and be self-motivated. In addition, they must have solid typing or keyboarding skills and be familiar with computers, duplicating machines, and other office machines.

Successful Legal Receptionists share several personality traits, such as being friendly, tactful, composed, organized, reliable, and flexible.

Unions and Associations

Many Legal Receptionists join local, state, and national professional associations to take advantage of networking opportunities, training programs, job listings, and other professional services and resources. For example, Legal Receptionists are eligible to join NALS, a national society that serves the interests of legal support professionals. For contact information, see Appendix V.

Tips for Entry

1. If your high school has a work-experience program, talk with the program director about the possibility of being placed in a law office as a general office clerk.
2. Consider taking clerical training programs at community colleges or other postsecondary programs to develop and improve your office skills. Many community colleges offer certificate or degree programs for various legal support occupations such as Legal Receptionists.
3. Many law offices have Web sites on the Internet. Check out some of them to get an idea of what different law offices do and how they are organized. To get a list of relevant Web sites, enter the keywords *law office* or *law firm* in a search engine.

LEGAL WORD PROCESSOR

CAREER PROFILE

Duties: Use computers or other machines to produce legal documents, correspondence, and other materials; perform other duties as required

Alternate Title(s): Legal Document Processor

Salary Range: $19,000 to $44,000

Employment Prospects: Good for highly skilled individuals

Advancement Prospects: Fair

Prerequisites:

    Education or Training—High school diploma; some college background preferred

    Experience—Previous word processing work experience is required

    Special Skills and Personality Traits—Typing or keyboarding skills; reading comprehension, grammar, proofreading, communication, and self-management skills; be reliable, flexible, detail-oriented, hardworking

CAREER LADDER

```
┌─────────────────────────────────┐
│   Senior Legal Word Processor   │
│ or Legal Word Processing Supervisor │
└─────────────────────────────────┘

┌─────────────────────────────────┐
│      Legal Word Processor       │
└─────────────────────────────────┘

┌─────────────────────────────────┐
│         Word Processor          │
└─────────────────────────────────┘
```

Position Description

Legal Word Processors operate computers, word processors, or typewriters to produce legal documents, correspondence, memorandums, reports, tables, mailing labels, and other materials. Many of these legal support professionals are employed by law firms as well as by legal departments in corporations, government agencies, courts, and other organizations. Some Legal Word Processors are hired on a contractual basis through temporary office placement agencies.

Because of the legal content of the materials, they are knowledgeable about legal terminology as well as about the required legal formatting for different materials. Their job requires typing at fast and accurate speeds. In fact, many Legal Word Processors type at 80 words or more per minute.

Legal Word Processors typically handle large volumes of work each day, working under heavy deadlines. Lawyers, paralegals, legal administrators, and other legal staff give them rough drafts or dictation tapes from which to transcribe notes. They enter the notes by keyboarding or using other devices, such as optical scanners. If there are any questions or concerns about the notes, Legal Word Processors check back with the proper staff member.

Most Legal Word Processors use complex word processing systems to create and edit documents, tables, and so forth. Many also use spreadsheet, presentation, and graphic software to produce graphics and exhibits.

Legal Word Processors are responsible for performing quality checks on printed documents before giving them to attorneys or other staff. They make sure that documents follow the required formats and standards. They proofread materials, locating and correcting errors in spelling, grammar, and punctuation.

In smaller offices, Legal Word Processors may provide other office support, such as filing, reception work, and mail distribution. Some Legal Word Processors perform additional support roles such as those of a legal secretary or legal receptionist.

The nature of their job requires them to sit for long periods of time in front of computer monitors. Their work involves repetitive motion. They may be prone to eyestrain, carpal tunnel syndrome, neck injuries, and back injuries, hence many employers provide them with ergonomically designed workstations. In addition, Legal Word Processors are occasionally stressed because of tight deadlines.

Legal Word Processors work full time or part time. In large law firms, Legal Word Processors might work different shifts that may include evening, night, and weekend shifts.

Salaries

Salaries for Legal Word Processors vary, depending on such factors as their education, experience, job duties, employer, and geographical location. According to the May 2005 *Occupational Employment Statistics* (OES) survey, by the U.S. Bureau of Labor Statistics (BLS), the estimated annual salary for most word processors, overall, ranged between $19,200 and $43,550. The estimated annual mean salary for word processors working in the legal service industry was $36,820.

Employment Prospects

The BLS reports in its May 2005 OES survey that an estimated 153,580 word processors were employed in the United States. About 10,270 word processors worked in the legal services industry, one of five industries that employed the highest number of word processors.

Most jobs become available as Legal Word Processors resign, or transfer to other jobs or positions. Opportunities are best for those with highly technical skills.

Advancement Prospects

Legal Word Processors can advance to senior and supervisory positions. Most pursue advancement by receiving higher wages and professional recognition.

Depending on their ambitions, Legal Word Processors can obtain additional education and experience to become legal secretaries, legal administrators, and even lawyers.

Education and Training

Legal Word Processors should have at least a high school diploma or a general equivalency diploma. Many employers prefer that word processors have some college background.

Employers typically provide new Legal Word Processors with on-the-job training.

Experience, Skills, and Personality Traits

Employers require that applicants for entry-level positions have word processing experience. For higher-paying positions, employers generally hire Legal Word Processors with one or more years of work experience in law offices or other legal settings.

Candidates need outstanding typing or keyboarding skills; minimum speed requirements vary with the different employers. They also need reading comprehension, grammar, and proofreading skills, as well as good communication skills. In addition, they need excellent self-management skills—such as the ability to handle pressure, meet deadlines, and work independently.

Successful Legal Word Processors share several common personality traits, such as being reliable, flexible, detail-oriented, and hardworking.

Unions and Associations

Legal Word Processors can join professional associations to take advantage of networking opportunities, continuing education programs, and other professional services and resources. NALS is a national society that Legal Word Processors are eligible to join. Those word processors who also perform legal secretary duties can belong to the Legal Secretaries International, Inc. For contact information for these two organizations, see Appendix V.

Tips for Entry

1. High school courses that can help you prepare for this occupation are keyboarding or typing, word processing, English, math, and business.
2. To gain experience, you might sign up with temporary office placement agencies.
3. Being familiar with legal terminology and procedures can enhance your employability. You may find appropriate courses at community colleges or in continuing education programs.
4. You can learn more about the legal field on the Internet. You might start by visiting these Web sites: All Law.com, http://www.alllaw.com, and Law.com, http://www.law.com. For more links, see Appendix VI.

INFORMATION TECHNOLOGY (IT) PROFESSIONAL

CAREER PROFILE

Duties: Maintain all computer systems, equipment, software, networks, and so on; provide technical support; perform duties as required

Alternate Title(s): Systems Analyst, Database Administrator, Desktop Support Technician, or other title that reflects a particular occupation

Salary Range: $24,000 to $146,000

Employment Prospects: Good

Advancement Prospects: Fair

Prerequisites:

Education or Training—A college degree or college background required or preferred

Experience—Previous experience in legal settings

Special Skills and Personality Traits—Customer service, interpersonal, communication, writing, problem-solving, and self-management skills; patient, friendly, analytical, resourceful, organized, flexible, self-motivated

CAREER LADDER

```
┌─────────────────────────────────┐
│     Legal Technology Manager     │
└─────────────────────────────────┘

┌─────────────────────────────────┐
│     IT Professional (Law Office) │
└─────────────────────────────────┘

┌─────────────────────────────────┐
│             Trainee              │
└─────────────────────────────────┘
```

Position Description

Lawyers and their staff use technology to help them complete a wide range of legal and nonlegal tasks more efficiently and effectively. They use various applications to draft legal documents, invoice clients, monitor budgets, and organize litigation cases. They conduct legal research on databases found on CD-ROMs and the Internet, as well as communicate electronically with clients. Hence, many law offices employ Information Technology (IT) Professionals to maintain all computer systems and ensure that the equipment, software, and networks function smoothly each day. In addition, they provide technical support to lawyers and staff as needed.

IT Professionals have various responsibilities (such as technical support or systems analysis), and so perform different tasks. Depending on a law office's budgets and specific needs, there may be one or more IT Professionals on staff. The following are a few of the IT Professionals that are more commonly found in law offices:

Systems analysts configure computer systems to meet the specific needs of lawyers and their staff. They continually look at ways to enhance computer systems so that they serve law offices more efficiently. Additionally, they are responsible for resolving problems with the systems. Large law offices may employ several systems analysts to support the separate needs of finance, practice, and other departments.

Database administrators develop and maintain the various database systems used in the law office, such as accounting, practice management, and case management systems. They monitor systems, archive and back up information, update systems, troubleshoot problems, make necessary repairs, and perform other tasks. They also make sure that all confidential information stored in the databases is safe and secure.

Network administrators maintain and support various types of networking systems for communicating between computers inside and outside the law offices. These include local area networks (LANs) for intraoffice communication; wide area networks (WANs) that connect office computers to computers outside the office; and internetworks, such as the Internet, that connect office computers to various networks at the same time. Network administrators also provide technical support to lawyers and staff, such as upgrading required software on individual computers, setting up e-mail accounts, troubleshooting new applications, and responding to security problems such as viruses and hacker attacks.

Computer support specialists provide technical support to lawyers and staff regarding their individual computers. These specialists troubleshoot problems with equipment and applications on an individual basis, in person or on the phone. They also upgrade and install hardware and software for individuals as well as answer questions about using computers and software.

Technical trainers are responsible for providing technical instruction to lawyers and staff. Their duties also include developing training programs and preparing training materials.

Legal technology managers oversee the daily operations of IT departments. They plan, coordinate, and manage all computer and IT activities, as well as keep up with the latest technologies and determine how they may help their employers' legal and non-legal needs. These managers are also responsible for supervising and directing the work of the IT specialists and office staff. Depending on the size of the organization, there may be two or more technology managers. The main legal technology manager may be known as the chief technology officer.

All IT Professionals are responsible for keeping up with developments in technology. They also maintain their skills by obtaining necessary training to learn new skills.

IT Professionals work part time or full time. In large firms with nationwide offices, IT Professionals may work different shifts, including evening, night, and weekend hours. On occasion, IT Professionals work longer hours to complete their tasks. Some law offices require IT Professionals to be on call to assist lawyers and staff for system emergencies.

Salaries

Salaries for IT Professionals vary, depending on their position, job duties, experience, employer, geographical location, and other factors.

According to the May 2005 *Occupational Employment Statistics* (OES) survey, by the U.S. Bureau of Labor Statistics (BLS), the estimated annual salary ranges for most of the following positions were:

- network administrators—$37,790 to $93,270
- database administrators—$35,400 to $100,930
- computer support specialists—$24,230 to $67,640

- computer systems analysts—$43,080 to $102,750
- computer and information systems managers—$57,300 to $145,600

Employment Prospects

Besides law firms and corporate law departments, IT Professionals are employed by court systems, government agencies, community legal services programs, and other legal and legal-related organizations. Some IT Professionals in legal settings are independent contractors or consultants. Others are hired on a temporary basis through legal staffing agencies or firms that offer legal technology support services on a contractual basis.

The use of technology in the legal industry is steadily growing as increasingly more lawyers and law firms set up sophisticated computer and network systems. Opportunities are particularly favorable for skilled IT Professionals who are experienced working in law firms and other legal settings. In general, most positions become available as IT Professionals advance to higher positions, transfer to other jobs, or leave the workforce for various reasons. As their IT needs grow, employers create additional staff positions and/or outsource technological support work.

Advancement Prospects

IT Professionals can advance to senior, supervisory, and managerial positions, which may require obtaining positions with other employers. Advancement opportunities are better with large organizations. Professionals with entrepreneurial ambitions can become independent consultants or owners of firms that offer consulting or contracting services.

Education and Training

Educational requirements vary with the different occupations as well as among different employers. Most employers prefer to hire candidates who have college degrees in computer science or other related fields, or who have some college training along with qualifying work experience.

Most employers provide technical training programs, which may also include sending IT Professionals to outside workshops, seminars, and classes.

Experience, Skills, and Personality Traits

Generally, employers prefer to hire candidates who have previous experience in legal settings. They must also be familiar with the types of legal and nonlegal needs particular to lawyers and law offices.

IT Professionals require excellent customer service, interpersonal, and communication skills, as they must be able to explain technical concepts in clear and nontechnical language. Additionally, IT Professionals need strong writing, problem-solving, and self-management skills.

Some personality traits that successful IT Professionals share are being patient, friendly, analytical, resourceful, organized, flexible, and self-motivated.

Unions and Associations

Many IT Professionals join professional associations at local, state, and national levels to take advantage of networking opportunities, training programs, and other professional services and resources. Some national societies include the International Legal Technology Association, the Association for Computing Machinery, and the Association of Support Professionals. For contact information, see Appendix V.

Tips for Entry

1. While in college, participate in internship programs. Try to obtain placements in law firms or legal departments.
2. Enroll in training and continuing education programs to pick up new technical skills.
3. To enhance their employability, many IT Professionals obtain professional certification through recognized organizations. See Appendix II for some groups.
4. You can learn more about the area of legal technology on the Internet. To find relevant Web sites to browse, enter the keywords *legal technology* or *law office technology* in a search engine. For some links, see Appendix VI.

LEGAL SECRETARY

CAREER PROFILE

Duties: Provide administrative support to lawyers; perform clerical tasks; perform other duties as required

Alternate Title(s): Lawyer's Assistant, Administrative Assistant, Executive Assistant

Salary Range: $23,000 to $57,000+

Employment Prospects: Good

Advancement Prospects: Good

Prerequisites:

Education or Training—High school diploma

Experience—Previous experience in law office settings or several years of general secretarial experience

Special Skills and Personality Traits—Typing, shorthand, computer, writing, communication, organizational, time management, and interpersonal skills; diplomatic, conscientious, flexible, adaptable, trustworthy

CAREER LADDER

```
┌─────────────────────────────────────┐
│  Senior Legal Secretary, Law Office  │
│       Manager, or Paralegal          │
└─────────────────────────────────────┘

┌─────────────────────────────────────┐
│           Legal Secretary            │
└─────────────────────────────────────┘

┌─────────────────────────────────────┐
│        Junior Legal Secretary        │
└─────────────────────────────────────┘
```

Position Description

Legal Secretaries provide attorneys with clerical and administrative support to ensure the smooth and efficient delivery of legal services. They are specially trained secretaries who are well-versed in legal terminology and procedures.

Some Legal Secretaries work directly with one attorney, while others provide support to several lawyers in a law office or legal department. Their work involves contact with clients, attorneys, court personnel, and the general public. They perform a wide variety of tasks, usually working with minimal supervision. Their duties vary from office to office, depending on the particular needs of the attorneys.

One major duty that all Legal Secretaries perform is the preparation of highly confidential legal materials, such as contracts, court papers, correspondence, memorandums, and reports. They take dictation directly from lawyers or transcribe lawyers' handwritten or taped notes, then process final documents on typewriters, word processors, or computers. Secretaries check documents for completeness and accuracy of information, bringing any facts or data that may be incorrect to the attention of the attorneys. Secretaries also edit materials for correct sentence construction, grammar, spelling, and punctuation.

Another major responsibility for Legal Secretaries is the maintenance of lawyers' daily schedules and court-appearance calendars. They arrange appointments and meetings for attorneys and often make travel arrangements for them. Secretaries are also aware of deadlines, depositions, and other significant events, and remind lawyers of their commitments, as well as the need for any preparation for particular cases.

Most Legal Secretaries are in charge of setting up and maintaining administrative and legal file systems. This includes both paper and electronic files and records. They might also handle bookkeeping duties, such as keeping a record of time, money, or services rendered by attorneys. On occasion, they may be asked to record and transcribe minutes of meetings and conventions. Legal Secretaries also perform routine clerical tasks. They answer telephones; greet visitors; screen calls and visits; open, review, and distribute incoming mail; maintain office supplies; and so on.

In some offices, Legal Secretaries act as office managers or as supervisors of the legal clerical staff. Their duties might then include supervising and training staff, making daily work assignments, setting up office policies and procedures, and approving vacation or other leave.

Legal Secretaries might also perform paralegal duties for attorneys. For example, they might do legal research, compile documents or data to support pleadings, prepare questions for initial client interviews, prepare exhibits for court cases, file legal documents with the courts, or maintain law libraries.

Legal Secretaries work part time or full time. They often work overtime to help lawyers meet their deadlines.

Salaries

Salaries for Legal Secretaries vary and depend on such factors as their education, experience, employer, and geographical location. The U.S. Bureau of Labor Statistics (BLS) reports in its May 2005 *Occupational Employment Statistics* (OES) survey that the estimated annual salary for most Legal Secretaries ranged between $23,380 and $57,510. According to the Legal Secretaries International, Inc. Web site (in 2006), the base salary ranges from $20,000 for beginning secretaries in non-urban areas to $65,000 for experienced secretaries in large metropolitan areas.

Employment Prospects

Legal Secretaries find employment with law firms, corporate law departments, public-interest legal services, courts, banks and financial institutions, educational institutions, and government agencies. About 265,000 Legal Secretaries were employed in the United States, according to the BLS's May 2005 OES survey.

Opportunities are favorable for qualified Legal Secretaries. According to some experts in the field, in 2006, the demand for Legal Secretaries is greater than the supply. The BLS projects an average growth (about 9 to 17 percent) for legal secretaries through 2014. In addition to job growth, replacements will be needed for Legal Secretaries who retire, advance to higher positions, or transfer to other jobs.

Advancement Prospects

Legal Secretaries can advance to supervisory positions. With additional training and experience, they can become legal office administrators, paralegals, patent agents, abstractors, or title examiners. Another career option for these legal support professionals is to enroll in law school and pursue a law career.

Education and Training

The minimum education requirement is a high school diploma or general equivalency diploma. Some employers require two-year or four-year college degrees. Many employers prefer candidates who have completed a legal secretary program (or related program) in business schools, vocational-technical institutes, or community colleges.

Employers usually provide orientation training to new employees. Throughout their careers, many Legal Secretaries enroll in continuing education and training programs to update their skills and knowledge.

Experience, Skills, and Personality Traits

For entry-level positions, employers look for candidates who show the ability to learn quickly and work independently. They generally prefer candidates who have worked previously in legal settings or have several years of general secretarial experience, performing complex tasks.

Legal Secretaries need strong typing and shorthand skills, as well as computer skills, particularly with word processing, spreadsheets, and database applications. They also need superior writing, communication, organizational, time management, and interpersonal skills. Furthermore, they must have excellent judgment, which is needed to make critical decisions in their work. Being diplomatic, conscientious, flexible, adaptable, and trustworthy are a few personality traits that successful Legal Secretaries share.

Unions and Associations

Many Legal Secretaries join professional associations to take advantage of networking opportunities, continuing education programs, and other professional services and resources. Some national societies include NALS, Legal Secretaries International, Inc., and International Association of Administrative Professionals. For contact information, see Appendix V.

Tips for Entry

1. To prepare for the Legal Secretary profession in high school, take courses in business and computers. If available, take a shorthand class and basic law class.
2. To enhance their employability, many Legal Secretaries obtain voluntary certification through recognized organizations. See Appendix II for some groups.
3. One way to gain work experience in legal settings is through work assignments with temporary employment agencies.
4. To learn more about legal secretaries, you might start by visiting these Web sites: Legal Secretaries International, Inc., http://www.legalsecretaries.org, and NALS, http://www.nals.org. For more links, see Appendix VI.

PARALEGAL

CAREER PROFILE

Duties: Provide such substantive legal support as conducting legal research and preparing legal documents; perform other duties as required

Alternate Title(s): Legal Assistant, Paralegal Specialist; a title that reflects a practice area such as Corporate Paralegal or Real Estate Legal Assistant

Salary Range: $26,000 to $65,000

Employment Prospects: Excellent

Advancement Prospects: Good

Prerequisites:

Education or Training—College degree or certificate in paralegal studies

Experience—Varies with the different employers

Special Skills and Personality Traits—Research, writing, communication, organizational, interpersonal, teamwork, and computer skills; be analytical, detail-oriented, trustworthy, self-motivated, flexible, compassionate

CAREER LADDER

```
┌─────────────────────────┐
│    Senior Paralegal     │
│   or Paralegal Manager  │
└─────────────────────────┘

┌─────────────────────────┐
│        Paralegal        │
└─────────────────────────┘

┌─────────────────────────┐
│   Entry-level Paralegal  │
└─────────────────────────┘
```

Position Description

Paralegals, or legal assistants, have been trained in substantive and procedural law and are qualified to perform various legal tasks. They may be involved in transactional matters, such as drafting contracts or reviewing trust instruments, or they may work on civil litigation or criminal defense cases. However, paralegals, unlike attorneys, cannot practice law. Paralegals cannot offer legal advice. They cannot accept clients or represent clients in courts, and paralegals cannot establish legal fees.

Paralegals perform their legal work under the supervision and direction of licensed attorneys. They may execute any legal task assigned by attorneys, such as:

- assist with case planning, development, and management
- interview clients to obtain background information
- conduct legal research
- prepare legal documents, pleadings, and correspondence
- analyze and interpret contracts, wills, motions, briefs, and other legal documents
- investigate the facts in a case or a legal matter
- locate and interview witnesses
- summarize depositions and testimonies of witnesses
- prepare clients for court hearings or other proceedings

Like lawyers, Paralegals are involved in the different practice areas of law—such as civil litigation, criminal law, corporate law, family law, immigration law, employment law, intellectual property law, real estate law, and estate law. After several years of work experience, Paralegals usually specialize in one or more practice areas.

Many Paralegals are employed by solo practitioners and law firms. Many others work in corporate legal departments, court systems, government agencies, community legal services programs, banks, insurance companies, real estate firms, trade associations, and other organizations.

The types of duties that Paralegals perform vary among the different work settings. Corporate Paralegals perform tasks, such as drafting financial reports or analyzing employee benefit plans, that are related to the legal needs of private corporations. Paralegals in government agencies collect evidence for agency hearings, prepare information guides on agency regulations, and analyze legal material, among many other duties. Paralegals in community legal services programs often work as advocates and perform such tasks as obtaining government benefits for clients.

Some Paralegals play a dual role in law offices, performing duties of a Paralegal and legal secretary for attorneys. Paralegals in supervisory positions oversee paralegal staff. And in some offices, supervisors may provide direction to other legal support staff as well.

Paralegals are responsible for keeping current with changes in the law, technology, and other developments that may affect their work, as well as for pursuing their professional growth. They read legal and professional journals, network with colleagues, participate in professional conferences, and enroll in continuing education programs.

Paralegals work part time or full time. They may be required to work overtime to help attorneys meet deadlines.

Salaries

Salaries for Paralegals vary, and depend on such factors as their education, experience, employer, and geographical location. According to the U.S. Bureau of Labor Statistics (BLS), in its May 2005 *Occupational Employment Statistics* (OES) survey, the estimated annual salary for most Paralegals ranged between $26,270 and $65,330.

Employment Prospects

The BLS reports in its May 2005 OES survey that an estimated 217,700 Paralegals were employed in the United States. Nearly 75 percent were employed in the legal services industry.

Job growth for Paralegals is predicted to increase by 27 percent or more through 2014, according to the BLS. In addition, opportunities will become available as Paralegals advance to higher positions, transfer to other jobs, or retire.

Advancement Prospects

Paralegals can advance to supervisory and managerial positions. Many realize advancement by receiving higher pay and greater responsibilities, which may require seeking positions with other employers.

Paralegals can pursue other legal-related careers such as litigation support managers, real estate brokers, compliance inspectors, and mediators. They also have the option to earn a law degree and become practicing lawyers.

Education and Training

Depending on the employer, entry-level applicants may be required to possess at least an associate degree, a bachelor's degree, or a professional certificate in paralegal studies. Employers may hire candidates with degrees in other fields, if they have completed a certain number of months of in-house training as Paralegals. Employers may also accept candidates without college degrees if they have completed a certain number of years of in-house training as legal assistants or if they have a minimum number of years of law-related experience under the supervision of lawyers.

Entry-level Paralegals usually receive on-the-job training, working under the supervision of experienced Paralegals. Large employers may also provide them with formal classroom training.

Experience, Skills, and Personality Traits

Many employers prefer to hire candidates who have prior experience working in legal settings. They may have gained their experience through internships, work-study programs, part-time employment, or volunteer work. Paralegals must have excellent research, writing, and communication skills as well as organizational, interpersonal, and teamwork skills. Increasingly, more employers require that Paralegals have computer skills in legal research, word processing, spreadsheets, and database management. Being analytical, detail-oriented, trustworthy, self-motivated, flexible, and compassionate are some personality traits that successful Paralegals share.

Unions and Associations

Paralegals can join local, state, or national professional associations to take advantage of networking opportunities, professional certification programs, training programs, and other professional resources and services. Some national societies include the National Association of Legal Assistants, the National Paralegal Association, the American Alliance of Paralegals, Inc., and the Standing Committee on Paralegals (part of the American Bar Association). For contact information, see Appendix V.

Tips for Entry

1. To enhance their employability, many Paralegals obtain professional certification through recognized organizations. See Appendix II for specific programs.
2. Take advantage of the resources that are available at the career center at your college. For example, counselors can help you create a job search plan as well as strengthen your job search skills.
3. One source for learning about job openings is professional associations. Many local and state groups maintain job listings.
4. Learn more about the Paralegal profession on the Internet. You might start by visiting the American Alliance of Paralegals Web site at http://www.aapipara.org. For more links, see Appendix VI.

LEGAL ADMINISTRATOR

CAREER PROFILE

Duties: Manage and oversee the daily business functions and administrative operations in a law office or legal department; perform duties as required

Alternate Title(s): Law Office Manager, Law Department Administrator, Chief Office Administrator, Executive Director

Salary Range: $33,000 to $113,000

Employment Prospects: Good

Advancement Prospects: Fair

Prerequisites:

Education or Training—A college degree is preferred

Experience—Several years of office management experience, preferably in law settings; experienced or knowledgeable in business services, human resources, financial management, and other areas

Special Skills and Personality Traits—Supervisory, leadership, administrative, management, teamwork, interpersonal, communication, writing, and computer skills; be energetic, composed, organized, hardworking, loyal, creative

CAREER LADDER

```
┌─────────────────────────────────┐
│   Chief Office Administrator     │
│     or Executive Director        │
└─────────────────────────────────┘

┌─────────────────────────────────┐
│      Legal Administrator         │
└─────────────────────────────────┘

┌─────────────────────────────────┐
│  Assistant Law Office Manager    │
│ or other legal management position│
└─────────────────────────────────┘
```

Position Description

Legal Administrators are responsible for the smooth and efficient management of the daily administrative operations in law offices, law firms, legal departments, and legal services programs.

They are responsible for executing the vision and philosophy of law partners, chief lawyers, or executive officers. These managers establish office rules and procedures. They identify changing needs for their organizations and plan for them accordingly. They also make recommendations to law partners or executive officers about ways to make cost-effective improvements to business operations. In some law firms, Legal Administrators participate in law practice management meetings to make plans and strategies for developing further business for the firms.

Legal Administrators also manage all business functions. Some of these functions are:

- office services, which includes all office support (such as word processing, filing, mail distribution, greeting clients, and answering phones) needed by lawyers, paralegals, and other staff
- human resources, which includes the recruitment and selection of all staff, salary and benefits administration, employee relations, and professional development
- financial management, which includes preparing and monitoring annual budgets; handling payroll, billing, and collections; tax reporting; and maintaining bank relations
- facilities management, which includes the planning and maintenance of physical space, purchasing equipment and office supplies, and taking care of mail and records storage needs
- information systems, which includes all technology and telecommunications systems
- marketing, which includes the planning, developing, and execution of marketing strategies and activities for the organization

In smaller offices, Legal Administrators are responsible for overseeing all management functions. In larger offices, they may be responsible for one or a few major functions and supervise managers of other functions. For example, a Legal Administrator might directly manage all functions but human resources and technology.

Legal Administrators act as liaisons between attorneys and the legal support staff. Their job also involves providing supervision and guidance to their legal support staffs, and establishing a working environment that motivates individuals and fosters teamwork.

These managers are also responsible for handling problems and issues as they arise. For example, they might need to deal with a staff conflict, improve the organization's information technology security program, or seek a more reliable overnight delivery service.

Legal Administrators might work beyond their 40-hour week in order to complete necessary tasks.

Salaries

Salaries for Legal Administrators vary, depending on such factors as their experience, education, employer, and geographical location. Specific salary information for this occupation is unavailable, but these managers generally earn salaries similar to administrative services managers. According to the May 2005 *Occupational Employment Statistics* survey, by the U.S. Bureau of Labor Statistics, the estimated annual salary for most administrative services managers ranged between $32,770 and $113,150.

Employment Prospects

Legal Administrators are employed by law firms, corporate law departments, legal services programs, government agencies, and other organizations. Most opportunities become available as Legal Administrators retire, resign, or transfer to other positions.

Advancement Prospects

Many Legal Administrators pursue career growth by earning higher wages, advancing to positions with more complex responsibilities, or obtaining jobs with the organizations of their choice. Entrepreneurial individuals can become independent consultants or owners of legal management consulting firms.

Education and Training

Most employers require or prefer that candidates have an associate or bachelor's degree or have some college background. They especially look for candidates who have completed course work in business administration or management, finance, human resources, technology, or marketing.

Throughout their careers, Legal Administrators enroll in training and continuing education programs to develop and maintain their skills and expertise.

Experience, Skills, and Personality Traits

Employers seek candidates who have several years of office management experience, preferably in law settings. Candidates should have experience in or be knowledgeable about business services, human resources, financial management, and other areas of business operations.

Legal Administrators need excellent supervisory, leadership, administrative, and management skills. They also need strong teamwork, interpersonal, and communication skills, as they must work well with attorneys, legal support personnel, and others. In addition, they must have competent writing and computer skills. Being energetic, composed, organized, hardworking, loyal, and creative are some personality traits that successful Legal Administrators share.

Unions and Associations

Many Legal Administrators belong to professional associations to take advantage of networking opportunities, and other professional services and resources. The Association of Legal Administrators and NALS are two national societies that serve the interests of this occupation. For contact information, see Appendix V.

Tips for Entry

1. To enhance their employability, many Legal Administrators obtain professional certification through recognized organizations. See Appendix II for some groups.
2. Build up a network of contacts from school, professional organizations, conferences, and so on. Call, write, or e-mail your contacts when doing your job search. Many of them may know of current or upcoming vacancies.
3. Learn more about law office management on the Internet. You might start by visiting the Association of Legal Administrators Web site at http://www.alanet.org. For more links, see Appendix VI.

HUMAN RESOURCES MANAGER
(LAW FIRM)

CAREER PROFILE

Duties: Oversee administrative functions that relate to personnel, such as staff recruitment and training, compensation and benefits administration, and compliance with employment laws; perform duties as required

Alternate Title(s): Director of Human Resources, Personnel Director

Salary Range: $41,000 to $140,000

Employment Prospects: Good

Advancement Prospects: Fair

Prerequisites:

Education or Training—A bachelor's degree

Experience—Previous work experience in law firms or other professional services; supervisory experience; knowledgeable about labor and employment laws

Special Skills and Personality Traits—Leadership, administrative, management, interpersonal, teamwork, communication, writing, and computer skills; tactful, calm, fair-minded, ethical, persuasive, friendly, flexible

CAREER LADDER

```
┌─────────────────────────────────┐
│   Director of Human Resources   │
│   or Law Office Administrator   │
└─────────────────────────────────┘

┌─────────────────────────────────┐
│     Human Resources Manager     │
└─────────────────────────────────┘

┌─────────────────────────────────┐
│    Human Resources Specialist   │
└─────────────────────────────────┘
```

Position Description

Many law firms have Human Resources Managers who oversee all administrative functions relating to the employees of a law firm. These managers act as the link between top management (employers) and employees, and are responsible for executing their firm's personnel policies and requirements.

Human Resources Managers are responsible for a wide range of duties that may include:

• designing and administering compensation and benefits programs such as health insurance and pension plans
• developing and coordinating programs for the welfare of employees, such as programs promoting workplace safety and health practices, car pooling and transportation, child care, and counseling services
• overseeing the recruitment and selection process for new staff positions

• developing and coordinating staff training, including orientation programs for new employees and professional development programs
• coordinating job performance evaluations of lawyers and support staff
• assisting top management in the development of personnel policies and procedures
• making sure that their firm is in compliance with the appropriate local, state, and federal employment laws
• investigating workplace issues and concerns such as employee grievances
• providing guidance and advice to all managers, supervisors, and attorneys about handling employee relations issues
• maintaining all employee records

Human Resources Managers are also responsible for the direction and supervision of their staff, which may include human resources specialists as well as office and administrative personnel. In some law firms, one manager, or director, oversees the work of several Human Resources Managers who perform specific human resources functions, such as employee training programs or compensation and benefits administration.

Human Resources Managers generally work a standard 40-hour week. On occasion, they may work in the evenings and on weekends to complete projects.

Salaries

Salaries for Human Resources Managers vary, depending on such factors as their experience, education, employer, and geographical location. Specific salary information for these law firm managers is unavailable. However the estimated annual salary for most Human Resources Managers was reported by the U.S. Bureau of Labor Statistics (BLS), in its May 2005 *Occupational Employment Statistics* survey, as follows:

- compensation and benefits managers—$39,910 to $122,330
- training and development managers—$40,830 to $128,780
- all other human resources managers—$49,820 to $139,600

Employment Prospects

Most opportunities for Human Resources Managers in law offices become available as individuals retire, resign, or transfer to other positions. New positions are usually created by small and medium-sized firms as they grow and require the need of experienced Human Resources Managers.

According to the BLS, employment for Human Resources Managers (in all industries), is expected to increase by 18 to 26 percent through 2014.

Advancement Prospects

Most Human Resource Managers pursue advancement by seeking positions with higher salaries and more complex responsibilities, or by being employed in the top law firms. The ultimate goal for some managers is to become human resources consultants, operating their own businesses.

Education and Training

Many employers require candidates to possess at least a bachelor's degree in human resources, human resources administration, labor relations, business administration, liberal arts, or another related field.

Most managers enroll in continuing education and training programs throughout their careers to develop and strengthen their skills and expertise.

Experience, Skills, and Personality Traits

In general, employers look for candidates who have previous human resources experience in law firms or with other professional services. They also have several years of supervisory experience. In addition, they have a thorough knowledge of labor and employment laws.

Human Resources Managers need excellent leadership, administrative, and management skills. They also require superb interpersonal, teamwork, and communication skills, as well as strong writing and computer skills. Furthermore, they must be able to work well with people of different backgrounds, abilities, and education.

Some personality traits that successful Human Resources Managers share are being tactful, calm, fair, ethical, persuasive, friendly, and flexible.

Unions and Associations

Many Human Resources Managers belong to local, state, and national professional associations in order to take advantage of professional services and resources as well as networking opportunities. One such national organization is the Society for Human Resource Management. Law office Human Resource Managers are also eligible to join the Association of Legal Administrators. For contact information, see Appendix V.

Tips for Entry

1. Obtain internships in human resources departments to gain experience.
2. Many Human Resources Managers got their start by working as human resources clerks while in college.
3. Many Human Resources Managers obtain professional certification through recognized organizations. See Appendix II for some groups.
4. You can learn more about the human resources field on the Internet. You might start by visiting the Society for Human Resource Management at http://www.shrm.org. For more links, see Appendix VI.

MARKETING MANAGER (LAW FIRM)

CAREER PROFILE

Duties: Plan, develop, and execute marketing strategies and activities; perform various duties as required

Alternate Title(s): Marketing Coordinator, Marketing Director

Salary Range: $49,000 to $146,000

Employment Prospects: Good

Advancement Prospects: Poor

Prerequisites:

Education or Training—A bachelor's or advanced degree

Experience—Several years of marketing experience in law firms or other professional services

Special Skills and Personality Traits—Leadership, teamwork, interpersonal, communication, analytical, writing, and computer skills; positive, self-motivated, tactful, persuasive, decisive, persistent, creative, flexible

CAREER LADDER

```
┌─────────────────────────────────┐
│   Marketing Director or Legal    │
│     Marketing Consultant         │
└─────────────────────────────────┘

┌─────────────────────────────────┐
│        Marketing Manager         │
└─────────────────────────────────┘

┌─────────────────────────────────┐
│ Marketing Coordinator or Marketing │
│    Manager (non-law firm)        │
└─────────────────────────────────┘
```

Position Description

To succeed in business, law firms must be able to continually bring in new clients. For this reason, many law firms hire Marketing Managers who are experts in the area of promoting legal services. They help law firms plan, develop, and execute marketing strategies and activities that would most effectively influence target audiences to hire their firms.

The responsibilities of Marketing Managers vary, depending on the needs of their employers as well as their levels of expertise. Legal Marketing Managers typically oversee the development of all promotional activities. They create promotional tools such as brochures, newsletters, and attorney biographies. They manage public relations tasks, such as writing and distributing press releases about their firm's activities to the media. They also coordinate advertising projects for print, radio, and other media. In addition, many Marketing Managers assist in the design of their law firm's Web site as a promotional tool.

Another typical area of responsibility is the promotion of events, such as seminars, open houses, and conferences, where lawyers meet with potential clients, as well as current ones, to talk about the legal services they provide. Marketing Managers might also assist in the planning and coordination of these events.

Legal Marketing Managers are also responsible for conducting market research for different purposes. For example, they might survey current clients to measure their satisfaction with their lawyers' performance. Or, they might conduct research to find out the potential market for new legal services that lawyers would like to offer.

Many Marketing Managers also have the duty of developing education and training programs for attorneys and staff, covering topics such as client service, marketing, and presentation skills.

In law firms that have several practice areas, Marketing Managers may also have the responsibility of helping the different practice groups develop and execute marketing activities.

Most legal Marketing Managers are responsible for monitoring budget expenses throughout the year. This may also include budgets for practice groups and individual lawyers. In some law firms, Marketing Managers prepare, or help in the preparation of, the annual marketing budget.

In addition, Legal Marketing Managers perform a wide range of routine duties. Some of these tasks are:

- providing guidance and supervision to marketing staff
- managing relationships with outside vendors such as advertising agencies, graphic designers, or public relations consultants
- maintaining database systems for mail lists, referral sources, client and industry analysis, attorney biographies, and other information
- attending marketing meetings for different practice areas
- preparing presentation materials, such as visual and hand-out materials, for attorneys' speaking engagements

Marketing Managers sometimes work evenings and weekends to complete their projects. Some of their tasks may involve traveling to different cities or states.

Salaries
Salaries for Marketing Managers vary, depending on their job duties, experience, education, geographical location, and other factors. Specific salary information for law firm managers is unavailable. However, the estimated annual salary for most Marketing Managers, in all industries, ranged between $48,590 and $145,600, according to the U.S. Bureau of Labor Statistics, in its May 2005 *Occupational Employment Statistics* survey.

Employment Prospects
Many legal Marketing Managers are employed by law firms, while others work for agencies that offer marketing services to attorneys and other professionals. Law firms will create new positions to meet their growing needs. Most opportunities become available as managers retire, advance to higher positions, or transfer to other jobs.

Advancement Prospects
Legal Marketing Managers pursue advancement by earning higher salaries, receiving greater responsibilities, and gaining professional recognition. This generally requires moving from one law firm to the next. The top goal for some managers is to become consultants or owners of marketing firms that offer legal marketing services.

Education and Training
Minimally, legal Marketing Managers must possess a bachelor's degree, which may be in any field. For example, marketing, advertising, public relations, journalism, psy-chology, liberal arts, and business administration, are a few subjects in which Marketing Managers might have degrees. Some managers also have law degrees.

Throughout their careers, Legal Marketing Managers enroll in training and education programs sponsored by trade associations and colleges to develop and improve their skills.

Experience, Skills, and Personality Traits
Minimum requirements vary with the different employers. In general, they look for candidates who have several years of marketing experience in law firms or other professional services.

Legal Marketing Managers require the ability to see the big picture as well as to pay attention to details. They should have strong leadership, teamwork, interpersonal, and communication skills as they must be able to work well with attorneys, staff, clients, media, and others. In addition, they need strong analytical, writing, and computer skills.

Some personality traits that successful Legal Marketing Managers share are being positive, self-motivated, tactful, persuasive, decisive, persistent, creative, and flexible.

Unions and Associations
Many Legal Marketing Managers join local, state, and national organizations that serve their field, such as the Legal Marketing Association and the American Marketing Association. They are also eligible to join the Association of Legal Administrators, an organization that serves all types of legal administrators. These different organizations offer various types of professional services and resources as well as opportunities for networking with colleagues. (For contact information for the above organizations, see Appendix V.)

Tips for Entry
1. Continue to build and develop your computer and Internet skills.
2. Talk with Legal Marketing Managers to learn more about their jobs. Also find out what courses you should take in college, and what types of work experiences might prepare you for their profession.
3. Contact attorney bars and professional associations for job listings, as many of them also post announcements for non-lawyer positions.
4. You can learn more about the legal marketing field on the Internet. Enter the keywords *legal marketing* or *lawyer marketing* in any search engine to get a list of Web sites. For some links, see Appendix VI.

LEGAL TECHNOLOGY CONSULTANT

CAREER PROFILE

Duties: Provide technology consulting services such as assessing the automation needs of law offices and providing suggestions for new or improved systems; perform duties as required

Alternate Title(s): None

Salary Range: $39,000 to $123,000

Employment Prospects: Good

Advancement Prospects: Poor

Prerequisites:

   Education or Training—No standard requirements

   Experience—Several years of technology expertise

   Special Skills and Personality Traits—Interpersonal, communication, writing, presentation, and self-management skills; small business skills for business owners; be patient, friendly, analytical, organized, self-motivated, flexible, creative

CAREER LADDER

```
┌─────────────────────────────────────┐
│  Senior Legal Technology Consultant  │
└─────────────────────────────────────┘

┌─────────────────────────────────────┐
│     Legal Technology Consultant      │
└─────────────────────────────────────┘

┌─────────────────────────────────────┐
│     Legal Technology Specialist      │
│             or Manager               │
└─────────────────────────────────────┘
```

Position Description

Legal Technology Consultants are experts in the area of office automation (or technology) for the law office. They are hired on a contractual basis by law firms, corporate law departments, and other legal and legal related programs and organizations. These consultants help lawyers determine how technology can most effectively meet their legal, office, and administrative needs. In addition, these consultants educate their clients about unfamiliar technologies so that they can make informed decisions.

Legal Technology Consultants provide several areas of service for lawyers. One area is making recommendations for improving a law office's automation systems. Consultants start by performing assessments of the lawyers' business management and practice management needs. They gather information about a law office's current automation systems, its problems and limitations, the office's immediate needs and long-range goals, and so forth. This involves talking with lawyers, secretaries, legal administrators, information system administrators, and other staff members. Consultants then prepare an assessment report that defines the office's goals and objectives, summarizes problem areas and limitations of the automation systems, and provides recommendations for improving systems. Consultants also provide a budget and schedule for purchasing and installing the new systems.

Coordinating the purchase of a law office's new information system is another service that Legal Technology Consultants provide. They contact prospective vendors, asking vendors to send them proposals, which include estimated costs and time schedules. Consultants review all proposals and prepare an evaluation report, providing comparisons of equipment and costs and a synopsis of strengths and weaknesses of each vendor.

Many Legal Technology Consultants also provide the service of overseeing the installation of new automation systems in the law office. Their tasks may include negotiating prices, and warranty provisions; ensuring that vendors meet schedules and perform their obligations; managing the conversion of data from the old system to the new one; coordinating quality tests; and, developing training programs.

Many law offices retain Legal Technology Consultants to advise lawyers on how to make changes to their systems as needed.

Some Legal Technology Consultants are solo practitioners, while others are associates or partners in legal technology firms. They are considered independent consultants; that is, they are not connected in any way with vendors or manufacturers of computer products.

Self-employed consultants and business owners are responsible for the daily administration of their businesses. They handle such tasks as setting consulting fees, supervising staff, paying bills and taxes, invoicing clients, bookkeeping, and maintaining office space.

Legal Technical Consultants may work part time or full time. Many Consultants travel to different cities and states to meet and work with clients.

Salaries

Salaries for Legal Technology Consultants vary, depending on such factors as their experience, personal ambition, and geographical location. Salary information for this occupation is unavailable, but Legal Technology Consultants generally receive earnings similar to management analysts. According to the U.S. Bureau of Labor Statistics, in its May 2005 *Occupational Employment Statistics* survey, the estimated annual salary for most management analysts ranged between $38,650 and $123,300. The estimated annual mean wage was $88,740 for consultants who provide management and technical consulting services.

Employment Prospects

Although law office technology is a young field, job opportunities are expected to grow in the coming years. Increasingly more law firms and law departments are seeing the need for setting up technology systems in their offices. Additionally, many law firms that are already technologically savvy are increasing their budgets to keep their systems up to date.

Advancement Prospects

Associate consultants can advance to such senior positions as partnership in a firm. Another option is to start their own consulting businesses after gaining several years of experience.

In general, Legal Technology Consultants realize advancement by earning higher wages and gaining professional recognition.

Education and Training

There are no standard educational requirements for Legal Technology Consultant. Many consultants have bachelor's degrees in different fields. Some also have law degrees.

Legal Technology Consultants are responsible for their professional development. They do independent study, network with colleagues, participate in conferences, and enroll in training and continuing education programs.

Experience, Skills, and Personality Traits

Legal Technology Consultants enter this field from different backgrounds—lawyers, paralegals, legal administrators, engineers, economists, and legal technology specialists. Along with having several years of technology expertise, they have an understanding of the way the legal profession works.

Legal Technology Consultants must have the ability to describe technical terms in nontechnical language. They also need excellent interpersonal and communication skills, as they must be able to work well with people of different backgrounds and abilities. In addition, they must have strong writing and presentation skills as well as superior self-management skills. The self-employed and business owners should also have good small business skills. Successful Legal Technology Consultants share several personality traits such as being patient, friendly, analytical, organized, self-motivated, flexible, and creative.

Unions and Associations

Legal Technology Consultants join professional associations to take advantage of networking opportunities, training programs, and other professional services and resources. Some technology associations are the Society for Information Management and the International Legal Technology Association. Many consultants join bar associations, such as the American Bar Association. Some also join the Association of Legal Administrators, a professional society for legal management professions. For contact information for the above organizations, see Appendix V.

Tips for Entry

1. Get basic information technology training in either hardware or software, then obtain legal technology training from consultants in the field.
2. Take basic law courses in college or continuing education programs to become familiar with the needs of lawyers.
3. Many technology consultants enhance their credibility by obtaining product certifications and professional certification in management consulting.
4. Establish your reputation. For example, you might make presentations at conferences for lawyers or write articles about legal technology for legal publications.
5. Use the Internet to learn more about legal technology. To find relevant Web sites, enter the keywords *legal technology* or *legal technology consultants* in a search engine. For some links, see Appendix VI.

LEGAL SEARCH CONSULTANT

CAREER PROFILE

Duties: Find qualified attorney candidates for legal employers; perform duties as required

Alternate Title(s): Headhunter, Job Recruiter

Salary Range: $26,000 to $79,000+

Employment Prospects: Fair

Advancement Prospects: Poor

Prerequisites:

Education or Training—A bachelor's degree; many possess a law degree

Experience—Lawyer, job recruiter, or career counselor experience preferred; experience in, or knowledgeable about, the legal industry

Special Skills and Personality Traits—Interpersonal, interviewing, negotiation, observational, communication, and listening skills; can handle rejections; have good instincts; be reliable, honest, ethical, persistent, enthusiastic, trustworthy, self-motivated, resourceful

CAREER LADDER

```
┌─────────────────────────────────────┐
│  Principal Legal Search Consultant   │
└─────────────────────────────────────┘

┌─────────────────────────────────────┐
│      Legal Search Consultant         │
└─────────────────────────────────────┘

┌─────────────────────────────────────┐
│        Law Firm Recruiter            │
│    or Legal Search Associate         │
└─────────────────────────────────────┘
```

Position Description

Legal Search Consultants are headhunters who offer job recruiting services to law firms, corporate law departments, and other organizations. Their expertise is finding the best attorney candidates that match their clients' requirements for associate, partner, or in-house counsel positions.

Legal Search Consultants generally receive job orders from their clients that state specific information about their job openings, such as type of position, job duties, salaries, and advancement prospects. To get a better sense of the best candidates for a client, Legal Search Consultants research the employer. They learn as many details as they can—the employer's mission and goals, areas of practice, types of clients, work values, working styles, and so on. The headhunters provide this information to prospective candidates so that they can decide whether they might be compatible with an employer.

Legal recruiters begin their search for potential attorney candidates by first producing a list of names, which can sometimes be up to 100 or more. To find qualified candidates, Legal Search Consultants go through their databases and contacts of attorneys, law firms, legal departments, and so forth. Their initial search may include candidates all over the state, country, and world. They also list potential candidates who are not actively searching for new positions. At the end of the screening process, headhunters present résumés of only the top candidates to their clients.

Headhunters go through résumés and choose attorneys who best match the requirements of their clients. They call up these individuals and find out if they may be interested in the job openings. Most headhunters meet with interested individuals to learn more about them as well as to provide them with more information about the job opening and the employer.

Legal Search Consultants work closely with candidates whom they will be presenting to their clients. They review candidates' résumés and help revise résumés if necessary. They prepare prospective candidates for their interviews and coach them on their interviewing techniques. When their candidates are offered a job, Legal Search Consultants may assist them with salary and benefits negotiations.

Legal Search Consultants typically conduct attorney searches for several job openings at a time. In small and mid-size firms, they generally perform all aspects of an attorney search. In large firms, researchers and associates assist with the research and initial screening process.

Many Legal Search Consultants specialize in the type of attorney searches that they conduct. For example, they may recruit for certain positions (such as lateral transfers or partners), certain practice areas (for example, intellectual property), or only for law firms or corporations.

Performing legal search work usually requires long hours. Travel to other cities or states may be necessary to meet with clients and potential candidates.

Salaries

In addition to their salaries, most Legal Search Consultants earn a commission fee for every successful placement that they make. The commission is a percentage of a position's gross annual salary during the first year. Specific salary information for Legal Search Consultants is unavailable. According to the May 2005 *Occupational Employment Statistics* survey, by the U.S. Bureau of Labor Statistics, the estimated annual salary for most employment, recruitment, and placement specialists ranged between $25,960 and $78,930.

Total earnings for legal recruiters vary each year, depending on such factors as their annual salary, their ambition, and the actual number of placements. Top Legal Search Consultants can earn six-figure annual incomes or more.

Employment Prospects

In general, the legal recruiting field is highly competitive and changes constantly, following the marketing trends for attorneys. Most Legal Search Consultants work in small firms with one to five headhunters. Opportunities usually become available to replace recruiters who have advanced to higher positions, transferred to other jobs, or who have left the workforce for various reasons. Recruiting firms will create additional positions to meet their growing needs.

Advancement Prospects

Associate recruiters may rise to senior positions. They may also be offered a partnership in their firms. Another option for Legal Search Consultants is to start their own recruiting agencies.

Most Legal Search Consultants measure success by gaining professional reputations and by earning higher incomes.

Education and Training

Legal Search Consultants hold bachelor's degrees; many also possess law degrees.

Typically, novices learn on the job, receiving supervision and mentoring from senior headhunters.

Experience, Skills, and Personality Traits

Legal Search Consultants usually have years of experience as lawyers, job recruiters, or career counselors. They have solid experience in, or knowledge about, the legal industry.

To succeed in this field, headhunters must have excellent interpersonal, interviewing, negotiation, and observational skills. In addition, they need superior communication and listening skills. They also can handle rejections. Furthermore, they have an instinct for making matches between candidates and clients that are highly compatible.

Some personality traits that successful consultants share are being reliable, honest, ethical, persistent, enthusiastic, trustworthy, and self-motivated.

Unions and Associations

Many Legal Search Consultants join local, state, and national professional associations to take advantage of networking opportunities, education programs, publications, and other professional resources and services. One such national organization is the National Association of Legal Search Consultants. For contact information, see Appendix V.

Many Legal Search Consultants also join professional organizations for attorneys and law firms to network with potential clients, as well as to keep up with developments in the legal services industry.

Tips for Entry

1. Obtain work as a researcher or an internship with a legal recruiting firm to see if it is a field that might interest you.
2. To find reputable recruiting firms for whom you'd like to work, ask for recommendations from law firm recruiting coordinators.
3. Use the Internet to learn more about legal recruiting. To find relevant Web sites, enter any of these phrases into a search engine: *legal recruiting, legal headhunter,* or *legal search consultants.* For some links, see Appendix VI.

LITIGATION SUPPORT PROFESSIONALS

DEMONSTRATIVE EVIDENCE SPECIALIST

CAREER PROFILE

Duties: Create demonstrative exhibits for court trials; perform duties as required

Alternate Title(s): Legal Graphic Artist; Graphic Designer, Medical Illustrator, Animator, or other title that reflects a particular specialty

Salary Range: $15,000 to $93,000

Employment Prospects: Good

Advancement Prospects: Good

Prerequisites:

Education or Training—A solid formal education in speciality; on-the-job training

Experience—Several years of professional experience

Special Skills and Personality Traits—Communication, interpersonal, teamwork, self-management skills; business skills for self-employed specialists; be intelligent, patient, calm, organized, hardworking, open-minded, flexible

CAREER LADDER

```
┌─────────────────────────────┐
│  Senior Specialist, Manager, │
│  or Independent Contractor   │
└─────────────────────────────┘

┌─────────────────────────────┐
│ Demonstrative Evidence Specialist │
└─────────────────────────────┘

┌─────────────────────────────┐
│   Demonstrative Evidence     │
│     Specialist Trainee       │
└─────────────────────────────┘
```

Position Description

Demonstrative Evidence Specialists are professional graphic designers, illustrators, medical illustrators, photographers, animators, videographers, and other visual artists. They create demonstrative exhibits, or demonstrative evidence, for lawyers to use in court trials. These may include graphs, charts, illustrations, photographs, audiotapes, videotapes, and computer-generated graphics. Demonstrative Evidence Specialists may create one, dozens, or hundreds of demonstrative exhibits for a trial.

A demonstrative exhibit depicts specific facts that have been presented in sworn testimony by witnesses or experts. For example, a lawyer may show a computer animation that recreates the scene of an automobile accident as presented by a key witness. By using oral and visual testimonies together, lawyers believe that jurors can understand abstract concepts better and remember those concepts when they deliberate on a verdict in the jury rooms. Many lawyers also use demonstrative exhibits in their opening and closing statements.

Demonstrative Evidence Specialists work closely with lawyers and with expert witnesses. They generate demonstrative exhibits for a wide range of criminal and civil cases. Thus, along with having artistic talents and skills, specialists must be able to break down complex concepts presented by lawyers and experts and translate them into visual aids that communicate the ideas clearly and simply. Specialists help determine what concepts need to be communicated visually and in what form (such as an illustration, chart, or animation) that they should be presented.

Demonstrative Evidence Specialists produce demonstrative exhibits that are based on testimony or physical evidence. Attorneys provide them with witness statements, photographs, accident reports, medical records, and other relevant documents. Specialists must pay close attention to every detail. The details must be accurate and correct, as well as be relevant to the issues involved in the case. Otherwise, the demonstrative evidence may not be admissible in court. In addition, specialists must ensure that their designs do not mislead jurors or judges in any way.

Demonstrative Evidence Specialists may be called to testify at trials. As expert witnesses, they testify that the demonstrative evidence that they created is accurate, unbiased, and represents the actual evidence.

Most Demonstrative Evidence Specialists are independent contractors. Depending on the legal market in their areas, they may do projects for other industries. Independent contractors must also handle the tasks of running a business. Their duties include bookkeeping, maintaining project files, invoicing clients, paying bills and taxes, ordering supplies, generating new business, and so forth.

Demonstrative Evidence Specialists work part time or full time. It is not uncommon for specialists to work nights and weekends to complete projects for lawyers.

Salaries

Salaries for Demonstrative Evidence Specialists vary, depending on such factors as their specialty, experience, employer, and geographical location. Specific salary information for this profession is unavailable, but an approximation can be obtained by looking at the salaries for different visual artists. For example, the U.S. Bureau of Labor Statistics reported in its May 2005 *Occupational Employment Statistics* survey that most of the following artists earned an estimated annual salary that fell within these ranges:

- graphic designers, $23,160 to $67,660
- illustrators, $19,580 to $79,950
- multi-media artists and animators, $29,680 to $93,060
- photographers, $15,240 to $53,900

Employment Prospects

Demonstrative Evidence Specialists may be independent contractors or employees of litigation support firms that offer demonstrative evidence services.

Demonstrative Evidence Specialists are part of a relatively young field, which has been steadily growing since the 1980s. Job opportunities are expected to continue growing as increasingly more lawyers need visual aids as tools for trials, as well as for mediations, arbitrations, and settlements.

The demand for experienced Demonstrative Evidence Specialists is currently high.

Advancement Prospects

In large firms, specialists can advance to project management positions, such as project managers, art directors, and operations directors. The goal of many Demonstrative Evidence Specialists is to own successful firms.

Education and Training

Demonstrative Evidence Specialists come from various backgrounds, including art, advertising, law, and communications. Generally, specialists have a solid, formal education in graphic design, illustration, animation, or related fields.

Entry-level specialists receive on-the-job training. Throughout their careers, specialists enroll in continuing education and training programs to increase their knowledge and update their skills.

Experience, Skills, and Personality Traits

In general, employers seek candidates with several years of professional experience. Candidates also demonstrate the ability to understand complex ideas and to design exhibits that can be easily understood by judges and jurors.

Demonstrative Evidence Specialists need excellent communication, interpersonal, teamwork and self-management skills. Being intelligent, patient, calm, organized, hard working, open-minded, and flexible are some of the personality traits that successful specialists share.

Unions and Associations

Demonstrative Evidence Specialists join professional associations to take advantage of professional services and resources, as well as opportunities to network with colleagues. One national organization dedicated to this field is the Demonstrative Evidence Specialists Association. The Association of Medical Illustrators, the Evidence Photographers International Council, and the American Guild of Court Videographers are some other professional associations that different specialists might join. For contact information, see Appendix V.

Tips for Entry

1. One way to break into the field is to get an internship with an established Demonstrative Evidence Specialist.
2. Having a variety of competent multimedia skills may enhance your employability.
3. Before starting your own business, learn how big a market is available for your services. Survey lawyers in the area about their needs for your particular services.
4. Use the Internet to learn more about the field. This includes learning about various firms and the type of services they offer. To find relevant Web sites, enter the keywords *demonstrative evidence* in any search engine. For some links, see Appendix VI.

LEGAL VIDEOGRAPHER

CAREER PROFILE

Duties: Videotape sworn statements of witnesses for civil or criminal cases; provide lawyers with other legal video services as needed; perform other duties as required

Alternate Title(s): Legal Video Specialist, Forensic Videographer, Court Videographer, Video Court Reporter

Salary Range: $19,000 to $57,000

Employment Prospects: Excellent

Advancement Prospects: Poor

Prerequisites:

Education or Training—Legal videography training

Experience—Professional videography experience

Special Skills and Personality Traits—Interpersonal, communication, self-management skills; business skills for independent contractors; be friendly, cooperative, patient, detail-oriented, ethical, professional

CAREER LADDER

> Senior Legal Videographer, Supervisor, or Independent Operator

> Legal Videographer

> Trainee

Position Description

Many litigation attorneys use the services of Legal Videographers to videotape depositions for civil or criminal cases. Depositions are sworn testimonies that witnesses give to lawyers before court trials begin and which lawyers may enter as evidence in trials. Traditionally, depositions are presented in written form, but now federal courts and many state courts allow lawyers to submit videotaped depositions. Sometimes lawyers are able to make pretrial settlements because of how witnesses appear on videotape. To ensure the high quality of videotaped depositions, lawyers seek Legal Videographers who are skilled in videography, as well as have a thorough knowledge about court procedures and the requirements for preparing and presenting legal video evidence.

Legal Videographers use camera operation, lighting, audio, editing, and shot planning—all specialized areas of video production—to provide the most effective visual record for the judge or jury to view. Videotaped depositions, unlike written depositions, allow judges and jurors to see and hear how witnesses deliver their testimony.

With each deposition, Legal Videographers first meet with lawyers to discuss what their needs are. If possible,

they look at the room where the deposition will be taken. The specialists then decide what kinds of equipment they will need and whether they may need additional assistance.

On the day of the deposition, Legal Videographers arrive early, set up their equipment, and take a test run to make sure everything is in working order. In taping a deposition, Legal Videographers follow specific court procedures to ensure that the videotaped deposition may be admitted as evidence at the trial. Videographers must tape a deposition as simply as possible. If it appears that a videographer was using techniques to influence the viewers, the videotaped deposition can be thrown out of court.

Upon completion of a deposition, Legal Videographers make backup copies of the videotaped deposition. They give the original tapes and backup copies to the attorneys, who will submit the original tape as evidence before the court.

In addition to videotaping depositions, Legal Videographers offer other legal video services to lawyers. For example, lawyers may hire videographers to videotape:

- clients who wish to videotape their wills
- scenes of incidents, proof of damages, or evidence of insurance fraud

- mock trials, in which lawyers do a practice run of their case before volunteers acting as pretend jurors
- "day-in-the-life" documentaries that show how personal injuries have changed daily routines of persons seeking compensatory damages

Self-employed Legal Videographers are responsible for managing their business operations. This includes buying and maintaining equipment, record keeping, invoicing clients, paying bills and taxes, and generating new business.

Legal Videographers work irregular hours. Their job also requires that they travel constantly, sometimes to different cities and states.

Salaries

Earnings for Legal Videographers vary, depending on such factors as their experience, employer, and geographical location. Formal salary information for this occupation is unavailable, but a general approximation can be gained by looking at what video equipment technicians earn. The U.S. Bureau of Labor Statistics reported in its May 2005 *Occupational Employment Statistics* survey, that the estimated annual salary for most video equipment technicians ranged between $19,350 and $57,340.

Employment Prospects

The legal videography field has been growing steadily and, according to some experts, the demand for professional Legal Videographers is greater than the number that are available. The majority of Legal Videographers are independent operators. Staff positions may be found with video services, court reporting firms, and litigation support companies that offer legal video services. Large law firms, usually in major cities, sometimes hire staff Legal Videographers.

Advancement Prospects

Advancement opportunities for employees are limited to openings for lead and managing positions. As independent contractors, Legal Videographers generally pursue advancement by gaining professional recognition, offering additional professional services, and earning higher incomes.

Education and Training

New entrants into this field must be trained in such areas as the basics of legal video (including techniques for videotaping depositions), laws governing legal video, legal procedures and paperwork, and basic legal and technical vocabulary. Legal videography training might be obtained through apprenticeships or internships under professional Legal Videographers, or through completion of training programs offered by professional associations or other organizations.

Throughout their careers, Legal Videographers enroll in training and continuing education programs to build up their skills and expertise.

Experience, Skills, and Personality Traits

Entry-level Legal Videographers should already be professional videographers.

Legal Videographers need excellent interpersonal and communication skills for their work. They should also have strong self-management skills—the ability to work well with others, prioritize tasks, meet deadlines, and handle stressful situations. Additionally, independent contractors must have good business skills. Being friendly, cooperative, patient, detail-oriented, ethical, and professional are some personality traits that successful Legal Videographers share.

Unions and Associations

Many Legal Videographers join professional associations to take advantage of networking opportunities, training programs, and other professional services and resources. Some national societies include the American Guild of Court Videographers, the National Legal Video Association, and the National Court Reporters Association. For contact information, see Appendix V.

Tips for Entry

1. Take basic video training courses that are offered at your high school or in community youth programs. You might also find basic courses at local community colleges or continuing education programs.
2. Talk with different Legal Videographers to learn more about their profession.
3. To enhance their employability and professional credibility, many Legal Videographers obtain professional certification through recognized organizations. See Appendix II for some certification programs.
4. One way to spread the word about your business is to network with lawyers, Legal Videographers, court reporters, and other litigation support professionals.
5. You can learn more about the legal videography field on the Internet. To find pertinent Web sites, enter these keywords in a search engine: *legal video* or *legal videography.*

PRIVATE INVESTIGATOR

CAREER PROFILE

Duties: Provide investigative services; seek facts and evidence to support clients' cases; perform duties as required

Alternate Title(s): Private Detective; a title that reflects a specialty such as Legal Investigator

Salary Range: $19,000 to $62,000

Employment Prospects: Good

Advancement Prospects: Poor

Prerequisites:

Education or Training—High school diploma; on-the-job training

Experience—Previous law enforcement, military, or security experience preferred

Special Skills and Personality Traits—Interviewing, interrogation, interpersonal, communication, writing, research, computer, and self-management skills; be independent, professional, objective, curious, honest, responsible, flexible

Special Requirements—Private investigator's and firearms licenses may be required

CAREER LADDER

```
┌──────────────────────────────────────┐
│  Private Investigation Agency Owner   │
└──────────────────────────────────────┘

┌──────────────────────────────────────┐
│        Private Investigator           │
└──────────────────────────────────────┘

┌──────────────────────────────────────┐
│     Private Investigator Trainee      │
│   or Assistant Private Investigator   │
└──────────────────────────────────────┘
```

Position Description

Private Investigators are trained professionals who offer investigative services to their clients, such as conducting background checks on individuals, finding missing persons, or collecting specific information about a person's activities. Litigation lawyers typically employ Private Investigators to search out facts and evidence that may help support their criminal or civil cases. Private Investigators who specialize in conducting legal investigations are also known as legal investigators.

Conducting a legal investigation involves various tasks. For example, Private Investigators might:

- gather and review appropriate documents and records—for example, police reports, medical charts, driving records, and bank statements
- examine scenes where personal injuries, accidents, or other incidents related to a case had taken place
- conduct research for background information on people, which may involve doing research on computer databases and the Internet
- locate and interview potential witnesses
- conduct surveillance or undercover work

When they gather evidence, Private Investigators must follow certain legal procedures. Otherwise, the evidence may not be admissible in court. They are also responsible for maintaining accurate, well-detailed notes about their investigations, as well as providing lawyers with verbal or written progress reports.

Many Private Investigators also perform other litigation support tasks. Some investigators, for instance, serve processes to defendants and witnesses. Or lawyers may ask Private Investigators to find appropriate expert witnesses for their cases. On occasion, Private Investigators testify as expert witnesses about facts or issues related to the cases that they have investigated for lawyers.

Many Private Investigators are self-employed or independent contractors, and so are responsible for managing their businesses. They perform duties such as bookkeeping, invoicing clients, paying bills and taxes, supervising and training support staff, and generating business.

Private Investigators travel constantly. Their job sometimes requires traveling to different cities and states. They work irregular hours, including early mornings, late nights, weekends, and holidays to complete their tasks.

Salaries

Annual earnings for Private Investigators vary, depending on such factors as their experience, fees, and geographical location. In addition, independent investigators must factor in the cost of operating a business. According to the May 2005 *Occupational Employment Statistics* (OES) survey, by the U.S. Bureau of Labor Statistics (BLS), the estimated annual salary for most Private Investigators ranged between $19,230 and $61,520.

Employment Prospects

Private Investigators are either employees or owners of private investigation agencies. Legal investigators may be staff members of legal firms. According to the BLS' May 2005 OES survey, an estimated 33,720 Private Investigators were employed overall in the United States.

The BLS reports that jobs for Private Investigators are expected to increase by 18 to 26 percent through 2014. Job openings will also become available as investigators retire or enter other professions. The competition is keen due to the high number of law enforcement and military personnel who retire and start a second career in this field. As the rate of litigation increases in the United States, the demand for Private Investigators should also grow among legal services.

Advancement Prospects

Most Private Investigators realize advancement by earning higher wages and through professional recognition. For many, the top goal is to become successful detective agency owners.

Education and Training

Private Investigators should have at least a high school diploma or a general equivalency diploma. Many employers prefer candidates who have a college background. In fact, many Private Investigators have associate or bachelor's degrees in various fields.

Entry-level Investigators receive on-the-job training. Throughout their careers, many investigators enroll in courses, seminars, and workshops to increase their knowledge and update their skills.

Special Requirements

Private Investigators may be required to possess a state or local private investigator's license to practice. Trainees are covered by the licenses of the investigators for whom they work. Private Investigators who plan to carry firearms must possess the proper state license. For specific licensing information, contact your state private investigator licensing agency or a local law enforcement agency.

Agency owners must maintain the proper business licenses required by their community and state. For more information on business licenses, contact your city hall.

Experience, Skills, and Personality Traits

Employers usually prefer to hire candidates who have work experience in law enforcement, the military, security, or another related field. Candidates who have experience in conducting investigations are also preferred.

Private Investigators need excellent interviewing, interrogation, interpersonal, and communication skills. They must also have strong writing and computer skills. In addition, they need superior self-management skills, such as the ability to handle stressful situations, prioritize tasks, make sound judgments, and meet deadlines. Successful investigators share several personality traits such as being independent, professional, objective, curious, honest, responsible, and flexible.

Unions and Associations

Many Private Investigators belong to professional associations to take advantage of networking opportunities, training programs, and other professional services and resources. The National Association of Legal Investigators, the National Association of Investigative Specialists, and the Council of International Investigators are some societies that investigators might join. For contact information, see Appendix V.

Tips for Entry

1. Become familiar with the law and court procedures. You might do independent study by reading legal books and periodicals. You might also take classes in college or continuing education programs.
2. Contact private investigators in your area about trainee positions.
3. To enhance their employability and professional credibility, many Private Investigators obtain professional certification through recognized organizations. See Appendix II for some certification programs.
4. Learn more about Private Investigators on the Internet. You might start by visiting these Web sites: The Private Investigators Portal, http://www.infoguys.com, and National Association of Legal Investigators, http://www.nalionline.org. For more links, see Appendix VI.

PROCESS SERVER (PRIVATE)

CAREER PROFILE

Duties: Deliver legal papers to defendants or witnesses; follow court procedures and state laws and rules for serving processes; perform other duties as required

Alternate Title(s): None

Salary Range: $30,000 to $80,000

Employment Prospects: Good

Advancement Prospects: Poor

Prerequisites:

    Education or Training—High school diploma; on-the-job training

    Experience—No experience required for entry-level positions

    Special Skills and Personality Traits—Interpersonal, communication, reading, writing, math, self-management, and business skills; professional, reliable, energetic, self-motivated, friendly, courteous, and persistent

    Special Requirements—State or local license, certification, or registration may be required; state driver's license; business license, permit, or bond may be required

CAREER LADDER

```
┌─────────────────────────────────┐
│   Process Serving Firm Owner     │
│   or Independent Contractor      │
└─────────────────────────────────┘

┌─────────────────────────────────┐
│   Process Server (subcontractor) │
└─────────────────────────────────┘

┌─────────────────────────────────┐
│            Trainee               │
└─────────────────────────────────┘
```

Position Description

Process Servers are responsible for delivering summons, complaints, subpoenas, or other processes to individuals in a professional and timely manner. A process is a court order that commands a person to appear in court for specific reasons.

When attorneys file lawsuits for their clients, they are required to notify the defendants—the parties being sued—about the court actions by presenting them with a court summons and complaint. Attorneys usually hire Process Servers to perform the task of serving these court documents in person to the defendants. Attorneys also use Process Servers to deliver subpoenas to individuals, which order them to testify as witnesses at depositions or trials.

Process Servers must follow court procedures for serving processes, which vary with every state and federal jurisdiction. Additionally, they must deliver legal papers in a timely manner. In general, Process Servers serve the legal papers to the names listed on the processes. They try to serve papers to defendants at their homes or workplaces. Some defendants may be hard to locate; some are trying to avoid being served. On such occasions, Process Servers must come up with creative ways to serve the papers. For example, they might follow persons to restaurants or other public places to serve them their papers. Or, they might go to people's houses early in the mornings and serve them the papers just as they walk out the door for work.

In some jurisdictions, Process Servers may use alternative ways to serve processes when defendants are not available. For example, some courts allow Process Servers to hand legal papers to an adult who lives at a defendant's home with the directions to give it to the defendant.

Process Servers must complete a proof of service for each paper that they serve, which is then returned to the court. The proof may be a court form or an affidavit that states to whom a paper was served, and when and where it was served.

The workload for Process Servers differs from one day to the next. For example, one day they may have 10 processes to deliver in different cities of a county, and on another day they may have 20 processes to deliver within a 10-mile radius.

Most Process Servers are independent contractors. Some own process service companies. Many are self-employed and work on a contractual basis for law firms, private investigation agencies, or process service companies.

As independent contractors, private Process Servers are responsible for various business tasks. For example, they invoice clients, pay bills and taxes, generate new business, and maintain their offices. If they use subcontractors (other Process Servers), they are responsible for supervising them and paying their fees. They also take care of recruiting and selecting new subcontractors, as well as training them.

Process Servers work part time or full time. Their hours are flexible, which may include working evenings and weekends. Because their job requires a lot of travel, they must have dependable and insured cars.

Salaries

Process Servers receive a fee for each paper that they serve. Fees vary, depending on the geographical location and competition in an area. According to Alan Crowe, administrator of the National Association of Professional Process Servers, fees generally range from about $25 to $50 nationwide. It is not uncommon for independent contractors to earn between $30,000 and $80,000, depending on their fees, location, personal ambition, business costs, and other factors.

Employment Prospects

Most process service companies hire Process Servers as subcontractors rather than salaried employees. Subcontracting opportunities are generally favorable as the turnover rate is high.

Advancement Prospects

Opportunity for advancement is limited to becoming an owner of a process service company.

Depending on their ambitions and interests, Process Servers might pursue other legal-related careers, such as becoming court clerks, law enforcement officers, lawyers, or criminal justice social workers.

Education and Training

Process Servers should have at least a high school diploma or a general equivalency diploma. Many professionals have college degrees or college backgrounds. Some Process Servers also have law degrees.

Entry-level Process Servers receive on-the-job training.

Special Requirements

In some states, Process Servers must hold a process-serving license. Many local governments require that Process Servers be certified or registered within their jurisdictions. To learn specific requirements for the location where you wish to work, contact a local Process Server or your local sheriff's office.

Process Servers may also be required to obtain local business licenses, permits, or surety bonds.

Experience, Skills, and Personality Traits

For entry-level positions, many companies hire individuals without any previous experience. To start a business, Process Servers should have several years of experience, because attorneys prefer to use established professionals.

Process Servers need effective interpersonal and communication skills, as they must be able to relate well with people from many backgrounds. They also strong reading, writing, and math skills. Additionally, they need excellent self-management skills—the ability to work independently, follow instructions, handle stressful situations, prioritize tasks, and meet deadlines. Furthermore, as independent contractors, they should have adequate business skills.

Some personality traits that successful Process Servers share are being professional, reliable, energetic, self-motivated, friendly, courteous, and persistent.

Unions and Associations

Professional associations for Process Servers are available at the state and national levels. They offer opportunities for networking with colleagues, as well as various professional services and resources. Two national organizations are the National Association of Professional Process Servers and the International Process Servers Association. For contact information, see Appendix V.

Tips for Entry

1. Contact process serving firms in your area for work.
2. Read business-management books to learn what is needed to be successfully self-employed. You might also check out continuing education programs for class offerings on starting a business.
3. You can learn more about the private process server industry on the Internet. You might start by visiting these Web sites: National Association of Professional Process Servers, http://www.napps.com; and International Process Servers Association, http://www.processervers.com. To learn about other links, see Appendix VI.

TRIAL CONSULTANT

CAREER PROFILE

Duties: Develop trial strategies for lawyers; conduct pretrial and posttrial studies; assist with jury selection; perform other duties as required

Alternate Title(s): Jury Consultant, Jury and Trial Consultant, Litigation Consultant

Salary Range: $100 to $500 per hour

Employment Prospects: Good

Advancement Prospects: Poor

Prerequisites:

Education or Training—Advanced degrees

Experience—Several years of experience in their specialty; familiarity with the law and legal systems

Special Skills and Personality Traits—Analytical, time management, interpersonal, teamwork, communication, interviewing, report-writing, and presentation skills; business skills for self-employed consultants; be self-motivated, organized, creative, flexible

CAREER LADDER

```
┌─────────────────────────────┐
│   Senior Trial Consultant    │
│  or Independent Contractor   │
└─────────────────────────────┘

┌─────────────────────────────┐
│      Trial Consultant        │
└─────────────────────────────┘

┌─────────────────────────────┐
│   Junior Trial Consultant    │
└─────────────────────────────┘
```

Position Description

Trial Consultants help attorneys prepare their clients' cases for trials by providing lawyers with an idea of how jurors may perceive their cases. These consultants are experts in human dynamics, and are trained to observe how jurors react to words, images, and sound. They advise lawyers on matters such as jury selection, credibility of witnesses, and presentation styles. They also help lawyers develop trial strategies that would most effectively influence jurors to deliberate in their clients' favor.

Trial Consultants provide services to lawyers before, during, and after trials. Pretrial services might include conducting surveys to measure the feelings that a community has about issues related to a court case. Another service is developing and coordinating focus groups and mock trials before which lawyers briefly present their arguments. Trial Consultants analyze responses and provide lawyers with a written report that includes profiles of the best and worst type of jurors to have sitting in their trials.

Other pretrial services that Trial Consultants might offer are:

- reviewing the documents, depositions, and other case materials, and providing lawyers with an opinion on how well they may do in a trial
- assisting lawyers in preparing witnesses for depositions and trials
- coaching lawyers on how to present themselves before jurors, as well as how to use exhibits and technology to their advantage in court
- drafting questions to ask potential jurors

Many Trial Consultants advise lawyers as trials occur. Lawyers might ask consultants to help them during the actual jury selection. Trial Consultants sit in the courtroom and provide lawyers with immediate feedback about potential jurors. Lawyers might also hire consultants to monitor their trials. They provide daily feedback so that lawyers can make necessary changes in their presentations.

Some Trial Consultants also offer posttrial research services. They design questionnaires about case themes, exhibits, witnesses, and other aspects of a trial. Then, when the trial is complete, they interview jurors for their feedback.

Different consultants offer different services, depending on their backgrounds and expertise, so it is common for several Trial Consultants to collaborate on a case, each providing services in their particular strengths or areas.

Many Trial Consultants are independent contractors, or self-employed. Some are employees of trial (or litigation) consulting companies, while others work as in-house Trial Consultants for large law firms. Self-employed consultants must handle tasks related to running their businesses, including drafting business contracts, maintaining client records, invoicing clients, paying bills and taxes, and generating new business.

Many Trial Consultants write articles and books about their field, as well as give lectures and presentations at programs, seminars, and conferences. Some Trial Consultants also maintain an academic career as professors or adjunct lecturers.

Trial Consultants work part time or full time. They sometimes travel to different cities and states to work with clients.

Salaries

Annual earnings for Trial Consultants vary, depending on such factors as their experience, personal ambition, and geographical location. Formal salary information for this occupation is unavailable.

Trial Consultants usually charge hourly fees that vary according to the types of services they provide. Most consultants earn between $100 and $500 per hour.

Employment Prospects

The Trial Consultant field has been growing steadily since the 1980s. In recent years, the American Society of Trial Consultants has developed practice standards and guidelines for a number of trial consulting services that has contributed to the establishment of this field. According to an expert in the field, opportunities should continue to grow for Trial Consultants, as increasingly more attorneys require trial consulting services.

Advancement Prospects

Staff consultants can advance to senior and managing positions, becoming responsible for specific projects, supervising others, and generating new business for their firms. Some consulting firms also offer opportunities for consultants to become principal consultants or partners.

Many Trial Consultants' goal is to have their own successful consulting firms.

Education and Training

Trial Consultants typically have master's and doctoral degrees in social psychology, sociology, communications, marketing, and other related fields. Some Trial Consultants also hold law degrees.

Trial Consultants continually develop their skills and expertise through independent study, by networking with colleagues, and by attending professional seminars and conferences.

Experience, Skills, and Personality Traits

Generally, employers hire candidates who have several years of experience in their areas of specialization. They also prefer candidates who are familiar with the law and legal systems.

To become independent contractors, Trial Consultants should have several years in the field on a full-time basis. Lawyers typically are more confident about choosing consultants who have been exposed to a variety of cases.

Trial Consultants need excellent analytical, time management, interpersonal, teamwork, and communication skills. They also must have strong interviewing, report-writing, and presentation skills. Additionally, self-employed consultants need good business skills. Being self-motivated, organized, creative, and flexible are some personality traits that successful consultants share.

Unions and Associations

Many Trial Consultants are members of the American Society of Trial Consultants and the American Psychology-Law Society, a division of the American Psychology Association. (For contact information, see Appendix V.) Many Trial Consultants also belong to bar associations. By joining professional organizations, these consultants are able to take advantage of various professional services and resources, as well as opportunities for networking with colleagues.

Tips for Entry

1. Talk with Trial Consultants to learn more about their work and how they got into the field.
2. While in college, obtain internships with litigation consulting firms.
3. Contact trial consulting firms directly about staff positions or contractual positions. (Small firms sometimes hire Trial Consultants on a contractual basis.)
4. You can learn more about the Trial Consultant field on the Internet. To find relevant Web sites, enter the keywords *trial consultant* or *jury consultant* in any search engine. For some links, see Appendix VI.

LITIGATION CONSULTANTS AND EXPERT WITNESSES

LITIGATION CONSULTANT

CAREER PROFILE

Duties: Provide various pretrial services that help lawyers prepare for trials; may provide testimony as an expert witness; manage business operations

Alternate Title(s): Litigation Specialist, Forensic Consultant, Expert Witness; a title that reflects a profession such as Real Estate Appraiser or Forensic Accountant

Salary Range: $100 to $300+ per hour

Employment Prospects: Good

Advancement Prospects: Poor

Prerequisites:

    Education or Training—College degrees and training appropriate to an occupation

    Experience—Extensive work experience in field

    Special Skills and Personality Traits—Interpersonal, writing, communication, presentation, and business skills; be competent, credible, articulate, positive, calm, fair, and objective

    Special Requirements—Professional licensure or certification may be required, depending on occupation

CAREER LADDER

```
┌─────────────────────────────────────┐
│       Litigation Consultant          │
└─────────────────────────────────────┘

┌─────────────────────────────────────┐
│     New Litigation Consultant        │
└─────────────────────────────────────┘

┌─────────────────────────────────────┐
│ Senior, Administrative, or Management│
│      Position (in a workplace)       │
└─────────────────────────────────────┘
```

Position Description

Lawyers handle litigation cases that may involve issues about which they lack sufficient technical knowledge. To ensure that they prepare the best cases for their clients, lawyers may hire one or more Litigation Consultants. These are experts in their particular fields—nursing, family counseling, psychiatry, plastic surgery, criminology, trace evidence examination, pathology, computer forensics, accounting, stock trading, electrical engineering, pilot procedures, crash reconstruction, art restoration, physical security, and real estate appraising, among others.

Litigation Consultants are independent contractors or employees of litigation consulting firms. They offer various pretrial services that help lawyers prepare their civil and criminal cases. For example, they might:

- analyze and evaluate a case to help lawyers determine whether it should be brought to trial
- review a case to help lawyers identify the issues and facts

- educate lawyers about the subject matter so they can fully understand the issues of a case
- help lawyers develop effective strategies for a case
- gather physical evidence
- interview eyewitnesses
- conduct research for additional data to support a case
- conduct tests or experiments to prove or disprove certain facts or issues; for example a criminalist expert tests blood samples to determine if the blood found at a crime site matches the defendant's blood type
- locate and recruit other expert witnesses who would be appropriate for testifying about specific issues of a case
- prepare reports that lawyers would use with motions and other pretrial court proceedings or in settlement negotiations
- formulate a list of questions that lawyers would ask witnesses for the opposing party
- prepare demonstrative evidence (such as diagrams, models, or computer animation) that help juries and judges understand specific issues of a case

Many Litigation Consultants also offer expert witness services. That is, they provide sworn testimony at arbitrations, depositions, or trials. Expert witnesses are used for one of two purposes in court trials. One is to provide technical information so that the judges or juries can better understand the particular issues of a case. The second is to provide an expert opinion on a particular issue or fact in a case. Expert witnesses are expected to explain technical concepts and vocabulary in terms easy to understand.

To be an expert witness, a Legal Consultant must have the appropriate experience, knowledge, skills, education, or training that gives the consultant the expertise to testify about a specific issue. Although they are hired by either the plaintiff or defendant, expert witnesses provide testimony that is impartial and unbiased. They are ethically bound not to support or oppose the arguments of either party.

Not all expert witnesses are Litigation Consultants. Many doctors, criminologists, engineers, forensic scientists, researchers, and others offer expert witness services as a supplemental activity to their occupation or practice.

As independent contractors, Litigation Consultants are responsible for managing their business operations. Their tasks include billing clients, paying bills and taxes, maintaining offices and equipment, generating new business, and so on.

Litigation Consultants work flexible hours. Many offer their services statewide or even nationwide.

Salaries

Salaries for staff consultants vary, depending on such factors as their education, experience, employer, and geographical location. Salary information for Litigation Consultants is unavailable.

Annual gross income for independent consultants is based on the total fees that they have earned on their projects. They usually charge an hourly rate, which is based on the types of services they provide, their specialty, the competition for their services, and other factors. In general, the hourly fees for litigation consulting services range from $100 to $300 or more per hour. The fees for expert witness services can be as much as $2,000 or more per hour for highly reputable consultants.

In addition, many consultants bill clients for out-of-pocket expenses such as photocopying expenses, telephone calls, and travel costs.

Employment Prospects

Opportunities for Litigation Consultants, in general, are favorable throughout the nation. The prospects for consultants within any location depend on the demand for their particular expertise and on the number of similar consultants in the area.

Advancement Prospects

Litigation Consultants realize advancement by earning higher incomes and receiving high accolades for their work.

Many also measure success in terms of being sought out by lawyers for very complex or publicized cases.

Education and Training

Litigation Consultants have completed the appropriate education and training that is required for their particular professions. Throughout their careers, they enroll in continuing education and training programs to develop and maintain their professional skills and expertise.

Special Requirements

Litigation Consultants hold the appropriate licensure and certification that is required for their occupations. For example, physicians have valid medical licenses in the states where they practice.

Experience, Skills, and Personality Traits

Professionals typically become Litigation Consultants after many years of experience in their fields. Many have retired or resigned from senior, administrative, or management positions to start litigation consulting and expert witness services.

Litigation Consultants need excellent interpersonal skills to work well with lawyers. Additionally, they need strong writing, communication, and presentation skills. As independent contractors, consultants need strong business skills. Personality traits that successful consultants share are being competent, credible, articulate, positive, calm, fair, and objective.

Unions and Associations

Litigation Consultants join professional associations that serve their particular fields, such as criminology, forensic accounting, heart surgery, psychiatry, aerospace engineering, or recreation. By joining societies, they can take advantage of networking opportunities and other professional services and resources.

Tips for Entry

1. Join professional associations and participate in their various activities.
2. Market your services directly to lawyers. For example, you might list yourself in expert witness databases on the Internet.
3. To enhance their credibility, many Litigation Consultants obtain professional designations from recognized professional organizations in their field. Many also teach, give presentations, as well as write articles and books about their subject matter.
4. On the Internet, you can learn more about Litigation Consultants. To get a list of relevant web sites, enter any of these keywords in a search engine: *expert witnesses* or *litigation consulting*. For some links, see Appendix VI.

APPRAISER

CAREER PROFILE

Duties: Assess the value of property, conduct research, and prepare reports; provide expert witness testimony; may perform litigation consulting services; perform other duties as required

Alternate Title(s): A title that reflects a specialty area, such as Real Estate Appraiser, Jewelry Appraiser, Art Appraiser, Business Appraiser, or Horse Appraiser

Salary Range: Salaries vary, depending on specialty area

Employment Prospects: Good

Advancement Prospects: Fair

Prerequisites:

Education or Training—Apprenticeship or training under professional Appraisers

Experience—Highly experienced and knowledgeable in specialty area

Special Skills and Personality Traits—Interpersonal, communication, writing, research, computer skills; be impartial, trustworthy, curious, and resourceful

Special Requirements—State license or certification required for real estate appraisers

CAREER LADDER

```
┌─────────────────────────┐
│    Senior Appraiser     │
└─────────────────────────┘

┌─────────────────────────┐
│       Appraiser         │
└─────────────────────────┘

┌─────────────────────────┐
│    Appraiser Trainee    │
└─────────────────────────┘
```

Position Description

Appraisers are often retained by lawyers to provide expert witness testimony in litigation cases. Their expertise lies in providing professional opinions on the value of tangible and intangible property—real estate, automobiles, aircraft, machinery, gems, jewelry, artwork, antiques, toys, furniture, quilts, books, businesses, mines, oil fields, public utilities, patents, trademarks, and so on. These professionals typically specialize in appraising one or several types of property.

Appraisers do not establish the value of property. Their job is to prepare a well-documented report, or appraisal, that states their opinions of how much a property is currently worth. The appraisal process begins with an inspection or examination of a property. Then appraisers conduct research to find out what the current prices are for similar properties in the local area, as well as regionally, statewide, and nationally. Their research includes reading market reports, searching computer databases, interviewing experts in the specialty area, and so on.

As expert witnesses, Appraisers testify only about issues that are related to the value of the property in question. At the start of their assignment, attorneys give them specific instructions about their tasks and the raw data (such as business documents) that they need to complete their appraisal. Appraisers submit written reports for review by the courts and the lawyers, as well as for questioning by the opposing lawyers in sworn depositions. Sometimes cases are settled before reaching trial.

At trials, they present their information so that judges and juries can easily understand technical concepts and terms. Appraisers sometimes use demonstrative exhibits to illustrate difficult concepts more clearly. Appraisers can expect to be cross-examined by the opposing lawyers who do their best to discredit their testimony.

Many Appraisers also offer litigation consulting services, such as:

- providing technical assistance to lawyers; for example, answering questions about the appraisal process
- reviewing cases at the beginning of litigation to provide lawyers with an idea of further research and analysis that may be required
- documenting the value of the property in question
- preparing appraisal reports of the property that lawyers can use for pretrial proceedings and trials, as well as settlement negotiations
- reviewing appraisals presented by opposing parties. (Typically, if Appraisers will be providing expert testimony, they may avoid reviewing the opposing appraisals to ensure their objectivity.)
- conducting research for additional new data

Appraisers work full time or part time.

Salaries

Earnings for Appraisers vary, depending on such factors as their specialty, experience, and geographical location. In general, independent contractors, or self-employed Appraisers, earn hourly fees for their work, while employees earn an annual salary.

Most real estate appraisers earn an estimated annual salary that ranges between $23,020 and $83,480, according to the May 2005 *Occupational Employment Statistics* survey by the U.S. Bureau of Labor Statistics. Salary information for the other types of Appraisers is unavailable.

Employment Prospects

Professional Appraisers are employed by government agencies, insurance companies, accounting firms, real estate companies, auction houses, and other organizations. Many Appraisers are independent contractors.

Staff positions usually become available as Appraisers retire, resign, or move on to other positions. The opportunities for independent Appraisers depend on the demand for their specialization in their geographical area and the number of Appraisers locally available.

Advancement Prospects

Appraisers may advance in any number of ways, depending on their ambitions and interests. Individuals with managerial and administrative interests can seek such positions within their organizations. Individuals with entrepreneurial ambitions can become independent consultants or owners of appraisal firms.

Education and Training

Appraisers complete a training period or apprenticeship in their areas of specialization under professional Appraisers. Their training programs also include study in appraisal theory, principles, procedures, ethics, and law.

Special Requirements

Real estate appraisers must possess a professional license or certification. Some states also require trainees to obtain a real estate trainee appraisal license. For information about requirements, contact the state regulating board in the jurisdiction where you wish to work.

Experience, Skills, and Personality Traits

Professional Appraisers are highly experienced and knowledgeable in their specialty areas. They are up to date with the latest appraisal standards and are familiar with local, regional, national, and even international markets.

Appraisers need excellent interpersonal and communication skills, as well as strong writing, research, and computer skills. Successful Appraisers share personality traits such as being impartial, trustworthy, curious, and resourceful.

Unions and Associations

Appraisers join professional associations that serve their areas of specialization. These associations offer professional certification, continuing education programs, networking opportunity, and other professional services and professional resources. Some national associations are

- American Society of Appraisers (general)
- International Society of Appraisers (personal property)
- Appraisers Association of America, Inc. (personal property)
- National Association of Independent Fee Appraisers (real estate)
- National Association of Master Appraisers (real estate)
- National Association of Jewelry Appraisers
- American Society of Farm Managers and Rural Appraisers
- Institute of Business Appraisers

For contact information, see Appendix V.

Tips for Entry

1. Talk with professional Appraisers in the discipline in which you wish to work to learn specific information. You may also be able to find someone willing to take you on as a trainee or an apprentice.
2. Network with professional Appraisers in the different disciplines. Most Appraisers refer clients to other Appraisers who can serve their specific needs.
3. Many Appraisers obtain professional certification from professional organizations to enhance their credibility and employability. For information about some certification programs, see Appendix II.
4. Learn more about the appraisal industry on the Internet. Two web sites to visit are: American Society of Appraisers, http://www.appraisers.org; and Appraisal Foundation, http://www.appraisalfoundation.org. For more links, see Appendix VI.

BUSINESS APPRAISER

CAREER PROFILE

Duties: Assess the value of businesses and intangible business assets; may provide litigation consulting or expert witness services; perform other duties as required

Alternate Title(s): Business Valuation Expert, Business Valuator, Valuation Analyst

Salary Range: $100 to $250+ per hour

Employment Prospects: Fair

Advancement Prospects: Good

Prerequisites:

Education or Training—College degree preferred

Experience—Prior work experience in performing business appraisals

Special Skills and Personality Traits—Analytical, time management, research, interviewing, writing, communication, interpersonal, and customer service skills; persistent, attentive, objective, impartial, ethical, and reliable

Special Requirements—Florida requires a real estate license; professional certification recommended

CAREER LADDER

```
┌─────────────────────────────────┐
│   Principal Business Appraiser  │
└─────────────────────────────────┘

┌─────────────────────────────────┐
│       Business Appraiser        │
└─────────────────────────────────┘

┌─────────────────────────────────┐
│            Trainee              │
└─────────────────────────────────┘
```

Position Description

Business Appraisers specialize in assessing the value of businesses, whether they are start-up companies, small businesses, professional services, mid-size companies, or multinational corporations. These business valuation experts also appraise the value of intangible assets—such as copyrights, patents, trademarks, securities, goodwill, contracts, and franchises—that businesses own. Business Appraisers do not assign a value to a business or business asset. Instead, their job is to provide clients, who may be attorneys, business owners, individuals, government officials, or others, with an independent and unbiased opinion of how much a business or a business asset is currently worth.

Business Appraisers work for clients on a contractual basis in the areas of taxation, business transactions, litigation, and regulatory compliance issues. They perform appraisals for such purposes as estate planning, charitable contributions, institutional financing, purchases, sales, company mergers, acquisitions, partner buy-outs, divorce settlements, personal injury lawsuits, bankruptcy, and meeting financial regulations.

These valuation experts perform meticulous research for their appraisals. They collect and examine financial data about businesses, including their assets, liabilities, profits, and tax burdens. These experts also seek background information to learn more about the businesses, what their competition is like, what the current prices are for similar businesses, and so on. Their research involves reading market reports and searching databases as well as interviewing employees, customers, suppliers, vendors, subject-matter experts, government officials, and others.

Depending on the needs of their clients, Business Appraisers prepare an oral or written report, or both. They provide their appraisals in a cost-effective and timely manner. They are expected to give accurate and precise appraisals, and to present technical concepts in language that is understandable to clients and others who are unfamiliar with the technical terms.

In performing their appraisals, these experts follow standards and guidelines that are established by recognized appraisal organizations to which they belong. Additionally, they comply with the requirements of their clients, courts, and government agencies. Furthermore, Business Appraisers must remain independent in their opinions to maintain the credibility of their appraisal. In other words, they do not advocate the views of their clients.

Besides business valuation services, many Business Appraisers offer litigation support services. Attorneys hire these experts to perform any number of services, such as educating lawyers about the appraisal process; reviewing cases to determine what further research and analysis is needed; preparing appraisal reports for settlement negotiations; and reviewing appraisals conducted by the other party. With these appraisers' assistance, lawyers are often able to settle cases before they reach the trial stage.

Many Business Appraisers also offer expert witness services to attorneys, who may call upon them to testify at depositions, in court trials, before administrative hearing boards, or at alternative dispute resolution sessions. They give testimony for one of two purposes. They might provide technical information to help judges and jurors better understand the issues of the case; or they might be asked to offer their expert opinion on a particular issue or fact in a case.

To qualify as expert witnesses, Business Appraisers must possess appropriate education or training, experience, knowledge, skills, and professional credentials that are recognized by court or administrative judges.

Beginning appraisers usually begin as staff analysts and researchers, and perform such duties as industry research, data assembly, and financial statement analysis. As they gain experience, they may help appraisers draft reports.

Business Appraisers usually juggle several assignments at a time. In addition to their appraisal duties, they are also responsible for generating new business and retaining clients.

Some experts perform business appraisals on a part-time basis, while working as a certified public accountant or other occupation. Full-time Business Appraisers work 40 hours per week occasionally put in additional hours to complete their tasks or meet deadlines. Many experts are required to travel away from their office to meet with clients or to conduct interviews.

Salaries

Annual earnings for Business Appraisers vary, depending on such factors as their experience; whether they are independent contractors, partners, or associates; the types of services they offer; the demand for their services; and their geographical location. Formal salary information for this profession is unavailable. Like most appraisers, Business Appraisers charge an hourly rate or a flat fee per project. Many of them charge $100 to $250 or more per hour, depending on the type of services they provide. Fees for litigation consulting and expert witness services are usually at the higher rate.

Employment Prospects

The business valuation field is relatively new; it emerged about 20 years ago. It has grown and evolved rapidly, according to some experts in the field. Most Business Appraisers are independent practitioners or work in small firms. Some are employed by accounting firms, financial institutions, investment firms, and regulatory agencies.

According to the Institute of Business Appraisers Web site, the business appraisal market is on the rise due to various factors, including the growth in business start-ups, the increasing number of litigation cases that require business valuation, and the growing demand for appraisals for acquisitions, mergers, and sales of businesses.

Advancement Prospects

Business Appraisers seek advancement opportunities according to their ambitions and interests. As they gain experience, many appraisers develop expertise in certain types of appraisals (such as mergers and acquisitions), or in specific areas (such as intellectual property) or industries.

In firms, appraisers can advance to become principals and partners. Individuals with entrepreneurial ambitions pursue careers as independent practitioners or owners of appraisal firms. To advance to ownership level, individuals must have an outstanding ability to generate significant fees and new clients.

Some Business Appraisers use their experience as stepping-stones to other careers. For example, they may choose to become financial analysts, actuaries, bank officers, or college professors.

Education and Training

There are no formal educational requirements for individuals to become Business Appraisers. However, to obtain professional certification, individuals must possess a bachelor's degree in a qualifying field, which varies with the different appraisal organizations that grant certification. Many Business Appraisers possess a bachelor's or advanced degree in accounting, finance, business, or another related discipline.

Many Business Appraisers have learned the knowledge and skills of their profession through courses taught by professional organizations, which are made up of practicing Business Appraisers. Some of them completed a training period or apprenticeship under professional appraisers.

Throughout their careers, Business Appraisers enroll in continuing education programs and training programs to update their skills and knowledge.

Special Requirements

In Florida, Business Appraisers are required to possess a valid real estate license. As of 2006, no other states require Business Appraisers to hold a professional license.

To demonstrate their professional credibility as business valuation experts, Business Appraisers are encouraged to seek professional certification from a recognized appraisal organization. Appraisers who provide expert witness services typically hold one or more professional designations. For information about certification programs for Business Appraisers, see Appendix II.

Experience, Special Skills, and Personality Traits

Many Business Appraisers have backgrounds as certified public accountants, financial analysts, business brokers, and real estate appraisers, among other business professions. They usually entered the business valuation field after several years of performing business appraisals in their work.

To be effective at their work, Business Appraisers must have strong analytical, time management, research, interviewing, and writing skills. They also need effective communication, interpersonal, and customer service skills, as they must work well with attorneys, business people, and others from diverse backgrounds.

Some personality traits that these appraisers share include being persistent, attentive, objective, impartial, ethical, and reliable.

Unions and Associations

Many Business Appraisers belong to professional associations to take advantage of networking opportunities, continuing education, professional certification, and other professional services and resources. Some societies that serve Business Appraisers include the Institute of Business Appraisers, the American Society of Appraisers, the American Institute of Certified Public Accountants, and the National Association of Certified Valuation Analysts. For contact information, see Appendix V.

Tips for Entry

1. As a high school student, you can begin finding out if business valuation may be a field that interests you. Talk with Business Appraisers to learn about their work and how they entered the field. Also ask them to suggest courses that would be helpful in developing the proper skills and knowledge. To find Business Appraisers in your area, contact a professional business appraisal society.
2. Contact Business Appraisers directly about apprenticeship opportunities.
3. Join a professional association and begin building a network. Often times job opportunities are learned through word-of-mouth.
4. Use the Internet to learn more about the business valuation field. You might start by visiting the Web site for the Business Valuation Discipline, which is part of the American Society of Appraisers. The URL is http://www.bvappraisers.org.

CRASH RECONSTRUCTION CONSULTANT

CAREER PROFILE

Duties: Examine and reconstruct traffic collisions; prepare reports for attorneys; may provide expert witness testimony; perform duties as required

Alternate Title(s): Accident Reconstruction Specialist, Collision Reconstructionist

Salary Range: $100 to $200 per hour+

Employment Prospects: Good

Advancement Prospects: Poor

Prerequisites:

Education or Training—Completion of training programs from recognized institutions; ongoing training and continuing education programs

Experience—Several years of experience in crash reconstruction units in law enforcement agencies; or engineering background

Special Skills and Personality Traits—Communication, analytical, report-writing, business skills; problem solver, dedicated, methodical, detail-oriented, innovative

Special Requirements—A private investigator license may be required in some states

CAREER LADDER

```
┌─────────────────────────────────────┐
│   Crash Reconstruction Consultant    │
└─────────────────────────────────────┘

┌─────────────────────────────────────┐
│   Crash Reconstruction Specialist    │
│       (law enforcement agency)       │
└─────────────────────────────────────┘

┌─────────────────────────────────────┐
│    Crash Reconstruction Trainee      │
│       (law enforcement agency)       │
└─────────────────────────────────────┘
```

Position Description

Crash Reconstruction Consultants are experts in analyzing traffic accidents and reconstructing what took place during the collisions. (A traffic collision may involve automobiles, trucks, motorcycles, bicycles, as well as pedestrians.) Lawyers hire their consulting services for civil or criminal cases, such as personal injury lawsuits or manslaughter charges, that involve traffic crashes.

Crash Reconstruction Consultants often work on cases in which the accidents may have occurred several months or years ago. They analyze traffic crashes to answer specific questions that are related to the issues of a case. For example: How fast were the drivers going? Did the plaintiff try to avoid the collision? Was the defendant's view of the pedestrian blocked? Were the car headlights on at the time of the crash?

To reconstruct a traffic crash, consultants examine physical evidence, such as skid marks and vehicle parts. They also review police reports, eyewitness testimony, photographs of the accident site, and other sources of information. They carefully piece together the data and rebuild the events of the collision. Their work involves investigative techniques, as well as the use of math formulas and scientific laws and principles. They might also recreate a crash, using similar vehicles, to set a clearer understanding of what took place.

Crash Reconstruction Consultants provide lawyers with detailed reports that include diagrams, models, computer animations, or other visual aids to illustrate their findings. Lawyers often use these reports to negotiate settlements with the opposing side.

Many Crash Reconstruction Consultants also offer expert witness services. They may provide testimony at depositions, trials, or alternative dispute resolution sessions. As expert witnesses, Consultants give opinions only on the specific issues that they are being asked. They present technical concepts in nontechnical terms so that the judge or jury can understand the issues. Consultants often use demonstrative exhibits (diagrams, photographs, models, and so forth) to help them explain technical concepts more clearly.

Along with their consulting services, many Crash Reconstruction Consultants write articles and books about their discipline. Many also teach courses at universities, conduct training workshops for law enforcement officers, and give presentations at conferences and meetings.

As business owners or independent contractors, Crash Reconstruction Consultants are responsible for overseeing their business operations. They perform tasks such as billing clients, paying taxes and bills, record keeping, maintaining their office space and equipment, and generating new business.

Crash Reconstruction Consultants have flexible hours. They sometimes work long hours to meet deadlines. They may travel to different cities and states to meet with clients, survey traffic scenes, or testify in court.

Salaries

Crash Reconstruction Consultants charge hourly fees, which typically range from $100 to $200 per hour or more. Their fees are based on such factors as experience, the services offered, and geographical location. Many Consultants charge a flat fee for the creation of demonstrative exhibits.

Employment Prospects

Most Crash Reconstruction Consultants are self-employed or owners of consulting firms. Attorneys and insurance companies hire them on a contractual basis.

Advancement Prospects

In consulting firms, individuals generally advance through the ranks as consultants, project managers, and partners. Independent consultants realize advancement through the growth of their businesses, by earning higher incomes, and by being recognized for the high quality of their work.

Education and Training

Many consultants received their training while serving as traffic accident reconstructionists in law enforcement agencies. Many of them completed basic and advanced training programs from such nationally recognized institutions as the Institute of Police Technology and Management, the Northwestern University Center for Public Safety, or the Texas Engineering Extension Service.

Other Crash Reconstruction Consultants have engineering degrees in automotive engineering, civil engineering, mechanical engineering, or other engineering fields.

Throughout their careers, Crash Reconstruction Consultants enroll in training and continuing education programs to develop and maintain their skills and expertise.

Special Requirements

No professional licensure is required to become a Crash Reconstruction Consultant. However, some states may require that they hold a private investigator license. For licensure information, contact the business licensing department in the state where you wish to practice.

Experience, Skills, and Personality Traits

The majority of Crash Reconstruction Consultants are former law enforcement officers who served many years in their agencies' traffic crash reconstruction detail. Some consultants come to this field from engineering backgrounds.

Crash Reconstruction Consultants need excellent communication, analytical, and report-writing skills. To succeed in business, they also need adequate business skills. Some personality traits that successful consultants share are being a problem solver, as well as being dedicated, methodical, detail-oriented, and innovative.

Unions and Associations

Crash Reconstruction Consultants join professional associations to take advantage of networking opportunities with colleagues as well as professional services and resources. Some societies are:

- American Society of Safety Engineers
- International Association of Accident Reconstruction Specialists
- National Association of Professional Accident Reconstruction Specialists
- National Association of Traffic Accident Reconstructionists and Investigators
- Society of Accident Reconstructionists

For contact information, see Appendix V.

Tips for Entry

1. Helpful courses to take in high school are math and physics.
2. If you plan to become an independent contractor, enroll in courses or workshops about running a small business to help you succeed.
3. Many Crash Reconstruction Consultants obtain professional certification to enhance their credibility and employability. For information about some certification programs, see Appendix II.
4. You can learn more about traffic reconstructionists on the Internet. You might start by visiting the Accident Reconstruction Network Web site at http://www.accidentreconstruction.com. For more links, see Appendix VI.

CRIMINOLOGIST

CAREER PROFILE

Duties: Conduct studies on crime and the law; provide litigation consulting and expert witness services; perform other duties as required

Alternate Title(s): Professor of Criminology, Professor of Criminal Justice

Salary Range: $33,000 to $109,000

Employment Prospects: Fair

Advancement Prospects: Fair

Prerequisites:

Education or Training—Advanced degree; doctorate required for academic teaching

Experience—Many years of research and teaching experience in a particular area of study

Special Skills and Personality Traits—Analytical, concentration, writing, interpersonal, and communication skills; creative, curious, observant, detail-oriented, objective, open-minded

CAREER LADDER

```
┌─────────────────────────────────────┐
│  Criminologist—Expert Witness and    │
│      Litigation Consultant           │
└─────────────────────────────────────┘

┌─────────────────────────────────────┐
│           Criminologist              │
└─────────────────────────────────────┘

┌─────────────────────────────────────┐
│         Doctoral Student             │
└─────────────────────────────────────┘
```

Position Description

Criminologists are experts in the area of crime and the law. Many of them offer litigation consulting and expert witness services to attorneys.

Criminologists are sometimes confused with criminalists, or forensic scientists. Criminalists are part of the criminology discipline, but their expertise is in the examination of physical evidence (such as blood, DNA, bullets, latent prints, and questioned documents) that is found at crime scenes. Criminalists have backgrounds in physical or life science and work in crime labs. Criminologists, on the other hand, are social scientists. Some work as researchers or policy advisers for law enforcement agencies and other government organizations, but most Criminologists are academicians who teach and conduct research in colleges and universities.

In general, Criminologists are engaged in the scientific study of the making of criminal laws, the breaking of these laws, and society's reaction to criminal activity. They research such questions as: What makes certain people commit a specific kind of crime? What causes teenagers

to join gangs? How do different neighborhoods respond to crime? What might be the future trend for a particular type of criminal activity? The results of their studies help law enforcement agencies, correction facilities, social work organizations, legislators, and others to design effective programs to prevent crime, apprehend criminals, and rehabilitate delinquent or criminal behavior.

Criminologists specialize in studying one or a few areas of crime. Some of those areas include violent crime, domestic violence, white-collar crime, cyber crime, youth gangs, race and crime, women and crime, victimization, deviance, prison subcultures, correctional rehabilitation, policing, the criminal court system, alternative justice programs, and crime prevention. Some Criminologists devote their time to developing and improving effective research methods for studying clues in the crime lab as well as at the crime scene.

In conducting their studies, Criminologists perform various duties, such as designing research projects, collecting data, analyzing and interpreting information, writing reports, and completing administrative tasks. They also share the results of their studies by publishing articles and books as well as by giving presentations at professional conferences. Criminologists often conduct research in conjunction with law enforcement agencies and governmental criminal justice programs.

Attorneys often seek Criminologists to serve as expert witnesses in civil or criminal cases. They offer opinions on criminal behavior related to the specific issues of the particular cases. However, they can testify only after the court has ascertained that they have the required expertise, skills, knowledge, training, or education.

Some Criminologists offer other types of litigation consulting services. For example, they might interview defendants and family members to gather evidence for specific issues. Or they might review all the records of a case to help lawyers develop trial strategies.

Academic Criminologists have flexible work hours. They divide their time between teaching, conducting research, writing, and consulting.

Salaries

Salaries for Criminologists vary, depending on their experience, education, employer, and geographical location. Specific salary information for this occupation is unavailable. However, they earn wages similar to sociologists. According to the May 2005 *Occupational Employment Statistics* survey, by the U.S. Bureau of Labor Statistics (BLS), the estimated annual salary for most sociologists ranged between $33,000 and $109,350.

Employment Prospects

Most Criminologists work in colleges and universities as part of the teaching and research staff in the criminology or criminal justice departments. Criminologists are also employed by law enforcement agencies, correctional facilities, criminal justice research institutes, and crime prevention programs.

In general, openings become available as Criminologists retire, resign, or transfer to other positions. The competition for jobs in all work settings is keen.

Advancement Prospects

As academicians, Criminologists can advance through the ranks as instructor, assistant professor, associate professor, and full professor.

Many Criminologists pursue advancement by earning higher incomes and professional recognition. Some also measure success in terms of being sought out to provide expert witness testimony in highly complex or publicized trials.

Education and Training

Criminologists hold a master's or doctorate degree in criminology, criminal justice, sociology, psychology, or other related field. Most practicing Criminologists have earned a doctoral degree, which is a requirement for teaching positions in four-year colleges and universities. Attorneys generally look for Criminologists with doctorates to provide expert witness testimony.

Experience, Skills, and Personality Traits

Attorneys typically choose as expert witnesses Criminologists who have a solid reputation for their expertise in their area of study. They usually have many years of teaching and research experience and have published articles and books in their subject matter. Lawyers also look for Criminologists who have a balance of academic and practical experience.

Along with teaching and researching skills, Criminologists have superior analytical, concentration, and writing skills. They also have excellent interpersonal and communication skills. Some personality traits that successful criminologists share are being creative, curious, observant, detail-oriented, objective, and open-minded.

Unions and Associations

Many Criminologists belong to professional associations to take advantage of networking opportunities, training programs, professional publications, and other professional resources and services. Some associations that Criminologists join are the American Society of Criminology, the Western Society of Criminology, the Academy of Criminal Justice Sciences, and the American Sociological Association. For contact information, see Appendix V.

Tips for Entry

1. As an undergraduate, talk with criminology professors or an adviser of the criminology or sociology graduate program at your college. Find out what classes you should take to prepare for a graduate program.
2. Gain experience in the field of criminology and criminal justice by obtaining appropriate internships. Talk with your adviser or college career counselor for help finding available opportunities.
3. As a student, begin building up a network of professionals and others whom you can contact about job openings.
4. Learn more about criminology on the Internet. You might start by visiting the American Society of Criminology Web site at http://www.asc41.com. For more links, see Appendix VI.

FORENSIC ACCOUNTANT

CAREER PROFILE

Duties: Analyze and interpret financial evidence; provide lawyers with litigation consulting services, which may include expert witness services; perform duties as required

Alternate Title(s): Forensic Examiner

Salary Range: $33,000 to $90,000+

Employment Prospects: Excellent

Advancement Prospects: Fair

Prerequisites:

    Education or Training—A bachelor's degree; on-the-job training

    Experience—Accounting and auditing experience

    Special Skills and Personality Traits—Analytical, investigative, organizational, communication, report-writing, and interpersonal skills; be curious, creative, persistent, discreet, honest, and open-minded

    Special Requirements—Certified Public Accountant (CPA) license may be required

CAREER LADDER

```
┌────────────────────────────────┐
│   Senior Forensic Accountant,  │
│      Department Manager,        │
│    or Independent Contractor    │
└────────────────────────────────┘

┌────────────────────────────────┐
│      Forensic Accountant        │
└────────────────────────────────┘

┌────────────────────────────────┐
│   Assistant Forensic Accountant │
└────────────────────────────────┘
```

Position Description

Forensic Accountants are specialists in the area of investigative accounting. They use accounting, auditing, and investigative skills to analyze and interpret financial records. Many attorneys hire Forensic Accountants to advise them with financial issues related to civil or criminal litigation cases that they are handling. These accountants are involved in a wide range of issues, such as personal injury, medical malpractice, divorce, contract disputes, product liability claims, fraud, and embezzlement.

Forensic Accountants perform a number of litigation consulting services for attorneys. For example, they might:

- analyze financial records to determine specific issues such as the amount of losses or damages, the flow of funds between particular people and organizations, or the accuracy of financial statements
- gather evidence, which requires extensive review of various financial records and business documents
- interview witnesses

- determine what financial documents lawyers should ask the opposing party to provide
- write well-documented reports that lawyers can use as a basis for pretrial motions and proceedings as well as negotiation settlements
- create, or oversee, the development of demonstrative exhibits (such as charts and diagrams)
- educate lawyers on the basic concepts of accounting principles
- provide expert witness testimony at arbitrations, depositions, and trials

Forensic Accountants also offer investigative accounting services to individuals, law enforcement agencies, government agencies, insurance companies, banks, corporations, and other organizations. For example, they might investigate fraud cases (such as securities fraud, insurance fraud, and kickbacks) for law enforcement agencies. Or they might review financial records for businesses to help them determine if they should declare bankruptcy.

Forensic Accountants are self-employed or work for accounting companies, including firms that exclusively provide forensic accounting services. Lawyers may hire Forensic Accountants on a contractual basis.

Forensic Accountants often work longer than 40 hours a week to complete their projects for clients.

Salaries

Salaries for Forensic Accountants vary, depending on their education, experience, geographical location, and other factors. According to the May 2005 *Occupational Employment Statistics* survey by the U.S. Bureau of Labor Statistics, the estimated annual salary for most accountants and auditors ranged between $33,170 and $89,550. Some experts in the field say that highly experienced and reputable Forensic Accountants can make up to $100,000 or more a year.

Employment Prospects

In addition to being self-employed or working for accounting or law firms, Forensic Accountants may find employment with banks, insurance companies, financial companies, private corporations, law enforcement agencies, and government agencies, among other institutions.

Since the 1980s, forensic accounting has been one of the fastest-growing disciplines in the field of accounting. The demand for qualified Forensic Accountants is expected to increase through the coming years, as companies seek to hire staff or consultants to conduct internal financial investigations to prevent and detect fraud. In addition, Forensic Accountants are continually needed to assist attorneys with civil and criminal litigation cases involving such areas as securities investigations, health care fraud, business fraud, and intellectual property theft.

Advancement Prospects

In accounting firms, Forensic Accountants can advance to senior and managing positions, and in many firms can become partners. The top goal for some Forensic Accountants is to become successful independent operators or owners of their accounting firms.

Education and Training

Many Employers prefer or require that Forensic Accountants have a bachelor's degree in accounting or have completed general accounting courses.

Entry-level Forensic Accountants are trained on the job. Throughout their careers, accountants enroll in continuing education and training programs to develop and maintain their skills and expertise.

Special Requirement

Many employers require that candidates possess the certified public accountant (CPA) license. For licensure information, contact your state board of accountancy.

Many employers also prefer to hire candidates who possess professional certification, such as the certified fraud examiner (CFE) designation, granted by the Association of Certified Fraud Examiners. For information about this and other professional certification programs, see Appendix II.

To maintain professional designations, Forensic Accountants must complete a minimum of continuing professional education credits.

Experience, Skills, and Personality Traits

For entry-level positions, employers look for candidates who have accounting and auditing experience. Candidates demonstrate the ability to make sensible judgments and should be able to visualize the whole picture of a case as well as examine the many fine details.

Forensic Accountants demonstrate strong analytical, investigative, and organizational skills. They also have excellent communication, report-writing, and interpersonal skills. Being curious, creative, persistent, discreet, honest, and open-minded are some personality traits that successful Forensic Accountants share.

Unions and Associations

Many Forensic Accountants belong to local, state, and national professional associations to take advantage of networking opportunities as well as professional services and resources. Some national societies are the Forensic Accountants Society of North America, the Association of Certified Fraud Examiners, the American Institute of Certified Public Accountants, and the Association of Insolvency and Restructuring Advisors. For contact information, see Appendix V.

Tips for Entry

1. Start gaining experience by obtaining internships with firms that offer forensic accounting services.
2. Check out job listings at Web sites of professional accounting associations, as well as in professional publications.
3. You can learn more about forensic accounting on the Internet. To find relevant Web sites, enter the keywords *forensic accounting* or *forensic accountant* in any search engine. For some links, see Appendix VI.

FORENSIC PSYCHOLOGIST

CAREER PROFILE

Duties: Vary, depending on the work setting—for example, may provide assessment and treatment services, conduct research, or provide consulting services; provide expert witness testimony; may provide litigation consulting services

Alternate Title(s): None

Salary Range: $34,000 to $99,000

Employment Prospects: Good

Advancement Prospects: Fair

Prerequisites:

    Education or Training—A doctorate in psychology

    Experience—To be expert witnesses, several years of experience in area of specialization; familiarity with the law and legal procedures

    Special Skills and Personality Traits—Research, communication, interpersonal, teamwork, and presentation skills; be patient, adaptable, analytical, compassionate

    Special Requirements—A psychologist license or certification is required to provide assessment and treatment

CAREER LADDER

```
┌─────────────────────────────────────────┐
│ Senior Forensic Psychologist, Program    │
│ Director, or Private Practitioner        │
└─────────────────────────────────────────┘

┌─────────────────────────────────────────┐
│ Forensic Psychologist                    │
└─────────────────────────────────────────┘

┌─────────────────────────────────────────┐
│ Doctoral Student                         │
└─────────────────────────────────────────┘
```

Position Description

Forensic Psychologists are trained in the areas of psychology and law. They are often retained by lawyers to provide expert witness testimony on psychological issues that are related to their cases. These experts may testify for civil or criminal cases about such issues as trial competency, domestic violence, drug dependence, psychosocial motivations, child abuse, paranoid disorders, or malingering.

Forensic Psychologists perform different roles in the legal and court systems. Some are clinical psychologists, working in correctional facilities, psychiatric hospitals, and other forensic units. Their primary duty is assessing and treating juvenile and adult criminal offenders. Other clinical Forensic Psychologists have private practices, working with children, adults, and families.

Many Forensic Psychologists are researchers and educators, working in universities, medical schools, hospitals, research institutes, and clinics. Others are jury consultants, working independently or with trial consulting firms. Their expertise is in helping lawyers select jurors that may be more sympathetic to their clients.

Some Forensic Psychologists work with law enforcement agencies, helping with criminal investigations. They do criminal profiling, which is creating psychological profiles of typical offenders of certain crimes. Some experts work with court systems, performing various duties, such as evaluating defendants for their ability to stand trial or investigating cases of abused or neglected children.

As expert witnesses, Forensic Psychologists testify only on issues for which the court has qualified them as being experts. Attorneys use Forensic Psychologists for one of two purposes. One is to explain specific psychological concepts so that judges and juries can fully understand the issues of the case. The other is to present their opinions about defendants based on their professional evaluations.

Many Forensic Psychologists offer litigation consulting services as a supplementary activity. However, they are ethically bound to provide either consulting or expert witness services on a case, but not both. This is to prevent a conflict of interest, as well as to ensure that their testimony as expert witnesses is objective and unbiased.

In addition to their primary activity (such as research, clinical work, or trial consulting), many Forensic Psychologists devote time to teaching classes and training workshops. Many also make presentations at conferences and write articles and books.

Salaries

Salaries for Forensic Psychologists vary, depending on factors such as their experience, work setting, nature of their work, and geographical location. Most clinical psychologists earned an estimated annual salary that ranged between $34,040 and $99,270, according to the May 2005 *Occupational Employment Statistics* survey by the U.S. Bureau of Labor Statistics. The estimated annual salary for most psychology postsecondary teachers ranged between $31,710 and $98,340. The basic pay range in 2006 for entry-level clinical psychologists employed by the Federal Bureau of Prisons was $46,189 to $85,578.

Consultants usually charge an hourly rate for their services. The rates may vary from $100 to $300 per hour, depending on a Forensic Psychologist's reputation and the competition for their consulting and expert witness services in their area.

Employment Prospects

Opportunities are expected to grow steadily for Forensic Psychologists in all work settings, particularly for those holding doctoral degrees. Some experts predict that the highest demand for Forensic Psychologists shall come from attorneys, courts, and lawmakers.

Advancement Prospects

In general, supervisory and management opportunities for Forensic Psychologists are to be found in the various work settings. For example, in a prison, an entry-level staff psychologist can rise up through the ranks to become the psychology department chief or even the top administrator at the prison.

Education and Training

Individuals who wish to become Forensic Psychologists should generally hold a doctoral degree in psychology. Those interested in clinical, or applied, psychology usually earn a doctor's in psychology degree (Psy.D.), while those devoted to doing research generally earn a doctor of philosophy degree (Ph.D.). Opportunities are available for Forensic Psychologists with a master's degree in clinical psychology, but they usually work under the supervision of doctoral personnel.

Formal training for doctoral-level Forensic Psychologists involves several years. Students first earn a bachelor's degree in psychology or other behavioral science field. They then complete a one- or two-year master's program in psychology, followed by a three-year doctorate program. Students wishing to become clinical psychologists usually complete a four-year doctorate program in clinical psychology, followed by a one-year internship.

Special Requirements

Forensic Psychologists who provide forensic assessment and treatment services must be licensed or certified psychologists in the states where they practice. Professional licensure or certification is not necessary for those who are primarily consultants, educators, researchers, or policy makers. Having a state license, however, may enhance a Forensic Psychologist's credibility as an expert witness.

Experience, Skills, and Personality Traits

To be expert witnesses, Forensic Psychologists normally have several years of experience in their area of specialization. In addition, they are familiar with the law and legal procedures.

Forensic Psychologists must have excellent research, communication, and interpersonal skills. They also need strong teamwork skills, as they work with various professionals in their particular work settings. As expert witnesses, Forensic Psychologists need good presentation skills and must be able to explain psychological concepts in clear and understandable words to nonpsychologists. Some personality traits that successful Forensic Psychologists share are being patient, adaptable, analytical, and compassionate.

Unions and Associations

Many Forensic Psychologists join professional associations to take advantage of professional resources and services as well as opportunities to network with peers. Two national organizations that serve the interests of Forensic Psychologists are the American Academy of Forensic Psychology and the American Psychology-Law Society, a division of the American Psychological Association. For contact information, see Appendix V.

Tips for Entry

1. Find out if this field is right for you before starting a graduate program. Read about forensic psychology. Also talk with some professionals.
2. As an undergraduate student, talk with psychology professors or a psychology adviser for the graduate program at your college. Find out what classes you should take to prepare yourself for a graduate program.
3. You can learn more about forensic psychology on the Internet. You might start by visiting the American Psychology-Law Society Web site at http://www.ap-ls.org. For contact information, see Appendix VI.

LEGAL NURSE CONSULTANT (LNC)

CAREER PROFILE

Duties: Provide litigation consulting services in the area of health care; may provide expert witness testimony; as independent consultants, manage business operations; perform duties as required

Alternate Title(s): None

Salary Range: $39,000 to $79,000+

Employment Prospects: Good

Advancement Prospects: Fair

Prerequisites:

Education or Training—Legal Nurse Consultant training programs are available

Experience—Several years of clinical or surgical experience preferred

Special Skills and Personality Traits—Analytical, research, report-writing, communication, interpersonal, computer, and self-management skills; business skills for independent consultants; be organized, detail-oriented, ethical, patient, determined, resourceful

CAREER LADDER

Independent Legal Nurse Consultant

Legal Nurse Consultant

Registered Nurse

Position Description

Legal Nurse Consultants offer consulting services to law firms, insurance companies, and others that require expert assistance with medical issues related to civil or criminal litigation. These highly experienced registered nurses work on a wide range of cases, including personal injury, heart surgery, medical malpractice, negligence, elder abuse, product liability, and worker's compensation, among other types of medically related cases.

Legal Nurse Consultants offer various types of consulting services, such as:

- reviewing medical records and other documents to determine issues, such as liability and standards of care
- working with financial experts to identify damages and related costs of services
- educating lawyers about health care facts and issues related to their cases
- conducting research to answer questions about health-related issues
- interviewing health care practitioners and patients

- assisting lawyers with writing motions, briefs, interrogatories, demand letters, and other legal documents
- organizing and summarizing medical records and other medical materials needed for litigation
- developing and preparing demonstrative exhibits such as charts and diagrams
- preparing a list of questions that lawyers would ask the expert witnesses for the opposing party
- locating appropriate health practitioners who can provide expert witness testimony for specific issues in a case

Some LNCs also offer expert witness services to attorneys. At depositions and trials, LNCs provide testimony about issues for which the court has qualified them as experts. When serving in the capacity of a nurse expert, LNCs may not provide the hiring attorneys with any litigation consulting services. This is to prevent a conflict of interest, as well as to ensure that their testimony as an expert witness is objective and unbiased.

Most LNCs are independent contractors who provide services on a contractual basis. They may perform their work at home or at their clients' offices. As small business owners, they must handle various business tasks. For example they keep records, pay bills and taxes, invoice clients, maintain files, and generate new business.

LNCs work part time or full time. Many Legal Nurse Consultants continue working as registered nurses.

Salaries

Earnings for LNCs vary, depending on such factors as their experience, job status (employee or independent contractor), personal ambition, and geographical location.

Independent contractors earn hourly fees that generally range from $45 to $150 per hour, according to the Widener University School of Law Legal Education Institute Web site (http://www.law.widener.edu/lei_lnc/index.shtml).

Staff LNCs earn salaries that are similar to pay with registered nurses. The U.S. Bureau of Labor Statistics reports in its May 2005 *Occupational Employment Statistics* survey that the estimated annual salary for most registered nurses ranged from $38,660 to $79,460.

Employment Prospects

The majority of LNCs are independent contractors. They may be self-employed or owners of legal nursing consulting firms. Some LNCs are staff members at law firms, insurance companies, government agencies, or health care institutions.

The LNC field is a young field which has grown steadily as a specialty since 1989. Experts expect this field to continue growing for years to come. Increasingly, attorneys are utilizing the services of LNCs more than those of medical doctors because it is more cost effective.

Advancement Prospects

Staff LNCs can advance to supervisory and administrative positions. Independent consultants generally pursue advancement by earning higher incomes and by gaining professional recognition among colleagues and lawyers.

Education and Training

There is no standard educational requirement to become Legal Nurse Consultants. LNCs may have associate, bachelor's, or advanced degrees in nursing.

Prospective LNCs can obtain basic training by enrolling in LNC certificate programs, which are offered by two-year and four-year colleges, universities, private postsecondary schools, and professional associations. These programs provide students with a basic knowledge of law and legal procedures relevant to performing LNC duties. Students also learn practical skills, such as legal research, legal writing, and working with medical records.

Throughout their careers, LNCs enroll in workshops, seminars, and courses to update their skills and knowledge.

Experience, Skills, and Personality Traits

Lawyers prefer hiring LNCs who have several years of clinical or surgical experience, which includes interpreting medical records.

Legal Nurse Consultants need strong analytical, research, and report-writing skills, as well as excellent communication and interpersonal skills. Having good computer skills is also necessary. In addition, they have strong self-management skills, such as the ability to manage multiple tasks, meet deadlines, and work independently. Independent consultants should have good business skills.

Successful Legal Nurse Consultants share several personality traits such as being organized, detail-oriented, ethical, patient, determined, and resourceful.

Unions and Associations

Legal Nurse Consultants join professional associations such as the American Nurses Association and the American Association of Legal Nurse Consultants. (For contact information, see Appendix V.) As members of professional associations, LNCs can take advantage of education programs, networking opportunities, and other professional services and resources.

Tips for Entry

1. Entry into an LNC certificate program may require that an applicant have worked a minimum number of years as a practicing registered nurse.
2. To enhance their employability and professional credability, many LNCs obtain professional certification. For information about some programs, see Appendix II.
3. Let lawyers in your area know about your services. Send brochures or flyers about yourself to local lawyers as well as local bar associations. Also prepare press releases to local newspapers and legal publications.
4. You can learn more about the profession on the Internet. To find relevant Web sites enter the keywords *legal nurse consultant* in any search engine. For some links, see Appendix VI.

COURT SUPPORT STAFF

BAILIFF (LOCAL AND STATE COURTS)

CAREER PROFILE

Duties: Preserve order in courtrooms during trial proceedings; maintain security in courtrooms and surrounding areas; perform other duties as required

Alternate Title(s): Court Officer, Marshal

Salary Range: $17,000 to $56,000

Employment Prospects: Fair

Advancement Prospects: Fair

Prerequisites:

Education or Training—High school diploma; completion of bailiff training

Experience—One or more years of law enforcement experience; knowledgeable about court security, court functions, and court proceedings

Special Skills and Personality Traits—Interpersonal, computer, communication, and self-management skills; courteous, tactful, firm, reliable

Special Requirements—Peace officer certification

CAREER LADDER

```
┌─────────────────────────┐
│     Senior Bailiff       │
└─────────────────────────┘

┌─────────────────────────┐
│        Bailiff           │
└─────────────────────────┘

┌─────────────────────────┐
│     Bailiff Trainee      │
└─────────────────────────┘
```

Position Description

Bailiffs are law enforcement officers who are responsible for preserving order in courtrooms during trial proceedings, as well as maintaining the security of the courtrooms and the surrounding areas. Bailiffs also provide protection to the judges and jurors, and ensure that criminal defendants are safe and secure.

Sheriff's offices are usually responsible for providing bailiff services to local and district courts. In some municipal courts, police departments handle the bailiff services. State police departments typically provide bailiff services for state supreme courts. (In federal courts, the court security and bailiff duties are provided by the U.S. Marshals Service.)

Bailiffs perform a wide variety of tasks before, during, and after court proceedings. They usually work in teams of two or more. Before each court session, Bailiffs inspect courtrooms for security and cleanliness. They seat witnesses and jurors in specific areas of the courtroom. They open each session of court by announcing the entrance of the judge. Bailiffs swear in witnesses before they testify in court. They escort juries between courtrooms and jury rooms during court proceedings, as well as stand guard outside the jury rooms.

Bailiffs guard criminal defendants throughout court proceedings. They escort defendants between the holding cells and the courtrooms. They also make sure that holding cells at the courts are secure and free of any contraband. Some Bailiffs have the duty of transporting prisoners between the court and the jail.

When juries are making their deliberations, Bailiffs make sure that jurors have no contact with other people besides themselves. They accompany jurors to all meals and remain with them during the meals. If a jury must be sequestered overnight, Bailiffs arrange for meals, lodging, and transportation for the jurors.

Bailiffs work closely with judges and the court staff to make sure that the courts operate efficiently and safely. In some courts, security measures involve screening individuals before they can enter the courtroom. Bailiffs might operate weapon detection devices or perform hand searches. As certified law enforcement officers, Bailiffs have the authority to arrest persons who disturb the court proceedings or break security violations either inside or outside the courtrooms. Bailiffs also take charge during medical emergencies, bomb threats, fire alarms, and other emergencies.

Bailiffs are also responsible for various clerical tasks. For example, they complete security reports, photocopy documents, log information on court forms, or update databases in a computer system. Some Bailiffs are in charge of arranging with the jail staff to make prisoners available for court. Furthermore, Bailiffs may be asked by judges to run such errands as summoning lawyers to judges' chambers, delivering court files, or fetching supplies.

Bailiffs work 40 hours a week, sometimes working additional hours when required.

Salaries

Salaries for Bailiffs vary, depending on such factors as their experience, job duties, rank, employer, and geographical location. The estimated annual salary for most Bailiffs ranged between $17,320 and $55,690, according to the May 2005 *Occupational Employment Statistics* survey by the U.S. Bureau of Labor Statistics.

Employment Prospects

Bailiff duty is a voluntary assignment in sheriff's offices and state police departments. Some local police departments also have bailiff units. Opportunities generally become available as Bailiffs retire, resign, or transfer to other positions. Courts may request additional Bailiffs to fit staffing needs as long as funding is available.

Advancement Prospects

Law enforcement officers have the opportunity to develop a career according to their personal interests and ambitions. They can advance in rank as well as in pay scale. Law enforcement officers can stay with this detail as long as they are qualified for the job or until they request a transfer to other assignments. Supervisory and administrative positions are limited to unit coordinator positions.

Education and Training

The minimum education requirement for law enforcement officers is a high school diploma or general equivalency diploma. Some agencies also require that peace officers have an associate degree or some college background.

New Bailiffs typically complete specialized training that includes classes in legal matters, arrest procedures, firearms training, process serving, and security training.

Special Requirements

Bailiffs are required to be certified law enforcement officers—sheriff's deputies, local police officers, or state police officers (or state troopers). They earn their certification upon completion of basic training at a law enforcement academy.

Experience, Skills, and Personality Traits

Depending on the law enforcement agency, candidates generally need one to three years of law enforcement experience. They also are knowledgeable about court security, court functions, and court proceedings. In addition, they demonstrate a professional appearance and demeanor, as well as the ability to make sound judgments.

Bailiffs must have excellent interpersonal and communication skills in order to work well with judges and other court employees. They also need good computer skills. In addition, Bailiffs need strong self-management skills—such as the ability to understand and follow directions, work independently, and handle stressful situations.

Being courteous, tactful, firm, and reliable are a few personality traits that successful Bailiffs share.

Unions and Associations

Bailiffs typically join local, state, and national professional associations to take advantage of professional services, resources, and networking opportunities. Two national associations that serve law enforcement officers are the American Deputy Sheriffs' Association and the Fraternal Order of Police. For contact information, see Appendix V.

Tips for Entry

1. Would you like to get an idea of what it may be like to be a Bailiff? Contact the courts in your area to learn about their volunteer programs. Many courts use volunteers to help Bailiffs with some of their more routine duties.
2. As a deputy's sheriff or police officer, talk with the commander in charge of bailiff detail. Let him or her know about your interest, even if you are not yet eligible.
3. Many law enforcement agencies have Web sites. To find the Web site for a specific agency, enter its name in any search engine. For example, *Los Angeles County Sheriff's Office, Seattle Police Department,* or *New York State Police.*

COURT ADMINISTRATOR

CAREER PROFILE

Duties: Oversee all nonjudicial administrative functions; assist judges in defining the court's goals, objectives, policies, and procedures; perform duties as required

Alternate Title(s): Court Executive Officer, Court Manager, Clerk of the Court, Director of the Administrative Office of the Court, or a title that reflects the type of court for which they work, such as Criminal Court Administrator, Family Court Administrator, or Municipal Court Administrator

Salary Range: $38,000 to $146,000

Employment Prospects: Good

Advancement Prospects: Good

Prerequisites:

Education or Training—A bachelor's degree; a master's degree or Institute of Court Management certification, for positions in larger, complex court systems

Experience—Three to eight years court administration experience; two to four years of supervisory experience

Special Skills and Personality Traits—Leadership, supervisory, management, interpersonal, writing, communication, analytical, and problem-solving skills; be composed, organized, analytical, hardworking, creative

CAREER LADDER

```
┌─────────────────────────────────────┐
│        Court Administrator           │
│ (in a larger, complex court system)  │
└─────────────────────────────────────┘

┌─────────────────────────────────────┐
│        Court Administrator           │
└─────────────────────────────────────┘

┌─────────────────────────────────────┐
│        Assistant or Deputy           │
│        Court Administrator           │
└─────────────────────────────────────┘
```

Position Description

Court Administrators hold high-level management positions in local, state, federal, and tribal court systems. Their job is to ensure that all nonjudicial activities are operating in an organized, efficient, and effective manner every day. These managers are known by various titles, such as *Court Executive Officer* or *Director of the Administrative Office of the Court.* The job title for federal Court Administrators is *Clerk of the Court.*

Court Administrators work closely with the judges to define their court's goals and objectives, as well as to develop appropriate policies and procedures, which they implement accordingly. They also participate in planning and developing new and improved court services, programs, and activities. They oversee various administrative functions such as fiscal management, personnel administration, space and equipment management, automation (or information systems), record and information management, jury operations, community relations, and media relations. Depending on the size of their court, Court Administrators directly manage some or all of the administrative functions.

Court Administrators are responsible for a wide range of duties. Some of these responsibilities include:

• organizing, directing, and coordinating the various court activities, such as court reporting services, court interpreting programs, case processing, and court security
• planning and managing annual budgets
• providing supervision and guidance to nonjudicial employees, including clerks, technicians, law clerks, supervisors, and program managers, among others

- hiring and firing personnel
- developing and coordinating employee training programs
- directing records management activities such as the creation of court forms
- reviewing and approving (or rejecting) service contracts with vendors
- conducting special studies (as directed by judges), which includes preparing statistical data and analysis as well as writing reports
- obtaining grant funding for new court programs
- serving as liaison to other courts, legislatures, law enforcement agencies, the news media, the general public, and others

Furthermore, Court Administrators are responsible for keeping up with developments in the court administration field, as well as furthering their own professional development. They enroll in training programs, participate in professional conferences, network with colleagues, read professional journals and books, and so on.

Court Administrators work independently, under the supervision of presiding, or chief, court judges. They generally work a 40-hour week, but sometimes work nights and weekends to complete their various tasks.

Salaries

Salaries for Court Administrators vary, depending on such factors as their experience, job duties, employer, and geographical location. Earnings are typically higher in metropolitan areas.

No formal salary surveys are available for Court Administrators. However, a look at the earnings of other management occupations can give a general idea of what Court Administrators may earn. According to the May 2005 *Occupational Employment Statistics* survey, by the U.S. Bureau of Labor Statistics, the estimated annual salary for most management occupations ranged between $37,800 to $145,600 per year.

Employment Prospects

The field is continually growing, and opportunities are available for Court Administrators in small courts as well as in larger, complex court systems. Most opportunities become available as Court Administrators retire, resign, or transfer to other positions.

Advancement Prospects

Court Administrators pursue advancement by seeking positions with higher salaries and more complex responsibilities. This usually involves transferring from one court to the next. Court Administrators can also advance to top management positions in state administrative offices, which oversee the state court systems.

Education and Training

Employers generally require candidates to have at least a bachelor's degree. Course work in public administration, court management, business administration, law, criminal justice, or related fields is highly desirable.

Educational requirements for Court Administrator positions in complex court systems usually include a master's degree in public administration, court administration, or related field. Many employers also accept candidates who have completed the Institute for Court Management's court executive development program. (For information about this program, visit the program Web site at http://www.ncsconline.org/D_ICM/icmindex.html.)

Experience, Skills, and Personality Traits

Depending on the employer, Court Administrators need three to eight years of court administration experience with two to four years of supervisory experience. In addition, they have experience in or are knowledgeable about the different areas of court operations, such as human resources, financial management, information systems, facilities management, and customer service practices.

Court Administrators must have excellent leadership, supervisory, and management skills. They also need effective interpersonal skills to work well with judges, court support staff, attorneys, other government agencies, the media, and the public. In addition, they have effective writing, communication, analytical, and problem-solving skills. Being composed, organized, analytical, hardworking, and creative are a few personality traits that successful Court Administrators share.

Unions and Associations

Many Court Administrators join professional associations to take advantage of networking opportunities and other professional services and resources. Some groups that they might join are the American Bar Association, the National Association for Court Management, the Federal Court Clerks Association, or the International Association for Court Administration. For contact information, see Appendix V.

Tips for Entry

1. Talk with Court Administrators to learn more about their jobs.
2. Many Court Administrators worked their way up through the ranks of court clerks, supervisors, and department managers.
3. Learn more about court administration on the Internet. You might start by visiting the National Association for Court Management Web site at http://www.nacmnet.org. For more links, see Appendix VI.

COURT ANALYST

CAREER PROFILE

Duties: Conduct studies; gather, analyze, and interpret data; make recommendations based on findings and conclusions; perform other duties as required

Alternate Title(s): Management Analyst, Administrative Analyst, Program Analyst, Court Specialist

Salary Range: $39,000 to $123,000

Employment Prospects: Fair

Advancement Prospects: Fair

Prerequisites:

Education or Training—Bachelor's degree in business, public administration, judicial administration, or another related field; on-the-job training

Experience—Prior work experience in administrative or management analysis required

Special Skills and Personality Traits—Research, statistical analysis, proposal writing, computer, problem-solving, communication, interpersonal, and teamwork skills; curious, logical, detail-oriented, dependable, tactful, and courteous

CAREER LADDER

```
┌─────────────────────────────────────┐
│   Senior or Principal Court Analyst  │
└─────────────────────────────────────┘

┌─────────────────────────────────────┐
│            Court Analyst             │
└─────────────────────────────────────┘

┌─────────────────────────────────────┐
│   Assistant or Junior Court Analyst  │
└─────────────────────────────────────┘
```

Position Description

Court Analysts are among the court administrative personnel that assist in the efficiency and effectiveness of state and federal court systems. Their role is to provide expert analysis in the planning, development, implementation, and evaluation of court programs, policies, and procedures. These professionals conduct special studies and projects related to the different aspects of court operations, such as jury management, case management, sentencing guidelines, court reporter certification, alternative dispute resolution, budget development, court finance, personnel administration, and court system management and administration. Their work involves performing general research, compiling and analyzing data, and providing solutions based on their findings and conclusions.

Court Analysts are assigned to a wide range of projects. For example, they may be involved in performing budgetary or records management studies; appraising organizational policies, structure, functions, practices, or work methods; evaluating existing court programs for ways to improve court management and the delivery of court services; or examining proposed legislation and administrative regulations for their impact on courts

These analysts perform a wide range of tasks, which vary according to their experience and skills level. Their duties may include:

- planning and designing research projects
- gathering and verifying the accuracy of information and statistical data
- analyzing and interpreting information
- preparing recommendations based on research findings and conclusions
- preparing correspondence, statistical reports, briefing papers, and other written materials
- presenting analysis, findings, and recommendations orally or in written form
- assisting in the development of grant proposals to fund special projects
- developing procedures for quality control of data bases
- attending meetings for court committees, task forces, or work groups

Court Analysts may be assigned to work on projects or programs alone or as part of a team. As leaders, they supervise and direct the work of subordinate team members. Court Analysts are expected to establish working relationships with judges, court administrators, clerks of the court, members of judicial commissions and committees, and other officers of the judicial and criminal justice system. They also work with other analysts, managers, support staff, and other court employees.

Entry-level analysts are assigned to perform routine tasks, such as compiling, tabulating, and formatting statistical data, while working under the supervision of senior Court Analysts. As they gain experience, Court Analysts are assigned more difficult tasks as well as greater responsibilities, including being responsible for leading projects. Senior analysts may also be given the additional duty of supervising and directing the work of subordinate staff members.

Court Analysts usually perform work under the general supervision of a court program manager, court administrator, or a director of the court research and services department. They work a 40-hour week but put in additional hours as needed to complete tasks and meet deadlines.

Salaries

Salaries for Court Analysts vary, depending on such factors as their education, experience, employer, and geographical location. Specific salary information for these analysts is unavailable, but they generally earn salaries similar to management analysts. The estimated annual salary for most management analysts ranged between $38,650 and $123,300, according to the May 2005 *Occupational Employment Statistics* survey by the U.S. Bureau of Labor Statistics.

Employment Prospects

Court Analysts are employed by state and federal courts. Job openings usually become available when analysts transfer to other jobs, advance to higher positions, retire, or leave the workforce for various reasons. Courts occasionally create new analyst positions to meet growing needs as long as funding is available.

Advancement Prospects

Court Analysts can advance in any number of ways, depending on their ambitions and interests. They can be promoted to higher ranks and salary levels. They can become specialists in financial analysis, judicial planning, or other areas. They can also pursue supervisory, managerial, or administrative positions in judicial administration.

Education and Training

In general, employers prefer to hire candidates who possess a bachelor's degree in business, public administration, judi-

cial administration, criminology, statistics, political science, or another related field. Employers may hire candidates who have only a high school degree or with some college background if they have several years of qualifying work experience.

Entry-level analysts work under the guidance and supervision of experienced Court Analysts and supervisors.

Throughout their careers, Court Analysts enroll in continuing education programs and training programs to update their skills and knowledge.

Experience, Special Skills, and Personality Traits

In general, employers prefer to hire candidates who have a few years of professional experience performing administrative or management analysis, preferably in a court, justice agency, or governmental setting.

To do their work effectively, Court Analysts need strong research, statistical analysis, proposal writing, computer, and problem-solving skills. They also must have excellent communication, interpersonal, and teamwork skills, as they must be able to work well with many people from diverse backgrounds. Being curious, logical, detail-oriented, dependable, tactful, and courteous are some personality traits that successful Court Analysts share.

Unions and Associations

Many Court Analysts are members of a local union that represents them in negotiations with their employers. The union seeks favorable contractual terms relating to pay, benefits and conditions for their members. It also assists members with any grievances they may have with their employers.

Court Analysts may join professional associations that provide their members with continuing education programs, professional publications, networking opportunities, and other professional resources and services.

Tips for Entry

1. As a high school or college student, get an idea if you would like to work in a court setting. Many courts offer internship, work-study, and/or summer employment programs for students. Call a court directly, or ask your guidance or career center counselor for assistance in finding a position.
2. Many employers will allow candidates to substitute a master's degree in an appropriate field for one or more years of work experience.
3. Contact the human resources department of courts for which you would like to work. In addition to asking about job vacancies, request information about their selection process.
4. Use the Internet to learn more about justice administration. For a list of relevant links, enter any of these keywords in a search engine: *courts administrative office, court service division, or court services department*. For some links, see Appendix VI.

COURT CLERK

CAREER PROFILE

Duties: Provide administrative support to courts of law; perform clerical tasks such as typing, filing, distributing mail, and running errands; perform other duties as required

Alternate Title(s): Deputy Court Clerk, Court/Legal Clerk; a title that reflects specialized duties, such as Courtroom Clerk, Jury Clerk, or Case Processing Clerk

Salary Range: $19,000 to $45,000

Employment Prospects: Fair

Advancement Prospects: Good

Prerequisites:

Education or Training—A high school diploma; college background, legal clerical training, or paralegal training for higher-level positions

Experience—One to three years of general office experience; legal clerk experience for higher-level positions

Special Skills and Personality Traits—Reading, writing, and math skills; communication, interpersonal, teamwork, self-management skills; positive, enthusiastic, dependable, cooperative, detail-oriented, flexible

CAREER LADDER

```
┌─────────────────────────────┐
│    Senior Court Clerk       │
│    or Supervisor Clerk      │
└─────────────────────────────┘

┌─────────────────────────────┐
│  Court Clerk (Journey Level)│
└─────────────────────────────┘

┌─────────────────────────────┐
│  Court Clerk (Entry Level)  │
└─────────────────────────────┘
```

Position Description

Court Clerks provide administrative support in a court of law. In general, they are responsible for recording and processing legal documents, legal records, and court forms, as well as keeping legal records and files up to date. They may be assigned to work in court offices or courtrooms, under the general supervision of clerk supervisors, department managers, or judges.

They perform various clerical tasks that include typing correspondence, legal documents, and forms; preparing court letters for mailing; updating records; maintaining files; taking phone messages; distributing mail; running errands; and so on. They operate various office machines such as typewriters, photocopiers, fax machines, tape recorders, 10-key calculators, and multiline telephone systems. Court Clerks also use computers, working with word processing, spreadsheets, databases, and other software programs.

In addition, Court Clerks answer general questions over the phone or in person from the public, lawyers, government offices, and others. When requested by the judges, Court Clerks contact witnesses, attorneys, litigants, and others to obtain specific information for the court.

Depending on the size and needs of a court, the clerical staff may range from one or two clerks to hundreds. Their duties vary, depending on their positions as well as their abilities and experience. Here are just a few duties that Court Clerks might perform:

- schedule cases for hearings, conferences, and trials, as well as inform participants when and where they must appear in court
- review case files for all required records and documents, and request lawyers, litigants, or others to supply the missing information
- assist in the jury selection process, which involves tasks such as contacting jurors for service, conducting jury orientation, and recording daily attendance of jurors
- provide courtroom support during court trials—such as recording the court proceedings, administering oaths to witnesses, and acting as custodians of physical evidence

- record rulings and decisions on required forms after court trials are complete, then process the records
- collect and process court fees, fines, and other payments received from defendants and others
- conduct research on criminal justice, FBI, department of motor vehicles, or other related computer databases for specific information
- prepare court processes (such as summonses, subpoenas, warrants, and writs) and secure a judge's signature on them
- supervise other Court Clerks

Some Court Clerks are identified by job titles that describe the duties that they perform. For example, courtroom clerks work primarily in the courtrooms, jury clerks perform duties related to jury selection, and civil processing clerks specialize in preparing civil processes.

Court Clerks generally work 40 hours a week. In courts where sessions are scheduled during evening hours, Court Clerks may work evenings.

Salaries

Salaries vary, depending on factors such as their experience, job duties, and geographical location. According to the May 2005 *Occupational Employment Statistics* survey, by the U.S. Bureau of Labor Statistics, the estimated annual salary for most Court Clerks ranged between $19,270 and $45,150.

Employment Prospects

Court Clerks are employed by local, state, federal, and tribal courts. Most opportunities become available as clerks retire, resign, or transfer to other positions. On occasion, courts create additional positions to fit staffing needs if funding is available.

Advancement Prospects

Court Clerks can advance to senior and supervisory clerk positions. With additional experience and training, they can become judicial assistants, legal secretaries, administrative assistants, paralegals, and lawyers. For those with managerial ambitions, courts offer middle management and high-level management positions, such as program managers, deputy clerks (or deputy court administrators), clerks of court, and court administrators.

Education and Training

For entry-level positions, a high school diploma or general equivalency diploma is required. For higher-level Court Clerk positions, employers usually require some college background, legal clerical training, or paralegal training.

Throughout their careers, Court Clerks enroll in training and continuing education programs to develop their skills and expertise.

Experience, Skills, and Personality Traits

Employers generally require one to three years of general office experience, depending on the position for which one is applying. Legal clerk experience is usually required for higher-level positions. In addition, employers prefer candidates who are knowledgeable about court functions, court procedures, legal forms, and legal terminology.

Court Clerks should have adequate reading, writing, and math skills. They also need strong communication, interpersonal, teamwork, and self-management skills. Being positive, enthusiastic, dependable, cooperative, detail-oriented, and flexible are some personality traits that successful Court Clerks share.

Unions and Associations

Many Court Clerks join professional associations to take advantage of training programs, professional publications, networking opportunities, and other professional services and resources.

Two national organizations available for Court Clerks are NALS and the International Association of Clerks, Recorders, Election Officials, and Treasurers. Federal clerks might join the Federal Court Clerks Association. For contact information, see Appendix V.

Tips for Entry

1. Enroll in appropriate classes to develop and improve your office skills. Many community colleges offer certificate or degree programs in court operations and legal office practices.
2. Many courts have open recruitment for Court Clerk positions.
3. To find job listings for federal Court Clerk positions, visit the U.S. Office of Personnel Management Web site at http://www.usajobs.opm.gov.
4. You can learn more about courts on the Internet. You might start by visiting these Web sites: U.S. Courts, http://www.uscourts.gov; and National Center for State Courts, http://www.ncsconline.org. For more links, see Appendix VI.

COURT INTERPRETER

CAREER PROFILE

Duties: Provide oral translations in court proceedings for witnesses or litigants who have limited English language skills; perform other tasks as required

Alternate Title(s): Judicial Interpreter, Official Court Interpreter, Legal Interpreter

Salary Range: $21,000 to $62,000, for staff positions

Employment Prospects: Good

Advancement Prospects: Poor

Prerequisites:

Education or Training—Completion of a court interpretation program

Experience—Previous court interpreting experience may be required or preferred

Special Skills and Personality Traits—Highly proficient in English and another language and knowledgeable about the cultures of the non-English speakers; interpersonal, communication, and public speaking skills; business skills for independent contractors; be respectful, articulate, sincere, truthful

Special Requirements—State or federal certification or registration may be required

CAREER LADDER

```
┌─────────────────────────────┐
│   Senior Court Interpreter   │
│   or Program Coordinator     │
└─────────────────────────────┘

┌─────────────────────────────┐
│      Court Interpreter       │
└─────────────────────────────┘

┌─────────────────────────────┐
│   Court Interpreter Trainee  │
└─────────────────────────────┘
```

Position Description

In the U.S. court system, when witnesses or litigants in court trials are unable to communicate effectively in the English language, Court Interpreters may translate for them. Many courts have staff Court Interpreters or use freelancers on a contractual basis. They are fluent in English and one or more other languages—Spanish, American Sign Language, Vietnamese, Thai, Russian, Korean, Mandarin, Japanese, Ilocano, Polish, Arabic, Hindi, Ukrainian, Serbo-Croatian, Tongan, Farsi, Greek, Navajo, Haitian Creole, or Portuguese, among others.

Court Interpreters provide their services for various criminal and civil cases. For example, they interpret testimony for witnesses, defendants, or plaintiffs in murder trials, drug trials, domestic violence cases, landlord and tenant disputes, arson trials, child support hearings, and small claims cases.

In addition to court trials, Court Interpreters are also used during arraignments, pretrial hearings and conferences, depositions, and probation meetings.

Court interpretation is a difficult task. Court Interpreters interpret the everyday language of witnesses who come from diverse backgrounds. They deal with the legal terminology of judges and attorneys, as well as handle the technical vocabulary of police officers, forensic scientists, and various expert witnesses. Court Interpreters are expected to do accurate, word-for-word oral translations. They do not change, nor do they add anything to, what is said by speakers. In addition, Court Interpreters preserve the tone and level of language of the speakers.

Court Interpreters perform three types of court interpreting. One is called consecutive interpreting, in which they translate statements into English or the second language after the speaker has finished speaking. Another type is simultaneous interpreting, in which Court Interpreters translate a speaker's statements as the person is speaking. The third type is sight interpreting, which is used when Court Interpreters read a document written in one language while translating it orally into another language.

As officers of the court, Court Interpreters must follow court policies as well as an ethical code of professional responsibility. They maintain an impartial attitude at all times. In other words, they do not become emotionally involved with the participants or the cases. In addition, Court Interpreters do not express personal opinions nor act as an advocate for either party in a case.

Staff Court Interpreters perform other duties as required by their employers. For example, they might interpret and translate technical, medical, legal, and other documents for judges and court staff. They may also provide interpretation for public inquiries in the clerk offices or over the telephone. They also perform various clerical tasks, such as filing and maintaining records of their interpreting and translating activities.

Freelance Court Interpreters are responsible for managing various business tasks. Such tasks include paying bills and taxes, invoicing clients, and generating new business. Many independent contractors also offer their services to private attorneys, public defenders, law enforcement agencies, social service agencies, hospitals, health care facilities, and others.

Staff Court Interpreters work a standard 40-hour week. Freelancers are employed on an as-needed basis, and hence work flexible work hours.

Salaries

Staff Court Interpreters receive salaries, while freelancers are paid by the hour or per diem (by the day). Earnings vary, depending on factors such as their experience, employer, and geographical location. Federal courts generally pay higher wages than local, state, or administrative courts. According to the May 2005 *Occupational Employment Statistics* survey, by the U.S. Bureau of Labor Statistics, the estimated annual salary for most interpreters overall ranged between $20,540 and $61,770.

Employment Prospects

Freelance positions are more readily available than staff positions. Opportunities are available in local, state, and federal courts as well as with administrative boards in government agencies. Court interpreters are also employed by court interpretation services.

The demand for qualified Court Interpreters is strong, particularly in cities with large immigrant populations. Spanish-language interpreters are the most in demand nationally. The demand for other language interpreters vary, depending on the geographical location.

Advancement Prospects

Supervisory and management opportunities for staff Court Interpreters are limited. Generally, Court Interpreters realize advancement by making higher earnings and through professional recognition.

Education and Training

Prospective Court Interpreters typically complete court interpreter training programs that focus on specialized vocabulary and interpreting skills. Enrollment in these programs requires that students already be highly proficient in the second language.

Throughout their careers, Court Interpreters participate in voluntary and mandatory training and continuing education programs to increase their interpreting skills and expertise.

Special Requirements

Court Interpreters may be required to be certified or registered by a federal or state court before they can obtain employment. Requirements vary from court to court. For information about federal Court Interpreter certification, contact a federal court in your area. For information about state court certification, contact your local courts. You can also check Appendix II for some certification programs.

Experience, Skills, and Personality Traits

Many employers prefer to hire candidates who have work experience as a staff or freelance interpreter in court or non-court settings. Employers generally look for candidates who possess an extensive vocabulary and have general knowledge about various subjects. Candidates are also familiar with legal terminology and court proceedings.

Court Interpreters must be highly proficient in reading, writing, speaking, and listening for both English and a second language. In addition, they are familiar with various dialects and idiomatic expressions in both languages. They are also knowledgeable about the cultural differences, regionalisms, and issues of the non-English speakers.

Court Interpreters need effective interpersonal and communication skills, as well as strong public speaking skills. Additionally, independent contractors should have adequate business skills. Being respectful, articulate, sincere, and truthful are a few personality traits that successful Court Interpreters share.

Unions and Associations

Many Court Interpreters are members of local, state, and national professional associations. These organizations offer networking opportunities as well as various professional services and resources. Some national organizations are the Translators and Interpreters Guild, the American Translators Association, and the National Association of Judiciary Interpreters and Translators. For contact information, see Appendix V.

Tips for Entry

1. To find court interpretation programs, check out the colleges and universities in your area. You might also contact local or state court interpreter associations to learn about available training programs.

2. To learn about job opportunities, requirements, and application processes, contact a court interpreter's office directly. If a court has no such office, than ask to talk with the person in charge of hiring court interpreters.

3. You can learn more about court interpreting on the Internet. To find relevant web sites, enter any of these keywords in a search engine: *court interpreting, judiciary interpreting,* or *court interpreter.* For some links, see Appendix VI.

COURT REPORTER

CAREER PROFILE

Duties: Make a verbatim record of court proceedings; produce official court transcripts; perform other duties as required

Alternative Title(s): Official Court Reporter; Real-Time Court Reporter or other title that reflects a specialty

Salary Range: $20,000 to $79,000

Employment Prospects: Good

Advancement Prospects: Fair

Prerequisites:

Education or Training—A high school diploma; completion of a court reporting program

Experience—Varies with different employers

Special Skills and Personality Traits—Organizational, computer, English, and self-management skills; be honest, patient, disciplined, resourceful

Special Requirements—May require state or other professional certification

CAREER LADDER

Senior or Managing Court Reporter

Court Reporter

Entry-Level Court Reporter or Court Reporter in other settings

Position Description

Court Reporters are responsible for creating and producing official records of proceedings in local, state, and federal courts. These women and men may be court staff members or independent contractors (or freelancers). Court employees usually go by the title *Official Court Reporter*.

Court Reporters record, word for word, what defendants, plaintiffs, witnesses, lawyers, judges, and jury members say during court proceedings. They may be assigned to record court trials, hearings, or conferences for civil, criminal, juvenile, family, and other types of court cases. To ensure the accuracy of their work, Court Reporters do not become emotionally involved or affected by the cases that they hear.

Most reporters use the machine, or stenotype, reporting method to make verbatim records. They take shorthand notes at speeds of 225 or more words per minute on stenotype machines. Unlike typewriters or computer keyboards, reporters press several keys at the same time on the stenotype machine keypad (similar to playing chords on a piano) to record words or phrases phonetically. Their notes are produced on paper tape, as well as an electronic format such as a computer disk. If at any time they have trouble taking

notes, they stop the proceedings immediately and request that people speak slower, speak louder, repeat themselves, and so forth.

Some Court Reporters do real-time reporting. Their stenotype machines are connected to computers which simultaneously translate their notes into unedited text. The text can be viewed instantly on other computer screens by judges, lawyers, persons with hearing impairments, and others. Other Court Reporters use electronic sound recording devices that are placed throughout a room to pick up voices. These reporters monitor the recording process to ensure the quality of the taping as well as to take notes to identify speakers.

Court Reporters are responsible for transcribing their notes into formal transcripts, which lawyers and judges request to help them with their cases. Producing transcripts usually takes one to three hours for every hour of taking stenotype notes. During busy times or when transcripts must be produced quickly, Court Reporters usually hire freelance court reporters and scopists (editors) for assistance.

Most reporters use computer-aided transcription (CAT) software to translate their shorthand notes into the text format that the courts require. The CAT program contains a personalized dictionary of court reporters' stenotype symbols, words, and phrases. The program translates all stenotype symbols that it recognizes into text. The reporters translate unfamiliar symbols and add them to their CAT dictionary.

Court Reporters make sure that the transcripts are accurate and clear. They research any items that are vague, check for correct spelling of names and words, make sure that unfamiliar or technical terms and citations were taken down precisely, and so forth. The reporters proofread final transcripts, and have them certified by notary publics as being complete, true, and accurate. If a Court Reporter is a notary public, he or she does the certification.

Official Court Reporters are usually assigned to specific judges. In addition to their reporting duties, they perform various administrative tasks, such as reviewing court transcripts, keeping a log of records, maintaining an inventory of court reporting equipment and supplies, purchasing items as needed, and performing clerical and secretarial tasks as assigned by judges, managing court reporters, or other superiors.

Freelance Court Reporters are responsible for the daily management of their businesses. They perform such duties as invoicing clients, paying bills and taxes, bookkeeping, maintaining their equipment and supplies, and generating new business. Along with performing contractual work for courts, freelancers might be contracted by attorneys to take depositions, as well as by legislative bodies and other groups that require verbatim records of meetings, conventions, and other proceedings.

All Court Reporters are responsible for updating their skills and knowledge as well as keeping up with technology and developments in their field. They accomplish this by enrolling in training programs, networking with peers, attending professional conferences, reading professional journals, and so on.

Official Court Reporters may be hired on a full-time or a part-time basis. They usually have a regular 40-hour work schedule, while freelancers have a more flexible schedule, which may include working evenings or weekends. Court Reporters sometimes need to work long hours to produce transcripts within a certain timeframe.

Salaries

Earnings for Court Reporters vary, depending on such factors as their experience, job status (staff or freelance), employer, and geographical location. According to the May 2005 *Occupational Employment Statistics* survey by the U.S. Bureau of Labor Statistics (BLS), the estimated annual salary for most Court Reporters ranged between $20,370 and $78,590.

In addition to their salaries or court reporting fees (for freelance individuals), Court Reporters earn income by producing transcripts for attorneys and others. They generally earn a per-page fee for their transcripts.

Employment Prospects

In addition to courts, Court Reporters can find employment with court reporting services, law firms, government legislatures, government agencies, television networks, cable stations, and educational institutions.

Staff positions generally become available as Court Reporters retire or transfer to other jobs. The BLS reports that job opportunities should be excellent due to there being more job openings than qualified applicants. It predicts that job growth for this occupation will increase by 9 to 17 percent through 2014.

Opportunities are readily available for freelancers as well as permanent employees in other settings. Court Reporters with real-time reporting experience are in demand in all settings.

Advancement Prospects

Senior and supervisory positions are available, but rather limited. Most Court Reporters realize advancement through higher pay and professional recognition. Some reporters consider employment with the federal courts or government legislatures as their ultimate career goals. Others strive to become freelancers or owners of court reporting services. Many pursue alternative careers in their field, becoming scopists, medical transcriptionists, television closed captionists, or rapid text entry specialists in the business world.

Education and Training

The minimum educational requirement is a high school diploma or general equivalency diploma. Many Court Reporters have associate or bachelor's degrees.

Many employers prefer to hire candidates who have successfully completed a court-reporting program. Court reporter programs are offered by two-year and four-year colleges as well as by public and private vocational programs and technical schools. Some institutions also offer online and distance learning options for court reporting programs.

The length of a program varies from two to four years, depending on a student's ability to master court reporting skills and to pass proficiency tests on the stenotype machine.

Special Requirements

Many states require that Court Reporters hold state Certified Court Reporter (CCR) or Certified Shorthand Reporter (CSR) certification. Some states require the Registered Professional Reporter (RPR), a nationally recognized certification that is granted by the National Court Reporters Association. Some states require that Court Reporters obtain a notary public license. For specific certification and licensure information, contact the state board of examiners of court reporters or a court reporting association in the state where you wish to practice.

Federal courts generally require or prefer that Court Reporters have RPR certification.

Experience, Skills, and Personality Traits

Experience requirements for entry-level positions vary from court to court. At the federal court level, entry-level candidates need a minimum of four years experience as state court reporters, freelancers, or a combination of staff and freelance work. They should have prime court reporting experience, such as working on criminal cases or highly-publicized litigation cases.

Court Reporters need strong organizational, computer, and English (grammar, spelling, and punctuation) skills. They also need excellent self-management skills—be self-motivated, work well under pressure, meet deadlines, and so on. Being honest, patient, disciplined, and resourceful are some personality traits that successful Court Reporters share.

Unions and Associations

Court Reporters join professional associations to take advantage of networking opportunities, continuing education pro-grams, and other professional services and resources. Along with local and state associations, Official Court Reporters might join the National Court Reporters Association. Official Court Reporters at the federal level might join the United States Court Reporters Association. For contact information, see Appendix V.

Tips for Entry

1. To find a listing of accredited programs, see Appendix I.
2. Many courts maintain an eligibility list of temporary Court Reporters to fill part-day or full-day positions as reporters are needed. Contact each court for which you would like to work about their requirements and hiring process for these per diem positions.
3. Contact local, state, or federal personnel offices directly for information about Official Court Reporter vacancies or requirements.
4. Learn more about official court reporting on the Internet. To get a list of relevant Web sites, enter the keywords *official court reporters* or *court reporting* in a search engine. For some links, see Appendix VI.

JUDICIAL ASSISTANT

CAREER PROFILE

Duties: Perform administrative, secretarial, and clerical duties for judges

Alternate Title(s): Judicial Secretary, Legal Secretary

Salary Range: $23,000 to $58,000

Employment Prospects: Fair

Advancement Prospects: Good

Prerequisites:

Education or Training—A high school diploma; legal secretary or paralegal training is desirable

Experience—One or more years of secretarial experience, preferably in a legal setting; familiarity with court systems, legal terminology, and legal documents

Special Skills and Personality Traits—Proficiency in business English, grammar, punctuation, and spelling; communication, interpersonal, teamwork, organizational, and self-management skills; be positive, tactful, patient, responsible, reliable, detail-oriented

CAREER LADDER

```
┌─────────────────────────────────┐
│    Senior Judicial Assistant    │
│   or Administrative Assistant   │
└─────────────────────────────────┘

┌─────────────────────────────────┐
│        Judicial Assistant       │
└─────────────────────────────────┘

┌─────────────────────────────────┐
│  Judicial Assistant (entry-level) │
└─────────────────────────────────┘
```

Position Description

Judicial Assistants help judges in local, state, federal, and tribal courts oversee judicial activities so that courts work effectively and efficiently every day. Their job is to provide judges with administrative, secretarial, and clerical support.

Their duties vary, depending on their experience and abilities as well as the particular needs of the judges. Many Judicial Assistants fulfill the role of liaison for judges. They are the judges' contact person for attorneys, law enforcement officers, other judge's offices, court administrators, social service agencies, the general public, the media, and others. Judicial Assistants provide general information about court policies and procedures in person or over the phone. They also give out information about court activities to appropriate personnel. In addition, they notify appropriate professionals, such as social service workers, whom judges are appointing to cases.

Most Judicial Assistants are responsible for preparing correspondence, legal documents, administrative reports, and court forms, such as court processes, court orders, and affidavits. They use typewriters, word processors, or computers to produce final products from written drafts, notes, dictation tapes, or oral instructions. They make sure that their work follows proper formats and guidelines. They also check for completeness and accuracy of facts, as well as for correct grammar, punctuation, and spelling. Many Judicial Assistants are also assigned the task of preparing routine reports, forms, and correspondence for judges to review and sign.

Most Judicial Assistants manage the court and professional calendars for judges. These assistants schedule appointments for hearings, conferences, and trials, as well as mark the dates for committee meetings, professional events, and other professional conferences. They keep judges current with any date changes and cancellations.

Many Judicial Assistants help judges with case management. They update information in case files. They advise judges, attorneys, or litigants about any lack of information, and may remind them about filing deadlines. Judicial Assistants also review case files before scheduled hearings for accuracy and completeness of information as well as for compliance with required formats.

Here are a few other duties that Judicial Assistants might perform:

- conduct routine research for legal documents
- assist with jury management
- prepare the official record of court proceedings
- help maintain law libraries
- make travel and lodging arrangements for judges
- receive and process court fines
- supervise and train clerical staff
- assist judges with the preparation of budgets

Judicial Assistants also perform a wide variety of routine clerical tasks. These include distributing mail, photocopying, answering telephones, ordering office supplies, maintaining files, updating databases, and so on.

Judicial Assistants may be assigned to serve one judge or several judges. They typically work 40 hours a week.

Salaries

Salaries for Judicial Assistants vary, depending on such factors as their education, experience, employer, and geographical location. Specific salary information for this occupation is unavailable, but Judicial Assistants generally receive earnings similar to legal secretaries. According to the U.S. Bureau of Labor Statistics, in its May 2005 *Occupational Employment Statistics* survey, the estimated annual salary for most legal secretaries ranged between $23,380 and $57,510.

Employment Prospects

Judicial Assistants are hired by local, state, federal, and tribal courts. Most opportunities become available as assistants retire, resign, or transfer to other positions. On occasion, courts may create new positions to meet staffing needs, as long as funds are available.

Advancement Prospects

Judicial Assistants generally realize advancement by earning higher wages and being assigned complex responsibilities.

With additional experience and education or training, Judicial Assistants can pursue related careers, by becoming paralegals, lawyers, clerks of courts, or court administrators.

Education and Training

Judicial Assistants must have a high school diploma or a general equivalency diploma. Having additional legal secretarial or paralegal training is considered highly desirable by many employers. For higher-level positions, employers generally prefer candidates with college degrees or college backgrounds.

Judicial Assistants receive on-the-job training. Throughout their careers, they enroll in training and continuing education programs to enhance their skills.

Experience, Skills, and Personality Traits

Employers generally prefer to hire entry-level candidates who have one or more years of general secretarial experience, preferably in a legal setting. They also seek candidates who are familiar with court functions and procedures as well as legal terminology and documents.

Judicial Assistants must be highly proficient in business English, grammar, spelling, and punctuation. They also need strong communication, interpersonal, and teamwork skills in order to work well with judges, lawyers, and others of various backgrounds. Furthermore, assistants should have excellent organizational and self-management skills—such as the ability to work independently, prioritize tasks, understand and follow instructions, and handle stressful situations.

Being positive, tactful, patient, responsible, reliable and detail-oriented are some personality traits that Judicial Assistants share.

Unions and Associations

Many Judicial Assistants join professional associations to take advantage of networking opportunities, training programs, and other professional services and resources. Some national societies include NALS, Legal Secretaries International, Inc., and International Association of Administrative Professionals. For contact information, see Appendix V.

Tips for Entry

1. Having work experience as a legal secretary, paralegal, or legal clerk may enhance your chances of obtaining a Judicial Assistant position.
2. Some courts have open recruitment for Judicial Assistant positions. Applicants who successfully pass the selection process are placed on an eligibility list, from which candidates are chosen when openings become available.
3. Contact courts directly to learn about job openings and their application processes.
4. Use the Internet to learn more about the court systems. For general information about state courts, visit the National Center for State Courts Web site at http://www.ncsconline.org. For information about federal courts, visit the U.S. Courts Web site at http://www.uscourts.gov. For more links, see Appendix VI.

SCOPIST

CAREER PROFILE

Duties: Provide support services to court reporters; edit and produce first drafts of court transcriptions; perform other duties as required

Alternate Title(s): None

Salary Range: $12,000 to $40,000+

Employment Prospects: Good

Advancement Prospects: Poor

Prerequisites:

Education or Training—A high school diploma; on-the-job training or completion of a scopist training program

Experience—Familiarity with court reporting procedures, legal terminology, and machine shorthand; knowledge of computer-aided transcription (CAT) software

Special Skills and Personality Traits—Computer, English, communication, and self-management skills; business skills for independent contractors; be self-motivated, reliable, flexible, honest, impartial, discreet

CAREER LADDER

```
┌─────────────────────────────┐
│   Senior Scopist (staff)    │
│  or Independent Contractor  │
└─────────────────────────────┘

┌─────────────────────────────┐
│      Scopist (staff)        │
│  or Independent Contractor  │
└─────────────────────────────┘

┌─────────────────────────────┐
│ Scopist Trainee or Court Reporter │
└─────────────────────────────┘
```

Position Description

Court reporters are responsible for taking notes of court proceedings and producing those notes into certified court transcripts. When court reporters are too busy to transcribe and edit their notes, they use the services of Scopists who are independent contractors or staff members in court reporting firms. The Scopists' job is to produce accurate transcript drafts according to the specifications of the court reporters.

The court reporters take notes on stenotype machines that are attached to a computer system. Court reporters give Scopists a copy of their files on disks. Some court reporters transfer their files directly to Scopists' computers via a modem connection or through e-mail attachments. Court reporters also provide Scopists with court exhibits, such as audio tapes and documents, for them to use as reference materials.

Scopists work with computer-aided transcription (CAT) software which translates shorthand notes into the English language according to the program's dictionary. Court reporters each have their own personalized CAT dictionaries of stenotype symbols, words, and phrases. Scopists are responsible for updating CAT dictionaries with any new terms or phrases that the court reporters use in their court notes.

Scopists carefully read the software translations and make all necessary edits. They make sure that the proper words are being used. For example, a court reporter may have inputted the word *there,* but the text requires *their.* If any terms or passages are unclear in the drafts, Scopists alert court reporters by placing a note next to those items. Scopists also translate stenotype notes that the CAT program could not.

In addition, Scopists check for and fix typographical errors on the drafts. They make corrections in grammar and punctuation, using the same style as the individual court reporters. Scopists also check the spellings of proper names and technical terms by researching the court exhibits that were provided to them as well as dictionaries, directories, and other resources. Furthermore, Scopists make sure that the drafts follow proper court guidelines and formats.

Scopists return the edited drafts in the form that the court reporter wishes—on disks, as electronic files transferred via modem, or e-mail attachments.

Many Scopists also provide editing services for court reporters who do depositions. Some Scopists also offer editing services for real-time reporting and audio tape transcriptions.

Scopists are responsible for maintaining their skills, as well as keeping up with technology updates and developments in the court reporting profession. They read professional journals, enroll in training and continuing education programs, participate in professional conferences, network with colleagues, and so on.

Self-employed Scopists provide contractual services to official court reporters (those employed by the courts), court reporting firms, and independent court reporters. As independent contractors, Scopists manage various business tasks, such as invoicing clients, paying bills and taxes, keeping records, and generating new business. They are also responsible for buying and maintaining their own computer systems, printers, CAT software, reference materials, and other equipment and supplies.

Scopists often work nights and weekends, putting in long hours to meet deadlines.

Salaries

Earnings for Scopists vary, depending on factors such as their experience, abilities, ambition, and geographical location. Staff Scopists earn a salary, while freelance Scopists are paid an hourly rate, page rate, or a combination of both. In general, earnings for experienced Scopists range from $12,000 to $40,000 or more per year.

Employment Prospects

Most opportunities are available for freelance Scopists. Staff positions typically become available as Scopists resign or transfer to other positions. On occasion, court reporting firms create additional positions to fit staffing needs.

In general, the demand for Scopists parallels the demand for court reporters. In cities and regions where court reporters are in short supply, Scopists can usually expect to find more opportunities. Further, freelance Scopists need not be limited to work only in their local areas. With the capability of transferring computer files electronically, many Scopists are able to work for court reporters in distant cities and states.

Advancement Prospects

Most Scopists realize advancement by earning higher incomes and through professional recognition. For many, the top goal is to become successful independent contractors.

Education and Training

Scopists should have at least a high school diploma or general equivalency diploma.

Scopist training can be obtained in either of two ways. One is by on-the-job training in a court reporting firm. The other is by completing a scopist training program. Various scopist training programs are offered by postsecondary vocational and technical schools, community colleges, correspondence or Internet-based programs, and private tutoring programs.

Experience, Skills, and Personality Traits

To enter this field, Scopists must have a background in court reporting or be familiar with court reporting procedures and legal terminology. Scopists must also be familiar with stenotype, or machine shorthand. Additionally, they are able to operate the versions of CAT software used by the court reporters that hire them.

Scopists need excellent computer as well as English-language skills, including vocabulary, word usage, grammar, spelling, and punctuation. Scopists also need strong communication and self-management skills—the ability to meet strict deadlines, work under pressure, work independently, and so forth. Self-employed Scopists should have basic business skills.

Being self-motivated, reliable, flexible, honest, impartial, and discreet are some personality traits that successful Scopists share.

Unions and Associations

Scopists join professional associations, such as the National Court Reporters Association to take advantage of networking opportunities, training programs, and other professional services and resources. For contact information, see Appendix V.

Tips for Entry

1. Join local or state professional associations for court reporters. Network with them at meetings and conferences.
2. Let court reporters in your area know about your services. You might send brochures or flyers to court reporting firms and independent court reporters, as well as court reporting offices at state and federal courts in your area.
3. You can learn more about the scopist field, including available training programs, on the Internet. One Web site you might visit is Scopists.com at http://www.scopists.com. For more links, see Appendix VI.

CRIMINAL JUSTICE SUPPORT PROFESSIONALS

BAIL BOND AGENT

Duties: Sell bail bonds; interview potential clients; locate and return missing clients; as owners or managers, oversee business operations

Alternate Title(s): Bail Bondsman, Bail Agent

Salary Range: $24,000 to $113,000

Employment Prospects: Fair

Advancement Prospects: Poor

Prerequisites:

Education or Training—A high school diploma; on-the-job training

Experience—Prior experience may not be needed for entry-level positions

Special Skills and Personality Traits—Customer service, communication, interpersonal, math, writing, computer, and self-management skills; be confident, assertive, resourceful, detail-oriented, organized, persistent, professional

Special Requirements—Licensure by state department of insurance; appropriate business licenses

```
┌─────────────────────────────────┐
│  Senior Bail Bond Agent, Manager,│
│   or Bail Bond Agency Owner      │
└─────────────────────────────────┘

┌─────────────────────────────────┐
│         Bail Bond Agent          │
└─────────────────────────────────┘

┌─────────────────────────────────┐
│      Bail Bond Agent Trainee     │
└─────────────────────────────────┘
```

Position Description

For most crimes in the United States, defendants may be released from jail on bail until they are actually convicted. Bail is an amount of money set by judges based on the type of crime, the defendants' criminal histories, the likelihood of defendants fleeing the area, and other factors. By posting bail, criminal defendants promise to appear at the appointed times and places for their court hearings and trials. When defendants cannot pay bail, they seek the services of Bail Bond Agents. Also known as bondsmen, these professional men and women are state-licensed as surety insurance agents.

These agents take on the financial responsibility of assuring that the defendants will appear in court when required. They sell bail bonds to the defendants in the form of cash bonds or surety bonds, which are underwritten by an insurance company. They do not hand the bail bonds directly to the defendants, but rather agree to promise the courts that they, the Bail Bond Agents, will pay the full amount of the bail if defendants skip out of their court hearings or trials.

Bail Bond Agents carefully decide to whom they will sell bail bonds. They interview prospective clients—the defendants—as well as their lawyers, family members, or friends. If agents feel that defendants may flee, the agents won't take them as clients. Many Bail Bond Agents also refuse to take clients who are accused of committing certain crimes.

Agents charge a fee that is usually equivalent to 10 to 15 percent of the bail. For example, if bail is $10,000, an agent charging 10 percent would receive a $1,000 fee. Many Bail Bond Agents require that clients also put up collateral (such as a car, house, stocks, or money) which would go to the agents if defendants do not show up in court.

Once agents have posted bail for the clients, the courts release them to the agents' custody. Many agents make a point of monitoring their clients and reminding them about court dates. If clients skip out, Bail Bond Agents have the authority to locate and return them to jail. Courts give agents a certain time limit to find their clients.

Bail Bond Agents use various means to find their missing clients, now known as bail fugitives. They talk with family, friends, coworkers, and neighbors to learn about their likely whereabouts. On occasion, agents do surveillance work, which may mean sitting for hours or days, waiting for their clients to appear at a particular location. Agents also conduct research on computer and Internet databases to uncover old home addresses or other useful information. Many Bail Bond Agents hire the services of bail recovery agents, commonly known as bounty hunters, to help them locate missing clients.

Apprehending bail fugitives requires following rigid state regulations, which differ from state to state. For example, some states require that Bail Bond Agents first notify the county sheriff that they plan to apprehend a fugitive. Other states require that agents be accompanied by law enforcement officers. When agents locate fugitives in another state, they must follow the regulations governed by that state. Agents may, for example, be required to first register with local law enforcement agencies.

Many Bail Bond Agents are employees or subagents of bail bond companies. A large number of agents are owners of small independent agencies. Company owners and managers are responsible for overseeing business operations on a daily basis. They perform duties such as maintaining records, paying bills and taxes, keeping licenses up to date, generating new business, supervising staff, recruiting and training new staff, and maintaining the office space.

Bail Bond Agents work evening, late night, and weekend shifts. Many are available to the public 24 hours a day, seven days a week.

Salaries

Earnings for Bail Bond Agents vary, depending on factors such as their geographical location and the amount of competition in their area.

In general, salaries for Bail Bond Agents are similar to those earned by insurance sales agents. According to the May 2005 *Occupational Employment Statistics* survey, by the U.S. Bureau of Labor Statistics, the estimated annual salary for most insurance sales agents ranged between $23,630 and $113,290.

Employment Prospects

Most staff openings become available as agents retire or resign. Generally, as bail bond companies grow, they create additional positions.

The success rate for company owners depends on factors such as the local demand for bail bond services, the amount of competition, and the ambition and business sense of the individuals.

Advancement Prospects

Advancement prospects are rather limited for Bail Bond Agents. In large companies, they may advance to senior and managerial positions. Those with entrepreneurial ambitions might start their own bail bond companies.

Education and Training

Bail Bond Agents need at least a high school diploma or a general equivalency diploma. Many employers prefer applicants who have college backgrounds.

Entry-level Bail Bond Agents receive on-the-job training.

Special Requirements

Bail Bond Agents are usually required to possess a state license. In most states, the state department of insurance issues such licensure. Agents who sell surety bonds are licensed as surety insurance agents.

Licensing requirements for Bail Bond Agents vary from state to state. For example, applicants may be required to complete a minimum number of hours in training and/or pass a written examination to obtain a license. For specific information, contact your state department of insurance.

Experience, Skills, and Personality Traits

Many employers do not require any previous bail bond experience for entry-level positions.

Bail Bond Agents must have strong customer service skills and have a good sense for judging people's character. They also need strong communication and interpersonal skills, as they must meet people from varied backgrounds. Adequate math, writing, and computer skills are also important. Furthermore, they need excellent self-management skills—such as the ability to follow instructions, handle stressful situations, be independent, make decisions quickly, and meet deadlines. Some personality traits that successful agents share are being confident, assertive, resourceful, detail-oriented, organized, persistent, and professional.

Unions and Associations

Bail Bond Agents might join state professional associations to take advantage of networking opportunities and professional services and resources. Many also belong to the Professional Bail Agents of the United States, a national organization devoted to this profession. For contact information, see Appendix V.

Tips for Entry

1. Talk with Bail Bond Agents to learn more about the profession. You might also contact bail bond associations for information.
2. Many Agents have been hired because they were referred by staff members at a bail bond company.
3. Learn more about the bail bond industry on the Internet. You might start by visiting the Professional Bail Agents of the United States Web site at http://www.pbus.com. For more links, see Appendix VI.

CRIMINAL INVESTIGATOR

CAREER PROFILE

Duties: Enforce local, state, or federal criminal laws; conduct criminal investigations; perform duties as required

Alternate Title(s): Special Agent; a title that reflects a specific occupation such as Police Detective or FBI Special Agent

Salary Range: $33,000 to $89,000

Employment Prospects: Good

Advancement Prospects: Good

Prerequisites:

Education or Training—Educational requirements vary with every agency; new investigators complete criminal investigation training as well as on-the- job training

Experience—One or more years of law enforcement or criminal investigation experience required

Special Skills and Personality Traits—Analytical, problem-solving, crisis management, research, report-writing, interviewing, communication, interpersonal, and teamwork skills; be self-motivated, calm, honest, trustworthy, perceptive, and responsible

CAREER LADDER

```
┌─────────────────────────────────┐
│   Senior Criminal Investigator  │
└─────────────────────────────────┘

┌─────────────────────────────────┐
│      Criminal Investigator      │
└─────────────────────────────────┘

┌─────────────────────────────────┐
│   Criminal Investigator Trainee │
└─────────────────────────────────┘
```

Position Description

Criminal Investigators are responsible for solving crime, including robbery, theft, murder, stalking, domestic violence, kidnapping, fraud, forgery, arson, vice, narcotics, terrorism, and civil rights violations, among others. Their job is to conduct thorough investigations to find sufficient evidence to link suspects to crimes so that they can be arrested and prosecuted in courts of law.

These law enforcement officers are responsible for enforcing local, state, or federal laws. They are part of city, special jurisdiction (such as airport or campus), and tribal police forces, as well as of sheriff's offices and state police forces. Within the federal government, Criminal Investigators work in many federal agencies such as the Federal Bureau of Investigation, the U.S. Secret Service, the Drug Enforcement Administration, the Environmental Protection Agency, the U.S. Postal Service, the Internal Revenue Service, the Social Security Administration, the Immigration and Customs Enforcement, and the U.S. Food and Drug Administration. Criminal Investigators are also employed by local, state, and federal wildlife or natural resource conservation agencies.

Some Criminal Investigators work in offices of inspectors general, that are part of local, state, or federal government agencies. These inspectors investigate cases that involve employees who are suspected of violating rules or committing crimes.

Criminal Investigators perform challenging and dangerous work. They carry and use firearms in the performance of their duties.

These law enforcement officers execute duties that are particular to the agency in which they work. Many of their tasks are similar, regardless of where they work. Some of these tasks include:

- developing a plan of investigation
- examining the crime scene for facts and evidence
- interviewing suspects, witnesses, and others who may have information about a case

- reviewing police, crime lab, medical examiner, and other pertinent reports to determine if more information is needed
- examining records and files from various sources, such as government agencies and medical facilities, for pertinent information
- verifying facts about a case to ensure they have correct and accurate information about a suspect, victim, or crime scene
- analyzing information and evidence collected on a case
- conducting surveillance
- performing undercover work
- serving search warrants to individuals in order to perform a search of their property for specific items that may be proof that a crime has been committed
- making arrests or assisting with arrests
- keeping detailed and accurate notes of their investigations, maintaining files, and preparing written reports of their findings
- preparing cases for court trials
- providing testimony at depositions and trials about their findings

Criminal Investigators may handle a case alone or with a partner. On occasion, Criminal Investigators are assigned to work on cases with other law enforcement agencies. Cases may take several weeks, months, or years to solve. Some cases are never solved.

Many investigators travel to other locations, including other cities, states, and countries to solve their cases. Federal investigators may be reassigned to other field offices within their agency, which may be in the United States or in other countries.

Criminal Investigators are scheduled to work 40 hours a week but often put in additional hours to complete their duties. They often work nights, weekends, and holidays. Many of them are assigned to rotating shifts. Criminal Investigators are usually on call 24 hours a day.

Salaries

Salaries for Criminal Investigators vary, depending on such factors as their education, experience, employer, and geographical location. Investigators who live in metropolitan areas, such as New York, Chicago, or San Francisco, typically earn higher wages. According to the May 2005 *Occupational Employment Statistics* survey by the U.S. Bureau of Labor Statistics (BLS), the estimated annual salary for most Criminal Investigators ranged between $32,920 and $88,570.

Federal investigators earn a salary based on the general schedule (GS), a federal pay schedule that covers many federal employees. Depending on the agency, entry-level investigators may start at the GS-5, GS-7, or GS-9 level. Full-performance, or journey, investigators can progress up to either the GS-12 or GS-13 level. In 2006, the annual basic pay rates for law enforcement officers ranged from $31,075 (GS-5) to $85,578 (for GS-13).

Employment Prospects

The BLS reports that job growth for police and detectives is expected to increase by 9 to 17 percent through the period of 2004 through 2014.

Opportunities for Criminal Investigators are available with local, state, federal, and tribal law enforcement agencies. Job competition, however, is keen. Qualified candidates typically outnumber the positions that are available. Most openings are created to replace Criminal Investigators who advance to higher positions, retire, or resign. A law enforcement agency may establish additional positions to meet growing demands when funding becomes available.

All law enforcement agencies have a stringent selection process that usually includes the following: an oral interview, job-related aptitude and skills tests, a medical examination, a drug screening, a psychological review, a background investigation, and a polygraph examination.

Advancement Prospects

Criminal Investigators can advance in numerous ways. They are promoted in rank, as well as receive regular pay raises. As they gain experience, they can seek assignments of their choice. For example, they can ask for a transfer to a particular office or geographical location, or they can specialize in a particular area of investigations, such as narcotics or technology crime.

They can also pursue supervisory, managerial, or executive positions. Those at the local and state levels can rise through the ranks as lieutenants, captains, and so on up to the police chief or sheriff's position. At the city and county levels, the executive positions are either appointed or elected. Executive level positions at the state and federal levels are usually by appointment by the governor or president upon approval of the proper legislative body.

Education and Training

Educational requirements for Criminal Investigators vary with the different law enforcement agencies. The minimum requirement at some local and state agencies is a high school diploma or a high school equivalency diploma. Many agencies prefer to hire candidates with some college background or who possess a college degree (which may be an associate or a bachelor's degree) in law enforcement, criminal justice, or another related field.

At the federal level, the minimum requirement for entry-level applicants is usually a bachelor's degree in a field that a federal law enforcement agency prefers. For example, the FBI seeks candidates who hold a degree in law, accounting, computer science, or criminal justice, among other areas.

All recruits undergo a training program that may last several weeks or months, depending on the law enforcement agency. Local and state recruits usually attend a local law enforcement academy. Many federal agencies send recruits to the Federal Law Enforcement Training Center in Glynco, Georgia.

New Criminal Investigators normally receive on-the-job training while working under the supervision and guidance of experienced investigators.

Throughout their careers, Criminal Investigators enroll in continuing education programs and training programs to update their skills and knowledge.

Experience, Special Skills, and Personality Traits

Law enforcement agencies usually require that applicants be U.S. citizens. Applicants must also meet certain vision, weight, and height requirements. Age requirements vary with the different agencies. For example, to apply for most federal investigator positions, an applicant may not be 37 years old or older at the time of their appointment.

Depending on their agency's requirements, police officers, deputy sheriffs, state police, and conservation workers generally must have completed one or more years of patrol duty before they are eligible to apply for a detective position.

Requirements vary for the different federal agencies. In general, applicants should have prior experience working in law enforcement, and preferably in criminal investigations. Some agencies accept candidates without any law enforcement experience for entry-level positions, if they have three years of progressively responsible work experience.

To perform their work effectively, Criminal Investigators need strong analytical, problem-solving, crisis management, research, report-writing, interviewing, communication, interpersonal, and teamwork skills. Being self-motivated, calm, honest, trustworthy, perceptive, and responsible are some personality traits that successful Criminal Investigators share.

Unions and Associations

Many Criminal Investigators are members of a union that represents them in negotiations for better pay and working conditions as well as in grievance processes.

Criminal Investigators are also eligible to join professional associations to take advantage of networking opportunities, continuing education, professional certification, and other professional resources and services. Professional societies are available for officers locally, statewide, nationally, and internationally. Many societies serve their special interests, such as:

- American Deputy Sheriffs' Association
- Federal Criminal Investigators Association
- Federal Law Enforcement Officers Association
- Fraternal Order of Police
- High Technology Crime Investigation Association
- International Association of Arson Investigators
- International Association of Asian Crime Investigators
- International Association of Crime Analysts
- International Association of Women Police
- International Homicide Investigators Association
- National Black Police Association
  For contact information, see Appendix V.

Tips for Entry

1. While in high school or college, you can gain experience by volunteering or obtaining an internship with a local law enforcement agency.
2. Take criminal justice, law, computer science, logic, and forensic science courses to enhance and improve your investigative skills and knowledge.
3. You must have a clean criminal record to become a law enforcement officer.
4. If you are interested in working for a federal agency, contact it directly to learn about specific qualifications, job vacancies, and their application process.
5. Use the Internet to learn more about the law enforcement agency in which you would like to work. Most agencies have a Web site on which they provide information about themselves as well as post job vacancies. Some agencies also have on-line job applications. To find a particular law enforcement agency's Web site, enter its name in a search engine.

PRETRIAL SERVICES OFFICER

CAREER PROFILE

Duties: Assist courts to determine whether criminal defendants should be released before their trials; conduct pretrial investigations; supervise criminal defendants who are released from jail; perform other duties as required

Alternate Title(s): Detention Release Officer

Salary Range: $28,000 to $67,000

Employment Prospects: Good

Advancement Prospects: Fair

Prerequisites:

Education or Training—A bachelor's degree; on-the-job training for new officers

Experience—Previous work experience in court services, probation, criminal justice, or social services required or preferred; knowledge of case management and government and community resources

Special Skills and Personality Traits—Interviewing, research, communication, writing, computer, teamwork, and interpersonal skills; be energetic, self-motivated, analytical, objective, honest, ethical

CAREER LADDER

```
┌─────────────────────────────────────┐
│  Senior Pretrial Services Officer    │
└─────────────────────────────────────┘

┌─────────────────────────────────────┐
│     Pretrial Services Officer        │
└─────────────────────────────────────┘

┌─────────────────────────────────────┐
│  Pretrial Services Officer Trainee   │
│   or Pretrial Services Assistant     │
└─────────────────────────────────────┘
```

Position Description

In the U.S. criminal justice system, some defendants may be released from jail to await their court trials. It is the responsibility of Pretrial Services Officers to prepare unbiased pretrial reports that help judges determine whether criminal defendants should be detained or released. The pretrial reports provide judges with sufficient information to answer such questions as: If defendants are released, will they show up for their court hearings and trials, and will they stay out of trouble? Would they pose a danger to victims, witnesses, or the general community?

Pretrial Services Officers conduct thorough investigations for all cases that are assigned to them. They gather information about the defendants—their employment histories, criminal records, family relationships, residences, and so on. These officers conduct research by using various databases from government agencies, law enforcement agencies, credit report companies, and other sources. They also interview the defendants and verify facts by contacting employers, family members, law enforcement agencies,

financial institutions, school officials, and others. Officers may also talk with prosecuting attorneys to find out what the government's position is on releasing or detaining the defendants.

When the Pretrial Services Officers have completed their investigations, they evaluate the data to offer recommendations to the judges. The officers follow specific court guidelines as well as use risk assessment instruments. In addition to recommending whether defendants should be detained or released, these officers may suggest whether defendants should post bail bonds.

Pretrial Services Officers may recommend that the defendants' releases be based on certain conditions. For example, they must obtain mental health evaluations, participate in substance abuse treatment programs, find employment, or avoid the company of certain people. Officers may also recommend that the defendants' freedom of movement be restricted in such forms as curfews or house arrest.

Pretrial investigations and reports are completed prior to the defendants' first appearance before a judge. Hence, officers must perform their tasks quickly, yet make sure that their work is accurate and complete.

Pretrial Services Officers are also responsible for managing a caseload of criminal defendants who have been released from jail. The officers supervise the defendants until they have been acquitted, they begin their sentences, or when the criminal charges against them have been dropped.

As supervisors, Pretrial Services Officers are responsible for helping the defendants follow the conditions of their release. They provide the defendants with referrals to appropriate resources, such as employment counseling, drug treatment services, health clinics, or school programs. Officers also monitor their activities and movements by keeping regular contact with them in person and by telephone. If the defendants violate any of their conditions, Pretrial Services Officers inform the courts and prosecuting attorneys.

Pretrial Services Officers are responsible for other duties. For example, they develop community and government resources to whom they can refer criminal defendants for assistance, and make presentations about pretrial services to schools and community organizations. These officers also keep up with current criminal justice and social work issues and practices that are relevant to their work

Pretrial Services Officers work 40 hours a week, sometimes putting in additional hours to complete their various tasks.

Salaries

Salaries for Pretrial Services Officers vary, depending on factors such as their experience, education, employer, and geographical location. These officers earn wages similar to probation officers. The estimated annual salary for most probation officers ranged from $27,600 to $67,440, according to the May 2005 *Occupational Employment Statistics* survey by the U.S. Bureau of Labor Statistics.

Employment Prospects

Pretrial Services Officers are employed by state and federal court systems. Most opportunities become available as officers resign, retire, or transfer to other positions. Additional positions are occasionally created to meet staffing needs, as long as funding is available.

Advancement Prospects

Advancements in pretrial services offices are limited to a few supervisory and administrative positions. Most officers realize advancement by earning higher salaries and receiv-

ing more complex assignments. Many in state offices seek positions at the federal level.

Depending on their interests, Pretrial Services Officers can pursue other related career paths by becoming probation officers, correctional officers, law enforcement officers, social workers, and lawyers.

Education and Training

Employers generally prefer to hire candidates who possess a bachelor's degree in criminal justice, criminology, sociology, social work, psychology, or another related field.

New officers receive on-the-job training, while working under the guidance of experienced officers. Some employers also provide formal classroom training.

Experience, Skills, and Personality Traits

In general, employers require (or strongly prefer) that candidates have previous work experience in court services, probation, criminal justice, or social services. In addition, they must be knowledgeable about case management and about available social, legal, and health resources in the government and community.

Pretrial Services Officers need effective interviewing, research, communication, writing, and computer skills. In addition, they need strong teamwork and interpersonal skills, as they must work well with different people from various backgrounds. Being energetic, self-motivated, analytical, objective, honest, and ethical are a few personality traits that successful Pretrial Services Officers share.

Unions and Associations

Pretrial Services Officers join professional associations to take advantage of networking opportunities, training programs, and other professional services and resources. One national association that serves pretrial services practitioners is the National Association of Pretrial Services Agencies. For contact information, see Appendix V.

Tips for Entry

1. For federal positions, applicants must be 36 years old or younger at the time of their appointment.
2. Contact pretrial offices directly to learn about their job vacancies and the application process.
3. Learn more about pretrial services on the Internet. You might start by visiting the Pretrial Services Resource Center Web site at http://www.pretrial.org. For more links, see Appendix VI.

U.S. PROBATION OFFICER

CAREER PROFILE

Duties: Supervise probationers and parolees; make recommendations for sentencing offenders; conduct presentence investigations; perform other duties as required

Alternate Title(s): None

Salary Range: $34,000 to $90,000

Employment Prospects: Fair

Advancement Prospects: Poor

Prerequisites:

Education or Training—A bachelor's degree; on-the-job training

Experience—One to three years of progressive responsibility in probation, pretrial services, parole, corrections, or related fields

Special Skills and Personality Traits—Interviewing, research, communication, writing, teamwork, interpersonal, analytical, conflict management, and self-management skills; be courteous, honest, respectful, dedicated, realistic, objective

CAREER LADDER

```
┌─────────────────────────────────────┐
│   Senior U.S. Probation Officer      │
└─────────────────────────────────────┘

┌─────────────────────────────────────┐
│      U.S. Probation Officer          │
└─────────────────────────────────────┘

┌─────────────────────────────────────┐
│   U.S. Probation Officer Trainee     │
└─────────────────────────────────────┘
```

Position Description

U.S. Probation Officers are federal law enforcement officers whose job is to manage a caseload of offenders who have been placed under court supervision by the federal courts, the U.S. Parole Commission, or U.S. military authorities. These offenders are allowed to serve their court sentences in their communities as an alternative to imprisonment. The U.S. Probation Officers are responsible for monitoring their activities and movements to ensure the safety of the communities in which the offenders have been released.

U.S. Probation Officers supervise only offenders who have been convicted of federal crimes. Some are probationers—offenders who receive court supervision sentences instead of prison sentences. Others are parolees—offenders who have been conditionally released from prison before their sentence is complete. Probation officers provide supervision for probationers and parolees until they have completed their sentences.

All probationers and parolees are released from jail on certain conditions, which are specified in their supervision plans. For example, offenders may be required to obtain employment, finish educational programs, enroll in drug abuse or alcohol treatment programs, or obtain mental health counseling. Offenders may also be restricted as to where they may travel and with whom they may associate.

Probation officers help offenders meet the terms of their conditions by referring them to proper resources in government and community agencies. They also maintain regular personal contact with the offenders to ensure that they are following their supervision plans. Probation officers meet with the offenders in their offices, as well as visit the offenders in their homes and at their jobs.

Probation officers maintain accurate and up-to-date records on their probationers or parolees. They document meetings, the behavior of the offenders, and any significant events. In addition, they prepare and submit routine monthly and annual progress reports. They may propose changes to the conditions of the offenders' releases, such as adding or dropping treatment plans.

If offenders are suspected of having committed a violation of their probation or parole, officers conduct investigations accordingly. They report any violations to the proper authorities—the court, U.S. Parole Commission, or military authorities.

U.S. Probation Officers also have the major duty of helping federal judges determine the appropriate sentences for offenders. The officers conduct investigations to gather information about the offenders and the circumstances of the offenses that have been committed. They review court records, criminal history records, pretrial reports, treatment reports, and so on. They interview offenders and verify all facts. In addition, they interview law enforcement officers, attorneys, victims, family members, employers, clergy, community agencies, and others.

Applying appropriate federal laws and federal sentencing guidelines, U.S. Probation Officers assess the data and make recommendations for sentencing. Their recommendations may include probation, imprisonment, and fines.

U.S. Probation Officers perform other duties as required. For example, they might investigate parole plans for parolees who are under consideration for being released; supervise probationers transferring between federal districts; or develop community resources to which they can refer offenders.

U.S. Probation Officers sometimes work more than 40 hours per week to complete their various duties and meet deadlines. They may be required to work evenings and on weekends to supervise offenders. Travel is often necessary to visit offenders at their homes and jobs.

Salaries

Salaries for U.S. Probation Officers vary, depending on factors such as their experience, education, and geographical location. Officers who reside in areas with a higher cost of living typically earn higher wages. In 2006, annual salaries generally ranged between $34,000 and $90,000.

Employment Prospects

U.S. Probation Officers are employed by the various U.S. courts. Most opportunities become available as officers resign, retire, or transfer to other positions. Additional positions are occasionally created to meet staffing needs, as long as funding is available.

To become U.S. Probation Officers, applicants must be U.S. citizens. They must be under 37 years old upon the time of appointment. In addition, candidates must pass all steps of the selection process which includes an oral interview, FBI background investigation, medical exam, and drug screening.

Advancement Prospects

Supervisory and administrative positions are available for those interested in management duties. Most officers realize advancement by earning higher pay and receiving more complex responsibilities.

U.S. Probation Officers are required to retire at age 57. Many retirees pursue new careers in other fields that interest them.

Education and Training

Employers require that candidates have a bachelor's degree, preferably in a behavioral science discipline. In addition, employers may require that candidates have earned a master's degree, be currently enrolled in a master's program, or have completed a year of graduate-level courses.

New U.S. Probation Officers complete several weeks of training at the Federal Law Enforcement Training Academy in South Carolina. All officers receive in-service training each year.

Experience, Skills, and Personality Traits

In general, employers require one to three years of progressively responsible work in probation, pretrial services, parole, corrections, criminal investigation, substance abuse treatment, or related fields. In addition, candidates should be knowledgeable about the federal court system.

U.S. Probation Officers have excellent interviewing, research, communication, and writing skills. They also have strong teamwork and interpersonal skills as well as effective analytical, conflict management, and self-management skills. Being courteous, honest, respectful, dedicated, realistic, and objective are a few personality traits that successful officers share.

Unions and Associations

Many U.S. Probation Officers are members of professional associations to take advantage of networking opportunities, and other professional services and resources. Some associations that many join are the American Probation and Parole Association and the Federal Law Enforcement Officers Association. For contact information, see Appendix V.

Tips for Entry

1. Each U.S. Probation Office is responsible for its own hiring and recruitment. Contact the offices where you wish to work for information about job vacancies and requirements.
2. You might first gain employment as a probation officer at the local level. Then after a few years of experience, apply for a federal position.
3. Learn more about U.S. Probation Officers and their work on the Internet. You might start by visiting the U.S. Probation and Pretrial Services Web site at http://www.uscourts.gov/misc/propretrial.html. For more links, see Appendix VI.

VICTIM SERVICES SPECIALIST

CAREER PROFILE

Duties: Provide support services to crime victims; assist in the administration and development of victim assistance programs; perform other duties as required.

Alternate Title(s): Victim Advocate; Victim Assistance Counselor

Salary Range: $20,000 to $54,000

Employment Prospects: Good

Advancement Prospects: Poor

Prerequisites:

Education or Training—A bachelor's degree; victim assistance training

Experience—One or more years of experience, for staff positions

Special Skills and Personality Traits—Communication, listening, interpersonal, conflict management, and stress management skills; be brave, patient, trusting, respectful, flexible, resourceful, resilient

Special Requirements—State certification may be required

CAREER LADDER

```
┌─────────────────────────────────┐
│   Victim Assistance Program     │
│     Coordinator or Director     │
└─────────────────────────────────┘

┌─────────────────────────────────┐
│   Victim Services Specialist    │
└─────────────────────────────────┘

┌─────────────────────────────────┐
│   Volunteer, Intern, or Trainee │
└─────────────────────────────────┘
```

Position Description

In the United States, federal and state laws mandate that victims of crimes have certain rights. For example, crime victims have the right to be informed of the progress of court cases, and to be notified of changes in the status of the suspects or offenders. Victim Services Specialists are responsible for helping their clients handle the immediate and long-term effects of victimization. They work with children, teenagers, and adults. These specialists may be called out to crime scenes to provide crisis intervention to victims as well as to crime witnesses.

Victim Services Specialists provide various direct services to crime victims, while managing several cases at a time. Some of these services are:

• informing victims about how the criminal justice system works and what their rights are as crime victims

• providing victims with updates about the progress of court cases

• helping victims prepare to testify in court

• escorting victims to court appearances, and providing a safe and secure area for them during court proceedings

• helping victims apply for crime victim compensation programs as well as for restitution from the offenders

• helping victims obtain restraining orders

• notifying victims of the status of the offenders—such as their release from custody or eligibility for parole

• providing victims with counseling support

• referring victims to services they may require—such as legal assistance, special counseling, medical treatment, support groups, and housing services

• acting as liaisons between victims, and their families, and law enforcement agencies, correctional facilities, and other government agencies.

Some specialists provide services in one particular area of crime, such as domestic violence, sexual assault, homicide, or gang violence. Some specialists serve particular groups—for example, elderly victims, children, or victims of juvenile offenders.

These specialists also perform other duties. They assist in the administration of grant funds, the development of policies and procedures, the planning of new services and programs, and the creation of public information and training materials. They inform the general public about their programs, as well as act as liaisons with other victim assistance agencies. In addition, these specialists develop new legal, medical, emotional, and other resources to which they refer victims for help. They also keep up with trends and developments in the victim assistance field.

Victim Services Specialists often work additional hours at night and on weekends to help crime victims.

Salaries

Specific salary information is unavailable for Victim Services Specialists. Many are volunteers, and thus receive no compensation. Paid employees receive salaries comparable to other community and social services occupations. According to the May 2005 *Occupational Employment Statistics* survey, by the U.S. Bureau of Labor Statistics, the estimated annual salary for most community and social service specialists (not listed separately in the survey), ranged between $20,190 and $53,950.

Employment Prospects

Victim assistance programs are administered by prosecuting attorney's offices, corrections, law enforcement agencies, and community organizations. Most opportunities are for volunteer positions, but the number of paid staff positions is steadily increasing.

Most paid positions become available as Victim Services Specialists resign or transfer to other positions. Established programs occasionally create additional positions to meet staffing needs when funding is available. In addition, new victim assistance programs are continually starting throughout the country.

Advancement Prospects

Supervisory and administrative positions are available, but limited. Usually an advanced degree in social work or another related field is required for advancement.

Education and Training

Employers generally prefer to hire Victim Services Specialists who hold a bachelor's degree in psychology, social work, criminal justice, or another related field. In some states, specialists must meet minimum training requirements.

Special Requirements

Victim Services Specialists may be required to be state certified. For specific information, contact a victim services agency in the area where you wish to work.

Experience, Skills, and Personality Traits

Applicants for paid staff positions are generally required to have one or more years or experience providing victim assistance services. They are familiar with crime victim laws and court procedures. In addition, candidates have experience working with people from different cultural, social, and economic backgrounds.

Victim Services Specialists must have superior communication, listening, and interpersonal skills. They also need excellent conflict management and stress management skills. Successful Victim Services Specialists share several personality traits such as being brave, patient, trusting, respectful, flexible, resourceful, and resilient.

Unions and Associations

Victim Services Specialists join professional associations to take advantage of networking opportunities and other professional services and resources. Two national associations that many join are the National Organization for Victim Assistance and the Association of Traumatic Stress Specialists. For contact information, see Appendix V.

Tips for Entry

1. Gain experience by volunteering or interning with victim assistance services programs, such as rape crisis centers, battered women's programs, or child protective services agencies.
2. Many employers hire candidates who have successfully completed a background investigation. Some employers also require candidates to complete a polygraph examination, drug screening, and psychological test.
3. Use the Internet to learn more about victim assistance services. You might start by visiting the U.S. Office for Victims of Crime Web site at http://www. ojp.usdoj.gov/ovc. For more links, see Appendix VI.

JUVENILE COUNSELOR

CAREER PROFILE

Duties: Provide supervision, counseling, and case management services for the rehabilitation of juvenile offenders; perform other duties as required

Alternate Title(s): Juvenile Court Officer, Juvenile Probation Officer, Juvenile Caseworker, Juvenile Probation Counselor

Salary Range: $28,000 to $67,000

Employment Prospects: Good

Advancement Prospects: Fair

Prerequisites:

Education or Training—A bachelor's degree; on-the-job training

Experience—One or more years of experience working with children and teenagers

Special Skills and Personality Traits—Communication, listening, interpersonal, writing, interviewing, analytical, and self-management skills; be objective, stable, honest, respectful, concerned, ethical, dedicated

CAREER LADDER

```
┌─────────────────────────────┐
│     Senior of Supervisory    │
│     Juvenile Counselor       │
└─────────────────────────────┘

┌─────────────────────────────┐
│ Juvenile Counselor (Journey Level) │
└─────────────────────────────┘

┌─────────────────────────────┐
│ Juvenile Counselor (Entry Level) │
└─────────────────────────────┘
```

Position Description

Juvenile Counselors are employed by juvenile probation departments, which work closely with juvenile courts (or family courts). They provide these courts with supervision, case management, counseling, and other services related to the rehabilitation of juvenile offenders.

In the United States, juvenile courts are responsible for conducting legal proceedings against children under the age of 18 who are accused of violating criminal laws, such as vandalism, petty theft, burglary, assault, possession of guns, drug possession, manslaughter, or murder. Juvenile courts also address cases of chronic school truancy as well as cases of undisciplined youth whose parents or guardians are unable to control their disruptive behavior.

Juvenile offenders may be given sentences in juvenile correctional facilities or be placed under probation (or court supervision). The probation usually involves specific conditions, such as agreeing to meet certain expectations such as going to school, avoiding associations with certain persons, and being home by certain times. Their conditions may also include participating in counseling programs, performing community service, or enrolling in drug treatment programs. In addition, they may be required to make payments to injured parties.

Juvenile Counselors are responsible for providing supervision to juvenile offenders on probation. Their goals are to ensure the safety of the public, to assist the juveniles and their families in a program of rehabilitation, and to inspire a sense of responsibility in the offenders for their own acts. Juvenile Counselors usually manage 30 to 40 or more active cases, making personal contact with each juvenile on a regular basis. They help the youth meet the conditions of their probation plan by referring them to appropriate mental health counselors, education programs, community services, and other resources. They also counsel and advise juveniles on their behavior, responsibility, attitudes, goals, and other related concerns or problems. Juvenile Counselors investigate any suspected violations of the juveniles' probation, and when necessary, report violations to the proper authorities.

In addition, Juvenile Counselors monitor their clients' progress by talking with school officials, counselors, parents, and others. They also obtain copies of school records, treatment progress reports, and so forth. These counselors are responsible for maintaining accurate and up-to-date records on each of their cases, and submitting weekly or monthly reports about their caseload. When necessary, Juvenile Counselors testify in court about the progress of the youth that they supervise.

Juvenile Counselors perform other duties, which vary from department to department as well as within a department. Many counselors have the additional duty of helping judges determine the most effective and appropriate sentences for juvenile offenders. In addition, Juvenile Counselors suggest programs appropriate for the offenders' rehabilitation. Some counselors are also responsible for providing intake duties. They evaluate all juvenile violations and undisciplined behavior complaints to determine if there is enough evidence to warrant court action.

Juvenile Counselors have daily contact with various professionals, including judges, prosecuting attorneys, community agencies, law enforcement officers, school officials, and mental health counselors, among others. In addition, these counselors develop social, mental health, and other resources to which they can refer juveniles.

Juvenile Counselors often work evenings and on weekends to meet with clients and complete their tasks. Travel may be required to meet with youth, families, school officials, treatment providers, and others.

Salaries

Salaries for Juvenile Counselors vary, depending on factors such as their experience, education, employer, and geographical location. These officers earn wages similar to probation officers. The estimated annual salary for most probation officers ranged from $27,600 to $67,440, according to the May 2005 *Occupational Employment Statistics* survey by the U.S. Bureau of Labor Statistics.

Employment Prospects

Juvenile Counselors are employed by local and state juvenile probation departments. Most opportunities become available as Juvenile Counselors resign, retire, or transfer to other positions. When funding is available, agencies may create additional positions to meet staffing needs.

Advancement Prospects

Supervisory and administrative positions are available within juvenile probation departments.

Depending on their interests, Juvenile Counselors can also pursue other related careers by becoming schoolteach-

ers, school counselors, family therapists, law enforcement officers, or lawyers.

Education and Training

Employers generally require that candidates have a bachelor's degree, preferably in a behavior science discipline.

Entry-level Juvenile Counselors receive on-the-job training. Throughout their careers, Juvenile Counselors enroll in training seminars and continuing education classes to develop and enhance their skills and expertise.

Experience, Skills, and Personality Traits

In general, employers require that candidates have one or more years of experience working with children and teenagers. In addition, candidates must have general knowledge about juvenile laws, juvenile court procedures, and human behavior, as well as adolescent social structures and thinking patterns. Being familiar with social work principles of case management and with the social, legal, and health resources in the government and community is also desirable.

Juvenile Counselors must have excellent communication, listening, and interpersonal skills to work well with young people, judges, and others. They also need effective writing, interviewing, analytical and self-management skills. Being objective, stable, honest, respectful, concerned, ethical, and dedicated are a few personality traits that successful Juvenile Counselors share.

Unions and Associations

Juvenile Counselors join professional associations to take advantage of networking opportunities, training programs, and other professional services and resources. The American Probation and Parole Association and the American Correctional Association are two national associations that many Juvenile Counselors join. For contact information, see Appendix V.

Tips for Entry

1. Gain experience by interning in juvenile probation departments or volunteering in community-based youth programs that provide support services to juvenile offenders.
2. Many juvenile detention facilities hire temporary or on-call detention counselors to substitute for full-time counselors when they are absent. Contact juvenile probation departments for information.
3. Learn more about juvenile justice on the Internet. One Web site that you might visit is for the Office of Juvenile Justice and Delinquency Prevention at http://ojjdp.ncjrs.org. For more links, see Appendix VI.

CHILD PROTECTIVE SERVICES (CPS) CASEWORKER

CAREER PROFILE

Duties: Provide assessment, counseling, and case management services; perform other duties as required

Alternate Title(s): CPS Specialist, CPS Investigator

Salary Range: $24,000 to $59,000

Employment Prospects: Good

Advancement Prospects: Good

Prerequisites:

Education or Training—A bachelor's or master's degree in social work; in-service training

Experience—Previous experience working with child protective services

Special Skills and Personality Traits—Communication, listening, interpersonal, conflict management, interviewing, research, and self-management skills; be sincere, trusting, discreet, empathetic, resilient, sensitive, patient, flexible, objective

Special Requirements—Being licensed, certified, or registered social workers is required in some states

CAREER LADDER

> **Senior or Supervisory Child Protective Services Caseworker**

> **Child Protective Services Caseworker**

> **Child Protective Services Caseworker Trainee**

Position Description

Child Protective Services (CPS) Caseworkers are children's advocates. They are employed by child welfare agencies in their communities. Their job is to provide assessment, counseling, and case management services to children who have been abused or neglected or who are at risk of maltreatment. These social workers work with children as well as with their families.

CPS Caseworkers are authorized by law to investigate reports of abused and neglected children. Reports come from family members, teachers, law enforcement officers, and others who are concerned that children are being mistreated by their parents or guardians. CPS Caseworkers also receive court orders to look into such reports.

Their investigations involve interviewing children as well as the persons suspected of mistreating the children. Caseworkers also interview others (such as family members, school

officials, and law enforcement officers) to verify information. In addition, they review any relevant records, such as police or medical records, pertaining to the children, parents, and other persons living in the home. Caseworkers may request that children be given medical, psychological, or psychiatric examinations to establish whether abuse or neglect has occurred.

Upon completion of their investigations, CPS Caseworkers examine the data and rule whether maltreatment has occurred. If abuse or neglect is found, caseworkers may recommend that CPS agencies work with the families to resolve the problems. They may also recommend that petitions be filed in family court to remove children from their homes and place them temporarily in safer environments. In addition, CPS Caseworkers report any suspicions of criminal violations to appropriate law enforcement agencies.

CPS Caseworkers also have the duty to work with families to develop strategies for changing the conditions and behaviors within the homes that resulted in child abuse and neglect. For example, families may need assistance in child care, counseling, or public welfare, or individual family members may need job training, substance abuse treatment, or parenting classes. Caseworkers provide families with the proper services by referring them to the appropriate resources in their communities.

CPS Caseworkers meet with the families assigned to their caseload on a regular basis. They provide families with advice and counseling as well as monitor their progress. Caseworkers are responsible for keeping detailed records of their cases and preparing required forms and reports about their cases. If families fail to resolve their problems, CPS Caseworkers may recommend that children be placed permanently with other caregivers. In some cases, they may recommend that parent-child relationships be terminated.

CPS Caseworkers work a 40-hour week, but they occasionally work evenings and weekends to meet with clients or to complete their various tasks.

Salaries

Salaries for CPS Caseworkers vary, depending on factors such as their experience, education, and geographical location. According to the May 2005 *Occupational Employment Statistics* survey by the U.S. Bureau of Labor Statistics, the estimated annual salary for most child and family social workers, ranged between $23,610 and $59,200.

Employment Prospects

Openings for CPS Caseworkers usually become available as these professionals advance to higher positions, transfer to other jobs, or retire. Agencies occasionally create additional positions to meet staffing needs, as long as funding is available.

Job opportunities are favorable for this occupation. The turnover rate is generally high due to the emotional stress of the work, large caseloads, low wages, and other factors.

Advancement Prospects

With additional experience and education, CPS Caseworkers can advance to supervisory and administrative positions.

Depending on their interests, CPS Caseworkers can pursue other related careers, such as becoming child and family therapists, politicians, child welfare program directors, or family law attorneys.

Education and Training

Depending on the employer, candidates may need either a bachelor's or master's degree in social work.

CPS Caseworkers receive in-service training. In addition, most enroll in voluntary continuing education and training programs to develop their skills and expertise.

Special Requirements

In some states, CPS Caseworkers may need to be licensed, certified, or registered social workers. For specific licensure information, contact the regulatory board for social workers in the state where you wish to practice.

Experience, Skills, and Personality Traits

Employers generally prefer to hire candidates who have a few years of experience providing child protective services. In addition, candidates must be knowledgeable about child and adolescent development as well as about family development and dynamics. They should also have experience working with people of different backgrounds.

CPS Caseworkers need excellent communication, listening, and interpersonal skills. In addition, they must have strong conflict management skills, as well as adequate interviewing and research skills. Furthermore, they need superior self-management skills—such as the ability to work independently, make sound and timely decisions, handle stressful situations, and manage several tasks at the same time.

Being sincere, trusting, discreet, empathetic, resilient, sensitive, patient, flexible, and objective are some personality traits that successful CPS Caseworkers share. In addition, they are dedicated and compassionate about child welfare.

Unions and Associations

CPS Caseworkers join professional associations to take advantage of networking opportunities and other professional resources and services. Some national organizations that serve their needs are the American Professional Society on the Abuse of Children, the American Humane Association, and the National Association of Social Workers. For contact information, see Appendix V.

Tips for Entry

1. Gain experience by volunteering or interning with a social service agency, hospital, or therapeutic treatment program that works with abused and neglected children and their families.
2. To get an idea of what it might be like to be a CPS Caseworker, become a Court Appointed Special Advocate (CASA) volunteer. For information, contact a family court.
3. Learn more about the field of child protective services on the Internet. One Web site you might visit is the Child Welfare Information Gateway Web site at http://www.childwelfare.gov. For more links, see Appendix VI.

GUARDIAN AD LITEM (GAL)

CAREER PROFILE

Duties: Represent minor children in court proceedings; advocate for children's best interests throughout court proceedings; conduct investigations; perform duties as required

Alternate Title(s): Attorney Ad Litem, Law Guardian

Salary Range: Not applicable

Employment Prospects: Not applicable, volunteer position

Advancement Prospects: Not applicable

Prerequisites:

Education or Training—Completion of GAL training program

Experience—Prior experience working with at-risk children preferred

Special Skills and Personality Traits—Communication, interpersonal, teamwork, organizational, problem-solving, and self-management skills; impartial, objective, nonjudgmental, compassionate, flexible, and open-minded

CAREER LADDER

```
┌─────────────────────────────────┐
│        Guardian Ad Litem        │
└─────────────────────────────────┘

┌─────────────────────────────────┐
│     Attorney or other Profession │
└─────────────────────────────────┘
```

Position Description

Oftentimes in court cases that involve minor children, the children's interests are not represented. To ensure that the children's interests are represented, judges may appoint Guardians Ad Litem (GALs) to be the children's spokespersons. Their role is to protect the rights of the children as well as advocate for their best interests throughout court proceedings. GALs also make sure that the parties involved in the disputes, the court, and service providers work together to provide for the children's best interests.

GALs are trained volunteers. They work under the supervision of Guardian Ad Litem programs, which are part of state court systems. GALs are attorneys, social workers, psychologists, and others from different professions and backgrounds. In some courts, only attorneys are allowed to serve as GALs. Attorney GALs are sometimes known as attorneys ad litem or attorney guardians.

GALs are assigned to various types of court cases such as juvenile delinquency, child neglect, child abuse, domes-

tic violence, divorce, paternity, and contested inheritances. Guardians Ad Litem are not to be confused with children's legal guardians. While legal guardians are appointed by the court to care for the personal and financial interests of children, GALs support the interests of children only for the length of a court proceeding. Judges may also assign GALs to advocate for adults who are unable to understand the court proceedings so as to make choices that are in their best interest.

As officers of the court, GALs are official members of court proceedings. They work closely with attorneys, social workers, and other professionals who are involved in their assigned cases. As children's representatives, GALs attend all court hearings and trial sessions that are scheduled for their cases.

With each case, GALS are responsible for becoming familiar with it before it goes to trial or hearing. They meet with the children to find out their wishes. If they are too young to express themselves, GALs meet with others who are involved in the cases. GALs are also responsible for visiting the children on a regular basis to keep them informed of the proceedings, as well as to help them understand what is happening and what are their rights and options.

GALs make recommendations to the court about services and plans that would meet the best interests of the children. This involves conducting thorough investigations of children's past and current situations. They review court documents, medical records, school files, and other sources. They interview family members, friends, neighbors, babysitters, teachers, counselors, physicians, and others. They also observe interactions between children and their family members in home environments. GALs assess the information they have collected and develop recommendations, such as identifying appropriate community resources or social services that meet children's needs. GALs prepare written reports of their findings and recommendations, and submit them to the courts.

When judges order families to provide certain activities or services for their children, GALs monitor the families to ensure that they are in compliance. If any enforcement or change is required, GALs bring it to the attention of the proper court officer.

GALs are responsible for maintaining a confidential file on each of their cases. It includes documents from court case files as well as from other agencies. In addition, records of appointment schedules, interviews, intervention plans, and other required forms are kept within the case files.

Many GALs are assisted by court-appointed special advocates (CASAs). These are also volunteers, and are members of the community.

GALs work under the support of the GAL program and staff. They attend regular GAL meetings for supervision, evaluation, or training. These volunteers are expected to commit a minimum of hours per month to work on their assigned cases, including spending time with children and attending court hearings. Much of their work is done in the evenings and on weekends. They may accept as many cases as they can handle.

Salaries

Guardians Ad Litem are volunteers. In some courts, GALs are paid a nominal fee by either the parties that are involved or by the court. Many GALs, however, receive no compensation.

Employment Prospects

Volunteer opportunities vary with the different courts. Most courts are continually recruiting for volunteer Guardians Ad Litem, as it is often difficult to find qualified individuals to serve.

Individuals who are interested in volunteering usually submit an application, and then go through an interviewing process as well as a background check. If approved to be a GAL, individuals are then placed on a roster from which judges make assignments.

Advancement Prospects

There are no advancement prospects for Guardians Ad Litem. Many individuals use their volunteer work to gain valuable experience for their careers.

Education and Training

Candidates must successfully complete a basic training program before they are added to the roster of GAL volunteers. Training programs vary from court to court. Classroom instruction generally covers topics such as child development, child abuse and neglect, substance abuse, advocacy techniques, interviewing skills, courtroom procedure, and legal issues. Most training programs also require candidates to do court room observation and to shadow experienced GALs.

GALs must complete annual continuing professional education seminars or events to maintain their status as a volunteer.

Experience, Special Skills, and Personality Traits

Qualifications vary from court to court. In general, GAL programs seek volunteers who have experience working with children. Candidates show a concern for children at risk, as well as demonstrate sensitivity to people from all types of backgrounds.

GALs must have excellent communication and interpersonal skills, as they need to work well with children, parents, lawyers, judges, social workers, and others. Having strong teamwork, organizational, problem-solving, and self-management skills is essential as well. Being impartial, objective, nonjudgmental, compassionate, flexible, and open-minded are some personality traits that successful GALs have in common.

Unions and Associations

The National Court Appointed Special Advocate Association serves the interests of GALs and other court-appointed advocates. (For contact information, see Appendix V.) Similar societies at the state level are also available. By joining such an organization, GALs can take advantage of networking opportunities, research findings, publications, and other professional resources and services.

Tips for Entry

1. Learn as much as you can about a GAL program before you apply to be a volunteer. Make sure you understand the role you would play, the duties you would perform, and the time commitment you would need to make.

2. To gain experience working with children at risk in court proceedings, you might become a court appointed special advocate (CASA). In many courts, judges assign CASAs to assist Guardians ad Litem with their cases. For more information about CASA volunteers, contact the family court in your city or county.

3. Use the Internet to learn more about Guardians Ad Litem. To find relevant Web sites, enter the keywords *guardians ad litem, lawyers ad litem,* or *law guardians.* For some links, see Appendix VI.

EDUCATORS

LAW PROFESSOR

CAREER PROFILE

Duties: Teach law theory, practical lawyering skills, and/or clinical courses; research and write scholarly work; perform community service; perform other duties as required

Alternate Title(s): Instructor, Assistant Professor, Associate Professor, Professor

Salary Range: $40,000 to $146,000

Employment Prospects: Fair

Advancement Prospects: Fair

Prerequisites:
  Education or Training—A law (J.D.) degree
  Experience—Attorney experience required or preferred
  Special Skills and Personality Traits—Communication, presentation, interpersonal, organizational, and management skills; be enthusiastic, flexible, inspirational, independent, self-motivated, dedicated

CAREER LADDER

```
┌─────────────────────────────┐
│         Professor           │
└─────────────────────────────┘

┌─────────────────────────────┐
│     Associate Professor      │
└─────────────────────────────┘

┌─────────────────────────────┐
│     Assistant Professor      │
└─────────────────────────────┘

┌─────────────────────────────┐
│         Instructor           │
└─────────────────────────────┘
```

Position Description

Law Professors are educators and scholars. Their job is to teach students essential legal knowledge and basic lawyering skills. They also serve as role models and mentors. These educators impress upon students the responsibility they must uphold as future attorneys to promote both individual and social justice.

Most Law Professors are lawyers with experience in private practice, the court systems, public interest organizations, corporations, government agencies, and other institutions. Many Professors continue practicing law throughout their careers as legal educators.

Most Law Professors teach doctrinal, or theory, courses. These are courses in substantive areas, such as contracts, torts, civil procedure, constitutional law, criminal law, property law, family law, estate planning, intellectual property, commercial law, and environmental law. Some Law Professors provide instruction in such practical lawyering skills as legal research, legal writing, and negotiation. Others teach in clinical programs that provide students with hands-on experiences. Clinical professors supervise students as they handle family disputes, employment issues, criminal defense, appeals, and other cases.

All Law Professors are responsible for planning the courses that they teach. They prepare their course syllabi, outlines of what will be taught in the course. They assemble course materials, which may include the use of technology, such as the Internet. In addition, they plan for each class session, preparing lecture notes and designing exercises and assignments to reinforce students' learning. Other tasks include creating examinations, evaluating students' assignments, and providing students with feedback on their work.

Law Professors teach in various settings. For example, they may lecture about constitutional law to large groups of first-year students, work one-on-one with second-year students in legal writing workshops, or lead small groups of third-year students in discussion about commercial law.

Most professors hold formal office hours so students can meet with them individually. They are available to answer questions about class assignments, as well as to advise students about career options and opportunities.

Along with their teaching, Law Professors are expected to contribute to legal scholarship by authoring academic articles, student textbooks, and court opinions. Many professors are involved in one or more research projects on legal subjects that interest them.

Professors also perform community service. They serve on faculty committees for both the law school and the university with which a law school is connected. They get involved in boards and committees for professional bar associations, community groups, and other organizations. They offer expert advice to government agencies, nonprofit organizations, and others. Many of them also perform pro bono work to legal services, public defender's offices, and public interest organizations.

Law Professors work flexible hours, which may include teaching classes at night or on weekends. The total number of hours that they work may exceed 40 hours a week. This includes time spent teaching classes, holding office hours, preparing for classes, conducting research, and serving on committees.

Salaries

Salaries for Law Professors vary, depending on such factors as their experience, rank, and geographical location. The estimated annual salary for most law instructors ranged between $39,860 and $145,600, according to the May 2005 *Occupational Employment Statistics* survey, by the U.S. Bureau of Labor Statistics.

Employment Prospects

Job opportunities at law schools typically become available as Law Professors retire, resign, or transfer to administrative positions.

Law Professors may be hired for tenure-track or non-tenure track positions. When professors become tenured they are assured a job until they retire or resign. They cannot be fired from their job without just cause and due process. Non tenure track professors (usually skills and clinical instructors) are hired on a contractual basis. They receive limited-term contracts, usually for three years. The contracts are often renewable.

Advancement Prospects

Law Professors on tenure tracks can advance through the ranks as assistant professors, associate professors, and full professors. Those with administrative ambitions can become assistant and associate deans, and eventually become deans of law schools. Such positions can lead further to executive positions in the university administration.

Education and Training

Employers generally hire candidates who possess a juris doctor (J.D.) degree, preferably from a school accredited by the American Bar Association.

Law Professors are responsible for keeping up with developments in their specialties through independent study, networking with colleagues, and participating in professional conferences and workshops.

Experience, Skills, and Personality Traits

Law schools typically choose candidates who have excellent academic credentials. They also prefer that candidates have a speciality in the substantive areas that the law schools emphasize. Many schools require that candidate be experienced attorneys.

Law Professors need excellent communication and presentation skills, as well as strong interpersonal skills to work well with students, faculty members, administrators, and others. Additionally, they should have good organizational and management skills. Being enthusiastic, flexible, inspirational, independent, self-motivated, and dedicated are some personality traits that successful Law Professors share.

Unions and Associations

Law School Professors join various professional associations to take advantage of networking opportunities and other professional services and resources. Two organizations that represent legal educators are the Society of American Law Teachers and the Clinical Legal Education Association. They may also join higher education associations such as the American Association of University Professors.

Additionally, Law Professors join local and state bar associations, as well as profession associations such as the American Bar Association, the American Association for Justice, the National Asian Pacific American Bar Association, or the National Association of Women Lawyers.

For contact information for the above organizations, see Appendix VI.

Tips for Entry

1. One way to obtain teaching experience is to become an adjunct instructor. Many law schools hire part-time teachers to teach practical lawyering skills courses.
2. Representatives from most law schools attend a hiring convention sponsored by the Association of American Law Schools to interview and hire candidates for entry-level teaching positions. For more information, visit the group's Web site at http://www.aals.org.
3. Learn more about Law Professors on the Internet. One Web site to visit is Jurist: Legal News and Research at http://jurist.law.pitt.edu. For more links, see Appendix VI.

LEGAL WRITING INSTRUCTOR

CAREER PROFILE

Duties: Teach legal writing, legal research, legal reasoning, and legal analysis skills; prepare course syllabi and create course materials; critique students' assignments; perform other duties as required

Alternate Title(s): Legal Writing Professor, Professor of Legal Research and Writing, Lecturer

Salary Range: $40,000 to $146,000

Employment Prospects: Good

Advancement Prospects: Poor

Prerequisites:

Education or Training—A law (J.D.) degree

Experience—Law practice or judicial clerkship experience; teaching experience is preferred

Special Skills and Personality Traits—Interpersonal, listening, communication, teamwork skills; be tactful, patient, caring, dedicated, flexible, creative

CAREER LADDER

```
┌─────────────────────────────────────┐
│   Legal Writing Program Director     │
└─────────────────────────────────────┘

┌─────────────────────────────────────┐
│        Professor on a tenure         │
│        or non-tenure track           │
└─────────────────────────────────────┘

┌─────────────────────────────────────┐
│         Adjunct Instructor           │
└─────────────────────────────────────┘
```

Position Description

The ability to write about the law clearly, accurately, and concisely is a necessary skill for lawyers. Thus, many law schools hire Legal Writing Instructors who are experienced attorneys as well as legal educators who specialize in teaching legal writing. Legal Writing Instructors are sometimes called legal research and writing instructors because they teach more than legal writing skills. Their instruction also includes the basics of legal research, legal analysis, and legal reasoning skills. Through progressive lessons, students learn to research topics, analyze cases and statutes, reason and argue the facts, apply the law, and write their legal analysis in court briefs, office memorandums, and other legal documents. In addition, students learn about common legal writing formats and presentation styles.

Legal Writing Instructors usually follow a curriculum designed by the legal writing program director and senior legal writing faculty. The instructors, however, are responsible for preparing their course syllabi and designing course materials. Because theirs is a required course, Legal Writing

Instructors may be assigned from 30 to 70 students each semester. Full-time instructors usually teach two or more sessions each semester.

Instructors typically teach and demonstrate new skills, then assign students research and writing exercises to practice the skills. Instructors critique and evaluate their students' work. They also hold individual sessions with students to discuss their assignments and provide them with additional help.

Along with teaching, many Legal Writing Instructors conduct research projects and produce scholarly work about their field. They write books and articles about legal writing, teaching methodology, and other topics. Some law schools provide grants to support them with their research.

Many Legal Writing Instructors are adjunct, or part-time, instructors. They are typically practicing attorneys. They usually teach one legal writing course and spend only a few hours on campus. They generally are not given offices and rarely have a voice in school policies.

Some full-time instructors are hired as assistant or associate professors on a tenure track. When professors become tenured they are assured a job until they retire or resign. They cannot be fired without just cause and due process. Other full-time Legal Writing Instructors are hired on a contractual basis. Entry-level instructors receive one- to three-year contracts which may be renewable. Some law schools limit the number of years that Legal Writing Instructors may teach on their campus.

All Legal Writing Instructors work flexible hours, which may include working nights or weekends.

Salaries

Salaries for Legal Writing Instructors are generally lower than doctrinal professors in many law schools. Salaries vary, depending on their experience, rank, geographical location, and other factors. According to the May 2005 *Occupational Employment Statistics* survey, by the U.S. Bureau of Labor Statistics, the estimated annual salary for most law instructors ranged between $39,860 and $145,000.

Employment Prospects

The legal writing field is a young but growing one. Typically, adjunct and contractual positions are more available than tenure-track positions. Some in the field expect that more law schools will begin appointing Legal Writing Instructors to tenure track so as to keep experienced teachers.

Advancement Prospects

Advancement opportunities are limited to legal writing program directorships. Most instructors pursue advancement by being appointed on tenure track, by earning higher incomes, and by gaining professional reputations in their field.

Education and Training

Legal Writing Instructors hold juris doctor (J.D.) degrees; many also possess master of law (L.L.M.) degrees.

Instructors usually learn on the job as well as through mentoring with senior faculty members. Throughout their careers, Legal Writing Instructors enroll in training and education programs to develop their teaching skills and stay current with legal subjects.

Experience, Skills, and Personality Traits

Employers generally seek candidates who possess strong academic credentials and have lawyering experience. Some employers prefer candidates who have private practice or judicial clerkship experience. Many employers also favor candidates who have teaching experience.

Legal Writing Instructors need excellent interpersonal, listening, and communication skills to work well with students, fellow teachers, and others. They also need good teamwork skills. Being tactful, patient, caring, dedicated, flexible, and creative are some personality traits that successful Legal Writing Instructors share.

Unions and Associations

Many Legal Writing Instructors are eligible to join different associations to take advantage of networking opportunities and other professional resources and services. For example, they might join the Society of American Law Teachers, which represents law professors. They might also join the Legal Writing Institute. In addition, Legal Writing Instructors might belong to professional associations that serve the interests of all professors, such as the American Association of University Professors. For contact information for these organizations, see Appendix V.

Tips for Entry

1. While you are in law school, obtain a teaching assistant position in the legal writing program to gain experience.
2. Openings for adjunct positions in legal writing programs are often filled by word of mouth. Therefore, talk with current adjuncts to learn about current or future openings.
3. For information about job openings, contact the legal writing programs or faculty at the law schools where you would like to work.
4. You can learn more about legal writing and the instructor profession on the Internet. You might start by visiting the Legal Writing Institute at http://www.lwionline.org. For more links, see Appendix VI.

LAW SCHOOL DEAN

CAREER PROFILE

Duties: Act as both chief academic and administrative leader of law schools; perform duties as required

Alternate Title(s): Dean of School of Law

Salary Range: $40,000 to $131,000

Employment Prospects: Fair

Advancement Prospects: Fair

Prerequisites:

Education or Training—On-the-job training

Experience—Be a law professor; experience in academic administration required or highly preferred

Special Skills and Personality Traits—Leadership, management, administrative, fund-raising, listening, communication, interpersonal, and team building skills; be respectful, humble, appreciative, confident, positive, energetic, dedicated

CAREER LADDER

```
┌─────────────────────────────────────┐
│   University Provost or President    │
└─────────────────────────────────────┘

┌─────────────────────────────────────┐
│           Law School Dean           │
└─────────────────────────────────────┘

┌─────────────────────────────────────┐
│    Law Professor or Associate Dean   │
└─────────────────────────────────────┘
```

Position Description

Deans provide vision and leadership to law schools, which are generally part of public and private university systems. Their job is complex and challenging as they perform various duties and tasks each day.

Law School Deans serve two roles. As chief academic officers, they oversee the development of academic programs, curriculum, services, and activities. Unlike other academic deans, Law School Deans work directly with faculty members. (In other schools, academic deans work with department chairs.) They are responsible for providing supervision and guidance to faculty, motivating them to excel in teaching and scholarship.

The other role that Law School Deans play is that of chief administrative officer. They ensure that all operations are running smoothly and effectively. Law schools have many departments and services that are separate from the universities. For example, law schools have their own admissions and financial aid departments, libraries, and career centers. Assisting Deans with their administrative duties are such managers as associate and assistant deans, admissions officers, financial officers, and law library directors.

Law School Deans perform many administrative duties, such as:

- provide guidance and supervision to their administrative staff
- supervise support staff in their offices
- manage and develop budgets
- oversee the recruitment, hiring, retention, and firing of faculty, administrative staff, and other support staff
- provide for the professional development of academic and administrative staffs
- oversee the recruitment and selection of law students

Deans also actively lead in the role of development, or fund-raising, for their schools. For example, they meet with prospective donors in business and social meetings. They also participate in fund-raising activities, such as special alumni events. Furthermore, they motivate and assist faculty in writing proposals for research grants.

In addition, Law School Deans serve on university administrative councils and committees. As part of the university administration, deans help in the development of university policies.

Law School Deans are expected to be the primary spokespersons for their schools. They interact with local, state, and national attorney bars, as well as with alumni, businesses, community leaders, government agencies, media, and others. Additionally, they participate in legal, community, social, and other types of functions and events as representatives of their schools.

Deans often travel to other cities and states to attend conferences, meet with school supporters, make public presentations, and so forth. They can be expected to work evenings and weekends to complete their many routine tasks, attend meetings or functions, and handle various matters that need immediate attention.

Salaries

Salaries for Law Deans vary, depending on their experience, school budget, geographical location, and other factors. According to the May 2005 *Occupational Employment Statistics* survey, by the U.S. Bureau of Labor Statistics (BLS), the estimated annual salary for most postsecondary educational administrators, including deans, ranged from $39,510 to $131,250.

Employment Prospects

Opportunities generally become available as Deans resign, retire, or transfer to other positions. According to the BLS, competition for such prominent positions as academic deans is keen.

Advancement Prospects

Some Deans choose to return to teaching after one or two years because they dislike the pace of administrative work. Those who have further administrative ambitions can advance to such executive positions in a university as assistant provost, provost, and, eventually, president. Some Deans pursue deanships in other law schools that offer additional challenges, higher wages, or more professional prestige.

Education and Training

Deans typically learn their duties and tasks on the job. Many enroll in training workshops and education programs for deans, which are sponsored by professional associations such as the American Bar Association or the Association of American Law Schools.

Experience, Skills, and Personality Traits

Law schools usually choose deans who are tenured law professors with a distinctive record of teaching, scholarship, and service. Previous experience in academic administration may be required or highly preferred.

Law Deans must have strong leadership abilities and effective management skills, as well as excellent administrative and fund-raising skills. They also need superior listening, communication, interpersonal, and team building skills to work well with professors, administrators, donors, and others.

Being respectful, humble, appreciative, confident, positive, energetic, and dedicated are a few personality traits that successful Law Deans have in common.

Unions and Associations

Law School Deans join various professional and bar associations to take advantage of networking opportunities and other professional resources and services. Some organizations that they join, either as individuals or as school representatives, are:

- Association of American Law Schools
- American Bar Association—Section of Legal Education and Admissions to the Bar
- NALP
- Society of American Law Teachers
- American Association of University Administrators
- American Conference of Academic Deans

For contact information, see Appendix V.

Tips for Entry

1. Enroll in management classes or training programs to develop strong managerial skills.
2. Volunteer to serve on administrative committees at your law school, as well as at your university.
3. You can learn more about Law Deans on the Internet. To find relevant Web sites, enter *law school dean* into a search engine. For some links, see Appendix VI.

PARALEGAL EDUCATOR

CAREER PROFILE

Duties: Teach basic legal knowledge and skills in formal paralegal education programs; prepare course outlines and materials; perform other duties as required

Alternate Title(s): Paralegal Instructor, Legal Assistant Instructor, Legal Studies Professor

Salary Range: $40,000 to $146,000

Employment Prospects: Fair

Advancement Prospects: Poor

Prerequisites:

Education or Training—Many have bachelor's degrees along with law degrees or other advanced degrees

Experience—Several years of lawyering or paralegal experience; experience being paralegals or working with paralegals; have teaching experience or ability

Special Skills and Personality Traits—Communication, interpersonal, organizational, and self-management skills; patient, inspiring, versatile, resourceful, creative

Special Requirements—Community college teaching credential may be required; attorney license for lawyers

CAREER LADDER

```
┌─────────────────────────────────┐
│      Professor (tenured)        │
└─────────────────────────────────┘

┌─────────────────────────────────┐
│ Instructor or Assistant Professor│
│        (tenure track)           │
└─────────────────────────────────┘

┌─────────────────────────────────┐
│      Adjunct Instructor         │
└─────────────────────────────────┘
```

Position Description

Paralegal Educators are experienced attorneys and paralegals who train legal assistants, or paralegals, in formal paralegal education programs. They teach courses that provide students with basic legal knowledge and skills to succeed in entry-level paralegal positions. (Paralegals help lawyers with routine legal tasks, such as conducting legal research, interviewing clients, drafting legal documents, and maintaining legal records.)

These educators are part of different types of paralegal programs. Some are college degree programs (associate, bachelor's, or master's), while others are professional certificate programs. A program's curriculum typically covers legal research and writing, litigation, ethics, technology, contracts, and torts. Many programs include basic courses in real property, wills, estate planning, and family law as part of their core curriculum. In addition, most programs specialize in a few substantive courses (such as criminal law, elder law, immigration law, intellectual property law,

and employment law), which depend on the requirements of the legal markets in their communities. Furthermore, most paralegal programs require students to complete an internship or another clinical experience.

Paralegal Educators are assigned to teach one or more courses. They are responsible for developing a class outline or syllabus for each course, as well as for creating daily lesson plans, class assignments, and examinations. They check students' completed assignments and exams in a timely matter and provide them with feedback. They use various teaching methods to present their lessons, such as lecture, seminar, and role playing. They also use various forms of technology, including the Internet, to supplement their teaching.

Paralegal Educators evaluate and report student performance and progress as required by their programs. They meet with students individually to provide assistance with class work as well as to counsel students about career opportunities. Paralegal Educators also complete administrative tasks such as marking attendance, filing grades, and completing required paperwork. Some educators are responsible for supervising student interns.

Paralegal Educators are expected to work together as a team with the program director and other faculty members. They assist with the development of the paralegal program, which includes making decisions about curriculum, class schedules, annual budgets, and student recruitment. Many Paralegal Educators also assist with fund-raising activities and grant proposal writing.

Paralegal Educators may be hired as adjunct, or part-time, instructors. Some are hired full time but on limited-term contracts. Others are hired for a tenure-track position, usually at an assistant professor level. Tenured educators have job security. They cannot be fired without just cause and due process.

Many Paralegal Educators, whether full-time or part-time instructors, continue working as attorneys and paralegals.

Salaries

Salaries for Paralegal Educators vary, depending on such factors as their experience, education, type of employer, and geographical location. According to the May 2005 *Occupational Employment Statistics* survey by the U.S. Bureau of Labor Statistics (BLS), the estimated annual salary for most law instructors ranged between $39,860 and $145,600.

Employment Prospects

Paralegal Educators are hired by paralegal programs in public and private colleges, universities, and other postsecondary schools. About 1,000 programs exist in the United States, according to the BLS.

Opportunities for qualified Paralegal Educators should be favorable due to the continuous demand for paralegals. The BLS reports that job growth for the paralegal profession is expected to increase by 27 percent or more through 2014.

Advancement Prospects

For those interested in administrative duties, Paralegal Educators can become program coordinators or directors. Many Paralegal Educators measure their success through any or all of the following—job satisfaction, professional recognition, and higher incomes.

Education and Training

Most Paralegal Educators have bachelor's degrees, along with law degrees or other advanced degrees in education, paralegal studies, or related fields.

Throughout their careers, Paralegal Educators enroll in education and training programs to build their skills and knowledge for training future legal assistants.

Special Requirements

To teach in community college systems, Paralegal Educators may be required to obtain a state teaching credential. For specific information, contact the community colleges where you would like to teach.

Experience, Skills, and Personality Traits

Requirements vary from employer to employer. In general, candidates must be practicing lawyers or paralegals with several years of experience in their practice areas. Lawyers must have experience working with paralegals. In addition, candidates have teaching experience or are able to demonstrate teaching ability.

Paralegal Educators need excellent communication and interpersonal skills to work well with students, faculty and others. They also must have excellent organizational skills along with strong self-management skills—such as the ability to work independently, handle several projects and tasks at the same time, and meet deadlines.

Successful Paralegal Educators share several personality traits such as being patient, inspiring, versatile, resourceful, and creative. Furthermore, they are strongly committed to providing quality paralegal education programs.

Unions and Associations

Many Paralegal Educators belong to the American Association for Paralegal Education and the American Bar Association Standing Committee on Paralegals. (For contact information, see Appendix V.) These organizations, and other local and state professional societies, specifically represent the needs of Paralegal Educators. They offer professional resources and services, such as training programs, current research data, publications, and networking opportunities.

Tips for Entry

1. As a paralegal or lawyer, you might offer your services as a guest lecturer to local paralegal programs in order to gain teaching experience.
2. Because there are hundreds of different paralegal programs in different settings, learn more about a paralegal program before taking a teaching position. For example: Is the setting one in which you wish to work? Do the program's mission and goals match yours? Does the program meet the standards of quality set by local and national paralegal associations?
3. You can use the Internet to explore the various types of paralegal programs available. To find pertinent Web sites, enter either of these keywords in a search engine: *paralegal program* or *legal assistant program.*

JUDICIAL BRANCH EDUCATOR

CAREER PROFILE

Duties: Develop and manage continuing education programs for judges and court support staff; perform other duties as required

Alternate Title(s): Judicial Educator, Judicial Education Specialist, Judicial Education Coordinator, Judicial Education Manager

Salary Range: $27,000 to $76,000

Employment Prospects: Fair

Advancement Prospects: Poor

Prerequisites:

Education or Training—A bachelor's degree in education, court administration, or related field; a law degree or other advanced degree may be required

Experience—Experience developing adult training programs is desirable; experience working in the legal field or court systems

Special Skills and Personality Traits—Communication, teamwork, interpersonal, writing, project planning and computer skills; be self-motivated, determined, organized, dedicated, creative

CAREER LADDER

```
┌─────────────────────────────────┐
│   Program Manager or Director   │
└─────────────────────────────────┘

┌─────────────────────────────────┐
│  Senior Judicial Branch Educator │
└─────────────────────────────────┘

┌─────────────────────────────────┐
│     Judicial Branch Educator     │
└─────────────────────────────────┘
```

Position Description

Judicial Branch Educators are responsible for providing educational services in the federal, state and local courts. They develop and administer educational programs for judges and other court staff, including attorneys, public defenders, social workers, juvenile officers, bailiffs, interpreters, administrators, clerks, and so on. The programs provide participants with basic knowledge and skills that help them perform their duties effectively and efficiently. For example, Judicial Branch Educators have developed orientation programs for entry-level court judges, in-service workshops for court mediators, court interpreters training programs, jury management classes, and diversity workshops. They also develop seminars on issues that judges and other court staff handle, such as child abuse and neglect, domestic violence, and developments in science.

Judicial Branch Educators fulfill roles as curriculum developers, instructional designers, and program managers. They continually develop new programs, classes, and seminars as well as update current ones. They perform a wide range of duties that vary from court to court, as well as among staff members. Some major duties include:

- conducting assessments to determine the educational needs of judges and court staff
- assisting in planning overall delivery of education services
- developing curriculum, courses, and instructional materials in collaboration with instructors, subject-matter experts, and project managers
- managing education projects, which includes such tasks as finding instructors and vendors, negotiating contracts, coordinating logistics, handling registration, and ensuring that courses comply with laws, regulations, and rules
- developing and conducting course evaluations
- conducting training sessions for trainers

- maintaining a library of tapes, books and other judicial education and training materials
- serving as a resource on trends, research, and teaching methodologies
- creating newsletters or Web pages to provide judges, court staff, and the public with information about current court decisions, laws, and other legal developments

Senior educators have additional supervisory duties, while managers (or coordinators) are also responsible for the leadership and administration of the judicial education programs as a whole.

All Judicial Branch Educators are responsible for staying up to date with trends in judicial education, as well as with emerging social, technology, and professional issues that are relevant to the judges and court support staff.

Judicial Branch Educators generally work a 40-hour week.

Salaries

Salaries for Judicial Branch Educators vary, depending on such factors as their education and experience, the size and budget of the judicial education program, and their geographical location. Judicial Branch Educators with supervisory and management responsibilities can expect to earn higher wages.

Formal salary information for this occupation is unavailable. In general, the earnings for Judicial Educators are similar to those of training specialists. According to the May 2005 *Occupational Employment Statistics* survey, by the U.S. Bureau of Labor Statistics, the estimated annual salary for most training and development specialists ranged between $26,600 and $76,300.

Employment Prospects

Most opportunities become available as Judicial Branch Educators resign or transfer to other positions. As judicial education programs are established and expand throughout the states and federal court systems, additional positions will be created. Opportunities, in general, are dependent on the availability of funding.

Advancement Prospects

Judicial Branch Educators can advance to management and administrative positions, which may require transferring from one judicial education program to another. Many employers prefer that directors possess advanced degrees.

Education and Training

Minimally, Judicial Branch Educators must possess bachelor's degrees in education, court administration, or related fields. In addition, some employers prefer that Judicial Branch Educators hold law degrees or master's degrees in education or related fields.

Judicial Branch Educators enroll in training and education programs throughout their careers to further develop their skills and knowledge.

Experience, Skills, and Personality Traits

In general, employers prefer to hire candidates who have previous experience developing training programs for adults. Additionally, some employers require that candidates have experience working in the legal field or within the court systems.

Judicial Branch Educators need excellent communication, teamwork, and interpersonal skills to work well with judges, court administrators and staff, and others. They also need strong writing and project planning skills as well as competent computer skills. Being self-motivated, determined, organized, dedicated, and creative are some personality traits that characterize successful Judicial Branch Educators.

Unions and Associations

Judicial Branch Educators join professional societies, such as the National Association of State Judicial Branch Educators, to take advantage of professional resources and services. For example, professional associations generally offer opportunities for networking with colleagues, in addition to training programs and reports of current research projects. (For contact information for the above organization, see Appendix V.)

Tips for Entry

1. Enroll in courses about adult education theory and instruction.
2. Learn as much as you can about the court systems.
3. To learn more about judicial education programs on the Internet, visit JERITT: The Judicial Education Reference, Information and Technical Transfer Project at http://jeritt.msu.edu. For more links, see Appendix VI.

LAW SCHOOL CAREER COUNSELOR

CAREER PROFILE

Duties: Provide career counseling and job search advice to law students and alumni; coordinate programs and activities as assigned; perform other duties as required

Alternate Title(s): Career Services Counselor

Salary Range: $27,000 to $73,000

Employment Prospects: Fair

Advancement Prospects: Poor

Prerequisites:

> **Education or Training**—A bachelor's degree; a law degree or master's degree in counseling strongly preferred
>
> **Experience**—Previous experience in career counseling, student services, or law firm recruitment; lawyering experience preferred
>
> **Special Skills and Personality Traits**—Organizational, interpersonal, writing, communication, and computer skills; patient, objective, friendly, supportive, tactful, trustworthy, flexible, creative

CAREER LADDER

```
┌─────────────────────────────────┐
│   Assistant Director or Director │
│     of Career Services Center    │
└─────────────────────────────────┘

┌─────────────────────────────────┐
│   Law School Career Counselor    │
└─────────────────────────────────┘

┌─────────────────────────────────┐
│   Career Counselor or Attorney   │
└─────────────────────────────────┘
```

Position Description

Most, if not all, law schools have career services centers that help law students (and alumni) with planning their careers and with finding employment. Career counselors are part of the staff at these centers. Their job is to provide law students with career development counseling. They advise students of the various traditional and alternative legal careers that are available to them. They help students identify career options and develop their career plans. Those counselors work with students in individual or group counseling sessions.

Law School Career Counselors also assist students in finding employment. They help students find part-time or summer employment as well as internships. They aid graduating students and alumni with their searches for attorney positions, judicial clerkships, and nonlawyer positions.

Furthermore, career counselors advise students of ways to develop their job search strategies and techniques. These counselors plan, organize, and lead workshops on different job search skills, such as writing a résumé, networking, and organizing a job hunt. They work with students individually to help them develop their résumés or to build their job interviewing techniques. They also counsel students about various employment issues and concerns, such as salary negotiation, career satisfaction, and what to expect on their jobs as attorneys.

Career counselors perform other duties, which vary from one counselor to the next. For example, they might:

- help develop their center's career and job reference library, which usually includes print and electronic resources
- create print and nonprint materials about alternative careers, practice areas, job search techniques, and other topics
- coordinate recruitment programs, job fairs, career conferences, and other similar programs
- help in the development and implementation of new and ongoing services, programs, and activities

- maintain working relationships with students, faculty, alumni, legal employers, legal recruiters, and others
- represent the law school at professional conferences

Career counselors in law schools work part time or full time. They may be required to work evening hours to accommodate students who work and attend classes during the day.

Salaries

Salaries for Law School Career Counselors vary, depending on such factors as their experience, education, job duties, and geographical location. According to the May 2005 *Occupational Employment Statistics* survey by the U.S. Bureau of Labor Statistics, the estimated annual salary for most education and vocational counselors ranged between $27,040 and $73,420.

Employment Prospects

Job openings usually become available as counselors retire, resign, or transfer to other positions. The creation of additional positions depends on the need for more counselors at a school, along with the availability of funds.

Advancement Prospects

Law School Career Counselors with administrative and executive ambitions can pursue positions as program directors as well as deans of career services departments. This career path may require moving from one school to the next. They can also pursue other career paths by becoming private career counselors or law firm recruiters.

Education and Training

Most law schools strongly prefer that their career counselors have a juris doctor (J.D.) degree or a master's degree in counseling, student personnel, or related field. Schools sometimes choose candidates without advanced degrees if they have extensive experience in legal career counseling.

Throughout their careers, career counselors enroll in education and training programs to keep up with career development trends as well as to build their skills.

Experience, Skills, and Personality Traits

Law School Career Counselors generally have previous experience in career counseling, student services, or law firm recruitment. Many law schools prefer that candidates have previous legal experience, such as working in law firms or serving in judicial clerkships.

Career counselors need excellent organizational and interpersonal skills, as well as superior writing and communication skills. Additionally, they should have strong computer skills, including the ability to use the Internet. Being patient, objective, friendly, supportive, tactful, trustworthy, flexible, and creative are a few personality traits that successful career counselors in law schools share.

Unions and Associations

Law School Career Counselors join local, state, and national professional associations to take advantage of education programs, networking opportunities, and other professional services and resources. Some national groups that represent career counselors are the National Career Development Association and the American Counseling Association. As representatives of their law schools, career counselors might belong to NALP, the National Association for Law Placement. Many law school Career Counselors also join and actively participate in bar associations. (For contact information for the above societies, see Appendix V.)

Tips for Entry

1. As a high school or college student, find out if counseling is the right profession for you. You might, for example, participate in a peer counseling program.
2. Gain experience in the career counseling field by volunteering or working in school career centers, community job search training programs, or government employment offices.
3. You can learn more about law school career centers on the Internet, as many centers maintain Web pages. To find a list of Web pages, enter the keywords *law school career services* or *law school career development* in a search engine.

LIBRARIANS AND
INFORMATION SPECIALISTS

ACADEMIC LAW LIBRARIAN

CAREER PROFILE

Duties: Develop and maintain library collections in law schools; provide user services, technical services, and/or administrative services; perform other duties as required

Alternate Title(s): Reference Librarian, Technical Services Librarian, or other title that reflects a specialized area

Salary Range: $41,000 to $75,000

Employment Prospects: Good

Advancement Prospects: Fair

Prerequisites:

Education or Training—A master's degree in library science; a law degree may be required

Experience—Experience in law libraries or academic settings; knowledgeable about the legal system and familiar with legal materials

Special Skills and Personality Traits—Customer service, interpersonal, communication, teamwork, management, and organizational skills; be diplomatic, efficient, adaptable, versatile, detail-minded, creative

CAREER LADDER

```
┌─────────────────────────────────┐
│   Assistant or Associate Director│
│           of Library            │
└─────────────────────────────────┘

┌─────────────────────────────────┐
│      Senior Law Librarian       │
│      or Department Head         │
└─────────────────────────────────┘

┌─────────────────────────────────┐
│      Academic Law Librarian     │
└─────────────────────────────────┘
```

Position Description

Academic Law Librarians are responsible for running the law school libraries in public and private universities. These librarians serve the needs of law students and faculty as well as law school alumni, the local legal communities, and the general public.

Staffs of trained Academic Law Librarians develop and manage diverse collections of print and nonprint materials that support the various legal courses taught at their law schools. In addition, Academic Law Librarians are involved in the scholarly process. They assist law professors with research and teach law students the basics of legal research. Many Academic Law Librarians also produce their own scholarly work.

Law school library staffs are composed of various types of librarians. Academic Law Librarians who are responsible for user services deal directly with patrons. They are typically called reference librarians and public services librarians. They provide reference services to library users, manage the circulation and reserve rooms, and oversee computer facilities. They teach classes and workshops, as well as provide individual instruction on the use of print and electronic research tools, such as CD-ROMs and electronic databases. In addition, they provide faculty with help on their research projects. In many law schools, reference librarians also have the duty of teaching legal research courses to students.

Other Academic Law Librarians provide technical services for their libraries. They are responsible for acquiring new print and electronic materials, processing and cataloguing materials, and maintaining present collections. They implement and maintain automated circulation systems as well as online systems that allow access to library catalogs at other library systems. In addition, they perform other duties as required of their specific job title, such as acquisition librarian, catalog librarian, or computer services librarian.

Academic Law Librarians also provide administrative services to their libraries. Some librarians, such as library directors and department heads, perform administrative duties exclusively. They are responsible for developing library plans, policies and procedures, and budgets. Their many duties include coordinating library activities, negotiating contracts for services, materials, and equipment, supervising and training library staff, performing public relations duties, writing grant proposals, and so forth.

Many Academic Law Librarians, particularly reference librarians, hold faculty rank and tenure. (Tenure is job security; they cannot be fired without just cause and due process.) Like other academic faculty members, they are expected to conduct research projects, publish scholarly work, and participate in faculty and community service activities.

Academic Law Librarians have flexible work schedules that may include working some evenings and weekends.

Salaries

Salaries for Academic Law Librarians vary, depending on their experience, job duties, geographical location, and other factors. According to the 2004-05 salary survey by the Association of Research Libraries, the average annual salary for Academic Law Librarians ranged between $41,330 and $74,538.

Employment Prospects

In addition to academic libraries, law librarians are employed by law firms and corporate law departments. These special librarians also find employment with court systems, government libraries, and bar associations.

Opportunities for Academic Law Librarians generally become available as individuals retire, advance to higher positions, or transfer to other jobs. The job growth for librarians overall is projected to increase by 0 to 8 percent, according to the U.S. Bureau of Labor Statistics. However, the agency also reports that opportunities should be highly favorable due to the large number of librarians who are expected to retire within the next decade. Experts in law librarianship have expressed that this also holds true in their field.

Advancement Prospects

Academic Law Librarians can advance to such administrative positions as department heads and library directors within law schools. Academic Law Librarians have also been known to be appointed to deanships and other middle management positions in law schools. Law degrees are usually required to obtain such positions.

Law Librarians who are on tenure tracks receive promotional rankings as assistant professors, associate professors, or full professors.

Education and Training

Minimally, entry-level candidates must possess a master's degree in library and information science, preferably from a program accredited by the American Library Association. Some law schools prefer to hire candidates who also hold a juris doctor (J.D.) degree. Candidates for reference librarian positions may be required to possess a J.D. degree.

Experience, Skills, and Personality Traits

Generally, employers look for candidates who have professional experience in law libraries or academic settings. They also are knowledgeable about the legal system and familiar with legal materials. In addition, candidates have the appropriate qualifications for the specific position for which they apply. For example, teaching and legal research experience are typical requirements for Research Librarians.

Regardless of their position, Academic Law Librarians should have strong customer service, interpersonal, communication, and teamwork skills, as they must work well with students, faculty, staff, and others. In addition, they need excellent management and organizational skills.

Successful Academic Law Librarians share several personality traits, such as being diplomatic, efficient, adaptable, versatile, detail-minded, and creative.

Unions and Associations

Many Law Librarians join professional associations to take advantage of networking opportunities, training programs, professional publications, and other professional resources and services. The American Association of Law Libraries, the Association of Research Libraries, and the American Library Association are a few national organizations that Academic Law Librarians join. For contact information, see Appendix V.

Tips for Entry

1. Many professional associations, such as the American Association of Law Libraries and the Special Libraries Association, award scholarships to students to help them fund their education.
2. Law Librarians who are willing to relocate may have better chances of finding the positions that they want.
3. Learn as much as you can about a prospective employer before you go to your job interview. Check out both the Web sites for the law school library and the law school. If possible, spend time visiting the library and talking with the different librarians beforehand.
4. Use the Internet to learn more about academic law librarianships. You might start by visiting the American Association of Law Libraries Web site at http://www.aallnet.org. For more links, see Appendix VI.

LAW FIRM LIBRARIAN

CAREER PROFILE

Duties: Manage libraries in private law firms; provide information support to attorneys and other staff; conduct training workshops; perform other duties as required

Alternate Title(s): Information Resources Manager, Legal Information Specialist, Legal Researcher; a title, such as Reference Librarian or Electronic Services Librarian, that reflects a specialized area (usually in large firms)

Salary Range: $30,000 to $72,000

Employment Prospects: Fair

Advancement Prospects: Poor

Prerequisites:

Education or Training—A master's degree in library and information science

Experience—Law library, business library, or legal experience; strong foundation in technology

Special Skills and Personality Traits—Research, organization, writing, communication, customer-service, interpersonal, teamwork, and self-management skills; be enthusiastic, positive, resourceful, creative, flexible

CAREER LADDER

```
┌─────────────────────────────────┐
│        Library Director         │
└─────────────────────────────────┘

┌─────────────────────────────────┐
│       Law Firm Librarian        │
└─────────────────────────────────┘

┌─────────────────────────────────┐
│   Assistant Law Firm Librarian  │
│    or Academic Law Librarian    │
└─────────────────────────────────┘
```

Position Description

Law Firm Librarians are employed by private practices to provide library services to attorneys, paralegals, and other law firm staff members. They oversee private libraries that include collections of books, journals, and other printed materials as well as CD-ROMs, electronic databases, and legal-oriented Web sites. Law Firm Librarians may work alone or be part of a team of librarians and library technicians.

In most law firms, librarians are expected to manage all library operations—that is, to provide reference services, conduct research, catalog books, develop and maintain book collections and electronic sources, plan budgets, and negotiate vendor and services contracts, among other activities. In large law firms, law librarians may specialize in specific types of services, such as reference services or electronic services.

A major responsibility of law librarians is providing information support to their law firms. Because they are more familiar with the available resources in their libraries,

Law Firm Librarians are able to quickly direct attorneys and others to the materials or databases that provide them with the information they need.

Law Firm Librarians conduct both legal and nonlegal research for attorneys, which the attorneys may incorporate into legal briefs, memorandums, and other legal documents.

Typically, librarians must deliver requests for information promptly, and they must ensure that their information is correct and accurate. Librarians use both traditional sources (printed materials) and electronic sources (computer and online databases) in their research. They might also contact other law, special, academic, or public librarians, as well as subject-matter experts.

Many law librarians provide nonlegal research to other departments in a law firm. For example, they may be asked to gather information about prospective clients or estimate the costs of research services on business proposals.

Law Firm Librarians have the responsibility of planning training programs so law firm employees can use the library resources more effectively. They may put together a library orientation for summer interns, for example; or conduct a workshop on the use of new reference publications for legal support staff. Librarians provide one-on-one instruction as well as conduct group workshops on the use of CD-ROM technology and the World Wide Web.

Furthermore, law librarians promote the library services within their firms. They might develop brochures to describe databases and services. They might write newsletters to inform employees about new acquisitions and services, as well as about new research techniques. Many also create handbooks for using the various library resources.

Law Firm Librarians work part time or full time. Most have a flexible work schedule, adapting to the demands of attorney deadlines.

Salaries

Salaries for Law Firm Librarians vary, depending on their experience, education, job duties, geographical location, and other factors. According to the May 2005 *Occupational Employment Statistics* survey by the U.S. Bureau of Labor Statistics, the estimated annual salary for most librarians overall ranged between $29,740 and $71,890. The estimated annual mean salary for librarians working in legal services was $58,490.

Employment Prospects

Law firms add or reduce staff positions to meet their needs and demands. In general, opportunities in law firms become available as librarians resign or transfer to other positions.

Advancement Prospects

Advancement opportunities for Law Firm Librarians are limited to supervisory and administrative positions, which may require moving to other law firms. Most Law Firm Librarians realize advancement through job satisfaction and higher incomes.

Some Law Firm Librarians pursue entrepreneurial paths, offering legal research services, law library management services, or consulting services to law firms.

Education and Training

Some Law Firm Librarians do not have formal training, but instead learned on the job. They were originally paralegals and attorneys who increasingly took on more legal research and library responsibilities. However, most law firms today prefer to hire candidates who hold a master's degree in library and information science from schools accredited by the American Library Association. Law degrees are usually not required, though many Law Firm Librarians have juris doctor (J.D.) degrees.

Throughout their careers, Law Firm Librarians enroll in training and education programs to increase their legal knowledge and maintain their professional skills.

Experience, Skills, and Personality Traits

In general, employers look for candidates who have law library, business library, or legal experience, or are at least familiar with legal research terminology, techniques, and materials. In addition, candidates should have a strong foundation in technology, including the ability to use hardware, software, networks, and legal and nonlegal databases.

Law Firm Librarians need excellent research, organization, writing, and communication skills to do their work effectively. Having customer-service, interpersonal, and teamwork skills is also essential to their job, as they must work well with lawyers, legal staff, vendors, and others. Further, they must possess strong self-management skills—the ability to prioritize tasks, meet deadlines, handle stress, work independently, and so on.

Being enthusiastic, positive, resourceful, creative, and flexible are a few personality traits that successful Law Firm Librarians share.

Unions and Associations

Many Law Firm Librarians join local, state, and national professional associations to take advantage of networking opportunities, training programs, professional publications, and other resources and services. The American Association of Law Libraries, the American Library Association, and the Special Libraries Association are a few organizations that represent librarians in law firms. For contact information, see Appendix V.

Tips for Entry

1. Enroll in a few courses in paralegal studies to familiarize yourself with the law, legal research, legal terminology, and so forth.
2. Build a portfolio to present at your job interviews. Some items you might include are letters of recommendation, work or school projects, and published work.
3. You can learn more about law librarianship on the Internet. To find a list of relevant Web sites, enter the keywords *law librarianship* or *law firm librarian* in a search engine. For some links, see Appendix VI.

ELECTRONIC RESOURCES LIBRARIAN

CAREER PROFILE

Duties: Implement, manage, and acquire electronic resources that meet the legal research needs of library patrons; perform duties as required

Alternate Title(s): Electronic Services Librarian, Law Librarian

Salary Range: $30,000 to $72,000

Employment Prospects: Good

Advancement Prospects: Fair

Prerequisites:

Education or Training—Master's degree in library and information science; a juris doctor (J.D.) degree may be required

Experience—One or more years of professional librarian experience; experience with electronic resources, preferably with legal resources

Special Skills and Personality Traits—Problem-solving, organizational, time management, computer, writing, communication, interpersonal, teamwork, and customer service skills; analytical, flexible, self-motivated, courteous, patient, and enthusiastic

CAREER LADDER

```
┌─────────────────────────────────────┐
│          Senior Librarian           │
└─────────────────────────────────────┘

┌─────────────────────────────────────┐
│    Electronic Resources Librarian    │
└─────────────────────────────────────┘

┌─────────────────────────────────────┐
│             Librarian               │
└─────────────────────────────────────┘
```

Position Description

Most, if not all, law libraries today have a collection of electronic resources to support the legal and general research needs of their patrons. In law schools, electronic resources are also provided to support the teaching and scholarship requirements of faculty and students. Electronic resources include software, CDs, digital resources, and Web-based resources such as electronic journals, electronic indexes, legal databases (for example, Lexis or Westlaw), research guides, online encyclopedias, e-books, and data resources (for example, data involving criminal justice, business finance, jury verdicts, or the census). These collections also consist of electronic resources that are shared with other libraries. Library users may access these electronic resources within the library as well as from remote locations.

Electronic Resources Librarians are the men and women who are responsible for the day-to-day management of a library's collection of electronic resources. Those librar-

ians who specialize in the area of law work in law schools, law firms, corporate law departments, courts, government agencies, bar associations, and other legal and legal-related organizations.

Electronic Resources Librarians engage in a wide array of projects that involve the implementation, maintenance, and procurement of electronic resources. They perform a wide range of duties, which vary every day. For example, they may be assigned to:

• administer the access to subscriptions of online resources
• monitor and troubleshoot problems with the use of electronic resources
• negotiate licensing agreements for electronic resources with vendors
• arrange trial periods for new services
• evaluate electronic resources for their usefulness to and usage by patrons

- identify, evaluate, and recommend new legal and general electronic resources
- assist in the development of new services and programs using electronic resources
- catalog electronic resources
- develop and maintain the library's Web site
- promote the availability of new and current electronic resources to patrons
- develop library instructional programs
- act as liaison with information technology personnel and vendors

Some senior Electronic Resources Librarians also carry out supervisory duties. They are responsible for directing the work of subordinates and providing them with guidance and training. As supervisors, they perform regular evaluation reports of their staff and may be involved in the selection, hiring, and firing of personnel.

Electronic Resources Librarians work directly with library patrons. They assist users who need help finding appropriate electronic resources to complete their class or work assignments. These specialists provide individual instruction as well as workshops and library tours on the types of electronic resources that are available and how to use the different resources. Academic law librarians might instruct courses on the use of electronic resources in law research, or be guest lecturers. In addition, many academic librarians are assigned to work a shift at the reference desk where they perform general reference services. They provide reference service for both print and electronic sources.

Electronic Resources Librarians typically work collaboratively with other library staff members.

These librarians may be appointed to permanent or temporary positions. In academic settings, they may be hired on a tenure track or contractual basis. Librarians who hold tenured positions are expected to teach courses, conduct research projects, publish scholarly works, and participate in school and community service.

Electronic Resources Librarians work part time or full time. Most have flexible schedules. Academic librarians may be assigned work shifts that include evenings and weekends.

Salaries

Salaries for Electronic Resources Librarians vary, depending on their education, experience, job duties, geographical location, and other factors. According to the May 2005 *Occupational Employment Statistics* survey by the U.S. Bureau of Labor Statistics, the estimated annual salary for most librarians overall ranged between $29,740 and $71,890. The estimated annual mean salary for librarians working in legal services was $58,490, and for those working in colleges and universities, $52,110.

Employment Prospects

Opportunities generally become available as individuals advance to higher positions, transfer to other jobs, or retire. Employers will create additional positions to meet growing needs, as long as funding is available.

Advancement Prospects

Librarians in nonacademic settings can pursue supervisory and managerial positions. To fill such positions, they may be required to transfer to other workplaces.

Academic librarians usually have more opportunities for advancement. They can advance to become department heads and library directors, or be appointed to middle management and deanship positions. Those on tenure tracks receive promotional rankings as assistant professor, associate professor, and full professor. Academic librarians may also seek positions in educational technology or pursue opportunities in their school's information technology department.

Education and Training

Minimally, entry-level candidates must possess a master's degree in library and information science, preferably from a program accredited by the American Library Association. Many law libraries, law firms, and other legal employers prefer to hire candidates who also hold a juris doctor (J.D.) degree, preferably from a law school accredited by the American Bar Association.

Throughout their careers, Electronic Resources Librarians enroll in continuing education and training programs to update their skills and keep up with advancements in their field.

Experience, Special Skills, and Personality Traits

Depending on the employer, candidates may need one or more years of professional library experience. Many employers prefer to hire candidates who have experience working in law libraries. Candidates also need prior experience working with electronic resources, preferably with legal resources.

Electronic Resources Librarians must have effective problem-solving, organizational, and time management skills. In addition, their work requires that they have strong computer, writing, and communication skills. They also need excellent interpersonal, teamwork, and customer service skills, as these librarians must be able to work well with patrons, colleagues, vendors, and others from diverse backgrounds. Being analytical, flexible, self-motivated, courteous, patient, and enthusiastic are some personality traits that these librarians have in common.

Unions and Associations

Electronic Resources Librarians can join professional associations to take advantage of networking opportunities, continuing education programs, current research findings, and other professional resources and services. Some national societies that serve their interests include the American Association of Law Libraries, the American Library Association, the Association of Research Libraries, and the Special Libraries Association. For contact information, see Appendix V.

Tips for Entry

1. Develop computer skills in Web development and database management.
2. Some employers conduct informational interviews for job openings at the American Association of Law Libraries annual meeting. For more information, visit the organization's Web site at http://www.aallnet.org.
3. When you apply for a job, be ready to provide the names of three professional references. Be sure to have current contact information and job titles for your references.
4. Use the Internet to learn more about electronic resources that are used in law libraries. To find relevant Web sites, enter any of these keywords into a search engine: *law electronic services librarians, electronic resources law library,* or *law electronic resources.* For some links, see Appendix VI.

LAW LIBRARY TECHNICIAN

CAREER PROFILE

Duties: Assist librarians with providing user and technical services in law libraries; perform other duties as required

Alternate Title(s): Library Assistant, Library Associate

Salary Range: $15,000 to $42,000

Employment Prospects: Good

Advancement Prospects: Fair

Prerequisites:

    Education or Training—A high school diploma; an associate degree may be required

    Experience—Previous experience working in libraries; familiarity with legal terminology and legal systems; ability to operate computers and standard office equipment

    Special Skills and Personality Traits—Customer service, interpersonal, teamwork, communication, writing, and self-management skills; flexible, detail-oriented, organized, calm, patient

CAREER LADDER

```
┌─────────────────────────────────┐
│   Senior Law Library Technician  │
└─────────────────────────────────┘

┌─────────────────────────────────┐
│      Law Library Technician      │
└─────────────────────────────────┘

┌─────────────────────────────────┐
│             Trainee              │
└─────────────────────────────────┘
```

Position Description

Law Library Technicians are paraprofessionals who provide assistance in law libraries. They may work in law schools, law firms, courts, or government agencies. Technicians work under the supervision of law librarians as they perform various user and technical services.

Their duties vary, depending on their work settings and positions. Some of their duties might include:

- maintaining library stacks and reading rooms
- moving and arranging books
- answering general questions about reference materials
- teaching patrons on how to access data on computers
- maintaining computer databases
- retrieving information from computer databases
- receiving and processing books and other library materials
- helping with cataloging and coding of library materials
- handling interlibrary loan requests
- preparing materials for binding
- assisting librarians with producing brochures, newsletters, and other publications about the library
- transporting boxes of books

Law Library Technicians also perform routine office tasks. For example, they might file papers, sort and distribute incoming mail, operate office machines, and monitor inventory of office supplies.

Technicians in private firms and government agencies may assist in conducting legal and nonlegal research as well as in preparing bibliographies. Those working in law schools may specialize in helping librarians with either user services or technical services. They may also be assigned to supervise student employees.

Law Library Technicians work part time or full time.

Salaries

Salaries for Law Library Technicians vary, depending on such factors as their education, experience, employer, and geographical location. The Bureau of Labor Statistics (BLS) reported in its May 2005 *Occupational Employment Statistics* survey that the estimated annual salary for most library technicians ranged between $15,150 and $41,540. The estimated annual mean wage for technicians working in universities was $30,280, and for those working in legal services, $37,340.

Employment Prospects

The BLS predicts that the employment growth for library technicians should increase by 9 to 17 percent through 2014. Much of this will be due to advances in technology that allow employers to assign routine tasks, such as cataloging, to technicians. In addition to job growth, library technicians will be needed to replace those who transfer to other jobs, retire, or leave the workforce for various reasons.

Advancement Prospects

With additional experience and education, Law Library Technicians can advance to supervisory and administrative positions. Some library technicians pursue library degrees to become librarians.

Many career technicians realize advancement by earning higher wages, being assigned complex responsibilities, and enjoying job satisfaction and professional recognition.

Education and Training

Law Library Technicians must have at least a high school diploma or a high school equivalency diploma. Some employers prefer to hire candidates who possess an associate degree, preferably in library science.

Technicians are usually trained on the job. Many enroll in continuing education programs throughout their careers to develop their skills and expertise in librarianship further.

Experience, Skills, and Personality Traits

In general, employers look for candidates who have previous experience working in libraries. Candidates should also be familiar with legal terminology and legal systems, and be able to operate computers and standard office equipment.

Law Library Technicians need strong customer service, interpersonal, teamwork, communication, and writing skills. In addition, they must have excellent self-management skills, such as being able to work independently, follow directions, prioritize tasks, meet deadlines, and so forth.

Some personality traits that successful Law Library Technicians share are being flexible, detail-oriented, organized, calm, and patient.

Unions and Associations

Many library technicians join local, state, and national associations to take advantage of networking opportunities, training programs, professional publications, and other professional resources and services. Many Law Library Technicians belong to the Council on Library/Media Technicians and the American Library Association. For contact information, see Appendix V.

Tips for Entry

1. As a high school student, volunteer or obtain a part-time job in your school or public library. If your school has a work experience program, try to get a placement in a law office to see what it is like to work in such a setting.
2. Enroll in computer classes as well as in general courses at community colleges to expand your knowledge and skills. Also take courses in paralegal studies to familiarize yourself with the law and terminology.
3. Consider enrolling in an associate of arts degree program in library technology, if a local community college offers such a program.
4. Contact employers for whom you would like to work directly. Along with finding out about job vacancies, ask about their selection processes.
5. Use the Internet to learn more about the work of library technicians. You might start by visiting the Council on Library/Media Technicians Web site at http://colt.ucr.edu. For more links, see Appendix VI.

KNOWLEDGE MANAGER

CAREER PROFILE

Duties: Plan, develop, implement, and maintain knowledge management systems in a law firm; perform duties as required

Alternate Title(s): Knowledge Analyst, Knowledge Architect, Chief Knowledge Officer

Salary Range: $30,000 and $72,000

Employment Prospects: Fair

Advancement Prospects: Poor

Prerequisites:

Education or Training—Master's degree in library science and information may be required

Experience—Previous work as a law librarian with knowledge management and database management experience preferred

Special Skills and Personality Traits—Leadership, management, organizational, analytical, technology, writing, communication, interpersonal, teamwork, customer service, and self-management skills; outgoing, persuasive, detail-oriented, flexible, open-minded, enterprising, and creative

CAREER LADDER

```
┌─────────────────────────────┐
│   Senior Knowledge Manager  │
└─────────────────────────────┘

┌─────────────────────────────┐
│      Knowledge Manager      │
└─────────────────────────────┘

┌─────────────────────────────┐
│    Assistant or Associate   │
│      Knowledge Manager      │
└─────────────────────────────┘
```

Position Description

Knowledge is one of the most valuable assets that every law firm owns. It is all the information that attorneys at a law firm have and know about legal matters, cases, and clients, and which can be shared with others in the firm. Many law firms employ specialists known as Knowledge Managers to help them harness their intellectual assets to improve their efficiency and profitability.

Knowledge Managers envision how to connect people's knowledge through the aid of technology. In law firms, they are not only dealing with legal knowledge but also knowledge from the accounting, marketing, client development, administrative, and other departments. Their responsibilities include planning, developing, implementing, and maintaining knowledge management systems that allow attorneys and other staff members to access their law firm's knowledge easily from their computer desktops or remotely through the Internet. For example, lawyers might use their firm's knowledge management database to examine contracts similar to the ones they are working on, or to seek information about litigation consultants who were used by other attorneys, or to find out how much clients have been billed so that lawyers can negotiate settlements.

Knowledge Managers work with legal technology specialists to devise systems that attorneys and other staff can use as tools to help them accomplish their work more effectively. Because every law firm has different needs, Knowledge Managers seek to find the right balance of technology that accomplishes the goals and objectives of their employers. These specialists develop and put into practice various knowledge management strategies such as

- intranets—computer networks that are used to share information only within law firms
- Web portals, which are Web sites that act as the starting point to other resources on intranets or extranets

- intuitive search tools, including search engines, metasearchers, and directories
- data mining tools to search through databases
- weblogs, or blogs, which are journals or newsletters authored by individual lawyers or practice groups, who update them on a regular basis
- automated document assembly tools, which help attorneys draft routine tasks

Knowledge Managers are also in charge of the collection, storage, and flow of all the countless bits of information in law firms that lawyers, paralegals, legal administrators, marketing specialists, accountants, and other staff members create daily regarding legal, business, and marketing matters. Organizing the enormous amount of information is one of their major challenges. It involves identifying what information needs to be stored from databases, documents, records, policies, and procedures, as well as from knowledge that staff members have not put down in written form. Knowledge Managers also need to determine how to classify all of the knowledge into a context that is applicable to the various practice areas in a law firm.

To ensure they are meeting the informational needs of law firms, Knowledge Managers frequently communicate with attorneys and other staff members. These knowledge professionals attend meetings, use surveys, engage in one-on-one conversations, and apply other means to learn about staff priorities, the expectations that staff members have of knowledge management systems, what informational needs have changed, and other matters.

Knowledge Managers are responsible for keeping up with new and emerging knowledge management technologies and developments. They read books, journals, and other publications about the knowledge management field. They also attend workshops and conferences. In addition, they network with colleagues from other law firms as well as with knowledge professionals who work in other industries.

Knowledge leadership varies from one law firm to the next. In some law firms, a law librarian is assigned the additional duties performed by a Knowledge Manager. In some firms, the Knowledge Manager is the sole member of the knowledge staff, while in other firms, Knowledge Managers lead a staff of knowledge specialists. In law firms with a large knowledge staff, chief knowledge officers oversee the knowledge management operations. These officers are usually part of the information technology division.

Some Knowledge Managers perform dual roles in law firms. For example, they may also work in the capacity of a training manager or a compliance manager.

Entry-level employees are assistant or associate Knowledge Managers. In addition to working on Intranet design and implementation, many of them perform traditional law library functions such as reference services, legal research, and management of print and electronic resources collections.

Knowledge Managers work a 40-hour schedule but put in additional hours as needed to complete their tasks. Some Knowledge Managers are hired on a temporary basis.

Salaries

Salaries for Knowledge Managers vary, depending on such factors as their education, experience, employer, and geographical location. Specific salary information for this occupation is unavailable. In general, many of them earn salaries similar to librarians. The estimated annual salary for most librarians overall ranged between $29,740 and $71,890, according to the May 2005 *Occupational Employment Statistics* survey by the U.S. Bureau of Labor Statistics.

Employment Prospects

Knowledge management is a young field, which emerged during the 1990s. It is continually evolving as it grows. Opportunities for Knowledge Managers are available in various industries, in the United States, as well as worldwide.

Within legal services, job opportunities are mostly found in large law firms. Small and mid-size firms as well as corporate law departments sometimes hire knowledge professionals. In general, opportunities become available as Knowledge Managers transfer to other jobs, advance to higher positions, or leave the workforce for various reasons.

Many law firms do not have a staff of professionals dedicated to knowledge management. These firms usually assign their librarians to handle knowledge management issues and initiatives. As more law firms grasp the benefits of employing knowledge management professionals, the demand for Knowledge Managers will grow.

Advancement Prospects

Knowledge Managers can advance to supervisory and administrative positions, which may require seeking positions with other employers. Most professionals realize advancements through higher wages, job satisfaction, and professional recognition.

Individuals with entrepreneurial ambitions can become independent consultants or owners of firms that offer knowledge management consulting services.

Education and Training

Educational requirements vary among employers. Many employers prefer to hire candidates who have a master's degree in library and information science or another related degree. Some employers hire candidates who possess a bachelor's degree in library science or another discipline if they have qualifying work experience.

Many employers also prefer candidates who have completed course work or continuing professional education in knowledge management.

Throughout their careers, Knowledge Managers enroll in continuing education programs and training programs to update their skills and knowledge.

Experience, Special Skills, and Personality Traits

Employers usually prefer to hire candidates who have a few years of experience as law librarians in law firms, legal departments, academic law libraries, or other legal settings. They also seek candidates who have prior experience performing knowledge management and database management tasks.

The nature of their work requires Knowledge Managers to have excellent leadership, management, organizational, and analytical skills as well as superior technology and writing skills. They also need exceptional communication, interpersonal, teamwork, and customer service skills, as they must be able to work well with attorneys, paralegals, managers, and others from diverse backgrounds. Additionally, Knowledge Managers must have strong self-management skills such as the ability to prioritize multiple tasks, meet deadlines, understand and follow complex instructions, and work independently.

Some personality traits that successful Knowledge Manager share include being outgoing, persuasive, detail-oriented, flexible, open-minded, enterprising, and creative.

Unions and Associations

Knowledge Managers may join professional organizations to take advantage of networking opportunities, continuing education programs, and other professional services and resources. They are eligible for membership in the Knowledge Management Professional Society, an international society that serves knowledge professionals in all industries. Those with librarian backgrounds can belong to professional library societies such as the American Association of Law Libraries, the American Library Association, and the Special Libraries Association. For contact information, see Appendix V.

Tips for Entry

1. Talk with Knowledge Managers, particularly those working in law firms, to learn more about their jobs. Find out how they got into this field, and ask for suggestions on how to enter the field.
2. Oftentimes, jobs are found through word of mouth. When doing a job search, contact former co-workers, supervisors, and professors. Also talk with attorneys, law librarians, legal technology specialists, legal administrators, and others in the legal services.
3. Do your homework about a law firm before you go for an interview.
4. A law firm may have knowledge management professionals who work in their library or technology department.
5. Use the Internet to learn more about the knowledge management field. You might start by visiting these Web sites: Association of Knowledgework, http://www.kwork.org, and Knowledge Management Network, http://www.brint.com/km. For more links, see Appendix VI.

COMMUNICATIONS
PROFESSIONALS

LEGAL REPORTER

CAREER PROFILE	CAREER LADDER

Duties: Provide objective and accurate reports about people, events, issues, and other happenings in the legal community; perform duties as required

Alternate Title(s): Legal Journalist, Legal Affairs Reporter, Legal Correspondent

Salary Range: $18,000 to $71,000

Employment Prospects: Fair

Advancement Prospects: Fair

Prerequisites:

  Education or Training—A bachelor's degree; a law degree may be required or preferred

  Experience—Several years of journalism experience; legal experience is desirable

  Special Skills and Personality Traits—Writing, organization, research, communication, listening, interpersonal, computer, and self-management skills; be energetic, detail-oriented, patient, persistent, impartial, resourceful, composed, adaptable, creative

```
┌──────────────────────────────┐
│  Principal Reporter or Editor │
└──────────────────────────────┘

┌──────────────────────────────┐
│           Reporter            │
└──────────────────────────────┘

┌──────────────────────────────┐
│        Novice Reporter        │
└──────────────────────────────┘
```

Position Description

Legal Reporters provide the news about people, events, and issues in the legal community. They report on trials, court decisions, proposed bills, new regulations, legislative meetings, lawmakers, judges, attorneys, professional conferences, legal-related professions, and so on. Their job is to gather the facts and to summarize them clearly and comprehensively. The stories may take place at the local, state, or national level.

Many Legal Reporters write for trade publications (newspapers, magazines, and newsletters) that cover only legal topics and events in the legal community. The audience for these publications consists of attorneys and other legal professionals. Trade publications are available in printed or electronic formats. Some publications are nationwide, while others serve a particular state or region. Smaller publications usually specialize in a specific practice area such as employment, immigration, or public interest law.

Legal Reporters also write for the general daily newspapers as well as alternative weekly or monthly newspapers.

They are usually known as legal affairs reporters. A few Legal Reporters work for radio and TV stations and read their news reports on the air. Some Legal Reporters are freelance journalists.

Legal Reporters keep their eyes and ears open at all times for leads and tips for breaking news. They read press releases and announcements. They observe legislative meetings and court trials, as well as attend press conferences and other special events. In addition, they routinely talk with public relations staff and other sources in courthouses, legislatures, government agencies, professional associations, law firms, and other groups.

Legal Reporters are constantly under pressure to meet their deadlines. Thus, they gather details efficiently, yet thoroughly. They interview eyewitnesses as well as those who are directly involved in the events. Some reporters also take photographs for their stories. In addition, reporters conduct research for background information. For example, they consult with subject-matter experts, read books and articles, and search for information on the Internet.

Legal Reporters are able to organize their notes quickly and decide on the best structure for their stories. They write their stories so people can see, hear, smell, and feel as if they were there. They double-check dates and figures, the spelling of names and places, the correct professional titles of people, and other facts.

All journalists are responsible for reporting the news objectively, and for making sure that facts are accurate. Reporters and their publications can be sued for any untrue or libelous statements that they make. Thus, reporters find persons, documents, or other reliable sources that can verify information for them.

With the smaller legal publications, reporters may also be assigned to the editor role. As editors, they are responsible for putting together each issue. For example, they decide what stories should be covered, when stories are due, where stories should be placed in an issue, and what headlines should be. Editors also review stories to make sure they are newsworthy and accurate. They copyedit stories for clarity and length as well as for grammar, spelling, and punctuation errors.

Legal Reporters work long and irregular hours in order to follow up on story ideas or to meet deadlines.

Salaries

Salaries for Legal Reporters vary, depending on such factors as their experience, personal ambition, employer, and geographical location. According to the May 2005 *Occupational Employment Statistics* survey by the U.S. Bureau of Labor Statistics, the estimated annual salary for most reporters ranged between $18,300 and $71,220.

Employment Prospects

Opportunities are available for reporters in the different types of media, such as print, online, and television. In general, Legal Reporter positions become available as individuals retire, transfer to other jobs or advance to higher positions. Occasionally, opportunities open when legal newspapers add another news bureau or when legal newsletters are created.

Advancement Prospects

Legal Reporters generally realize advancement by earning higher incomes, receiving more complicated assignments, and being recognized for the high quality of their work.

Depending on their ambitions and interests, Legal Reporters may become columnists, special correspondents, legal analysts, and book authors, as well as editors, news bureau directors, and legal publishers. Legal Reporters might pursue other careers, becoming educators, attorneys, politicians, public relations professionals, or novelists.

Education and Training

Requirements vary, with the different employers. Minimally, Legal Reporters need a bachelor's degree in journalism, communications, or an other field. Many employers prefer to hire reporters with law degrees.

Experience, Skills, and Personality Traits

Employers generally require that applicants have several years of journalism experience. Having legal experience is desirable. Some employers are willing to hire lawyers without journalism experience if they demonstrate a willingness and an aptitude for reporting.

Legal Reporters need excellent writing, organizational, and research skills. Their job also requires that they have excellent communication, listening, and interpersonal skills. In addition, Legal Reporters should have adequate computer skills. Further, they need good self-management skills, such as the ability to handle stressful situations, meet deadlines, work independently, take initiative, and juggle various tasks. Being energetic, detail-oriented, persistent, impartial, resourceful, composed, adaptable, and creative are some personality traits that successful Legal Reporters share.

Unions and Associations

Many Legal Reporters join professional associations to take advantage of networking opportunities and other professional services and resources. Some national societies that serve the diverse interests of reporters include the Society of Professional Journalists, the Criminal Justice Journalists, the Investigative Reporters and Editors, the National Writers Union, and the American Society of Journalists and Authors. For contact information, see Appendix V.

Tips for Entry

1. Some courses that you might take in high school or college to prepare for a reporting career are journalism, English, and social studies.
2. As a student, obtain an internship or part-time job with a local newspaper or other news organization.
3. Build a portfolio of your published work, as publishers will want to see your writing samples.
4. Contact the publications where you would like to work about their job opportunities. Ask about both permanent and freelance positions that may be available.
5. Learn more about reporting careers on the Internet. You might start by visiting these Web sites: Investigative Reporters and Editors, http://www.ire.org; and The Working Reporters, http://www.workingreporter.com. For more links, see Appendix VI.

BOOK EDITOR

CAREER PROFILE

Duties: Develop and acquire new legal titles for publishers, general book publishers, or university presses; develop and edit manuscripts; maintain relationships with authors; perform other duties as required

Alternate Title(s): Acquisition Editor, Development Editor, Legal Editor, Case Law Editor, Attorney Editor

Salary Range: $27,000 to $85,000

Employment Prospects: Fair

Advancement Prospects: Good

Prerequisites:

Education or Training—A bachelor's degree; a law degree may be required or preferred

Experience—Book publishing experience; legal experience or background required or highly preferred

Special Skills and Personality Traits—Writing, research, interpersonal, communication, teamwork, and self-management skills; be tactful, creative, flexible, organized, detail-oriented, decisive, adaptable

CAREER LADDER

```
┌─────────────────────────────┐
│       Senior Editor         │
└─────────────────────────────┘

┌─────────────────────────────┐
│          Editor             │
└─────────────────────────────┘

┌─────────────────────────────┐
│ Assistant Editor; for Case Law │
│  Editors, Attorney or Law Student │
└─────────────────────────────┘
```

Position Description

Hundreds of new titles about law and legal topics are published each year by legal publishers as well as by general book publishers and by university presses. These include biographies, scholarly monographs, self-help legal books, law textbooks, legal manuals, practice guides, case reporters, code books, and so forth. Many publishers also publish non-print materials such as CD-ROMs, audiotapes, and online resources.

Book Editors are responsible for acquiring and developing new titles that meet their publishing house's mission and goals. They review proposals and manuscripts submitted by authors and agents, and recommend those that editors think are publishable to editorial committees, which accept or reject them. Book Editors also propose ideas for new titles and seek legal experts to develop book proposals and manuscripts.

Book Editors are responsible for overseeing the development of manuscripts. They work closely with authors as they first develop content outlines and later write their manuscripts. Editors review drafts and provide authors with suggestions and comments to improve the manuscripts. For example, they might point out gaps in logic, lack of focus, organizational problems, and unclear language. Editors monitor authors' progress to ensure that deadlines are being met.

Book Editors edit finished manuscripts for content and clarity. They also edit manuscripts so they meet their publishing house's formats and standards. Some editors copyedit and prepare manuscripts for production. Book Editors release final manuscripts to production departments, where manuscripts are turned into book pages for printing.

Editors usually manage several titles simultaneously, which requires working with several authors at a time. In addition, Editors perform a variety of related duties. They may:

- monitor the progress of manuscripts through the production and printing stages
- prepare editorial costs and schedules for individual titles

- help sales and marketing departments plan and develop promotions and publicity for new titles
- conduct research on markets, competition, legal trends, and developments in the legal publishing industry
- provide legal expertise and knowledge in product content as well as design and development of products

In some publishing houses, different Book Editors fill separate roles. Acquisition editors are in charge of acquiring new titles and maintaining relationships with authors. They also review manuscripts and may perform content editing. Development editors are responsible for editing manuscripts and overseeing their progress through the editorial and production stages.

Editors of case reporters are commonly called legal editors or attorney editors. (A case reporter is the published compilation of a court's decisions and opinions, also known as court reports.) They are responsible for all legal content. They provide legal analysis and interpretation, as well as write and edit case law summaries, notes, and headings.

Many editors travel to professional conferences to give presentations and workshops, or to work in publishers' booths to answer questions about the various products. Editors sometimes meet prospective authors at these conferences.

Editors often put in additional hours on evenings and weekends to meet deadlines.

Salaries

Salaries for Book Editors vary depending on such factors as their education, experience, and geographical location. According to the U.S. Bureau of Labor Statistics, in its May 2005 *Occupational Employment Statistics* survey, the estimated annual salary for most editors ranged between $26,910 and $85,230.

Employment Prospects

Editors of law and legal-related books are hired by legal publishers as well as by legal professional associations, such as the American Bar Association, which have publishing units. Many general book publishers and university presses hire editors to manage and oversee their line or division of legal titles.

Generally, opportunities become available as Book Editors advance to other positions or transfer to other publishing houses.

Advancement Prospects

Editors can advance to supervisory and management positions, such as managing editors, editorial directors, vice presidents, and publishers. Advancing through the ranks may require moving from one publishing house to the next.

Education and Training

Requirements vary among the different employers. Minimally, Editors must hold bachelor's degrees in any field. Most legal publishers prefer to hire editors who possess law degrees. They may hire candidates without law degrees if they have qualifying experience.

Experience, Skills, and Personality Traits

Acquisitions and developmental editors generally come up through the ranks of editorial assistants and assistant editors. To become editors of law and legal-related books, candidates should have legal experience or training. Employers may hire nonattorneys or those with no legal training if they have qualifying experience in legal publishing.

Editors need excellent writing and research skills for their jobs. They also must have strong interpersonal, communication, and teamwork skills, as they must work well with authors, editorial staff, and other departments. In addition, they need strong self-management skills, such as being able to meet deadlines, juggle several tasks at the same time, work independently, and handle stress.

Some personality traits that successful Editors share are being tactful, creative, flexible, organized, detail-oriented, decisive, and adaptable.

Unions and Associations

Many Editors join professional associations to take advantage of networking opportunities and various professional services and resources. Legal Book Editors are eligible to join the Association for Continuing Legal Education. For contact information, see Appendix V.

Tips for Entry

1. Contact publishing houses directly for information about job openings and job requirements.
2. Publishers sometimes hire development and legal editors for part-time and temporary (or freelance) positions.
3. Learn as much as you can about a publisher before being interviewed. Many publishers have Web sites on the Internet.
4. Use the Internet to learn more about the book publishing industry. You might start by visiting the Association of American Publishers Web site at http://www.publishers.org. For more links, see Appendix VI.

WEB DESIGNER

CAREER PROFILE

Duties: Develop and design Web sites and Web pages for information, e-commerce, marketing, or other purposes; perform duties as required

Alternate Title(s): Web Developer; a title that reflects a specialty such as Web Site Architect or Multimedia Designer

Salary Range: $40,000 to $100,000

Employment Prospects: Good

Advancement Prospects: Good

Prerequisites:

Education or Training—Varies, but usually a college degree required

Experience—Experience creating Web sites required; proficiency with HTML, scripting languages, and graphic design and layout software; understanding of visual communication and design

Special Skills and Personality Traits—Project management, organizational, writing, communication, interpersonal, teamwork, and self-management skills; creative, detail-oriented, precise, flexible, and patient

CAREER LADDER

```
┌─────────────────────────────┐
│     Senior Web Designer      │
└─────────────────────────────┘

┌─────────────────────────────┐
│        Web Designer          │
└─────────────────────────────┘

┌─────────────────────────────┐
│     Web Graphic Designer     │
└─────────────────────────────┘
```

Position Description

Attorneys, bar associations, legal societies, courts, law schools, legal publishers, law libraries, and legislatures are just some legal and legal-related groups that maintain a presence on the World Wide Web. They use their Web sites for various purposes, including information, e-commerce, marketing, and public relations. Web Designers are responsible for creating and designing these Web sites. They may be in-house staff members, employees of web design contracting or consulting services, or independent contractors.

Web Designers are involved in building Web sites from their conception to online publication. Their job is to produce Web sites that fulfill the visions of their clients or employers. These professionals combine design, illustration, art, and computer science to make high quality Web sites that are appealing and attractive to users as well as easy for them to access.

Depending on the size and complexity of a project as well as their experience, Web Designers work alone or as part of a Web development team. Experienced professionals may be designated as project team leaders.

Their projects go through several phases. First, Web Designers plan the overall design of Web sites. They work with project managers, programmers, information architects, marketing professionals, and others to determine the purpose and objectives of Web sites, their intended audience, how Web sites should look, the most efficient way for users to navigate Web sites, and other essential elements.

In the development phase, Web Designers gather information to learn more about the subject matter. They interview clients (or employers) and their staff, as well as seek relevant data and literature. They review brochures, slide presentations, or other written materials that they need to integrate into Web sites. Next, they design the structure, look, and feel of the sites. They create graphics, choose fonts and other visual elements, and design layouts. They may also incorporate animations, search engines, advertising, e-commerce features, and other essentials into Web sites. Additionally, these designers develop strategies that allow the sites to be modified as information and features need to be updated or changed. Their work also involves testing Web sites to ensure all hyperlinks and features function correctly. Clients or employers review Web Designers' final work. The designers make any changes that are requested before the Web sites are published.

Web Designers may also be assigned to maintain Web sites. Their job is to update sites as needed. For example, attorneys may want to announce additional services, provide new information, or change addresses at their Web sites.

Web Designers are responsible for completing their assigned projects in a timely manner and within the allocated budget. They are expected to work quickly but precisely and accurately as they create Web sites and web pages. They also provide regular work status reports to clients or employers as well as to other people involved in a project.

Entry-level Web Designers are assigned to perform routine tasks, such as creating navigational tools and other graphic elements for Web sites. As they gain experience and increase their skills, Web Designers are assigned more difficult tasks as well as greater responsibilities, including being responsible for designing entire Web sites. Experienced Web Designers may also specialize in a particular aspect of Web development. For example, many of them become user interface designers, who are responsible for how information is presented on Web sites, or Web site architects, who are responsible for helping companies meet their business goals through the Web environment.

All Web Designers are responsible for their own professional development. Through independent study, educational and training programs, and networking with colleagues, Web Designers keep up with technologies, techniques, and design standards that are continually being developed.

Independent contractors also have the duty of ensuring that their businesses run smoothly. They attend to such tasks as doing bookkeeping, pay bills and taxes, sending invoices to clients, maintaining office supplies and equipment, and generating new business.

Web Designers' work is oftentimes stressful, particularly when they are assigned to several projects at a time or when they must meet tight deadlines. Because they spend many hours working with computers, they may develop various physical problems such as eyestrain, back discomfort, and carpal tunnel syndrome.

Web Designers may work full time or part time. They may be employed permanently or on a temporary basis, which is usually for the length of the project on which they work. Many Web Designers put in more than 40 hours a week to complete their tasks and meet deadlines. Independent contractors usually travel to meet with clients at their offices.

Salaries

Salaries for Web Designers vary, depending on such factors as their education, experience, employer, and geographical location. According to the Wetfeet.com Web site (in May 2006), Web Designers generally earned between $40,000 to $100,000 per year.

Employment Prospects

Web Designers can find employment with small Web design firms, Internet consulting firms, and graphic design studios, as well as advertising, marketing, and public relations companies. Large law firms, legal publishers, courts, government agencies, and other legal-related establishments hire in-house Web Designers. Many Web Designers are independent contractors or owners of Web design firms.

Companies, institutions, and other organizations will continually hire Web Designers to create and maintain a presence for them on the Internet. Job opportunities in the legal industry, as well in every industry, are favorable for Web Designers who keep up with the newest technologies.

Advancement Prospects

Web Designers can advance in any number of ways, depending on their interests and ambitions. They can become technical specialists, project team leaders, supervisors, and managers. They can seek partnerships in consulting or design firms. Those with entrepreneurial ambitions can pursue their careers as independent contractors or owners of Web design companies.

Many Web Designers measure their success by earning higher incomes, through job satisfaction, and with professional recognition.

Education and Training

Educational requirements vary with different employers. Some employers require only an associate degree, while others prefer that candidates possess a bachelor's degree. The degree may be in Web design, computer science, graphic design, digital media, fine arts, or another related field. Employers may hire strong candidates with degrees in marketing, advertising, or other disciplines, if they have advanced computer training or qualifying work experience.

Experience, Special Skills, and Personality Traits

Requirements for entry-level Web Designers vary among employers. In general, they require that candidates have experience creating Web sites. Novice Web Designers may have gained their experience through professional certification programs, volunteer work, or part-time employment, for example. Entry-level candidates must be proficient with HTML, scripting languages (such as JavaScript), and graphic design and layout software (such as Adobe Photoshop and Dreamweaver). They must also have a fundamental understanding of visual communication and design. Many legal employers prefer that candidates have a general understanding of their fields.

Web Designers must have excellent project management, organizational, writing, and communication skills to be effective at their job. In addition, they need strong interpersonal and teamwork skills, as they must be able to work with many different people from various backgrounds. Web Designers also must have solid self-management skills, such as the ability to work independently, meet deadlines, prioritize multiple tasks, and understand and follow instructions.

Some personality traits that successful Web Designers have in common include being creative, detail-oriented, precise, flexible, and patient.

Unions and Associations

Web Designers can join professional associations to take advantage of professional certification, training programs, networking opportunities, and other professional resources and services. Two societies that they might join at the national (or international) level are the International Webmasters Association and the Society for Technical Communication. For contact information, see Appendix V.

Tips for Entry

1. While in high school, enroll in computer and art classes to start building up your skills.
2. Gain experience by volunteering to build Web sites for nonprofit organizations.
3. Many Web Designers enhance their employability by completing certification programs offered by software publishers.
4. Keep a portfolio of your best pieces of work. Prospective employers or clients will want to see examples of your creativity and technical skills.
5. Use the Internet to learn more about Web design work in the legal industry. To find relevant Web sites enter the keywords *legal web design* in a search engine. For some links, see Appendix VI.

MANAGERS AND ADMINISTRATORS

NONPROFIT ORGANIZATION (NPO) DIRECTOR

CAREER PROFILE

Duties: Provide organizational leadership and direction; oversee administrative operations; develop fund-raising; perform other duties as required

Alternate Title(s): Chief Executive Officer

Salary Range: $60,000 to $146,000

Employment Prospects: Good

Advancement Prospects: Good

Prerequisites:

Education or Training—A college degree in any field

Experience—Experience working in nonprofit settings; supervisory, administrative, and management experience

Special Skills and Personality Traits—Leadership, management, organizational, problem-solving, team building, interpersonal, communication, writing, business, and public relations skills; be creative, flexible, optimistic, visionary, self-motivated, diplomatic, dedicated

CAREER LADDER

```
┌─────────────────────────────┐
│     Executive Director       │
└─────────────────────────────┘

┌─────────────────────────────┐
│     Assistant Director       │
└─────────────────────────────┘

┌─────────────────────────────┐
│       Staff Member           │
└─────────────────────────────┘
```

Position Description

A nonprofit organization (NPO) is a group that sponsors a public interest or social concern for noncommercial purposes. In other words, an NPO is not engaged in making money from its promotions and activities. Examples of NPOs include public interest organizations, trade and professional associations, schools, community organizations, social services, religious groups, foundations, and charities. These organizations are involved in a wide range of areas, such as the arts, education, healthcare, animal rights, affordable housing, consumer rights, the environment, politics, and legal assistance for the poor.

NPO Directors are responsible for providing leadership and direction for their organizations. They also serve as the liaison between an organization's staff and its board of directors. NPO Directors work closely with their board of directors to formulate objectives, policies, and strategies that carry out an organization's mission and goals.

They oversee the development, delivery, and quality of the services, products, and programs that nonprofit organizations offer. For example, a community organization might offer a job training program, legal referral services, and youth counseling to its target clientele. In small organizations, NPO Directors perform some hands-on work. They might, for example, lead workshops, write educational pamphlets, or provide direct services to clients.

Additionally, NPO Directors plan, coordinate, and manage the day-to-day operations of their organizations. They work with staff to ensure that fiscal and administrative systems are running smoothly and efficiently. This includes planning and managing budgets, paying salaries, bills, and taxes, completing compliance reports, managing facilities, organizing business meetings, and so forth. In small and mid-size nonprofit organizations, NPO Directors may be responsible for overseeing all administrative duties, while in large organizations NPO Directors work with department managers.

NPO Directors are also responsible for managing human resources. They oversee the recruitment and hiring of paid and volunteer staff, as well as provide for training on an ongoing basis. Directors establish policies and procedures to comply with laws and regulations.

The continuing existence of nonprofit organizations depends on grants and donations. Consequently, fund-raising is a major duty of NPO Directors. They write and submit grant proposals, plan for fund-raising events, and meet with prospective donors.

NPO Directors are the spokespersons for their organizations. Therefore, public relations is another important duty they must handle. In addition, they develop and maintain various external relationships with government officials, donors, the media, other nonprofit organizations, their target clientele, and the community at large.

Each day is unique and challenging for NPO Directors. They continually juggle their various duties, working on multiple tasks and projects at the same time. They often work into the evenings and on weekends.

Salaries

Salaries for NPO Directors vary, depending on such factors as their experience, job duties, employer, and geographical location. According to the May 2005 *Occupational Employment Statistics* survey, by the U.S. Bureau of Labor Statistics, the estimated annual salary for most chief executive officers ranged between $59,990 and $145,600. A salary survey report by *The Nonprofit Times* reports the overall 2005 average salary for NPO executive directors as being $92,411.

Employment Prospects

About 1.5 million nonprofit organizations of all sizes exist in the United States. Job openings typically become available as NPO Directors retire, resign, or transfer to other positions. Opportunities should be favorable for qualified candidates in the coming years. According to some experts in the field a large number of NPO executives will be reaching retirement age over the next decade.

Advancement Prospects

NPO Directors typically realize advancement through professional recognition, higher salaries, the addition of more complex responsibilities, and the success of their organizations.

One career option for NPO Directors is to become nonprofit management consultants.

Education and Training

Many employers prefer that NPO Directors have bachelor's or advanced degrees in disciplines related to the services the organizations provide. For example, a family services organization may prefer its director to hold a master's degree in social services, or a legal services organization may require its director to have a law degree.

Throughout their careers, NPO Directors enroll in continuing education and training programs to develop and maintain their professional skills and expertise.

Experience, Skills, and Personality Traits

Employers generally choose candidates who have extensive experience working in nonprofit settings. Additionally, they should have several years of supervisory, administrative, and management experience in nonprofit settings.

NPO Directors must have excellent leadership, management, organizational, problem-solving, and team building skills. They also need superb interpersonal, communication, and writing skills along with good business and public relations skills. Some personality traits that NPO Directors share are being creative, flexible, optimistic, visionary, self-motivated, diplomatic, and dedicated.

Unions and Associations

NPO Directors join professional associations to take advantage of networking opportunities, continuing education programs, and other professional resources and services. One organization that represents nonprofit managers is the Alliance for Nonprofit Management. For contact information, see Appendix V.

Tips for Entry

1. In high school, you can start gaining experience by joining community youth groups that perform public service projects. Or volunteer with a nonprofit organization in your community that supports a cause in which you are interested—such as animal rights, environment, education, or library issues.
2. In college, obtain an internship with a nonprofit organization.
3. Talk with NPO Directors for recommendations of college courses that would be helpful in their work.
4. Use the Internet to find job listings nationwide. Some Web sites that post vacancies for staff as well as managerial and administrative positions in NPOs are: Idealist.org, http://www.idealist.org, ExecSearches.com, http://www.execsearches.com, and CEOupdate.com, http://www.ceoupdate.com.

ASSOCIATION EXECUTIVE

CAREER PROFILE	CAREER LADDER

Duties: Manage (or assist in the management of) the daily operations of a professional, trade, charitable, or philanthropic association; perform duties as required

Alternate Title(s): Executive Director, or a specific title, such as Director of Finance, that reflects a particular department

Salary Range: $133,000 to $146,000

Employment Prospects: Good

Advancement Prospects: Fair

Prerequisites:

Education or Training—A bachelor's degree or equivalent

Experience—Several years of executive management experience; knowledge of the trade of profession

Special Skills and Personality Traits—leadership, management team building, interpersonal, communication, writing, financial management, and public relations skills; be hardworking, analytical, organized, flexible, creative

```
┌─────────────────────────────┐
│      Executive Director      │
└─────────────────────────────┘

┌─────────────────────────────┐
│       Program Director       │
└─────────────────────────────┘

┌─────────────────────────────┐
│        Staff Position        │
└─────────────────────────────┘
```

Position Description

Association Executives are responsible for managing the nonprofit organizations known as associations, which serve groups of people or organizations that share a particular interest or concern. Many associations serve the interests of professionals and trades. Professional associations (or societies) represent groups of professionals, such as trial attorneys, probation officers, or business appraisers, while trade associations represent businesses, such as law firms or legal publishers. Professional and trade associations provide their membership with professional services and resources, such as training and educational programs, publications, the latest statistics and research about their industry, job listings, government advocacy, and networking opportunities. Other associations serve the interests of groups who share a particular philanthropic or charitable concern, such as poverty, health, education, animal rights, children's rights, or the environment.

Many professional and trade associations employ several Association Executives to run their operations. The following are some of the typical executive positions.

- The executive director oversees the total operations of an association—program development, human resources, finances, office management, and so on.
- The director of finance manages an associations's financial affairs.
- The director of communications manages all communications and public relations activities, such as producing association newsletters and other publications.
- The director of education develops and oversees various education programs that meet the needs of an association's membership.
- The director of membership oversees activities for recruiting new members as well as keeping current members.
- The director of conventions oversees the planning and coordination of all convention activities.
- The director of government relations manages the advocacy programs that promote an association's interests in state and federal legislation as well as relations with government agencies.

Depending on the size and budget of an association, Association Executives may manage one or several departments.

All Association Executives are responsible for fulfilling the mission and goals of their associations. They assist in the overall planning and development of their organization's programs and services. Further, all Association Executives perform similar duties for overseeing their particular departments. For example, they supervise and train staff members, plan and manage a departmental budget, and complete required reports.

Association Executives often work long hours, including evenings and weekends.

Salaries

Salaries for Association Executives vary, depending on such factors as their experience, education, position, and geographical location. According to May 2005 *Occupational Employment Statistics* survey by the U.S. Bureau of Labor Statistics, the estimated annual salary for most administrative services managers ranged from $32,770 to $113,150, and for general managers, from $40,060 to $145,600 per year.

Employment Prospects

In 2004, about 86,000 trade and professional associations as well as about 1 million charitable and philanthropic associations existed in the United States. An association may be organized to serve groups at the local, state, regional, national, or international level. The greatest concentration of associations are found in the metropolitan areas of Washington, D.C., New York City, and Chicago.

Opportunities generally become available as Association Executives retire, resign, or transfer to other positions. Associations occasionally create additional positions to meet their growing needs.

Advancement Prospects

Many Association Executives realize advancement through higher salaries, more responsibilities, and job satisfaction. Those aspiring to top positions become executive directors. Some executives climb through the ranks within their associations, while others move from one association to the next to attain top positions. Becoming association consultants or owners of association management companies are other career options for Association Executives.

Education and Training

Employers generally require that Association Executives have at least a bachelor's degree or an equivalency in education and experience. Association Executives typically hold college degrees that are relevant to the areas in which they work. For example, a director of communications might hold a journalism degree, while a director of government relations might possess a juris doctor (J.D.) degree.

Experience, Skills, and Personality Traits

Employers generally require that candidates have several years of executive management experience, particularly in association settings. They also look for candidates who are knowledgeable about the trades, professions, or charities that the associations serve.

Being an Association Executive requires excellent leadership, management, and team building skills, as well as superior interpersonal, communication, and writing skills. In addition, they should have adequate financial management and public relations skills. Being hardworking, analytical, organized, flexible, and creative are just a few personality traits that characterize successful Association Executives.

Unions and Associations

Association Executives might join professional associations that represent their profession, such as the partner organizations, ASAE and the Center for Association Leadership. (For contact information, see Appendix V.) Many also join professional associations that serve their specific field, such as education or marketing. By joining professional organizations, executives can take advantage of networking opportunities, training programs, and other professional resources and services.

Tips for Entry

1. As a college student, get involved with associations that represent your interests.

2. Many associations offer internships to college students. Contact local associations or talk to college career counselors to learn about intern opportunities.

3. Before you go to a job interview, learn as much as you can about a prospective employer. One valuable resource for learning more about an association is its Web site.

4. Use the Internet to learn more about working in the world of associations. You might start by visiting the ASAE and the Center for Association Leadership Web site at http://www.asaecenter.org. For more links, see Appendix VI.

LEGAL SERVICES MANAGER

CAREER PROFILE

Duties: Manage the daily operations of nonprofit legal assistance programs; may provide legal services; perform duties as required

Alternate Title(s): Executive Director, Deputy Director, Director of Litigation, Managing Attorney

Salary Range: $38,000 to $146,000

Employment Prospects: Fair

Advancement Prospects: Poor

Prerequisites:

Education or Training—A law (J.D.) degree

Experience—Several years experience providing legal services; legal administrative, management, and supervisory experience

Special Skills and Personality Traits—Leadership, fund-raising, team building, interpersonal, writing, communication, public speaking, and interpersonal skills; be organized, resourceful, analytical, sensible, dedicated

Special Requirements—Admission to the proper state bar association may be required.

CAREER LADDER

```
┌─────────────────────────────┐
│   Legal Services Manager    │
└─────────────────────────────┘

┌─────────────────────────────┐
│ Senior or Supervising Attorney │
└─────────────────────────────┘

┌─────────────────────────────┐
│       Staff Attorney        │
└─────────────────────────────┘
```

Position Description

Legal Services Managers are responsible for overseeing legal assistance programs that serve low-income clients. These nonprofit programs are funded through government grants, foundation grants, and private donations. They offer legal services for free (or for low fees) to clients on limited incomes. These programs provide legal counsel in substantive legal matters, such as family law, housing, public benefits, employment, elder law, and disability rights.

Many programs provide only civil legal services; some additionally work in specific legal areas or with certain clientele, such as the elderly. Some legal assistance programs also have a government relations component in which they perform lobbying activities in state and federal legislatures.

Legal Services Managers report directly to boards of directors who are responsible for establishing the goals, objectives, and policies for the programs. The Legal Services Managers' job is to assure the successful execution of their board's mission and policies.

Nonprofit legal services programs range from small offices with a few attorneys to large programs with several different offices in a city, region, or even the country. Regardless of their program size, all Legal Services Managers have many of the same duties. For example, they:

- administer office policies and procedures
- manage the various grants for their programs
- prepare and administer budgets
- supervise and support both legal and support staff
- monitor programs for compliance with applicable laws and regulations, as well as with the rules and policies of their different grants
- provide regular written and oral progress reports to the board of directors
- recruit, hire, and train attorneys, paralegals, and support staff
- develop and write grant proposals

- develop fund-raising projects
- build and maintain relationships with the local bar association, funding sources, and the community

In some programs, Legal Services Managers play a dual role. In addition to executing administrative and managerial responsibilities, they perform legal duties. They may provide direct services to clients or provide leadership counsel on major litigation.

Legal Services Managers often work evenings and weekends to complete reports and other administrative tasks, meet with board members and donors, attend social and community functions, and so forth.

Salaries

Salaries for Legal Services Managers vary, depending on such factors as their experience, job duties, their program's budget, and geographical location. Specific salary information for this occupation is unavailable. An idea of their earnings can be gained by looking at how much management occupations make. According to the May 2005 *Occupational Employment Statistic* survey, by the U.S. Bureau of Labor Statistics, the estimated annual salary for most management occupations ranged between $37,800 and $145,600.

Employment Prospects

In nonprofit organizations, the creation of new legal services programs is dependent on government grants and fund-raising. Job openings typically become available as managers resign, transfer to other positions, or retire.

Advancement Prospects

Legal Services Managers are the top positions in legal services programs. Further advancement may be measured in any number of ways, such as by earning higher incomes, obtaining management positions in larger programs, or receiving high accolades for the success of their programs.

Education and Training

The majority of Legal Services Managers are law school graduates. Many also hold a bachelor's degree in public administration, business administration, or a related field.

Throughout their careers, they enroll in continuing education and training programs to develop and maintain their professional skills and expertise.

Special Requirements

Most employers prefer to hire candidates who possess current membership in the state bar association that governs the jurisdiction in which they would work. They may hire qualified candidates from another state on the condition that they gain admission to the proper state bar within a certain timeframe.

For specific eligibility requirements, contact the state bar admission office where you wish to practice. See Appendix III for a list of offices.

Experience, Skills, and Personality Traits

Requirements vary from employer to employer. Having several years of experience providing legal services is usually required or strongly preferred. In addition, candidates need several years of legal administrative, management, and supervisory experience. Furthermore, they show a strong commitment to providing quality programs to low-income clientele.

Legal Services Managers need excellent leadership, fundraising, team building, and interpersonal skills, as well as superior writing and public speaking ability. Being organized, resourceful, analytical, sensible, and dedicated are a few personality traits that successful Legal Services Managers share.

Unions and Associations

Legal Services Managers join local, state, and national associations to take advantage of professional resources and services. These include opportunities for networking, education programs, publications, and job listings. Some national organizations that managers might join are the Management Information Exchange (MIE), the National Legal Aid and Defender Association, the American Bar Association, and the Association of Legal Administrators. For contact information, see Appendix V.

Tips for Entry

1. In high school and college, you can start getting experience working with low-income clientele. For example, you might volunteer or intern at senior centers, community programs, and social agencies.
2. In law school, obtain an internship with a legal services program.
3. As a lawyer in private practice, perform pro bono work to get an idea if you might like working in a legal services setting.
4. Use the Internet to learn more about legal services management. You might start by visiting the Management Information Exchange Web site at http://www.m-i-e.org. For more links, see Appendix VI.

DIRECTOR OF ADMISSIONS, LAW SCHOOL

CAREER PROFILE

Duties: Oversee the administration of the student admissions and enrollment programs; manage the daily operations of the admissions office; perform duties as required

Alternate Title(s): Dean of Admissions

Salary Range: $40,000 to $131,000

Employment Prospects: Fair

Advancement Prospects: Fair

Prerequisites:

    Education or Training—Master's degree in an appropriate field

    Experience—Several years of work experience in admissions as well as in management and leadership positions

    Special Skills and Personality Traits—Communication, interpersonal, leadership, management, team building, decision-making, problem-solving, computer, writing, presentation, marketing, and public relations skills; organized, flexible, open-minded, creative, dedicated, and energetic

CAREER LADDER

```
┌─────────────────────────────────┐
│   Vice President of Enrollment   │
│            Management            │
└─────────────────────────────────┘

┌─────────────────────────────────┐
│      Director of Admissions      │
└─────────────────────────────────┘

┌─────────────────────────────────┐
│   Assistant or Associate Director │
│          of Admissions           │
└─────────────────────────────────┘
```

Position Description

Every year, law schools admit new students to the various degree programs that they offer. The majority of new students enroll in a juris doctor (J.D.) degree program, which is the professional degree program for those who wish to become attorneys. Some students begin academic graduate degree programs, such as the master of laws (LL.M.) in specialties such as taxation and international law. Others continue their legal education in doctor of science of law (S.J.D.) or juridical science (J.S.D.) programs to become legal scholars. Many law schools also admit students to joint degree programs in which they earn their J.D. along with an advanced degree in another discipline, such as a master's in business administration (M.B.A.), master's in public administration (M.P.A), doctor of philosophy (Ph.D.), or doctor of medicine (M.D.) degree.

In law schools, Directors of Admissions oversee the recruitment and selection programs of new students. Their primary responsibilities include the development, administration, and implementation of such programs as well as the management of the daily operations of the admissions office. They also ensure that the admissions office operates consistently with their school's mission, administrative policies, and enrollment goals.

These directors perform a wide range of duties. For example, they:

- plan and execute goals, objectives, policies, and operating procedures for the admissions office
- manage budgets
- develop and implement a comprehensive student recruitment plan
- devise marketing strategies to attract top applicants from diverse backgrounds
- oversee the design and execution of recruitment events, projects, and activities
- coordinate the process of reviewing applications for admission to the selection of prospective students
- monitor and evaluate recruitment and selection programs, and seek ways to improve programs

Many of these directors also oversee the financial aid program, which helps students obtain scholarships, loans, or other financial assistance to pay for their education.

Many Directors of Admissions are involved in the actual recruitment and selection of students. For example, they might interview college students at recruiting events; answer questions about the admissions process by phone, e-mail, or in person; review applications; and assist in the selection of students.

Their job involves working closely with other administrators, faculty, advisers, classified staff, alumni, the legal community, and others in the recruitment and selection of prospective students. These directors also have contact with vendors, other law schools, professional organizations, and the general public.

As leaders of admissions offices, these directors are responsible for creating positive and respectful work environments. They are charged with supervising and directing the work of assistant managers, admissions counselors, administrative and clerical staff, and student workers. Directors of Admissions also provide for the training and professional development of all their staff. In addition, they participate in the recruitment, hiring, and firing of staff members.

Directors of Admission work 40 hours a week but put in additional hours as needed to fulfill their duties. They sometimes are required to attend events during evenings and on weekends. On occasion, they travel off-campus to perform duties, which may involve being away from home for several days or weeks.

Salaries

Salaries for admissions directors of law schools vary, depending on such factors as their education, experience, employer, and geographical location. According to the May 2005 *Occupational Employment Statistics* survey by the U.S. Bureau of Labor Statistics (BLS), the estimated annual salary for most educational administrators in higher education ranged between $39,510 and $131,250.

Employment Prospects

In general, job openings become available as Directors of Admissions retire, advance to higher positions, or transfer to other occupations. According to the BLS, opportunities among nonacademic administrative positions, such as admissions directors, are favorable because fewer people are interested in these positions. In addition, large numbers of educational administrators are expected to retire over the next decade.

Advancement Prospects

Directors of Admissions can advance in various ways. They can seek admissions director positions at larger or more prestigious schools. They can rise through the ranks as administrative deans, vice presidents, and presidents of law schools. They can also pursue other nonacademic administrative positions.

Education and Training

Educational qualifications vary with the different law schools. Most employers prefer to hire candidates who possess at least a master's degree in student personnel, higher education administration, or another related field. Some employers also accept candidates who possess a juris doctor (J.D.) degree. Employers sometimes hire strong candidates with only a bachelor's degree if they have qualifying work experience.

Throughout their careers, Directors of Admissions enroll in continuing education programs and training programs to update their skills and knowledge.

Experience, Special Skills, and Personality Traits

Employers typically seek candidates who have several years of experience working in college admissions, preferably in law schools. They also have work experience in management and leadership roles.

To work effectively with a variety of people from diverse backgrounds, Directors of Admissions need excellent communication and interpersonal skills. They also must have effective leadership, management, team building, decision-making, and problem-solving skills. In addition they need strong computer, writing, and presentation skills for their work. Having marketing and public relations skills is also essential.

Some personality traits that successful Directors of Admissions share include being organized, flexible, open-minded, creative, dedicated, and energetic.

Unions and Associations

Many law school Directors of Admissions join professional associations to take advantage of networking opportunities, training programs, and other professional services and resources. The American Association of University Administrators and the American Association of Collegiate Registrars and Admissions Officers are two national societies that they are eligible to join. For contact information, see Appendix V.

Tips for Entry

1. As a college student, obtain part-time work in your school's admissions office. Not only will you get an idea if this field is right for you, but you will also start gaining valuable work experience.
2. Many admissions officers began their careers as admissions counselors, and rose through the ranks as assistant and associate admission directors.
3. If you are willing to relocate, you may have greater chances of finding the position that you want.
4. You can learn about different admissions offices on the Internet. To get a list of Web sites, enter the keywords *law school admissions office.*

PROPERTY MANAGER

CAREER PROFILE

Duties: Oversee daily operations; enforce property owners' rules and policies; manage and negotiate contracts; comply with appropriate laws, regulations and codes; perform duties as required

Alternate Title(s): Facility Manager, Real Estate Manager; Apartment Manager, Condominium Manager, or other title that reflects a specific job

Salary Range: $20,000 to $91,000

Employment Prospects: Good

Advancement Prospects: Good

Prerequisites:

Education or Training—A college degree usually preferred; on-the-job training

Experience—Previous work experience required

Special Skills and Personality Traits—Business sense; management, organizational, negotiation, problem-solving, trouble-shooting, interpersonal, customer service, math, computer, writing, communication, and self-management skills; tactful, calm, positive, ethical, self-motivated, goal-oriented, persevering, creative, and resourceful

Special Requirements—Certification may be required for managers of federally subsidized housing

CAREER LADDER

```
┌─────────────────────────────┐
│   Senior Property Manager   │
└─────────────────────────────┘

┌─────────────────────────────┐
│      Property Manager       │
└─────────────────────────────┘

┌─────────────────────────────┐
│  Assistant Property Manager │
└─────────────────────────────┘
```

Position Description

Many individuals, groups, businesses, and organizations buy residential, commercial, and industrial property to rent or lease for investment purposes. Many of these owners prefer to hire Property Managers to run the daily operations of their property investments. These professional men and women are responsible for renting (or leasing) the properties as well as maintaining them. They are also responsible for protecting the owners' properties and ensuring that owners recover their investments, as well as making a profit.

Property Managers may be employed to oversee houses, apartment complexes, condominiums, office buildings, medical offices, shopping centers, warehouses, and industrial parks, among other residential, commercial, and industrial properties. They may manage one or several properties.

Their role is to act as liaison between property owners (who are also the landlords) and the tenants. Property Managers are responsible for attracting and selecting new tenants. They market vacant spaces by advertising them in newspapers, using a leasing agent, or by other means. These managers show vacancies to interested parties, collect and review applications, perform background checks on applicants, and complete and sign rental agreements.

It is the Property Managers' job to resolve any complaints or problems that tenants may have about their rental units. Property Managers are also expected to enforce the terms of rental or lease agreements. They inform tenants of any rules that they have broken. If tenants continue to break rules, Property Managers may serve them with eviction notices.

Property Managers are responsible for ensuring that properties are safe and properly maintained. They inspect equipment, buildings, and grounds (which may include recreational facilities such as swimming pools, gyms, and golf courses) on a regular basis to determine if maintenance or repairs are needed. When tenants terminate their leases, the managers inspect the conditions of the rental units, and decide what physical modifications or repairs are needed to make them ready to be rented again.

Property Managers plan, schedule, and coordinate all maintenance and repair work. They assign jobs and direct the work of maintenance staff. If jobs cannot be done by staff members, they hire specialists to perform the work. Property Managers are responsible for evaluating bids and negotiating contracts for such services as janitorial, groundskeeping, security, garbage removal, plumbing, and construction. Property Managers also monitor the job performance of the various contractors.

Property Managers are responsible for financial matters as well. They handle financial matters such as collecting rent from tenants and paying mortgages, taxes, insurance premiums, and maintenance bills. If they supervise staff, these managers take care of the payroll. They also prepare financial statements and reports for owners. In addition, many managers are involved in establishing rental rates and monitoring the profits and losses on properties.

Property Managers are also responsible for following various local, state, and federal laws and regulations. For example, they must be in compliance with fair housing and employment laws. They must also make sure that properties meet all governmental building codes and regulations.

Most Property Managers supervise a staff of office and maintenance workers. It is their responsibility to recruit, hire, and train new employees. Their supervisory duties also include conducting job performance evaluations.

Many Property Managers maintain offices on property sites. Those who manage apartment buildings, condominiums, and residential communities are often required to live on site. Some Property Managers are not involved with the daily management of operations. These professionals, known as real estate asset managers, are involved with the financial planning of property investments for owners. They engage in the purchasing, development, and disposition of property.

Property Managers work in offices, but they may spend much of their workday visiting the properties they oversee. For example, they may show vacancies to potential tenants, check the progress of construction projects, investigate tenant problems, or inspect units that have been vacated by tenants.

Their work can oftentimes be stressful. They handle various types of situations and crises at any time of the day or night, such as burst water pipes, lost power, natural disasters, and crime. Property Managers are expected to remain composed as they deal with angry, frustrated, unhappy, or otherwise emotional tenants, staff members, contractors, or others.

Property Managers may be employed full time or part time. They often work additional hours on evenings and weekends to complete their duties or handle emergencies. They do not receive overtime pay, but may receive compensatory time off.

Salaries

Salaries for Property Managers vary, depending on such factors as their education, experience, employer, and geographical location, as well as the type, size, and location of the property that they manage. According to the May 2005 *Occupational Employment Statistics* (OES) survey by the U.S. Bureau of Labor Statistics (BLS), the estimated annual salary for most Property Managers ranged from $20,100 to $91,050.

Depending on their line of work, Property Managers receive generous benefits in addition to their salaries. For example, apartment managers get a rent-free or reduced-rent apartment.

Employment Prospects

The BLS reports in its May 2005 OES survey that an estimated 154,230 property, real estate, and community association managers were employed in the United States.

Many Property Managers are self-employed. Many work for real estate companies and property management firms. Some are employed by real estate development companies, private corporations, and government agencies that possess buildings and properties for rent or lease.

Opportunities usually become available as Property Managers advance to higher positions, transfer to other jobs, or leave the workforce for various reasons. New positions are also created as employers' demands grow. According to the BLS, employment for property, real estate, and community association managers is expected to increase by 9 to 17 percent through 2014. The BLS further reports that the demand is expected to grow for Property Managers who have experience managing assisted-living facilities and retirement communities. This is partly due to the expanding population of older people during the period of 2004 to 2014.

Advancement Prospects

Property Managers can advance in numerous ways. They can earn higher incomes as well as move on to positions with greater responsibilities, such as running larger properties or supervising other Property Managers.

Property Managers may specialize in overseeing certain types of property, such as condominiums, shopping centers, or retirement communities. They may advance to real estate asset manager positions. They may pursue further education and appropriate licenses to become real estate agents, real estate brokers, or real estate lawyers. Entrepreneurial individuals may decide to start their own property management firms.

Education and Training

There is no standard educational requirement for individuals to become Property Managers. However, many employers prefer to hire candidates who possess an associate or bachelor's degree in business administration, finance, public administration, real estate, or another related field. Employers may hire strong candidates with liberal arts or other non-business degrees if they have qualifying work experience. Most employers provide new employees with training programs in which they learn about the basic concerns and obligations of their job as Property Managers.

Property Managers usually learn about project management on the job, as they work in such subordinate roles as an assistant property manager, a building superintendent, or an office worker in a property management firm.

Some colleges and universities offer professional certificate or degree programs in real estate or property management. Professional organizations, such as the Institute of Real Estate Management, also offer continuing education programs in property management for individuals interested in entering this field.

Many Property Managers enroll in continuing education and training programs throughout their careers to update their skills as well as to learn new ones for their job.

Special Requirements

Property Managers of public housing that is subsidized by the federal government are usually required to possess the public housing manager certification, which is granted by the national Center for Housing Management. Employers may hire candidates without this certification on the condition that they obtain it within a certain time period.

Experience, Special Skills, and Personality Traits

In general, employers hire candidates who have a few years of work experience managing properties, particularly properties similar to those they would be overseeing.

Property Managers are expected to have strong business sense. To be effective at their job, they need management, organizational, negotiation, problem-solving, and troubleshooting skills. In addition they need excellent interpersonal and customer service skills, as they must be able to work well with many people from diverse backgrounds. Having strong math, computer, writing, and communication skills is also essential for their line of work. Furthermore, Property Managers must have exceptional self-management skills, such as the abilities to handle stressful situations, work independently, understand and follow directions, and prioritize multiple tasks.

Some personality traits that successful Property Managers share include being tactful, calm, positive, ethical, self-motivated, goal-oriented, persevering, creative, and resourceful.

Unions and Associations

Many Property Managers join professional associations to take advantage of continuing education programs, job listings, publications, networking opportunities, and other professional services and resources. Some national societies that serve Property Managers include:

- Institute of Real Estate Management
- Community Associations Institute
- National Apartment Association
- Building Owners and Managers Association International
- National Association of Residential Property Managers

For contact information, see Appendix V.

Tips for Entry

1. Some courses that experts in the field suggest may be helpful to Property Managers are accounting, finance, marketing, public relations, psychology, and real estate.
2. To enhance their employability, many Property Managers have obtained professional certification through programs of recognized professional or trade associations. To learn about some certification programs, see Appendix II.
3. To learn about job openings, check newspaper classified ads as well as job listings at professional and trade associations that serve property management and real estate professionals.
4. Contact property management firms directly about job openings. To find establishments, check the yellow pages of telephone directories. Look under *property management* as well as *real estate management.*
5. Use the Internet to learn more about the property management field. To get a list of relevant Web sites, enter either of these keywords in a search engine: *property management* or *property managers.* For some links, see Appendix VI.

ANALYSTS AND EXAMINERS

ACTUARY

CAREER PROFILE

Duties: Examine data to determine the financial risk, uncertainties, and probabilities of future events; perform duties as required

Alternate Title(s): Actuarial Assistant, Actuarial Associate, Actuarial Consultant

Salary Range: $46,000 to $146,000

Employment Prospects: Good

Advancement Prospects: Good

Prerequisites:

Education or Training—A bachelor's degree; on-the-job training

Experience—Previous work experience may not be necessary for entry-level positions; completion of one or more actuarial examinations is preferred or required

Special Skills and Personality Traits—Problem-solving, project management, teamwork, communication, interpersonal, and computer skills; enthusiastic, adaptable, flexible, analytical, self-motivated, creative

CAREER LADDER

```
┌─────────────────────────────────────┐
│  Senior Actuary, Department Manager,  │
│       or Actuarial Consultant         │
└─────────────────────────────────────┘

┌─────────────────────────────────────┐
│              Actuary                  │
└─────────────────────────────────────┘

┌─────────────────────────────────────┐
│         Actuarial Assistant           │
└─────────────────────────────────────┘
```

Position Description

Actuaries study the financial risk, uncertainties, and probabilities of future events for their employers. Using mathematics, statistics, and financial theory, Actuaries define and analyze problems that may occur during the course of their employers' activities. They also help employers create programs that would be able to handle future financial loss.

Most Actuaries work in the fields of insurance, pension plans, and financial investments. Insurance Actuaries specialize in the different areas of insurance—life, health, property, casualty, or workers' compensation.

Actuaries work on a wide range of projects for their employers. For example, they might:

- determine the price at which a product should be sold
- calculate potential profits and losses for a new product
- project the cost of a loss over a number of years
- determine the financial risk involved in a business merger
- estimate the financial loss for an employer if a natural or human-made disaster should occur

- appraise the current value of an organization, a particular program, or specific inventory
- design new products or programs
- establish rating guidelines and risk categories
- estimate future cash flows, taxes, assets, or liabilities

Actuaries gather data from various sources to analyze. Along with numerical information, they read historical data, appropriate laws and regulations, and trends. They develop mathematical models to analyze problems. Actuaries then discuss their findings with executives, attorneys, marketing staff, and other employees. They explain complex, technical concepts in terms that are clearly understood.

As part of their job, Actuaries keep up with current legislation, economic and social trends, and developments in their industry.

Actuaries sometimes provide expert witness testimony at court trials, depositions, administrative hearings, legislative hearings, and arbitrations. For example, an Actuary might provide testimony about the value of a pension plan in a divorce case.

Actuaries work a standard 40-hour week.

Salaries

Salaries for Actuaries vary, depending on such factors as their education, experience, employer, and geographical location. According to the May 2005 *Occupational Employment Statistics* (OES) survey, by the U.S. Bureau of Labor Statistics (BLS), the estimated annual salary for most Actuaries ranged between $45,660 and $145,600 per year.

Employment Prospects

About 15,770 Actuaries work in the United States, according to the BLS's May 2005 OES survey. They are employed by insurance companies, actuary consulting firms, banks, financial institutions, government agencies, accounting services, and other organizations.

Employment in this occupation is predicted to increased by 18 to 26 percent through 2014, according to the BLS. Actuaries will also be needed to replace individual who retire, transfer to other jobs, or advance to higher positions.

Advancement Prospects

Actuaries can advance to supervisory and management positions, based on their experience, job performance, and professional status. Actuaries can also follow a career path as solo consultants or firm owners that provide actuarial services.

Actuaries obtain professional status by passing a series of examinations that are administered by professional actuary associations. There are two professional levels. The first level is Associate, which takes most Actuaries four to six years to achieve. The second level is Fellow, which takes a few more years to complete. The Casualty Actuarial Society grants the professional credential to those in the property and casualty practices. The Society of Actuaries grants the credential to those who practice in life insurance, health insurance, finance, investments, or pension plans.

Education and Training

Many Employers prefer to hire Actuaries who hold a bachelor's degree in mathematics, actuarial science, statistics, or another related field. Employers may hire candidates with nonmath degrees if they have passed one or more actuarial examinations.

Employers provide on-the-job training for entry-level positions.

Experience, Skills, and Personality Traits

Requirements vary from employer to employer for entry-level positions. Employers often hire college graduates with little or no experience, if they can demonstrate good business sense as well as show strong mathematical and technical aptitudes. Many employers prefer that candidates have completed one or more actuarial examinations.

Actuaries must have excellent problem-solving, project management, and teamwork skills as well as superior communication and interpersonal skills. In addition, they have strong computer skills, with the ability to use word processing, spreadsheet, statistical analysis, and other programs.

Successful Actuaries have several personality traits in common, such as being enthusiastic, adaptable, flexible, analytical, self-motivated, and creative.

Unions and Associations

Most Actuaries are members of one or more professional associations, such as the American Academy of Actuaries, American Society of Pension Professionals and Actuaries, Casualty Actuarial Society, Conference of Consulting Actuaries, and Society of Actuaries. (For contact information, see Appendix V.) By joining professional associations, Actuaries can take advantage of various professional services and resources, such as networking opportunities, job listings, and education programs.

Tips for Entry

1. As a college student, obtain an internship to see if the actuarial field is right for you. Visit your college career center for help in finding internships.
2. Many Actuaries recommend that students take courses in economics, business, computer science, and liberal arts in addition to mathematics courses.
3. Actuaries who wish to practice for pension plans must be licensed by the Joint Board for the Enrollment of Actuaries, part of the Internal Revenue Service. For further information visit its Web site at http://www.irs.gov/taxpros/actuaries/index.html.
4. You can learn more about Actuaries on the Internet. One pertinent Web site is Be an Actuary, http://www.beanactuary.com. For more links, see Appendix VI.

COMPLIANCE SPECIALIST

CAREER PROFILE

Duties: Ensure that employers are meeting appropriate local, state, and federal laws and regulations; perform duties as required

Alternate Title(s): Compliance Officer, Compliance Coordinator; a title that reflects a specific compliance area such as Public Utility Compliance Specialist or ADA (Americans with Disabilities Act) Specialist

Salary Range: $31,000 to $83,000

Employment Prospects: Good

Advancement Prospects: Fair

Prerequisites:

Education or Training—A bachelor's degree

Experience—Several years' experience in industry; previous experience in compliance, regulatory affairs, or another related field

Special Skills and Personality Traits—Leadership, interpersonal, communication, project management, organization, and writing skills; be independent, fair, ethical, analytical, credible, trustworthy, flexible

CAREER LADDER

```
┌─────────────────────────────────┐
│   Senior Compliance Specialist  │
│  or Compliance Program Manager  │
└─────────────────────────────────┘

┌─────────────────────────────────┐
│      Compliance Specialist      │
└─────────────────────────────────┘

┌─────────────────────────────────┐
│            Trainee              │
└─────────────────────────────────┘
```

Position Description

In the United States, local, state, and federal laws regulate how employers in the various industries must run their businesses. For example, employers must comply with various employment laws that cover equal opportunity, workplace safety, employee benefits, and other workplace issues. In addition, employers must follow specific laws and regulations that govern their industry. Employers who have government contracts or are receiving government funds must follow certain laws and regulations. Failure to comply with appropriate laws and regulations can result in employers being charged with violations and assessed heavy fines, as well as the possibility of being sued. Consequently, many employers hire one or more Compliance Specialists to ensure that they are properly following the laws and regulations.

Compliance Specialists are employed in many different industries—banks, securities, insurance, education, health care, biotechnology, pharmaceuticals, aviation, engineering, public utilities, municipalities, sports, casinos, retail, and so on. They usually are responsible for managing compliance programs pertinent to specific laws and regulations. For example, ADA Specialists make sure that employers are in compliance with the Americans with Disabilities Act (ADA), while environmental Compliance Specialists ensure that employers are meeting the required environmental laws and regulations.

Many duties vary among the different Compliance Specialists. Some responsibilities are the same, regardless of the industry in which they work or the compliance areas they cover. Some of these major responsibilities include:

- interpreting laws, regulations, and codes
- acting as a resource and consultant to managers and staff
- monitoring assigned projects, programs, and contracts for compliance with appropriate laws and regulations as well as with internal policies and rules
- developing, implementing, and maintaining compliance policies and procedures

- conducting audits to measure the effectiveness of monitoring systems
- developing and coordinating training and education programs to inform employees about current and revised laws and regulations as well as about compliance issues
- conducting investigations of complaints or suspicions that compliance is not being met
- maintaining accurate records
- writing correspondence and completing required reports and forms
- staying up to date with changes in laws and regulations as well as with court decisions and proposed legislation

Compliance Specialists generally work a standard 40-hour week.

Salaries

Salaries for Compliance Specialists vary, depending on such factors as their education, experience, job responsibilities, industry, and geographical location. According to the May 2005 *Occupational Employment Statistics* survey, by the U.S. Bureau of Labor Statistics (BLS), the estimated annual salary for most compliance officers ranged between $30,570 and $83,470.

Employment Prospects

The BLS predicts that the employment growth for compliance officers should increase by 9 to 17 percent through 2014. In addition to job growth, opportunities will become available as Compliance Specialists retire, advance to higher positions, or transfer to other jobs.

Advancement Prospects

Compliance Specialists can advance to supervisory and management positions. The top position in most organizations is the corporate compliance officer, which is usually a senior manager or executive officer.

Compliance Specialists with entrepreneurial ambitions can become independent consultants.

Education and Training

Employers generally require that Compliance Specialists possess bachelor's degrees in related fields.

Entry-level compliance officers receive on-the-job training.

Throughout their careers, Compliance Specialists enroll in education and training programs to develop their skills and expertise.

Experience, Skills, and Personality Traits

Requirements vary from employer to employer. In general, candidates must have several years of experience working in an industry. Additionally, they should have previous experience working in compliance, regulatory affairs, or another related field. Candidates also are able to demonstrate knowledge about appropriate laws and regulations.

Compliance Specialists must be able to work effectively with employees at every level, thus they must have excellent leadership, interpersonal, and communication skills. In addition they need superior project management, organization, and writing skills.

Some personality traits that successful Compliance Specialists share are being independent, fair, ethical, analytical, credible, trustworthy, and flexible.

Unions and Associations

Many Compliance Specialists join professional associations, such as the National Society of Compliance Professionals and the Health Care Compliance Association, that represent compliance professionals in their industry. (For contact information, see Appendix V.) By joining professional associations, they can take advantage of professional services and resources, such as education programs, certification programs, job listings, and networking opportunities.

Tips for Entry

1. Gain experience in the industry in which you would like to work. You might work with private companies, law firms (if a lawyer), or government agencies that regulate the industry.
2. Actively participate in professional associations that serve the industries in which you would like to work. For example, you might attend conferences, give presentations, write articles about compliance issues for publications, and so on.
3. You can learn more about different Compliance Specialists on the Internet. To find job descriptions about various Compliance Specialists, enter the keywords *compliance specialist* in a search engine.

CONTRACT ADMINISTRATOR

CAREER PROFILE

Duties: Oversee the management of various business agreements; draft, review, negotiate, and maintain contracts; perform other duties as required

Alternate Title(s): Contract Manager, Contract Specialist

Salary Range: $33,000 to $113,000

Employment Prospects: Good

Advancement Prospects: Fair

Prerequisites:

Education or Training—Bachelor's degree; a law degree, master's of business administration (MBA), or other advanced degree may be required

Experience—Contract administration experience; legal experience preferred; work experience in industry preferred

Special Skills and Personality Traits—Interpersonal, customer service, communication, negotiation, writing, computer, and self-management skills; be analytical, organized, detail-oriented, trustworthy, decisive, flexible

CAREER LADDER

```
┌─────────────────────────────┐
│     Contract Specialist      │
│    or Contract Manager       │
└─────────────────────────────┘

┌─────────────────────────────┐
│    Contract Administrator    │
└─────────────────────────────┘

┌─────────────────────────────────────┐
│ Associate Contract Administrator     │
│ or Contract Administrative Assistant │
└─────────────────────────────────────┘
```

Position Description

Contract Administrators are responsible for overseeing the management of business agreements for their employers. They administer various contracts, among them sales contracts, purchasing contracts, licensing agreements, service agreements, construction contracts, property leases, credit agreements, employment contracts, and insurance policies. Many Contract Administrators are also responsible for administering government contracts, as well as compliance records.

Contract Administrators perform a wide range of duties. They coordinate the contractual process; that is, they make sure that proposed contracts are forwarded to department managers and corporate attorneys for review and approval. Contract Administrators assist department managers with preparing business agreements, which may include the task of drafting contracts. These specialists also review contracts submitted by vendors, contractors, and others, and identify any business, legal, and financial issues that may concern their employers. In addition, Contract Administrators nego-

tiate the terms and conditions of contracts with vendors, contractors, and others.

Contract Administrators are also responsible for maintaining contracts. They process and file business agreements accordingly. They check that contractual requirements are being met and make sure that contracts are up to date. Furthermore, they respond to questions about the status of contracts, advise on contractual terms and conditions, and resolve any problems or issues in contracts.

Senior Contract Administrators may have the additional responsibility to act as lead team members. Their duties might include making work assignments to other team members, providing guidance and supervision, and evaluating their work. They may also serve as a primary resource for solving problems.

Contract Administrators work a 40-hour week. On occasion, they work overtime in order to meet deadlines. They may be required to travel to meet with vendors; in large companies, they may travel between their home office and branch offices.

Salaries

Salaries for Contract Administrators vary, depending on such factors as their experience, education, and geographical location. Specific information for these professionals is unavailable, but they earn salaries similar to administrative managers. According to the May 2005 *Occupational Employment Statistics* (OES) survey, by the U.S. Bureau of Labor Statistics (BLS), the estimated annual salary for most administrative managers ranged between $32,770 and $113,150.

Employment Prospects

Contract Administrators work for construction companies, publishing companies, retail stores, hospitals, financial services, government agencies, educational institutions, and various other organizations. Opportunities generally become available as Contract Administrators resign, advance to other positions, or transfer to other occupations.

Advancement Prospects

Contract Administrators typically advance through the ranks of their organization, holding different positions in contract administration and other administrative departments. They can become specialists, overseeing specific types of contracts such as licensing agreements or government contracts. They can also pursue management positions, which may require moving to other organizations. Those with higher ambitions can follow paths to executive positions, such as vice president of administrative services.

Education and Training

Educational qualifications vary from employer to employer. In general, candidates should possess a bachelor's degree in business, finance, accounting, or another related field, depending on the industry. Employers may accept unrelated degrees if candidates have completed relevant coursework or obtained professional certifications in contract administration. Some employers desire that candidates also hold a master's in business administration, a juris doctor (J.D.) degree, or another advanced degree.

Experience, Skills, and Personality Traits

Employers generally require that candidates have several years of experience in contract administration, purchasing, or another related area. Some employers prefer candidates with legal experience, either as lawyers or senior paralegals. In addition, work experience within an employer's industry is highly preferred.

Contract Administrators need superior interpersonal, customer services, and communication skills, as they must be able to work with diverse groups of people—managers, executives, lawyers, vendors, clients, and others. They also need excellent negotiation, writing, and computer skills. Furthermore, they should have strong self-management skills that include the ability to meet deadlines, manage multiple projects, prioritize tasks, handle stressful situations, and demonstrate initiative in their work.

Some personality traits that successful Contract Administrators share are being analytical, organized, detail-oriented, trustworthy, decisive, and flexible.

Unions and Associations

Contract Administrators join professional associations to take advantage of networking opportunities, training programs, and other professional services and resources. One organization that Contract Administrators might join is the National Contract Management Association. For contact information, see Appendix V.

Tips for Entry

1. Many individuals obtain additional training by enrolling in a graduate degree or a professional certificate program in contracts management.
2. To enhance their employability, many Contract Administrators obtain professional certifications granted by the National Contract Management Association. For more information, visit its Web site at http://www.ncmahq.org.
3. Learn more about contract administration on the Internet. To find relevant Web sites, enter the keywords *contract administration* in a search engine. For some links, see Appendix VI.

ELIGIBILITY WORKER
(FEDERALLY FUNDED PROGRAMS)

CAREER PROFILE

Duties: Determine eligibility of applicants to receive financial aid from public assistance programs; perform duties as required

Alternate Title(s): Eligibility Interviewer, Eligibility Specialist, Human Services Specialist

Salary Range: $24,000 to $46,000

Employment Prospects: Fair

Advancement Prospects: Poor

Prerequisites:

Education or Training—A high school diploma; on-the-job training

Experience—Requirements vary

Special Skills and Personality Traits—Communication, interpersonal, customer service, organizational, math, writing, and self-management skills; polite, tactful, patient, compassionate, fair, ethical, detail-oriented, analytical

CAREER LADDER

```
┌─────────────────────────┐
│  Senior or Supervisory  │
│    Eligibility Worker   │
└─────────────────────────┘

┌─────────────────────────┐
│    Eligibility Worker   │
└─────────────────────────┘

┌─────────────────────────┐
│         Trainee         │
└─────────────────────────┘
```

Position Description

Throughout the United States, local and state social service agencies sponsor public assistance programs that help individuals and families in need. These programs are funded with federal grants and must accomplish certain goals established by the federal government. One goal is to provide poor people with temporary financial assistance, including cash grants and financial aid for basic needs such as food, housing, child care, and health care. The other goal is to help recipients find permanent jobs so that they can support themselves and their families.

Eligibility Workers are responsible for determining if applicants qualify for federally funded public assistance programs. They interview applicants to obtain personal data and information needed to determine eligibility. This data includes documents, such as rent receipts, bank statements, or medical records, that may support applicants' current income status.

Eligibility Workers make sure all information is accurate and complete, then evaluate it according to the rules and regulations that govern the public assistance programs. Depending on the agency, Eligibility Workers may recommend or make the final decision about whether applicants are eligible to receive assistance, along with the type and amount of assistance that would be appropriate.

Eligibility Workers are also responsible for monitoring individual cases. (Many Eligibility Workers carry a caseload of 100 or more clients.) They meet with or call clients regularly, and sometimes conduct home visits. Eligibility Workers review cases routinely to determine if clients are still eligible for assistance, if benefits should be increased or decreased, or if other types of benefits may be needed. Eligibility Workers notify clients of any changes to their benefits.

Many Eligibility Workers are assigned the role of caseworker. They are responsible for helping clients become employable and self-sufficient and for monitoring their progress. Eligibility Workers assess clients' job skills and refer them to appropriate programs, such as job search training, vocational training, or work experience programs. They also help clients handle problems or obstacles that may keep them from finding work. This may entail getting proper clothing for job interviews, finding affordable child care, or being treated for substance abuse. Eligibility Workers refer clients to the appropriate social agencies and community resources that can help them.

Eligibility Workers perform a wide range of duties and tasks. For example, they prepare correspondence and reports; maintain accurate records and files for individual cases; and provide information about public assistance programs to prospective applicants, social workers, the general public, and the media. Eligibility Workers also keep up with changes in federal and state regulations, eligibility guidelines, and program policies and procedures.

Eligibility Workers are employed part time or full time. They may be assigned to a flexible work schedule, which includes working evenings and weekends.

Salaries

Salaries for Eligibility Workers vary, depending on such factors as their education, experience, job duties, and geographical location. According to the May 2005 *Occupational Employment Statistics* (OES) survey, by the U.S. Bureau of Labor Statistics (BLS), the estimated annual salary for most eligibility interviewers in government programs ranged between $23,620 and $46,330.

Employment Prospects

The BLS reports in its November 2004 OES survey that an estimated 86,620 eligibility interviewers were employed in the United States. In general, openings become available as Eligibility Workers retire, advance to higher positions, or transfer to other jobs. An agency may create additional positions to meet growing demands, as long as funding is available.

According to the BLS, employment for this occupation is expected to decline through 2014 because of the advancement in technology as well as changes in governmental programs. However, the employment of Eligibility Workers is also dependent on the health of the economy. During economic downturns, more people may need to apply for governmental aid which in turn increases the demand for qualified Eligibility Workers.

Advancement Prospects

Eligibility Workers can advance to supervisory and management positions, but opportunities in general are limited.

Many Eligibility Workers pursue such other careers as social workers, rehabilitation counselors, lawyers, paralegals, teachers, or law enforcement officers.

Education and Training

Most employers require or prefer that Eligibility Workers hold bachelor's degrees in social work, human services, or other related fields. Employers may choose candidates who have associate degrees or who have completed only some college course work, if they have qualifying work experience.

Entry-level Eligibility Workers learn policies, procedures, and regulations through both classroom and on-the-job training.

Experience, Skills, and Personality Traits

Requirements for entry-level positions vary among employers. For example, an employer may require that entry-level candidates have at least one year of experience determining eligibility for loans, financial assistance, or benefits.

Eligibility Workers need a variety of strong skills to perform their work well, including communication, interpersonal, customer service, organizational, math, and writing skills. They also need excellent self-management skills, such as the ability to work independently, handle stressful situations, and prioritize a variety of tasks. Being polite, tactful, patient, compassionate, fair, ethical, detail-oriented, and analytical are some personality traits that successful Eligibility Workers share.

Unions and Associations

Many Eligibility Workers belong to a union that represents them in contract negotiations with their employers. Many professionals also join professional associations to take advantage of networking opportunities and other professional resources and services. One such national society is the National Eligibility Workers Association. For contact information, see Appendix V.

Tips for Entry

1. Contact the local social services offices directly for information about job openings and the job application process. Some offices conduct ongoing recruitment for entry-level positions.
2. In some communities, fluency in a second language may give you an advantage in your job search.
3. Learn more about Eligibility Workers and public assistance programs on the Internet. You might start by visiting these Web sites: National Eligibility Workers Association, http://www.nationalnew.org; and Administration for Children and Families, http://www.acf.dhhs.gov. For more links, see Appendix VI.

ENROLLED AGENT (EA)

CAREER PROFILE

Duties: Prepare tax returns for individuals, small businesses, and others; represent clients before the IRS; perform duties as required

Alternate Title(s): Tax Preparer, Tax Practitioner, Tax Advisor

Salary Range: $16,000 to $53,000+

Employment Prospects: Good

Advancement Prospects: Fair

Prerequisites:

Education or Training—High school diploma

Experience—Several years of experience in tax preparation

Special Skills and Personality Traits—Self-management, computer, analytical, organizational, interpersonal, and communication skills; be friendly, courteous, tactful, patient, detail-oriented, ethical, and trustworthy

Special Requirements—Must be licensed by the U.S. Department of Treasury

CAREER LADDER

```
┌─────────────────────────────┐
│    Senior Enrolled Agent    │
└─────────────────────────────┘

┌─────────────────────────────┐
│       Enrolled Agent        │
└─────────────────────────────┘

┌─────────────────────────────┐
│        Tax Preparer         │
└─────────────────────────────┘
```

Position Description

Enrolled Agents (EAs) are specialized tax preparers who have the authority to practice before the Internal Revenue Service, the federal tax collection agency that is part of the U.S. Department of Treasury. Along with attorneys, enrolled actuaries, and certified public accountants, EAs may represent clients at IRS meetings to address questions and issues about their clients' income tax returns. Unlike the others, EAs are the only professionals licensed by the Department of Treasury. They have the authority to practice anywhere in the United States.

Many EAs are independent practitioners, while others work for tax preparation firms. These tax professionals offer their services to individuals, professionals, farmers, small businesses, corporations, nonprofit organizations, educational institutions, trusts, estates, and others that are required to report taxes. In addition to being experts in federal tax laws, EAs have expertise in state and local tax laws that govern the jurisdictions in which they work.

As tax preparers, Enrolled Agents are trained to prepare both state and federal tax returns for their clients. They are competent in interpreting and applying tax codes and regulations. Their work involves gathering information about their clients to determine the appropriate deductions, credits, and adjustments to make on their tax returns. They also review clients' income statements, financial records, and tax returns from previous years. In addition, EAs interview clients about their work, investments, work and personal expenses, home improvements, and other matters to get further information about potential deductible expenses and allowances as well as taxable income.

EAs fill out the appropriate tax forms and compute the taxes that their clients owe. When EAs are unsure of procedures, they check tax bulletins and law handbooks to obtain the answers. They might also contact the appropriate tax collection agency. EAs review their completed work before clients sign the tax forms. EAs make sure that they have applied tax codes and regulations correctly, computed figures accurately, and completed tax return forms thoroughly.

EAs are knowledgeable about local, state, and federal tax laws, regulations, and codes. They uphold tax laws and advise clients about any errors, omissions, or anything that is not compliant and about the consequences of not following the law.

These tax experts also offer clients assistance with tax problems, such as delinquent tax returns, unpaid taxes, and late tax payments that may arise with the IRS or state tax agencies. EAs may also help clients prepare for audits.

EAs have the authority to represent taxpayers with federal tax problems, including audits, collection processes, and appeals. EAs can represent clients whose tax returns they prepared as well as those who had their returns prepared by others.

EAs communicate directly with the IRS. They can prepare and file documents, correspond, and attend hearings and conferences on behalf of their clients. In fact, they can handle negotiations and other matters at meetings without the presence of their clients. They can work out compromises with the IRS on how much their clients can pay, as well as consent to payment schedules for their clients. EAs can also execute claims for refunds as well as receive refund checks for their clients.

Enrolled Agents are required to conduct their professional practice according to the rules stipulated by the Department of Treasury Circular 230: *Regulations Governing the Practice of Attorneys, Certified Public Accountants, Enrolled Agents, Enrolled Actuaries, and Appraisers before the Internal Revenue Service.* These professionals perform work in which they have no conflict of interest. They are expected to maintain a confidential relationship with their clients. In other words, they may not disclose any confidential information unless their clients have authorized it or they are legally obligated to do so by the proper authorities.

EAs may specialize by offering services to only certain clientele, such as professionals or health-care establishments. Some of them focus their practice on specific tax areas. Many EAs also offer financial planning and tax planning services to their clients. They advise clients on matters such as recordkeeping for tax purposes, as well as help them form strategies to minimize their tax liability.

In performing their work, EAs utilize computers and tax preparation software. They also access on-line resources, such as the IRS Web site, to obtain current tax information. These tax professionals use calculators, printers, fax machines, photocopiers, and other business and office machines.

The work of Enrolled Agents is often stressful, particularly during tax season (January through April). They must meet strict deadlines, as well as deal with clients who become emotional about their tax situations.

EAs work part time or full time.

Salaries

Salaries for Enrolled Agents vary, depending on such factors as their experience, employer, and geographical location. Specific salary information for this occupation is unavailable. In general, they earn more than tax preparers because of their greater expertise. The U.S. Bureau of Labor Statistics (BLS) reports in its May 2005 *Occupational Employment Statistics* (*OES*) survey that the estimated annual salary for most tax preparers ranged between $15,780 and $52,860. According to an expert in the field, experienced EAs can earn annual incomes in the six-figure range.

Employment Prospects

A large number of EAs are self-employed. Some are employed by national tax preparing chains, such as H&R Block as well as by local tax preparing offices. Some EAs work for accounting firms as bookkeepers or accountants.

The BLS reports that job growth for tax preparers is expected to increase by 9 to 17 percent through 2014. The BLS reports in its May 2005 OES survey that about 58,850 tax preparers were employed in the United States.

Opportunities in general are favorable for Enrolled Agents. Taxpayers will continually need tax experts to assist them with their tax problems with the IRS. And according to the National Association of Enrolled Agents Web site (http://www.naea.org), there are fewer than 35,000 EAs licensed to practice in the United States.

Advancement Prospects

Enrolled Agents with managerial and administrative talents and ambitions may be promoted to such positions within their firms. The top goal for some individuals is to become successful independent practitioners or owners of tax preparation firms. Many EAs measure their success by earning higher incomes and gaining professional recognition.

Education and Training

Educational requirements vary with the different employers. Minimally, tax preparers must possess a high school diploma.

Throughout their careers, Enrolled Agents sign up for continuing education programs and training programs to update their skills and knowledge.

Special Requirements

Enrolled Agents must be licensed by the U.S. Department of Treasury in order to practice before the IRS. To become eligible for this license, individuals must meet one of the following qualifications:

• They must have been employed by the IRS for at least five years in a position that involved interpreting and applying the federal tax code and its regulations.

- They must have passed the EA examination administered by the IRS. This two-day exam covers such areas as individual income taxes, partnerships, corporations, estate and gift tax, ethics, recordkeeping procedures, retirement plans, penalties, and collection procedures.

Qualified individuals submit an application to the IRS for an Enrollment Agent license. The IRS performs a thorough background investigation before accepting, or rejecting, applications.

To maintain their professional license, Enrolled Agents must complete a minimum number of hours of continuing professional education every three years. In 2006, the IRS required that EAs complete 72 hours.

Experience, Special Skills, and Personality Traits

Job requirements vary among different employers. In general, they seek candidates who have several years of work experience in their areas of expertise.

Enrolled Agents must have effective self-management skills, such as the ability to work well under stress, meet deadlines, understand and follow instructions, and work independently. Their work also requires strong computer, analytical, and organizational skills. Additionally, excellent interpersonal and communication skills are important, as they must be able to deal with people from diverse backgrounds. Being friendly, courteous, tactful, patient, detail-oriented, ethical, and trustworthy are some personality traits that successful Enrolled Agents have in common.

Unions and Associations

Enrolled Agents may join professional associations to take advantage of networking opportunities and other professional services and resources. Two national organizations that serve their interests include the National Association of Enrolled Agents and the National Association of Tax Professionals. For contact information for the above organizations, see Appendix V.

Tips for Entry

1. Some experts in the field suggest that individuals work one or more tax seasons to gain practical experience and knowledge about federal tax laws before taking the EA examination.
2. Some professional societies offer seminars or classes to help individuals prepare for the Enrolled Agent examination.
3. Many professional societies post job announcements in their publications and Web sites.
4. The IRS administers the EA examination once a year. Individuals wishing to take the test must apply, as well as pay a fee, within a certain time frame. For more information, visit the Office of Professional Responsibility Enrolled Agent Program Web site at http://www.irs.gov/taxpros/agents/index.html.
5. Learn more about Enrolled Agents on the Internet. You might start by visiting the National Association of Enrolled Agents Web site at http://www.naea.org.

EQUAL OPPORTUNITY (EO) OFFICER

CAREER PROFILE

Duties: Develop, implement, and administer equal opportunity programs and affirmative action plans; perform other duties as required

Alternate Title(s): EO Specialist, EO Coordinator, EO Director, Affirmative Action Officer

Salary Range: $31,000 to $83,000

Employment Prospects: Good

Advancement Prospects: Good

Prerequisites:

Education or Training—A bachelor's degree

Experience—Previous experience working with equal opportunity or affirmative action programs

Special Skills and Personality Traits—Writing, communication, teamwork, interpersonal, and self-management skills; be courteous, diplomatic, trustworthy, honest, flexible

CAREER LADDER

```
┌─────────────────────────────────┐
│       Program Manager           │
└─────────────────────────────────┘

┌─────────────────────────────────┐
│    Equal Opportunity Officer    │
└─────────────────────────────────┘

┌─────────────────────────────────┐
│    Trainee or Support Staff      │
└─────────────────────────────────┘
```

Position Description

In the United States, the civil rights of all individuals are protected in the workplace. According to federal and state laws, employers are required to provide equal opportunity to employees and job applicants regardless of their race, color, national origin, gender, religion, disability, or age. Employers may also be required to comply with other equal opportunity laws, regulations, and executive orders that cover other statuses of people, such as marital status, political beliefs, sexual orientation, or veteran status. To ensure that they are complying with government laws, employers may establish equal opportunity programs. Employers may also be required to establish affirmative action plans that describe their goals for ensuring that their employment practices (such as job recruitment, hiring, promotion, termination, disciplinary action, and compensation) are not discriminatory.

Equal Opportunity (EO) Officers are responsible for managing equal opportunity programs and affirmative action plans for employers. Some of their major duties include:

- developing policies that reflect employers' commitment to equity and nondiscrimination in the workplace

- designing and implementing training and education programs for all employees about equal opportunity principles and affirmative action policies
- creating internal audit and reporting systems for employment practices
- monitoring employment practices
- investigating and resolving internal complaints of discrimination
- keeping up to date with changes in equal opportunity laws and regulations

EO Officers perform various other duties, depending on their position. Lower-level EO Officers perform more routine tasks, such as conducting research, reviewing data, and preparing reports. They also provide support in developing and implementing programs, monitoring for compliance, and conducting investigations.

EO specialists are responsible for developing and administering one or more equal opportunity and affirmative action programs. For example, one EO specialist at a company coordinates the affirmative action plan and equal employment opportunity programs while another oversees the disability and veterans equal opportunity programs. EO specialists perform such tasks as developing program guidelines and procedures, evaluating the effectiveness of affirmative action plans and goals, designing and implementing training programs, providing guidance to department managers and supervisors, and acting as resources to executives, managers, and supervisors.

EO managers (or EO directors) are in charge of planning and directing the overall affirmative action plan and equal opportunity programs. They are responsible for ensuring that their employers are in compliance with all the appropriate laws, regulations, and executive orders. In addition, they act as their employers' liaison with government officials. EO managers also develop program policies and provide supervision and guidance to all EO Officers.

EO Officers generally work a standard 40-hour week.

Salaries

Salaries for EO Officers vary, depending on such factors as their education, experience, and geographical location. According to the U.S. Bureau of Labor Statistics, in its May 2005 *Occupational Employment Statistics* survey, the estimated annual salary for most compliance officers ranged from $30,570 to $83,470.

Employment Prospects

EO Officers are employed by corporations, educational institutions, government agencies, nonprofit organizations, and other institutions.

Job openings generally become available when EO Officers resign or transfer to other positions. Employers may create or cut positions, depending on the growth of their organizations.

Advancement Prospects

EO Officers can advance to management and executive-level positions in equal opportunity, which usually requires obtaining positions with other employers. Individuals with entrepreneurial ambitions may become consultants.

EO Officers can also pursue other careers in human resources, such as becoming labor relations specialists, human resource trainers, or employee benefits specialists.

Education and Training

Employers require that candidates hold bachelor's degrees. Some employers prefer that college degrees be in social science, behavioral science, public administration, or another related field. Many employers accept any college degree as long as candidates have qualifying work experience.

Throughout their careers, EO Officers enroll in training and continuing education programs to develop their skills and expertise.

Experience, Skills, and Personality Traits

Employers typically hire EO Officers who have previous experience working with equal opportunity or affirmative action programs. Additionally, they look for candidates who demonstrate knowledge of civil rights, affirmative action, and fair employment practices, laws, and regulations. Experience requirements vary, depending on the job position, responsibilities, employer, and other factors. For example, an employer may require at least one year of experience working with equal opportunity programs for entry-level positions; three years for specialist positions, and five or more years for program managers.

EO Officers need effective writing, communication, teamwork, and interpersonal skills. They must also have excellent self-management skills that include the ability to work with minimal supervision, handle stressful situations, take initiative, and meet deadlines. Being courteous, diplomatic, trustworthy, honest, and flexible are some personality traits that successful EO Officers share.

Unions and Associations

Many EO Officers join professional associations to take advantage of networking opportunities, and other professional resources and services. EO Officers are eligible to join societies, such as the Society for Human Resource Management, that represent human resources professionals. Some EO Officers also belong to societies that represent compliance officers, such as the American Association for Affirmative Action. For contact information, see Appendix V.

Tips for Entry

1. While in college, obtain internships or part-time jobs in human resources. Let your supervisor know of your interest in gaining experience working with equal opportunity programs.
2. Obtain information interviews with EO program managers at places where you would like to work. These interviews offer you the chance to learn more about the profession and job opportunities, as well as give employers a chance to meet you.
3. To learn more about equal employment opportunity, visit the U.S. Equal Employment Opportunity Commission Web site at http://www.eeoc.gov. For more links, see Appendix VI.

ETHICS OFFICER

Duties: Develop and implement policies, procedures, and activities for ethics program; act as resource and consultant; perform other duties as required

Alternate Title(s): Chief Ethics Officer, Ethics Director

Salary Range: $38,000 to $146,000

Employment Prospects: Fair

Advancement Prospects: Poor

Prerequisites:

Education or Training—No standard requirements, but many officers have law degrees

Experience—Extensive experience working within an industry; usually been employed several years in an organization

Special Skills and Personality Traits—Leadership, management, training, listening, communication skills; be open-minded, tolerant, sensitive, thoughtful

```
┌─────────────────────────────────┐
│        Chief Ethics Officer     │
└─────────────────────────────────┘

┌─────────────────────────────────┐
│          Ethics Officer         │
└─────────────────────────────────┘

┌─────────────────────────────────┐
│   Ethics Manager or Coordinator │
│  (for corporate divisions or    │
│           agencies)             │
└─────────────────────────────────┘
```

Position Description

Many employers have established ethics programs to promote among their employees the moral values and principles to which the employers are committed in conducting their business. Employers write a code of ethics (or code of business conduct) that states how employees are expected to perform their jobs in an honest and conscientious manner. The code also describes potential ethical problems that employees may face, such as conflicts of interest, noncompliance with government regulations, or witnessing illegal activities.

Ethics Officers are in charge of managing ethics programs. They are responsible for creating and implementing strategies and programs that reinforce the importance of an ethical work culture. Ethics Officers also make sure that contractors, vendors, and others with whom their employers do business are also familiar with their employers' code of ethics.

Ethics Officers perform a wide range of complex duties. For example, they:

- formulate ethics policies and procedures
- draft employers' code of business conduct
- review new government laws and regulations and recommend changes to their employers' ethical codes
- design and coordinate training and education programs to teach employees to understand the code of business conduct
- develop informational brochures, articles, and other print and multimedia material to reinforce awareness of ethical policies and procedures
- design internal reporting systems (such as telephone hot lines) that allow for employees and others to report suspected violations of the ethical code
- conduct or oversee investigations into any possible breaches of conduct

Ethics Officers act as resources and consultants to executive officers, assisting them with decision making. Ethics Officers have the responsibility of being their employers' conscience and pointing out any unethical aspects in business decisions.

In many organizations, Ethics Officers are also responsible for overseeing corporate compliance programs. Some Ethics Officers also address other concerns in the workplace, such as civil rights, environment, privacy, and labor issues.

Ethics Officers typically work closely with other operations, especially if their own office has limited resources. These include legal, human resources, internal audit, and security departments.

Ethics Officers report directly to the general legal counsel, chief executive officer, or an ethics committee. They work full time or part time.

Salaries

Salaries for Ethics Officers vary, depending on such factors as their education, experience, employer, and geographical location. Specific salary information for this occupation is unavailable, but they earn salaries similar to management professionals. The estimated annual salary for most management occupations ranged between $37,800 and $145,600, according to the May 2005 *Occupational Employment Statistics* survey by the U.S. Bureau of Labor Statics.

Employment Prospects

Ethics Officers are employed in many different industries—banks, securities, insurance, health care, biotechnology, retail, manufacturing, telecommunications, public utilities, education, nonprofit associations, and so forth. In addition, state and federal government agencies and local municipalities hire Ethics Officers.

Opportunities generally become available as individuals retire or transfer to other jobs.

Advancement Prospects

Ethics Officers typically realize advancement through higher incomes and job satisfaction. Some Ethics Officers become business ethics consultants.

Education and Training

Ethics Officers hold, at the minimum, bachelor's degrees. Many have law training and have earned juris doctor (J.D.) degrees. Others hold master's degrees in business administration or other fields. Some Ethics Officers also possess doctoral degrees.

Experience, Skills, and Personality Traits

Ethics Officers usually have had extensive experience working within their industry. In addition, many have worked for their organization several years in responsible positions of management. Ethics Officers come from different backgrounds, in such areas as corporate law, human resources, operations/administration, finance, accounting, and internal audit.

Ethics Officers should have excellent leadership, management, and training skills, as well as effective listening and communication skills. Being open-minded, tolerant, sensitive, and thoughtful are some personality traits that successful Ethics Officers share.

Unions and Associations

Many Ethics Officers join the Ethics and Compliance Officer Association and other state and national professional associations to take advantage of networking opportunities, education programs, and other professional services and resources. (For contact information for this society, see Appendix V.)

Tips for Entry

1. Many universities offer graduate programs in business ethics for ethics professionals and consultants who develop and administer corporate ethics programs.
2. Network with ethics officers, compliance officers, and executive-level officers to learn about job opportunities.
3. You can learn more about business ethics on the Internet. To find relevant Web sites, enter the keywords *business ethics* or *ethics officer* in a search engine. For some links, see Appendix VI.

INSURANCE CLAIMS PROFESSIONAL

CAREER PROFILE

Duties: Examine claims, conduct investigations, make settlements, and perform other duties as required

Alternate Title(s): Claims Representative, Claims Examiner, Claims Adjuster

Salary Range: $29,000 to $74,000

Employment Prospects: Good

Advancement Prospects: Fair

Prerequisites:

Education or Training—A bachelor's degree preferred; employer training program

Experience—Requirements vary for the different positions

Special Skills and Personality Traits—Interpersonal, communication, report-writing, computer, and self-management skills; be detail-oriented, observant, analytical, fair, judicious

Special Requirements—Licensure for independent adjusters may be required

CAREER LADDER

```
┌─────────────────────────────────────┐
│      Senior Claims Examiner          │
└─────────────────────────────────────┘

┌─────────────────────────────────────┐
│  Claims Examiner or Claims Adjuster  │
└─────────────────────────────────────┘

┌─────────────────────────────────────┐
│   Trainee or Claims Representative   │
└─────────────────────────────────────┘
```

Position Description

People buy different types of insurance policies—life, health, property, or liability—to cover the risk of loss or harm to their property and lives. When they experience loss or damage, they submit claims to their insurance companies. Insurance Claims Professionals are responsible for determining if customers' claims are covered by their policies. They also have the duty of assessing the facts and settling insurance claims.

Claims professionals are assigned several cases at a time. With each claim, they carefully examine the claim forms and supporting documents, such as medical records, for a disability claim, or estimate reports, for a car accident claim. They make sure that the forms are complete and the information is accurate and correct. They review the claimant's policy to ensure that it is still valid and to learn what losses a policy covers and the amount of insurance coverage that was purchased. In addition, claims professionals make sure that claims are not false or fraudulent. They verify the truth of a claim by contacting the claimant, doctors, employers, and others who may have information about the claim.

If more information is needed, Insurance Claims Professionals conduct further investigations. They may perform the investigations themselves or refer them to claims investigators. The investigations include interviewing claimants in person, inspecting sites or property, and reviewing police, hospital, and other records.

Upon completion of a review or investigation of a claim, claims professionals decide whether to accept or deny the claim. Furthermore, claims professionals have the authority to negotiate the amount of a settlement.

Different claims professionals perform specific duties. Claims representatives usually handle minor claims, and make contact with claimants by telephone or mail. They may also be assigned to coordinate information for more complex claims or gather and record information from claimants for senior staff members. Claims representatives normally work from insurance claims centers.

Senior claims professionals who work for life and health insurance companies are called claims examiners. These professionals are based in insurance headquarters and are usually assigned more complex claims.

Claims examiners investigate complex claims for life and health insurance companies. These professionals are usually based in insurance headquarters. Claims adjusters also investigate complex claims, but they work for property and liability insurance companies. They are based in branch offices. Some handle and settle claims by phone and mail. Others, known as field adjusters, travel to sites to inspect damaged property, interview claimants and witnesses, and read police reports and hospital records.

Claims examiners and claims representatives typically work a standard 40-hour week. Some insurance companies provide customer services 24 hours a day, seven days a week. In those companies, claims representatives may work shifts that include evenings and weekends. Claims adjusters sometimes put in 50 hours or more a week.

Salaries

Salaries for Insurance Claims Professionals vary, depending on such factors as their education, experience, job duties, and geographical location. The U.S. Bureau of Labor Statistics (BLS) reports in its May 2005 *Occupational Employment Statistics* (OES) survey that the estimated annual salary for most claims adjusters, examiners, and investigators ranged between $28,710 and $74,310.

Employment Prospects

According to the BLS's May 2005 OES survey, an estimated 234,030 claims adjusters, examiners, and investigators were employed in the United States. The BLS further reports that employment in these occupations should increase by 9 to 17 percent through 2014. Job openings will also become available as individuals retire, transfer to other jobs, or leave the workforce.

Advancement Prospects

With additional experience and training, claims representatives can advance to higher positions as claims examiners, adjusters, or investigators. Experienced claims adjusters may pursue careers as independent adjusters. Claims professionals with administrative ambitions may seek opportunities for supervisory and management positions.

Education and Training

Requirements vary for the different Insurance Claims Professional positions. Generally, employers prefer candidates with bachelor's degrees in liberal arts, business, or a field that is relevant to the type of claim being performed. For example, an engineering degree is desirable for a position dealing with industrial claims.

Insurance companies provide classroom training, on-the-job training, or both for entry-level positions.

Special Requirements

Some states require independent claims adjusters to be licensed. For specific information, contact the insurance commission in the state where you wish to work.

Experience, Skills, and Personality Traits

Requirements vary for the different claims positions. In general, employers prefer that candidates have some experience in claims work. Good candidates also demonstrate the ability to understand federal and state insurance laws. It is also helpful to have practical knowledge in the area of claims. For example, an automobile claims adjuster should have knowledge about cars and car repairs.

Insurance Claims Professionals must have excellent interpersonal and communication skills, as well as strong report-writing and computer skills. They also need good self-management skills—such as the ability to handle stressful situations, meet deadlines, work independently, and manage several tasks simultaneously.

Some personality traits that successful Insurance Claims Professionals share are being detail-oriented, observant, analytical, fair, and judicious.

Unions and Associations

Insurance Claims Professionals join professional associations to take advantage of professional services and resources. Two national associations that represent Claims Professionals are the International Claim Association and the National Association of Independent Insurance Adjusters. For contact information, see Appendix V.

Tips for Entry

1. Contact insurance companies directly for general job information, as well as job openings for trainee or entry-level positions in claims.
2. Many Insurance Claims Professionals obtain professional certification to enhance their employability. To learn about some certification programs, see Appendix II.
3. Many claims representatives started at an insurance company as an office clerk, gradually gaining work experience related to claims.
4. You can learn more about Insurance Claims Professionals on the Internet. To find pertinent Web sites, enter any of these keywords in a search engine: *insurance claims professionals, claims examiners, or claims adjusters.* For some links, see Appendix VI.

LEGAL MANAGEMENT CONSULTANT

CAREER PROFILE

Duties: Provide business advice and solutions to clients; conduct research and analysis; perform other duties as required

Alternate Title(s): Management Analyst, Research Associate

Salary Range: $39,000 to $123,000

Employment Prospects: Good

Advancement Prospects: Good

Prerequisites:

Education or Training—A bachelor's or advanced degree required; on-the-job training

Experience—Several years of experience working in legal management

Special Skills and Personality Traits—Leadership, time-management, analytical, problem-solving, research, writing, communication, interpersonal, teamwork, and customer service skills; creative, self-motivated, detail-oriented, assertive, personable, and ethical

CAREER LADDER

```
┌─────────────────────────────────────┐
│  Senior Legal Management Consultant  │
└─────────────────────────────────────┘

┌─────────────────────────────────────┐
│     Legal Management Consultant      │
└─────────────────────────────────────┘

┌─────────────────────────────────────┐
│  Research Associate or Junior Legal  │
│       Management Consultant          │
└─────────────────────────────────────┘
```

Position Description

In today's economy, lawyers cannot just be reputable practitioners to be successful. They must also have practices that operate efficiently and effectively every day. To meet the challenges of running and building a business, law firms, as well as legal departments, turn to Legal Management Consultants for assistance in improving their structure, productivity, and profits.

Many Legal Management Consultants are former attorneys, legal administrators, and legal managers. They have expertise in a wide array of business functions such as business strategies, finance, planning, human resources, client development, marketing, and information technology. They provide their services on a contractual basis to clients who range from solo practitioners starting up a new practice to large, well-established law firms and corporate law departments.

Legal Management Consultants are typically hired by clients who prefer to use temporary personnel to handle management projects for which they have no staff. Many clients also see the advantage of using consultants because they are free from the influence of company politics, and hence can remain objective.

Legal Management Consultants work on a variety of types of projects. For example, they may be involved in:

- formulating business plans
- conducting performance and profitability audits
- restructuring the organization for more efficiency
- designing improved billing and accounting systems
- evaluating automation, or technology, needs
- formulating solutions to human resources issues, such as employee benefits, grievance procedures, or employee incentives
- developing recruiting and retention strategies for attorneys, legal support staff, and nonlegal support staff
- planning marketing strategies to build up a client base
- advising on whether to buy or sell a law firm, or to merge with another firm
- studying the feasibility for a law firm to start up ancillary businesses
- planning attorney retreats

Consultants may be assigned to work on a project alone or as part of a team of consultants, depending on the nature and complexity of the project. They work closely with their clients' managers, attorneys, and other personnel.

Although projects vary, Legal Management Consultants perform similar procedures on each project. They identify and assess their clients' problems. They gather information by interviewing managers, attorneys, and other staff members; review materials from internal and external sources; and conduct studies and evaluations. They analyze and interpret information to develop recommendations for their clients. Consultants then prepare detailed written or oral reports of their findings and recommendations and present them to their clients. Sometimes clients retain consultants to implement the solutions they have suggested.

Novice consultants are assigned routine tasks while working under the supervision of experienced consultants. As they gain experience, they are given greater responsibilities and are assigned to lead positions. Senior consultants are usually involved in business development. They continually seek out new clients as well as maintain relationships with existing clients.

Legal Management Consultants work 40 hours a week, but often put in many more hours to perform their duties and meet deadlines. It is not uncommon for them to work nights and weekends. Consultants typically divide their time between their offices and their clients' worksites, which may be in another city, state, or country. Consultants sometimes spend several days or weeks completing tasks at their clients' sites.

Salaries

Salaries for Legal Management Consultants vary, depending on such factors as their education, experience, employer, and geographical location. According to the May 2005 *Occupational Employment Statistics* survey by the U.S. Bureau of Labor Statistics (BLS), the estimated annual salary for most management analysts, including management consultants ranged from $38,650 to $123,300.

In addition to their salaries, many Legal Management Consultants receive bonuses, which are based on their job performance.

Employment Prospects

Many Legal Management Consultants are self-employed or employees of small legal management consulting firms. Consultants may work for either small or big management firms that offer their services to other professions or industries.

The legal management consulting services industry is part of the larger management, scientific, and technical consulting services industry, which is the fifth fastest growing industry in the United States. The BLS predicts that this industry should increase by 60 percent within the period of 2004 and 2014. All areas of consulting, including legal management consulting, are expected to experience strong growth, according to the BLS.

In addition to job growth, opportunities for Legal Management Consultants will become available to replace individuals who have retired, advanced to higher positions, or transferred to other jobs. The competition for management consulting jobs, in general, is high because this occupation offers attractive salaries and prestige.

Advancement Prospects

Legal Management Consultants can rise through the ranks as research associates, consultants, managers, and partners. Consultants can also pursue supervisory and managerial positions. A master's degree or other advanced degree may be required for advancement. Those with entrepreneurial ambitions become independent consultants or start their own consulting firms.

Education and Training

Minimally, individuals need a bachelor's degree (usually in any field) to apply for a research associate position, which is an entry-level position. To qualify for a junior consultant position, a juris doctor (J.D.) degree or a master's degree in business administration or another related field is usually required. Some management firms waive the educational requirement, if candidates possess several years of qualifying experience.

Novice consultants receive on-the-job training while working under the supervision and guidance of experienced consultants. Some consulting firms may also provide formal classroom training programs.

Throughout their careers, Legal Management Consultants enroll in continuing education programs and training programs to update their skills and knowledge.

Experience, Special Skills, and Personality Traits

Most employers seek candidates who have several years of experience working in the area of management of law practices or legal departments. Management consulting firms occasionally hire recent graduates (with bachelor's or advanced degrees) to research associate or junior consultant positions. Entry-level candidates usually have relevant work experience that they have gained through employment, internships, or work-study programs.

To perform their work well, Legal Management Consultants must have excellent leadership, time management, analytical, problem-solving, research, writing, and communication skills. They also need effective interpersonal, teamwork, and customer service skills, as they must work well with clients, colleagues, and others from diverse backgrounds. Being creative, self-motivated, detail-oriented, assertive, personable, and ethical are some personality traits that Legal Management Consultants share.

Unions and Associations

Legal Management Consultants can join various professional associations to take advantage of networking opportunities, professional certification, continuing education programs, and other professional resources and services. One national society that serves the interests of management consultants in general is the Institute of Management Consultants USA. These consultants may also join the Association of Legal Administrators, the Legal Marketing Association, and other organizations that serve the interests of professionals involved in law firm management. For contact information for these organizations, see Appendix V.

Tips for Entry

1. Talk with Legal Management Consultants to learn more about their work and how they entered the field.
2. Gain practical experience by volunteering to do legal management consulting work with public interest organizations.
3. To enhance their employability, Legal Management Consultants might consider obtaining professional certification granted by the Institute of Management Consultants USA. For more information, visit its Web site at http://www.imcusa.org.
4. Use the Internet to learn more about legal management consulting. To find relevant Web sites, enter any of the keywords in a search engine: *legal management consultants, law firm management consulting,* or *law department management consulting.* For some links, see Appendix VI.

PATENT AGENT

CAREER PROFILE

Duties: Prepare patent applications; prosecute patents in the U.S. Patent and Trademark Office; perform other duties as required

Alternate Title(s): Patent Analyst, Patent Engineer, Patent Specialist

Salary Range: $30,000 to $146,000

Employment Prospects: Good

Advancement Prospects: Fair

Prerequisites:

Education or Training—A bachelor's degree; on-the-job training

Experience—Strong technical background; scientific or technical work experience is desirable

Special Skills and Personality Traits—Writing, analytical, communication, and interpersonal skills; be curious, detail-oriented, organized, flexible

Special Requirements—Be registered in the U.S. Patent and Trademark Office

CAREER LADDER

```
┌─────────────────────────────┐
│   Supervisory Patent Agent   │
└─────────────────────────────┘

┌─────────────────────────────┐
│         Patent Agent         │
└─────────────────────────────┘

┌─────────────────────────────┐
│           Trainee            │
└─────────────────────────────┘
```

Position Description

Patent Agents help clients obtain patents for new inventions, such as machines, medications, toys, food processes, plant varieties, shoe designs, and compositions of matter. Patents are legal documents that protect the rights of owners to sell their inventions exclusively. In other words, no one else can make, use, sell, or import patented inventions unless the owners first give their permission. (A patent is valid for a specific number of years.) In the United States, the authority for granting patents is the U.S. Patent and Trademark Office (USPTO), a federal office based in Washington, D.C.

Patent Agents serve clients who are inventors as well as those who own inventions—individuals, businesses, and others—but did not conceive or design them. These professionals represent clients in the USPTO where they are allowed to practice patent law. However, they are not attorneys. It is unlawful for them to provide legal services that are performed by lawyers, such as providing legal advice, negotiating licenses to use patented inventions, representing clients in court litigation, or filing appeals in courts.

Further, Patent Agents cannot practice law in federal or state courts.

Patent Agents offer clients two major services. One service is to prepare the patent application, upon which the granting of a patent is based. The application consists of a detailed description of an invention and the explicit claim to the invention. The claim describes the territory of use that belongs exclusively to the inventors. Patent Agents are responsible for drafting the application so that it is both technically and legally clear. To make sure the information is accurate, they consult with the inventors.

The other major service Patent Agents provide is the prosecution of patents. They represent their clients in the patent application process. Patent Agents are responsible for filing patent applications, responding to formal correspondence (called office actions) from the USPTO, meeting with examiners to discuss the merits of their clients' inventions, making sure all deadlines are met, and so forth. Patent Agents also counsel their clients on the progress of their applications.

Patent Agents work a standard 40-hour week, but sometimes put in additional hours to meet deadlines and complete tasks.

Salaries

Salaries for Patent Agents vary, depending on such factors as their education, experience, and geographical location. Specific income information for Patent Agents is unavailable, but a general idea can be gained by looking at what other legal occupations earn. According to the May 2005 *Occupational Employment Statistics* survey, by the U.S. Bureau of Labor Statistics, the estimated annual salary for most professionals within the legal occupation category ranged between $30,040 and $145,600.

Employment Prospects

Many Patent Agents are employed by law firms as well as by companies in various industries that are involved in research and development. Some Patent Agents work for academic institutions and government agencies. Others are employees of firms that offer patent prosecution services, and still others are solo practitioners.

Opportunities are favorable for qualified Patent Agents because of the continued growth in the creation of intellectual property.

Since the 1990s, intellectual property law has been one of the fastest growing areas of law and that growth is expected to continue for years to come. Some experts in the field report an increasing demand for experienced Patent Agents.

In general, opportunities become available as Patent Agents advance to higher positions, transfer to other jobs, retire, or leave the workforce for various reasons. Employers will create additional positions to meet growing needs for Patent Agents' services.

Advancement Prospects

Opportunities for supervisory and management positions are limited and usually requires obtaining positions with other employers. Many agents realize advancement through job satisfaction and by earning higher incomes.

Some Patent Agents earn juris doctor (J.D.) degrees and become patent attorneys.

Education and Training

Patent Agents must have at least a bachelor's degree in engineering, physics, chemistry, biochemistry, or other physical or natural science. Employers may also require that they possess an advanced degree in a science discipline.

Entry-level Patent Agents typically receive on-the-job training. Some employers provide education programs to help Patent Agents study for the USPTO entrance bar examination.

Special Requirements

No professional license is required to become a Patent Agent. However, a Patent Agent must register with the USPTO in order to practice law before it. This requires passing an entrance bar examination. For more information, visit the USPTO Web site at http://www.upsto.gov.

Experience, Skills, and Personality Traits

Requirements vary among the different employers. In general, candidates should have strong technical backgrounds. Having work experience in the science or technology fields in which they would be practicing patent law is desirable.

Patent Agents must have superior writing skills, including the ability to use technical and legal language clearly. They also need excellent analytical, communication, and interpersonal skills. Being curious, detail-oriented, organized, and flexible are some personality traits that successful Patent Agents share.

Unions and Associations

Many Patent Agents join local, state, and national professional associations in the industries in which they serve. Patent Agents are also eligible to join the National Association of Patent Practitioners. (For contact information, see Appendix V.) By joining professional associations, Patent Agents can take advantage of networking opportunities and other professional services and resources.

Tips for Entry

1. Some high school classes that may prepare you for this field are science, English composition, public speaking, and business law.
2. Directly contact employers for whom you would like to work. Ask about entry-level positions and their job application process.
3. You can learn more about Patent Agents on the Internet. You might start by visiting these Web sites: U.S. Patent and Trademark Office, http://www.uspto.gov; National Association of Patent Practitioners, http://www.napp.org; and Patent Law in the United States (by Bitlaw), http://www.bitlaw.com/patent.

TITLE EXAMINER, REAL ESTATE

CAREER PROFILE

Duties: Conduct research about the legal history of a property title; analyze legal instruments such as property deeds, wills, and liens; prepare reports of findings; perform other duties as required

Alternate Title(s): None

Salary Range: $21,000 to $64,000

Employment Prospects: Fair

Advancement Prospects: Poor

Prerequisites:

Education or Training—A high school diploma; on-the-job training

Experience—Previous experience performing title search and abstracting work

Special Skills and Personality Traits—Communication, interpersonal, teamwork, customer service, analytical, and organization skills; meticulous, detail-oriented, decisive, dedicated

Special Requirements—Licensure may be required

CAREER LADDER

```
┌─────────────────────────────────┐
│      Senior Title Examiner      │
│   or Department Supervisor      │
└─────────────────────────────────┘

┌─────────────────────────────────┐
│        Title Examiner           │
└─────────────────────────────────┘

┌─────────────────────────────────┐
│  Title Searcher or Title Abstractor  │
└─────────────────────────────────┘
```

Position Description

Title Examiners are part of the process of buying homes, land, commercial buildings, and other properties. In a real estate sale, the title to a property is formally transferred from the seller to the buyer. (A title is the legal document that states a person's true ownership of a property.) It is the responsibility of Title Examiners to check that the seller of a property is the legal owner. They research the legal history of the title and verify that the title is free and clear to transfer to a new owner.

Conducting title searches requires looking through public records in city and county offices. Title Examiners search through books and file cabinets as well as through computer databases to find required records. They review mortgages, deeds, wills, divorce decrees, court judgments, liens, tax records, land maps, and other legal instruments.

Title Examiners read public records closely and carefully. They make sure that the property being purchased matches the title that would be transferred to the new owner. They also look for any restrictions that may limit the use of a property, or if rights to the property have been already granted to others. In addition, Title Examiners learn if any mortgages, court judgments, and liens are on the property, and if property taxes or other assessments need to be paid.

After performing a title search, Title Examiners prepare a report, or abstract, of their findings. They summarize the facts and attach a list, or copies, of all the legal instruments that apply to the property.

Title Examiners are often faced with deadlines, as property buyers and sellers want to close sales as quickly as possible. Title Examiners usually work a standard 40-hour week.

Salaries

Salaries for Title Examiners vary, depending on such factors as their education, experience, and geographical location. According to the May 2005 *Occupational Employment Statistics* survey by the U.S. Bureau of Labor Statistics, the estimated annual salary for most Title Examiners ranged from $21,300 to $64,120.

Employment Prospects

Most real estate Title Examiners work for title companies. Some are employed by lawyers, banks, and local government offices. Some Title Examiners are independent contractors.

In general, positions become available as Title Examiners resign, retire, or transfer to other positions. Experts expect that fewer examiners may be needed because the increased use of technology will allow examiners to handle a heavier workload.

Advancement Prospects

Title Examiners have any number of career paths to choose, depending on their interests and ambitions. They may advance to supervisory or management positions within the title examination and search department of their company, or they may fill such positions in other organizations. Experienced Title Examiners might pursue freelance careers. With additional training and experience, they may pursue other careers within the title and real estate industry by becoming office managers, escrow officers, attorneys, insurance underwriters, or real estate agents.

Education and Training

Educational requirements vary from employer to employer. Minimally, Title Examiners must have a high school diploma or high school equivalency diploma along with qualifying experience. Employers generally prefer that candidates have completed some college courses.

Entry-level examiners typically receive on-the-job training, while working under the supervision of experienced Title Examiners.

Throughout their careers, Title Examiners enroll in courses and workshops to expand their knowledge and update their skills.

Special Requirements

Some states require Title Examiners to be licensed. For specific information, contact the state insurance commission in the state where you wish to work.

Experience, Skills, and Personality Traits

Depending on the employer, candidates may be required to have one or more years of experience performing title search and abstracting work. Candidates should be familiar with legal documents, descriptions, and terms relating to land titles and transactions.

Title Examiners must have adequate communication, interpersonal, teamwork, and customer service skills as they interact daily with coworkers and outside contacts (such as realtors, government officials, banks, and home sellers). In addition, they need strong analytical and organization skills.

Being meticulous, detail-oriented, decisive, and dedicated are some personality traits that successful Title Examiners share.

Unions and Associations

Many Title Examiners are members of state, regional, or national professional associations, such as the American Land Title Association. (For contact information, see Appendix V.) By joining professional associations, they can take advantage of such professional resources as training programs and networking opportunities.

Tips for Entry

1. To gain experience, apply for an office support position in a title company or real estate office or law firm that does title examination work. Let your supervisor know of your interest in becoming a title examiner. Show your willingness to learn how to do title searches.
2. Title searchers and title abstractors can advance to the position of Title Examiner.
3. Talk with Title Examiners about their work and how they broke into the field.
4. You can learn more about Title Examiners on the Internet. To find other relevant Web sites, enter the keywords *title examiners* or *title industry* in a search engine. For some links, see Appendix VI.

PROFESSIONS IN POLITICS

LEGISLATOR, STATE OR FEDERAL

CAREER PROFILE

Duties: Serve as an elected representative in the U.S. Congress or a state legislature; make federal or state laws; perform duties as required

Alternate Title(s): U.S. Senator, U.S. Representative, State Senator, State Representative

Salary Range: $0 to $165,000

Employment Prospects: Poor

Advancement Prospects: Fair

Prerequisites:

Education or Training—No standard requirements

Experience—Public service and community involvement

Special Skills and Personality Traits—Leadership, organizational, teamwork, interpersonal, communication, public speaking, and debate skills; ability to compromise; be outgoing, self-confident, popular, honest, dedicated, energetic, assertive

CAREER LADDER

```
┌─────────────────────────────┐
│     Federal Legislator       │
└─────────────────────────────┘

┌─────────────────────────────┐
│      State Legislator        │
└─────────────────────────────┘

┌─────────────────────────────┐
│   Local Elected Official,     │
│ Legislative Aide, or Any Occupation │
└─────────────────────────────┘
```

Position Description

In the United States, federal and state Legislators are responsible for making laws that govern the nation and the 50 states. They create laws to protect public safety and welfare; protect civil rights; provide for education, affordable health care, and social services; protect the environment; build and repair streets and freeways; assist small business owners; protect people in the workplace; raise or lower taxes; and so forth. As elected officials, Legislators propose and pass laws that are in the best interests of their constituents, the people whom they represent.

Federal Legislators are elected to serve in the U.S. Congress in Washington, D.C. They work in either one of the two Congressional chambers—the Senate, which is the upper house, and the House of Representatives, which is the lower house. State Legislators work in their state capitals. In 49 states, state Legislators are elected to serve in either one of two legislative chambers. The upper house is also known as the Senate; the lower house is called the House of Representatives, General Assembly, or House of Delegates. In Nebraska, the legislature is made up of only one house.

Along with making laws, Legislators perform other duties. Some of these responsibilities include:

- planning government budgets
- assessing taxes
- approving official appointments by executive officers
- regulating government activities
- conducting impeachment proceedings
- serving on committees (such as finance, education, or labor) that study prospective legislation

Legislators keep constituents informed about their activities through meetings, press releases, newsletters, Web sites, and other methods. They also ask constituents about their opinions regarding issues and proposed bills. In addition, Legislators assist constituents with their requests and questions. Legislators typically have offices in their capital as well as in their local districts. Almost all Legislators maintain a staff that provides office and legislative support.

U.S. Senators represent all the people who live in their state, and so are elected by voters statewide. U.S. Representatives are elected by voters in the districts where they live and which they represent. State legislators are elected by voters in the districts that they represent. Legislators are elected to serve terms that usually last from two to six years. They may seek reelection at the end of their terms. In some states, Legislators may run for only a limited number of terms.

At the state and national levels, candidates run for legislative offices as members of a political party—such as Democrat, Republican, Reform, or American Independent, party. Candidates begin campaign efforts several months, or even a few years, before an election. They use the television, radio, and print media, as well as distribute materials, to describe their qualifications and reasons for running for office. They make speeches before business, community, and social organizations, as well as meet voters at various public functions and events. Candidates also participate in public debates about issues that concern the communities they would represent. Furthermore, candidates raise money to pay for their political campaigns.

Legislators work long and varied hours, including evenings and on weekends. Each day is unique. They attend community, social, and charity functions; meet with lobbyists, other legislators, the media, and constituents; make public speeches; research issues; prepare reports; and attend meetings. Legislators often travel back and forth from their home state or district to the capital.

Salaries

Salaries for Legislators vary widely. In 2006, the annual salary for members of Congress was raised to $165,200. According to the National Conference of State Legislatures, annual compensation in 2005 for state Legislators ranged from no pay for New Mexico Legislators to $110,880 for California legislators. Many Legislators receive a per diem rate (per day) fee when they are in session.

Employment Prospects

There are 100 U.S. Senate positions, two from each of the 50 states. The number of U.S. Representatives and state legislative positions may increase or decrease depending on the population growth. In 2006, there were 435 U.S. representatives. The U.S. Bureau of Labor Statistics reports in its November 2004 *Occupational Employments Statistics* survey that there are an estimated, 3,640 state legislators in the United States.

Opportunities become available during elections. Any U.S. citizen who meets the age and residence requirements for an office may run for election.

Advancement Prospects

Many Legislators become career politicians, but much of their political success depends on their ability to win elections. Some Legislators pursue a career path of running for higher offices. For example, a state assemblyperson might run for state senate, then after several terms as a state senator run for the U.S. Senate or a state executive office.

Education and Training

There are no standard educational requirements for becoming state or federal Legislators. Most Legislators have bachelor's degrees as well as advanced degrees in various fields. Many Legislators possess law degrees.

Experience, Skills, and Personality Traits

Legislators come from various backgrounds—law, education, business, social services, health care, science, journalism, public advocacy, and other fields. Some Legislators have gained previous experience working as staff members for other politicians, by being legislative aides, chiefs of staffs, or political consultants

In general, voters choose candidates who have a track record of being involved in their communities. They also select candidates whose political principles and stances on social, economic, and other issues match theirs. Legislators need effective leadership, organizational, teamwork, interpersonal, communication, public speaking, and debate skills. They must also have the ability to make compromises. Being outgoing, self-confident, popular, honest, dedicated, energetic, and assertive are some personality traits that successful Legislators share. Further, they have a strong commitment to public service and are passionate about making changes for the best interests of the public welfare.

Unions and Associations

As members of their political parties, Legislators participate in meetings, committee work, and fund-raising activities. They also belong to various community organizations, charities, professional associations, and other organizations to take advantage of networking opportunities as well as to continually build a broad base of support.

Tips for Entry

1. Gain practical experience by working on political campaigns for candidates or initiatives in which you believe. Also, get involved in community groups, charities, and public service activities.

2. Gain experience by obtaining an internship or fellowship in a government office.

3. Use the Internet to learn more about how state and federal legislatures work. You might start by visiting these Web sites: U.S. Senate, http://www.senate.gov; U.S. House of Representatives, http://www.house.gov; and National Conference of State Legislatures, http://www.ncsl.org. For more links, see Appendix VI.

LOCAL ELECTED OFFICIAL

CAREER PROFILE

Duties: Serve as elected leaders in city and county governments; make and enforce laws, regulations, and codes; perform duties as required

Alternate Title(s): Mayor; City Council Member; County Commissioner, County Supervisor, County Freeholder (New Jersey)

Salary Range: $0 to $73,000

Employment Prospects: Poor

Advancement Prospects: Fair

Prerequisites:

Education or Training—No standard requirements

Experience—Public service and community involvement

Special Skills and Personality Traits—Leadership, teamwork, interpersonal, public speaking, and debate skills; ability to compromise; be outgoing, self-confident, popular, honest, dedicated, energetic, assertive

CAREER LADDER

```
┌─────────────────────────────────┐
│  State or Federal Elected Office │
└─────────────────────────────────┘

┌─────────────────────────────────┐
│      City Council or County      │
│      Board of Commissioners      │
└─────────────────────────────────┘

┌─────────────────────────────────┐
│ Member of a local board or       │
│ commission                       │
│ (such as the board of education) │
└─────────────────────────────────┘
```

Position Description

In the United States, local government is composed of two levels—county and municipality (city, village, or town). Both levels of local government are created by state governments and are under their authority. But it is the voters within each municipality and county who choose their local government leaders. Heading municipal governments are mayors and council members, while commissioners or supervisors govern county governments. (In Louisiana, counties are called parishes; in Alaska, boroughs.)

Local Elected Officials are responsible for making and executing laws that provide for the protection, safety, and general welfare of the citizens and the environment. They plan fiscal budgets as well as establish policies, objectives, and goals for running local governments. They also develop public services such as law enforcement, fire services, schools, hospitals, affordable housing, parks, public transportation, and waste treatment systems. In addition, they have the authority to assess and collect taxes. Furthermore, Local Elected Officials make sure that government operations are running smoothly and effectively each day.

The powers of Local Elected Officials vary, depending on the form of county or municipal government. In most county governments, the governing body consists of a board of one or more commissioners. The board performs both lawmaking and executive duties. In some counties, voters elect an executive officer who shares policy-making decisions with the board of commissioners.

The roles of mayor and city council vary among municipalities. In many city governments, the mayor and city council are two distinct offices. The mayor, as executive officer, determines government policy and runs the government while the city council makes municipal ordinances, or laws. In some municipalities, the mayor has limited powers and shares policy-making decisions with the city council. In other municipalities, the city council is the main governing body. The mayor, who may be elected or appointed, is a member of the council. A city manager is hired by the council to run the city.

Most local elections are nonpartisan. In other words, candidates do not run as members of political parties. Local Elected Officials usually are elected to serve an office term of two to four years. They may seek reelection at the end of their terms. In some communities, Elected Officials are limited in the number of terms they may serve.

When Elected Officials run for reelection, they must campaign extensively to convince voters that they are still the best candidates for office. They make speeches, meet with voters, participate in public debates, and so forth. They use the television, radio, and print media, as well as distribute materials, to describe their qualifications for office.

City council members and county commissioners work part time or full time in their elected positions. Many continue to hold down part-time or full-time jobs in their primary professions.

Local Elected Officials work irregular hours. They often work evenings and on weekends to attend meetings, review issues, prepare proposals, complete administrative tasks, fulfill official duties at community functions, and so forth.

Salaries

Salaries for Local Elected Officials vary widely. In some locations officials do not receive any salary. Specific salary information for these types of officials is unavailable. However, the estimated annual salary for most Legislators, including local officials, ranged between $11,820 and $72,700, according to the May 2005 *Occupational Employment Statistics* survey by the U.S. Bureau of Labor Statistics.

Employment Prospects

Opportunities become available with each local election. Any U.S. citizen who meets age and residence requirements may run for a city council or county board seat. To win, candidates must undertake campaigns that appeal to a broad base of local voters.

Advancement Prospects

Some Local Elected Officials serve for a few terms, accomplishing the goals for which the voters elected them (for example: cutting taxes, adding more social services, or enacting clean air laws). Other officials pursue a political career path, running for elected offices at progressively higher (local, state, and federal) levels.

Education and Training

There are no standard educational requirements for Local Elected Officials. Many hold associate, bachelor's, and advanced degrees in various disciplines.

Experience, Skills, and Personality Traits

Local Elected Officials come from different backgrounds—business, community services, law, and education, among others. Voters usually choose candidates who have a track record of being actively involved in their communities. They also select candidates whose political principles and stances on social, economic, and other issues match theirs.

Some skills that Local Elected Officials need are leadership, teamwork, interpersonal, communication, public speaking, and debate skills. In addition, they must have the ability to make compromises. Being outgoing, charming, sincere, honest, dedicated, energetic, creative, and flexible are some personality traits that successful Local Elected Officials share. Further, they have a strong desire to make changes that benefit their communities.

Unions and Associations

Local Elected Officials join state, regional, and national associations that serve city and county governments. Two national organizations are the National League of Cities and the National Association of Counties. These associations offer leadership training programs, opportunities to network with peers, and other professional services and resources. (For contact information, see Appendix V.)

Tips for Entry

1. Participate in your local government. For example, attend council meetings, apply for voluntary positions on city commissions, or get involved in the political issues that concern your community.
2. Many council members and county supervisors began their political careers by being elected or appointed to local school boards, special district boards, or other local government boards and commissions.
3. Join community organizations to gain public service experience and to take advantage of networking opportunities.
4. Use the Internet to learn more about how local government works. Many city and county governments have Web sites. To find a Web site for a city government, enter the name of the city and the phrase *city government* (for example, *Knoxville city government*). For a county government Web site, enter the name of the county and the phrase *county government* (for example, *San Benito county government*).

LEGISLATIVE ASSISTANT

CAREER PROFILE

Duties: Assist legislators with their decision making for proposed legislation; perform public relations duties; perform other duties as required

Alternate Title(s): Legislative Aide, Political Aide, District Aide, Field Representative

Salary Range: $30,000 to $45,000+

Employment Prospects: Fair

Advancement Prospects: Good

Prerequisites:

Education or Training—A bachelor's degree

Experience—Previous experience as interns, volunteers, or support staff in legislators' offices; knowledge of the legislative process and the issues that concern legislators

Special Skills and Personality Traits—Writing, research, organizational, teamwork, communication, interpersonal, self-management skills; be outgoing, energetic, enthusiastic, self-motivated, efficient, ambitious, creative, flexible

CAREER LADDER

```
┌─────────────────────────────────────┐
│ Legislative Director or Chief of Staff │
└─────────────────────────────────────┘

┌─────────────────────────────────────┐
│        Legislative Assistant         │
└─────────────────────────────────────┘

┌─────────────────────────────────────┐
│        Campaign or Legislative       │
│    Volunteer or Staff Member         │
└─────────────────────────────────────┘
```

Position Description

Legislative Assistants provide support to legislators so that they can effectively make laws that are in the best interests of their constituents. These assistants help legislators in all three levels of government. At the local level, they aid city council members and county supervisors. At the state and federal levels, they assist senators and representatives who serve in state legislatures or the U.S. Congress.

Legislators, at all levels of government, sponsor legislation as well as vote on proposed bills about funding, social programs, the environment, civil rights, individual rights, education, and other issues. Legislative Assistants are responsible for helping legislators stay on top of each proposed legislation. Some of their duties include:

- conducting research
- meeting with lobbyists, constituents, and others to gather accurate and factual information about the issues
- drafting proposed legislation
- attending legislative committee meetings and preparing reports of the proceedings

- analyzing bills and making recommendations to legislators on the best actions to make
- analyzing the voting records of other legislators
- keeping track of the status of proposed legislation
- keeping legislators informed about the needs and concerns of the legislators' constituents

Legislative Assistants may be assigned to handle several different bills or be in charge of one or more major issues, such as technology, children's rights, or health care.

Legislative Assistants are also responsible for helping constituents and the general public with questions or requests. For example, a constituent may want to know about government programs that help the elderly. Legislative Assistants conduct research and provide the information in person by phone, letter, or e-mail.

Many Legislative assistants handle public relations. They maintain relationships with the leaders and constituents in the home districts. In addition, the assistants keep constituents informed about legislators' activities and accomplishments through press releases, newsletters, Web sites, and other forms of communication. They also set up speaking engagements for legislators at schools, community centers, chambers of commerce, and community organizations, as well as at community events and other functions within their districts.

Many assistants are responsible for performing various office and administrative duties. These tasks vary from one office to the next. For example, they might answer phones and e-mail messages, greet visitors to the legislator's office, maintain the legislator's schedule, draft routine correspondence, and supervise interns and volunteers. Some assistants help legislators with their political campaigns. They may plan campaign activities, develop campaign materials, set up fund-raising events, and draft speeches.

At the local and state level, two or more legislators might share the services of one Legislative Assistant. In some states, legislators are allowed to hire only one assistant. Congress members typically hire several assistants. Federal and some state legislators have two staffs, one working in their capital offices and the other working in their district offices. District aides are responsible for keeping Legislators up to date with constituents' opinions and addressing constituents' requests.

Legislative Assistants work irregular hours. They often work in evenings and on weekends to complete specific assignments, attend meetings, and participate in social and community events on behalf of the legislators.

Salaries

Salaries for Legislative Assistants vary, depending on such factors as their experience, job duties, employer, and geographical location. Congressional assistants generally earn more than state and local legislative aides, and U.S. Senate aides typically receive higher salaries than House aides.

According to the Career Prospects in Virginia Web site, Legislative Assistants generally earn salaries between $30,000 to $45,000s. Senior assistants with ten or more years of experience may earn more.

Employment Prospects

Most opportunities become available after elections when newly elected legislators hire new staff members. Positions also become vacant when Legislative Assistants resign or transfer to other staff positions. In general, the turnover rate for assistant positions is high, but the competition is keen.

Advancement Prospects

Legislative Assistants can advance to top staff positions as chiefs of staff and legislative directors. Many employers prefer to hire top aides with an advanced degree in law, public policy, or another related field.

Many Legislative Assistants use their experience as stepping stones to other careers. Some of these careers include being politicians, political consultants, lobbyists, attorneys, journalists, public relations directors, and business executives.

Education and Training

Entry-level Legislative Assistants must have bachelor's degrees, which may be in any field. Legal Assistants who specialize in particular issues, such as the environment, have master's or doctorate degrees in appropriate fields. Some Legislative Assistants hold law degrees.

Experience, Skills, and Personality Traits

Legislators prefer to hire entry-level Legislative Assistants who have previous experience working in legislators' offices. They may have been interns or volunteers, or served in such support positions as legal correspondents or researchers. In addition, candidates must be knowledgeable about the lawmaking process as well as the specific issues that concern the legislators.

Legislative Assistants must have excellent writing, research, organizational, and teamwork skills. They also need strong communication and interpersonal skills to effectively handle meetings with constituents, lobbyists, interest groups, media, and others. In addition, they must have superior self-management skills. Successful Legislative Assistants have several personality traits in common, such as being outgoing, enthusiastic, energetic, self-motivated, efficient, ambitious, creative, and flexible.

Unions and Associations

Legislative Assistants are members of their political parties. Many actively participate in party meetings, events, and fund-raising activities.

Tips for Entry

1. You can begin gaining political experience as a student. For example, you might participate in student government, attend local government meetings, or work on political campaigns.
2. In high school or college, contact your state and congressional legislators to learn about temporary positions as pages or interns.
3. Succeeding in this field requires building and continually developing a network of contacts.
4. Learn more about the legislative process on the Internet. To learn about Congress, visit these Web sites: U.S. Senate, http://www.senate.gov; or U.S. House of Representatives, http://www.house.gov. To find Web sites for state legislatures, enter the name of a state and the word *legislature* in a search engine (for example, *Arizona legislature*).

LOBBYIST

CAREER PROFILE

Duties: Promote the interests of their clients or employers to law makers; perform duties as required

Alternate Title(s): Legislative Agent, Legislative Advocate, Public Advocate

Salary Range: $0 to $150,000+

Employment Prospects: Fair

Advancement Prospects: Poor

Prerequisites:

　Education or Training—No standard requirements

　Experience—Previous work experience in legislative settings preferred

　Special Skills and Personality Traits—Writing, communication, interpersonal, organizational, computer, and telecommunications skills; be friendly, diplomatic, energetic, persuasive, credible, flexible, creative

　Special Requirements—Registration with federal or state legislature is required

CAREER LADDER

```
┌─────────────────────────────────┐
│  Senior or Independent Lobbyist │
└─────────────────────────────────┘

┌─────────────────────────────────┐
│           Lobbyist              │
└─────────────────────────────────┘

┌─────────────────────────────────┐
│        Junior Lobbyist          │
└─────────────────────────────────┘
```

Position Description

Lobbyists are professional advocates who work in Washington, D.C., and in the 50 state capitals. Their job is to persuade lawmakers to sponsor legislation or to pass or oppose bills that would be in the best interests of their clients. For example, one Lobbyist might represent an environmental group that wants federal legislators to vote for certain pollution controls, while another Lobbyist might represent a manufacturer who wants those same legislators to oppose such controls.

Lobbyists perform lobbying services as either employees or contractors. They may represent small businesses, corporations, trade associations, labor unions, citizen groups, public interest organization, churches, charities, or foreign governments, among others.

These professional advocates handle a wide range of issues reflecting their wide range of clients. These may include education, senior citizens, civil rights, children, health care, the environment, gun control, public safety, scientific research projects, social programs, and foreign aid, among other issues.

Lobbyists maintain a highly visible presence in federal and state legislatures. They communicate constantly with lawmakers and their staff, by contacting them in person, or by phone, letters, faxes, and e-mail. They provide lawmakers with information that supports their clients' positions on specific issues or proposed bills.

In addition, Lobbyists are responsible for keeping tabs on bills that are relevant to their clients. They analyze proposed legislation and educate their clients on the key points. Lobbyists also perform other tasks. For example, they:

- conduct research on the issues that concern their clients
- prepare accurate, correct, and factual reports on issues for both clients and legislators
- collaborate with other organizations and groups to pass or defeat legislation
- attend legislative hearings
- monitor the progress of legislation and keep clients up to date with their status

Lobbyists use the media to generate public interest and awareness of the issues. They write press releases as well as newspaper and magazine articles. They may also appear on radio and TV talk shows. Some lobbyists do indirect lobbying, which involves organizing people to write or call their legislators on behalf of their clients.

Some Lobbyists provide regulatory advocacy services. That is, they lobby government agencies, such as a state insurance commission or the Environmental Protection Agency, that are proposing regulations which affect the interests of their clients.

Many Lobbyists are independent contractors or employed by lobbying firms or law firms that provide lobbying services. Independent Lobbyists work on a wide range of issues for various groups and organizations; they may be contracted to lobby a specific legislation or be retained to work on an ongoing basis. Other Lobbyists are employed by their clients and work on only those concerns that interest their clients.

Lobbyists work long hours, including nights and weekends, to complete various tasks as well as to meet with legislators and staff.

Salaries

Salaries for Lobbyists vary, depending on such factors as their education, experience, reputation, or employer (or clientele). Corporate Lobbyists typically earn higher salaries than public interest Lobbyists. In general, annual salaries range from zero for volunteer Lobbyists to $150,000 or more. Former politicians as well as highly experienced former legislative or executive branch staff members can realize salaries of $200,000 to $300,000 or more.

In addition to their salaries, many corporate in-house Lobbyists receive cash bonuses, stock options, and other benefits.

Employment Prospects

Lobbyists are employed by lobbying firms as well as by law firms. In-house Lobbyists work for corporations, trade and professional associations, political action committees, public interest organizations, and other organizations.

Competition for job openings is high. Opportunities usually become available as Lobbyists transfer to other jobs or are promoted. Employers may create additional positions to meet their growing needs.

Advancement Prospects

Most Lobbyists realize advancement by earning higher salaries and gaining reputations as effective advocates.

Experienced Lobbyists can pursue careers in other fields such as public relations, journalism, or education.

Education and Training

There are no standard educational requirements for individuals to become Lobbyists. However, most professionals hold bachelor's degrees, as well as advanced degrees in such areas as law, public policy, communications, public relations, education, and journalism.

Special Requirements

Lobbyists are required to register with the proper government office in Congress or the state legislature in which they want to work. In addition, Lobbyists must file regular reports on their activities, including information such as their expenses, whom they represent, and what bills they are trying to influence.

Experience, Skills, and Personality Traits

Employers prefer to hire junior Lobbyists who have several years of experience working on legislative staffs or in government agencies, or who have worked in positions as research assistants or issues analysts for lobbying organizations. Additionally, candidates demonstrate a thorough understanding of the legislative process.

Lobbyists need excellent writing, communication, computer, interpersonal, and organizational skills to perform well. Being friendly, diplomatic, energetic, persuasive, flexible, and credible are some personality traits that successful Lobbyists share.

Unions and Associations

Many Lobbyists join professional associations to take advantage of training programs, networking opportunities, and other professional resources and services. Two national professional associations that represent lobbyists are the American League of Lobbyists and the Women in Government Relations. For contact information, see Appendix V.

Tips for Entry

1. As a high school student, you can learn first hand what is involved in trying to change public policy by getting involved with an issue or cause at your school or in your local community.
2. To gain lobbying experience, obtain an intern position with a lobbying firm, public interest organization, or other group that has policy advocacy or similar departments.
3. Positions are mostly found through networking with other lobbyists.
4. You can learn more about the lobbying field on the Internet. One Web site you might visit belongs to the American League of Lobbyists at http://www.alldc. org. For more links, see Appendix VI.

PUBLIC INTEREST ADVOCATE

CAREER PROFILE

Duties: Promote public policies and legislation on behalf of the general public; identify issues, develop solutions, conduct research, and organize media events; perform other duties as required

Alternate Title(s): A title, such as Transportation Advocate or Environmental Advocate, that reflects a particular area

Salary Range: $0 to $35,000+

Employment Prospects: Good

Advancement Prospects: Fair

Prerequisites:

Education or Training—A bachelor's degree preferred

Experience—Previous experience working with public-interest organizations; knowledge of specific political issues and the lawmaking process

Special Skills and Personality Traits—Research, writing, computer, organizational, analytical, communication, and teamwork skills; enthusiastic, energetic, persuasive, patient, persistent, creative, flexible, positive

Special Requirements—Registration with federal or state legislatures may be required

CAREER LADDER

```
┌─────────────────────────────────────┐
│  Senior Advocate or Program Director │
└─────────────────────────────────────┘

┌─────────────────────────────────────┐
│      Public Interest Advocate        │
└─────────────────────────────────────┘

┌─────────────────────────────────────┐
│  Research Assistant, College Campus  │
│        Organizer, or Volunteer       │
└─────────────────────────────────────┘
```

Position Description

Public Interest Advocates work for public interest organizations that promote public policies and legislation they believe is in the best interest of the general public. These organizations support specific positions on education, children's issues, the environment, political reform, civil rights, transportation, consumer protection, and other areas. Public Interest Advocates may hold job titles that reflect the particular area in which they are working, such as consumer advocate, water quality advocate, democracy advocate, or transportation advocate.

Public Interest Advocates are responsible for identifying issues that can be presented to state or federal legislatures, government agencies, or other decision makers. They also have the duty of working on the campaigns to advance public policies. They perform a wide range of tasks that include:

- conducting research on issues
- writing comprehensive reports and studies about issues
- drafting proposed legislation
- developing solutions for public policies
- developing political strategies for getting public policies passed
- writing press releases
- organizing press conferences
- testifying in support of solutions at legislative hearings or at administrative hearings in government agencies
- lobbying lawmakers to pass legislation

In addition, Public Interest Advocates build political support. They network with other organizations and groups to create coalitions. Advocates also develop community relations by providing progress reports to local communities as well as by asking for feedback about their campaigns.

In addition, they encourage communities to participate in grassroots activities such as having people contact elected officials or putting together peaceful demonstrations.

Public Interest Advocates also perform other tasks. For example, they research and write grant proposals to raise funds for current and future advocacy campaigns. Further, they are responsible for keeping up with current developments in their subject areas.

Public Interest Advocates work long hours to complete their various duties. They sometimes work evenings and on weekends.

Salaries

Salaries for Public Interest Advocates vary, depending on such factors as their experience, employer, and geographical location. In general, Public Interest Advocates earn an annual salary that ranges from $25,000 to $35,000 or more. Many Public Interest Advocates are volunteers and do not receive any pay.

Employment Prospects

Opportunities for staff positions generally become available as Public Interest Advocates resign or transfer to other positions. In addition, employers create additional positions when they receive funding to maintain current programs or begin new programs. Volunteer positions are readily available.

Advancement Prospects

Advancement opportunities are limited to program directors (or coordinators) and assistants. Most Public Interest Advocates measure success through the satisfaction of making an impact in social changes.

Public Interest Advocates might choose to pursue related careers by becoming professional lobbyists, elected officials, legislative assistants, and executive officers of nonprofit organizations.

Education and Training

Most Public Interest Advocates have bachelor's or advanced degrees in various disciplines. They typically receive training on the job.

Special Requirements

Public Interest Advocates may be required to register with the federal government to lobby Congress or with a state government to lobby state legislators. In addition, they may be required to file regular reports on their activities, including information about their expenses and what bills they are trying to influence.

Experience, Skills, and Personality Traits

Employers require (or strongly prefer) that candidates have previous experience working with public interest organizations, especially on advocacy campaigns. In addition, candidates are knowledgeable about the issues that the employers advocate. They also have a thorough understanding of the legislative process.

Public Interest Advocates must have strong research, writing, and computer skills. In addition, they have effective organizational and analytical skills as well as excellent communication and teamwork skills.

Being enthusiastic, energetic, persuasive, patient, persistent, creative, flexible, and positive are a few personality traits that successful Public Interest Advocates share. Furthermore, they have a strong passion for and commitment to public interest issues.

Unions and Associations

The American League of Lobbyists and Women in Government Relations are two national professional associations that Public Interest Advocates are eligible to join. (For contact information, see Appendix V.) By joining professional associations, they can take advantage of network opportunities and other professional resources and services.

Tips for Entry

1. Start gaining experience in high school by getting involved in public interest issues that concern you.
2. Some entry-level positions (both paid and volunteer) that are available in public interest organizations are campus organizers, Web designers, writers, researchers, and public relations assistants. Many organizations also offer internships.
3. Many public interest employers do not have the budget to advertise widely for job openings. Thus, take the initiative and contact employers for whom you would like to work.
4. Learn more about public interest advocacy on the Internet. For example, you might visit the State PIRGs (Public-Interest Research Groups) Working Together Web site at http://www.pirg.org. For more links, see Appendix VI.

CAMPAIGN MANAGER

CAREER PROFILE

Duties: Oversee the day-to-day operations of a political campaign; perform duties as required

Alternate Title(s): Campaign Director

Salary Range: Unavailable

Employment Prospects: Fair

Advancement Prospects: Fair

Prerequisites:

Education or Training—On-the-job training

Experience—Previous campaign experience required

Special Skills and Personality Trails—Leadership, team building, communication, interpersonal, problem-solving, organizational, and self-management skills; focused, clever, sharp-witted, hardworking, dedicated, persistent, resilient, flexible, and creative

CAREER LADDER

```
┌─────────────────────────────────┐
│      Political Consultant        │
└─────────────────────────────────┘

┌─────────────────────────────────┐
│      Campaign Manager            │
└─────────────────────────────────┘

┌─────────────────────────────────┐
│  Assistant Campaign Manager      │
│  or a Campaign Department Director│
└─────────────────────────────────┘
```

Position Description

Campaign Managers are experts in overseeing the campaigns of political candidates who are running for local, state, or federal offices, from district school board member to the President of the United States. Campaign Managers also lead campaign operations to approve or reject initiatives, referendums, or propositions in local or state elections.

In any campaign, their job is to manage and coordinate the day-to-day operations. They make sure that campaigns are running smoothly and efficiently. They make certain that campaign messages are getting out to the voters in the form of direct mail, personal contact, advertisements, the media, the Internet, and other means. In addition, Campaign Managers ensure that campaigns have plenty of manpower—staff and volunteers—to perform campaign activities, as well as sufficient money to pay for operational needs and staffing.

Campaigns may start several months or years before an election. Campaign Managers are usually the first staff members to be chosen. Some of them are volunteers. Regardless of whether they are paid or work for free, Campaign Managers are responsible for planning, developing, implementing, and directing campaign strategies and activities. They work closely with candidates, staff members, volunteers, and political consultants to create a well-detailed and effec-

tive campaign plan that includes campaign objectives, staffing needs, timelines, budgets, fundraising goals, quantitative measures of progress, and descriptions of the activities (such as public speaking events and the use of the media and the Internet) to be conducted, among other things.

In presidential, gubernatorial, and other major and complex campaigns, political consultants are usually hired to formulate campaign strategies. The Campaign Manager's role is to lead staff and volunteers in executing the strategies successfully to win elections.

To run a political campaign, Campaign Managers engage in the coordination of several areas, including:

- field operations, which involve staff and volunteers making personal contact with the voters through door-to-door canvassing, phone calling, and providing information at campaign headquarters
- fund-raising events
- scheduling of candidates and their stand-ins for public events to meet with the voters
- communications, which involve the creation of press releases, advertisements, direct mailings, and other campaign materials
- media relations

- technology (such as Web sites and blogs) that is used to help promote the campaign message
- polling
- opposition research
- recruitment and management of staff, consultants, and volunteers
- compliancy with campaign laws and regulations

In most campaigns, Campaign Managers supervise one or more staff members who are in charge of different campaign areas. In larger campaigns that consist of hundreds of staff members, Campaign Managers usually oversee department directors (who manage specific campaign areas) and coordinators (who are in charge of certain functions within a department). In small campaigns, Campaign Managers are often responsible for handling all the details.

Campaign Managers do their best to create a respectful, positive, and energetic working environment. Along with the paid staff members, Campaign Managers direct the work of volunteers and interns. They do the routine, yet important, tasks that are needed for a successful campaign, such as stuffing and addressing envelopes, calling up voters on behalf of the campaign, distributing campaign flyers and leaflets to voters, and entering names, figures, and other data into databases. Campaign Managers also work closely with pollsters, media consultants, and other political consultants to ensure a successful campaign.

Campaign Managers communicate on a frequent basis with candidates, to provide them with the progress of their campaigns. Campaign Managers also hold regular staff meetings to review campaign plans, make changes in plans as needed, and to deal with possible problems.

Campaign Managers perform under highly intense conditions. Like the candidates they support, Campaign Managers are constantly under the public's eye. What they say and how they act and behave reflects directly upon the candidates. The work of Campaign Managers is fast-paced and often unpredictable. It can be particularly stressful during the last several weeks before elections. They are expected to labor long hours and sometimes work all night to complete their tasks. In state and federal elections, these professionals travel from city to city on the campaign trail.

For Campaign Managers, their job is done once an election takes place. Winning candidates sometimes offer them staff aide positions. Most professional Campaign Managers move on to work on other political campaigns.

Salaries

Compensation for Campaign Managers varies, depending on their experience, the number of successful political campaigns on which they have worked, the type of political campaigns that they organize, and other factors. Formal salary information about this occupation is unavailable.

However, salaries for Campaign Managers can range from no pay for volunteers to earnings of five- and six-figures per campaign. According to an on-line article in *New York Magazine,* Campaign Managers can earn up to $4,000 to $6,000 per month for running state senate races, and those heading U.S. senate campaigns may earn up to $25,000 per month.

Employment Prospects

Professional Campaign Managers are employed as independent contractors. Top managers sometimes take positions as political consultants.

Opportunities are readily available for Campaign Managers to run local, state, and federal political campaigns. Local campaigns for city council, county supervisor, sheriff, school board, and other local offices are sometimes run by volunteer Campaign Managers. In larger cities, many candidates hire professional Campaign Managers. Candidates for state and federal offices typically employ professional Campaign Managers.

Prospects are best for Campaign Managers who have a proven track record of campaign successes. In addition, individuals who are willing to relocate to other cities or states during a campaign election may have more opportunities to obtain positions that they desire.

Advancement Prospects

Many Campaign Managers measure their success through job satisfaction, professional reputation, campaign victories, higher incomes, and a demand for their services.

Depending on their interests and ambitions, Campaign Managers can advance in any number of ways. As they gain experience, they may seek opportunities in larger or major election campaigns. For example, managers of local political campaigns may seek staff opportunities, which may be junior positions, on state or federal campaigns. Campaign Managers can also specialize in particular campaigning areas, such as fund-raising or field operations, to become political consultants.

Some Campaign Managers seek positions in state or national party organizations (such as the Republican Party or the Green Party). Many individuals go back and forth between campaign and party positions. Other Campaign Managers use their experience to pursue other careers in politics, government, public relations, advertising, communications, or another that may interest them.

Education and Training

There are no educational requirement standards for individuals to become Campaign Managers. Many campaign professionals have bachelor's and advanced degrees in journalism, communications, political science, and other fields.

Many individuals receive their training under experienced Campaign Managers while working as staff members on different political campaigns.

Campaign workers typically learn their knowledge and skills through their work on different political campaigns. Most, if not all, Campaign Managers have performed several campaign roles under the supervision and guidance of experienced campaign staff members, including Campaign Managers and campaign consultants.

Experience, Special Skills, and Personality Traits

In general, political candidates prefer to hire Campaign Managers who have experience working on election campaigns similar to theirs, especially on winning campaigns. They seek individuals who are knowledgeable about the positions for which candidates are running and who are familiar with the issues that the candidates would address during their campaigns.

Because they must work effectively with many people from diverse backgrounds, Campaign Managers need excellent leadership, team building, communication, and interpersonal skills. Their work also requires superior problem-solving, and organizational, as well as self-management skills, such as the abilities to meet deadlines, handle stressful situations, work independently, and prioritize multiple tasks.

Some personality traits that successful Campaign Managers share include being focused, clever, sharp-witted, hardworking, dedicated, persistent, resilient, flexible, and creative.

Unions and Associations

The American Association of Political Consultants is a trade association that Campaign Managers are eligible to join. It offers members the opportunity to network with colleagues, as well as take advantage of various professional services and resources. For contact information, see Appendix V.

Tips for Entry

1. While in high school, you can start gaining valuable political campaign experience. You might run for a student body or class office, or perhaps help a friend campaign for office. In addition, read books and articles about the election process, and famous political campaigns as well as biographies about famous Campaign Managers or consultants.
2. Volunteer to work on campaigns for candidates or issues that interest you. Get involved in the different aspects of a campaign to build up your skills and knowledge.
3. To succeed in the field of campaign management, you will need to develop a network of personal contacts. Many campaign workers learn about paid positions through politicians, colleagues, and others.
4. Use the Internet to learn more about political campaigns and campaign management. To get a list of relevant links, enter any of these keywords in a search engine: *political campaigns, campaign management,* or *campaign manager.* For some links, see Appendix VI.

APPENDIXES

APPENDIX I
EDUCATION AND TRAINING RESOURCES ON THE INTERNET

Listed below are World Wide Web sources for education and training programs pertaining to some of the occupations in this book. To learn about education and training programs for other occupations, talk with school or career counselors as well as with professionals in the field. You can also look up schools in college directories produced by Peterson's or other publishers, which can be found in your school or public library.

Note: All Web site addresses were current at the time this book was being written. If you come across a URL that no longer works, enter the name of the organization in a search engine to find its new Web site.

GENERAL RESOURCES
The following Web sites provide links to various academic programs at colleges and universities in the United States.

- "Web U.S. Higher Education," a listing of two-year colleges, four-year colleges, and universities (maintained by the University of Texas at Austin), http://www.utexas.edu/world/univ.
- Peterson's, http://www.petersons.com
- The Princeton Review, http://www.princetonreview.com.
- GradSchools.com, http://www.gradschools.com.
- WorldWideLearn (online directory of education), http://www.worldwidelearn.com.

ACTUARIAL SCIENCE
The Society of Actuaries provides a listing of undergraduate and graduate programs in actuarial science at http://www.soa.org/ccm/content/?categoryID=1260076.

ALTERNATIVE DISPUTE RESOLUTION
- The Association for Conflict Resolution provides a list of family mediation training programs at http://www.acrnet.org.
- The Association of Attorney-Mediators has a listing of mediation training programs at http://www.attorney-mediators.org/train.html.

COUNT INTERPRETING
The American Translators Association provides a listing of court interpreting programs at http://www.atanet.org/bin/view.pl/30472.

COURT REPORTING
The National Court Reporters Association has a listing of court reporting programs at http://www.ncraonline.org.

COURT MANAGEMENT
The Institute for Court Management offers court management training programs. For more information, go to its Web site at http://www.ncsconline.org/D_ICM/icmindex.html.

CRIMINOLOGY
The American Society of Criminology provides a listing of graduate programs at http://www.asc41.com/GRADLINKS.html.

FORENSIC PSYCHOLOGY
The American Psychology-Law Society provides a listing of graduate programs in forensic psychology at http://www.ap-ls.org/students/graduateindex.html.

JUDICIAL EDUCATION AND TRAINING
The National Judicial College offers education and training programs for judges. For information, go its Web site at http://www.judges.org.

LAW
- The American Bar Association provides a listing of law schools at http://www.abanet.org/legaled/approved lawschools/approved.html.
- The Association of American Law Schools provides a listing of law schools at http://www.aals.org/about_memberschools.php.
- The Law School Admission Council provides a listing of law schools at http://www.lsac.org.
- The Findlaw for Students Web site has a listing of schools at http://stu.findlaw.com/schools.

LEGAL VIDEOGRAPHY
The American Guild of Court Videographers offers legal videography seminars. For information, go to its Web site at http://www.agcv.com.

LIBRARY AND INFORMATION SCIENCE

- The American Library Association provides a listing of graduate programs at http://www.ala.org/ala/accreditation/lisdirb/lisdirectory.htm.
- The American Association of Law Libraries provides a list of schools that offer law librarianship programs, including joint J.D. and master's in library and information science programs, at http://www.aallnet.org/committee/tfedu/list_1.html.

LIBRARY TECHNOLOGY

The Council on Library/Media Technicians has a listing of degree programs in library technology at http://colt.ucr.edu/ltprograms.html.

NONPROFIT MANAGEMENT

- Dr. Roseanne Mirabella, of the Department of Political Science, Seton Hall University, provides a listing of graduate programs in nonprofit management education at http://tltc.shu.edu/npo.
- Idealist.org provides a listing of graduate programs that offer a concentration in nonprofit management. The URL is http://www.idealist.org/npofaq/0/1492.html.

PARALEGAL

- The American Association for Paralegal Education provides a listing of paralegal programs at http://www.aafpe.org/m_search/index.asp.
- The Standing Committee on Paralegals, part of the American Bar Association, has a directory of paralegal programs at http://www.abanet.org/legalservices/paralegals/directory/home.html.
- FindLaw for Students Web site provides a database of paralegal programs at http://stu.findlaw.com/schools/paralegal.

PRIVATE INVESTIGATION

The Private Investigator Portal (by Infoguys.com) provides a listing of private investigator schools at http://www.infoguys.com/schools.cfm.

PUBLIC ADMINISTRATION

The National Association of Schools of Public Affairs and Administration has a database of graduate programs (including joint degree programs) at http://www.naspaa.org/students/graduate/schsearch.asp.

WEB DESIGN

The Web Design School Review Web site has a listing of schools offering degree programs in web design and development. Its URL is http://www.webdesignschoolreview.com.

PAYING FOR YOUR EDUCATION

Scholarships, grants, student loans, and other financial aid programs are available to help you pay for your postsecondary education. These programs are sponsored by government agencies, professional and trade associations, private foundations, businesses, and other organizations.

To learn more about financial assistance programs, talk with your high school guidance counselor or college career counselor. You might also consult college catalogs, as they usually include financial aid information. In addition, you might visit or contact the financial aid office at the institution where you plan to attend or are attending now. Lastly, check out these Web sites for financial aid information:

- FinAid, http://www.finaid.org.
- Information for Parents and Students (by the National Association of Student Financial Aid Administrators), http://www.studentaid.org.
- Student Aid on the Web (U.S. Department of Education Federal Student Aid), http://www.studentaid.ed.gov.
- The Student Guide (U.S. Department of Education), http://studentaid.ed.gov/students/publications/student guide/index.html.

APPENDIX II
PROFESSIONAL CERTIFICATION PROGRAMS

Professional certifications are granted by professional associations on a voluntary basis. Unlike occupational licenses, professional certification is not a mandatory state or local requirement for professionals to practice in their field. Employers may require or strongly prefer to hire candidates who possess particular professional certifications. Many individuals obtain professional certifications to enhance their employability.

To be eligible for professional certifications, individuals are usually required to have several years of work experience. They may need to complete courses, seminars, or workshops as well as pass professional examinations.

This appendix lists professional certification programs for some of the occupations in this book. To learn about other programs, talk with professionals, employers, and professional associations in the fields that interest you.

Note: All Web addresses were accessible while this book was being written. If a URL no longer works, you might find the new one by entering the name of the certification program or organization into a search engine.

APPRAISER
The American Society of Appraisers offers the Accredited Member (AM) and the Accredited Senior Appraiser (ASA) certification programs. For information, write to 555 Herndon Parkway, Suite 125, Herndon, VA 20170. Or call (703) 478-2228, or fax (703) 742-8471, or visit its Web site at http://www.appraisers.org.

BUSINESS APPRAISER
- The American Institute of the Certified Public Accountants offers the Accredited in Business Valuation (ABV) program. For information, write to Coordinator—ABV Certification Program, Harborside Financial Center, Plaza III, Jersey City, NJ 07311. Or call (201) 938-3823, option 2, or visit http://bvfls.aicpa.org on the Web.
- The American Society of Appraisers offers the Accredited Member (AM) and the Accredited Senior Appraiser (ASA) certification programs. For information, write to 555 Herndon Parkway, Suite 125, Herndon, VA 20170. Or call (703) 478-2228, or fax (703) 742-8471, or visit its Web site at http://www.appraisers.org.

- The Institute of Business Appraisers offers programs for these professional designations: Certified Business Appraiser (CBA), Master Certified Business Appraiser (MCBA), Accredited by IBA (AIBA), and Business Valuator Accredited for Litigation (BVAL). For information, write to P.O. Box 17410, Plantation, FL 33318. Or call (954) 584-1144, or fax (954) 584-1184, or visit its Web site at http://www.go-iba.org.
- The National Association of Certified Valuation Analysts offers the following certification programs: Certified Valuation Analyst (CVA), Accredited Valuation Analyst (AVA), and Certified Forensic Financial Analyst (CFFA). For information, write to 1111 Brickyard Road, Suite 200, Salt Lake City, UT 84106. Or call (801) 486-0600, or fax (801) 486-7500, or visit http://www.nacva.com on the Web.

CONTRACT ADMINISTRATOR
The National Contract Management Association offers programs for these professional designations: Certified Professional Contracts Manager (CPCM), Certified Commercial Contracts Manager (CCCM), and Certified Federal Contracts Manager (CFCM). For information, write to 8260 Greensboro Drive, Suite 200, McLean, VA 22102. Or call (800) 344-8096 or (571) 382-0082; or fax (703) 448-0939; or visit its Web site at http://www.ncmahq.org.

COURT INTERPRETER
- The American Translators Association offers a court interpreter certification program in several languages. For information, write to 225 Reinekers Lane, Suite 590, Alexandria, VA 22314. Or call (703) 683-6100, or fax (703) 683-6122, or visit its Web site at http://www.atanet.org.
- The CPS Human Resources Services offers the Federal Court Interpreter Certification Examination Program, which certifies Spanish interpreters. For information, write to Federal Court Interpreter Certification Program, 241 Lathrop Way, Sacramento, CA 95815. Or call (916) 263-3494, or visit its Web site at http://www.cps.ca.gov/fcice-spanish/index.asp.
- The National Center for State Courts (NCSC) administers the Consortium for State Court Interpreter Certification program, which certifies court interpreters in several lan-

guages in over 30 state court systems. For more information visit the NCSC webpage at http://www.ncsconline.org/D_Research/CourtInterp/CICourtConsort.html.

COURT REPORTER
The National Court Reporters Association offers programs in the following professional designations: Registered Professional Reporter (RPR), Registered Merit Reporter (RMR), Registered Diplomate Reporter (RDR), and Certified Real-time Reporter (CRR). For information, write to 8224 Old Courthouse Road, Vienna, VA 22182. Or call (800) 272-6272 or (703) 556-6272; or visit http://www.ncraonline.org on the Web.

CRASH RECONSTRUCTION CONSULTANT
The Accreditation Commission for Traffic Accident Reconstruction offers professional accreditation to individuals who meet its standards of experience and education, as well as successfully complete a practical and a theoretical examination. For information, write to P.O. Box 5436, Hudson, FL 34674. Or call (800) 809-3818, or visit its Web site at http://www.actar.org.

ELDER LAW ATTORNEY
The National Elder Law Foundation offers a program for the professional certification of elder law attorneys. For information, write to 1604 North Country Club Road, Tucson, AZ 85716. Or call (520) 881-1076, or fax (520) 325-7925, or visit its Web site at http://www.nelf.org.

FORENSIC ACCOUNTANT
- The American College of Forensic Examiners Institute offers the Certified Forensic Accountant (Cr.FA) program. For information, write to 2750 East Sunshine Street, Springfield, MO 65804. Or call (800) 423-9737 or (417) 881-3818; or fax (417) 881-4702; or visit http://www.acfei.com on the Web.
- The Association of Certified Fraud Examiners offers the Certified Fraud Examiner (CFE) program. For information, write to 716 West Avenue, Austin, TX 78701. Or call (800) 245-3321 or (512) 478-9000; or fax (512) 478-9297; or visit its Web site at http://www.acfe.com.
- The Association of Insolvency and Restructuring Advisors offers the Certified Insolvency and Reorganization Accountant (CIRA) program. For information, write to 221 Stewart Avenue, Suite 207, Medford, OR 97501. Or call (541) 858-1665, or fax (541) 858-9187, or visit its Web site at http://www.airacira.org.

FORENSIC PSYCHOLOGIST
The American Board of Professional Psychology offers board certification of forensic psychologists. For informa-

tion, write to 300 Drayton Street, 3rd Floor, Savannah, GA 31401. Or call (800) 255-7792 or (912) 234-5477; or fax (912) 234-5120; or visit http://www.abpp.org on the Web.

HUMAN RESOURCES MANAGER
The Human Resource Certification Institute offers programs in these professional designations: Professional in Human Resources (PHR), Senior Professional in Human Resources (SPHR), and Global Professional in Human Resources (GPHR). For information, write to 1800 Duke Street, Alexandria, VA 22314. Or call (866) 898-4724 or visit http://www.hrci.org on the Web.

INFORMATION TECHNOLOGY PROFESSIONALS
The Institute for Certification of Computing Professionals offers these certification programs: Associate Computing Professional (ACP), Certified Computing Professional (CCP), and Certified Data Management Professional (CDMP). For information, write to 2350 East Devon Avenue, Suite 115, Des Plaines, IL 60018, or visit its Web site at http://www.iccp.org.

INSURANCE CLAIMS PROFESSIONAL
The American Institute for Chartered Property Casualty Underwriters and the Insurance Institute of America offer these professional certification programs: Associate in Claims (AIC) and Associate in Insurance Services (AIS). For information write to 720 Providence Road, P.O. Box 3016, Malvern, PA 19355. Or call (800) 644-2101 or fax (610) 640-9576, or visit http:/www.aicpcu.org on the Web.

LEGAL ADMINISTRATOR
The Association of Legal Administrators offers the Certified Legal Manager (CLM) program. For information, write to 75 Tri-State International, Suite 222, Lincolnshire, IL 60069. Or call (847) 267-1252, or fax (847) 267-1329, or visit its Web site at http://www.alanet.org.

LEGAL MANAGEMENT CONSULTANT
The Institute of Management Consultants USA offers the Certified Management Consultant (CMC) program. For information, write to 2025 M Street NW, Suite 800, Washington, DC 20036. Or call (800) 221-2557 or (202) 367-1134; or fax (202) 367-2134; or visit its Web site at http://www.imcusa.org.

LEGAL NURSE CONSULTANT
- The American Association of Legal Nurse Consultants offers the Legal Nurse Consultant Certified (LNCC) program. For

information, write to 401 North Michigan Avenue, Chicago, IL 60611. Or call (877) 402-2562, or fax (312) 673-6655, or visit its Web site at http://www.aalnc.org.

- The American College of Forensic Examiners Institute offers the Certified Forensic Nurse (CFN) program. For information, write to 2750 East Sunshine Street, Springfield, MO 65804. Or call (800) 423-9737 or (417) 881-3818; or fax (417) 881-4702; or visit http://www.acfei.com on the Web.

LEGAL SUPPORT PROFESSIONAL

NALS offers the following certification programs: basic certification for legal professionals (ALS) and advanced certification for legal professionals (PLS). For information, write to 314 East 3rd Street, Suite 210, Tulsa, OK 74120. Or call (918) 582-5188, or fax (918) 582-5907, or visit its Web site at http://www.nals.org.

LEGAL VIDEOGRAPHER

- The American Guild of Court Videographers offers the following professional certification programs: Certified Deposition Video Specialist (CDVS), Certified Court Video Specialist (CCVS), and Certified Senior Court Videographer (CSCV). For information, write to 1628 East 3rd Street, Casper, WY 82601. Or call (800) 678-1990, or fax (307) 472-5048, or visit its Web site at http://www.agcv.com.
- The National Court Reporters Association offers the Certified Legal Video Specialist (CLVS) program. For information, write to 8224 Old Courthouse Road, Vienna, VA 22182. Or call (800) 272-6272 or (703) 556-6272; or visit http://www.ncraonline.org on the Web.

LITIGATION CONSULTANT

The American College of Forensic Examiners Institute offers the Certified Forensic Consultant (CFC) program. For information, write to 2750 East Sunshine Street, Springfield, MO 65804. Or call (800) 423-9737 or (417) 881-3818; or fax (417) 881-4702; or visit http://www.acfei.com on the Web.

MARKETING MANAGER (LAW FIRM)

The American Marketing Association offers the Professional Certified Marketer (PCM) program. For information, write to 311 South Wacker Drive, Suite 5800, Chicago, IL 60606. Or call (800) AMA-1150, or fax (312) 542-9001, or visit its Web site at http://www.marketingpower.com.

PARALEGAL

- NALS offers the Professional Paralegal (PP) program. For information, write to 314 East 3rd Street, Suite 210, Tulsa, OK 74120. Or call (918) 582-5188, or fax (918) 582-5907, or visit its Web site at http://www.nals.org.
- The National Association for Legal Assistants offers programs in these professional designations: Certified Legal Assistant (CLA) and Certified Paralegal (CP). For information, write to 1516 South Boston, Suite 200, Tulsa, OK 74119. Or call (918) 587-6828, or fax (918) 582-6772, or visit http://www.nala.org on the Web.
- The National Federation of Paralegal Associations offers the Registered Paralegal (RP) program. For information, write to P.O. Box 2016, Edmonds, WA 98020. Or call (425) 967-0045, or fax (425) 771-9588, or visit its Web site at http:/www.paralegals.org.

PRIVATE INVESTIGATOR

- The National Association of Legal Investigators offers the Certified Legal Investigator (CLI) program. For information, call (800) 266-6254 or visit its Web site at http://www.nalionline.org.
- The United States Association of Professional Investigators offers the Board Certified Professional Investigator (BCPI) program. For information, write to 1201 Pennsylvania Avenue NW, Suite 300, Washington, DC 20004. Or call (866) 958-7274 or (202) 393-5900; or fax (202) 478-2610, or visit its Web site at http://www.usapi.org.

PROPERTY MANAGER

The Institute of Real Estate Management offers the following certification programs: Certified Property Manager (CPM), Accredited Commercial Manager (ACM), and Accredited Residential Manager (ARM). For information, write to 430 North Michigan Avenue, Chicago, IL 60611. Or call (800) 837-0706, or fax (800) 338-4736, or visit its Web site at http://www.irem.org.

APPENDIX III
BAR ADMISSION OFFICES

To practice before a state or federal court, attorneys must possess the proper authorization. In this appendix, you will find contact information for the offices that handle applications for attorneys to practice law in the 50 states, the U.S. territories, and the District of Columbia, as well as in the federal court system.

Note: All contact information and Web site addresses were current when the book was being written. If you come across a URL that no longer works, you may be able to find an organization's new Web site by entering its name in a search engine.

A. STATE COURTS

In each of the 50 states (as well as the District of Columbia and the U.S. territories), attorneys must be first admitted to the bar of a state Supreme Court, the highest state court, before they can practice in the state. Requirements for entry vary from state to state, and usually entail passing an examination by the state board of law examiners and a background investigation.

ALABAMA

Admissions Office
Alabama State Bar
415 Dexter Avenue
Montgomery AL 36104
Phone: (334) 269-1515
http://www.alabar.org/admissions

ALASKA

Admissions Department
Alaska Bar Association
P.O. Box 100279
Anchorage, AK 99510
Phone: (907) 272-7469
Fax: (907) 272-2932
http://www.alaskabar.org

ARIZONA

Committee on Examinations and Committee on Character and Fitness
Arizona Supreme Court
1501 West Washington Avenue, Suite 104
Phoenix, AZ 85007
Phone: (602) 452-3971
http://www.supreme.state.az.us/admis

ARKANSAS

State Board of Law Examiners
625 Marshall Street
120 Justice Building
Little Rock, AR 72201
Phone. (501) 374-1855
Fax: (501) 374-1853
http://www.courts.state.ar.us/courts/ble.html

CALIFORNIA

Office of Admissions
State Bar of California
180 Howard Street
San Francisco, CA 94105
Phone: (415) 538-2300
or
1149 South Hill Street
Los Angeles, CA 90015
Phone: (213) 765-1550
http://calbar.ca.gov/state/calbar/calbar_generic.jsp?cid=10115

COLORADO

Board of Law Examiners
Colorado Supreme Court
1560 Broadway, Suite 1820
Denver, CO 80202
Phone: (303) 866-6626
http://www.coloradosupremecourt.com/ble/ble_home.htm

CONNECTICUT

Bar Examining Committee
State of Connecticut Judicial Branch
100 Washington Street
Hartford, CT 06106
Phone: (860) 706-5136; (800) 842-9710, for hearing and speech-impaired applicants
http://www.jud.state.ct.us/CBEC

DELAWARE

Board of Bar Examiners
Supreme Court of Delaware
820 North French Street, 11th Floor
Wilmington, DE 19801
Phone: (302) 577-7038
Fax: (302) 577-7037
http://courts.delaware.gov/bbe

DISTRICT OF COLUMBIA

Committee on Admissions
District of Columbia Court of Appeals
500 Indiana Avenue NW, Room 4200
Washington, DC 20001
Phone: (202) 879-2710
http://www.dcappeals.gov/dccourts/appeals/coa/index.jsp

FLORIDA

Florida Board of Bar Examiners
1891 Eider Court
Tallahassee, FL 32399
Phone: (850) 487-1292
Fax: (850) 414-6822
http://www.floridabarexam.org

HAWAII

Board of Bar Examiners
Supreme Court of Hawaii
417 South King Street
Honolulu, HI 96813
Phone: (808) 539-4977
http://www.courts.state.hi.us/index.jsp

IDAHO

Admissions Department
Idaho State Bar
P.O. Box 895
Boise, ID 83701
Phone: (208) 334-4500
http://www.state.id.us/isb

ILLINOIS

Illinois Board of Admissions to the Bar
625 South College Street
Springfield, IL 62704
Phone: (217) 522-5917
Fax: (217) 522-3728
http://www.ibaby.org

INDIANA

Board of Law Examiners
Indiana Supreme Court
South Tower, Suite 1370
115 West Washington Street
Indianapolis, IN 46204
http://www.in.gov/judiciary/ble

IOWA

Board of Law Examiners
Clerk of Iowa Supreme Court
1111 East Court Avenue
Des Moines, IA 50319
Phone: (515) 281-5911
http://www.judicial.state.ia.us/Professional_
    Regulation

KANSAS

Kansas Attorney Admissions
Kansas Judicial Center
301 SW 10th Avenue, Room 374
Topeka, KS 66612
Phone: (785) 296-8410
http://www.kscourts.org/clerkct/
    attyadmit.htm

KENTUCKY

Kentucky Office of Bar Admissions
1510 Newtown Pike, Suite 156
Lexington, KY 40511
Phone: (859) 246-2381
Fax: (859) 246-2385
http://www.kyoba.org

LOUISIANA

Committee on Bar Admissions
Louisiana Supreme Court
2800 Veterans Memorial Boulevard,
    Suite 310
Metairie, LA 70002
Phone: (800) 314-1530 or (504) 836-2420
Fax: (504) 834-1449
http://www.lascba.org

MAINE

Board of Bar Examiners
State of Maine
P.O. Box 140
Augusta, ME 04332
Phone: (207) 623-2464
Fax: (207) 622-0059
http://www.mainebarexaminers.org

MARYLAND

State Board of Law Examiners
2011 Commerce Park Drive
Annapolis, MD 21401
Phone: (410) 260-3640
http://www.courts.state.md.us/ble/index.
    html

MASSACHUSETTS

Massachusetts Board of Bar Examiners
3 Pemberton Square, Room 707
Boston, MA 02108
Phone: (617) 482-4466
Fax: (617) 542-5943
http://www.mass.gov/bbe

MICHIGAN

Board of Law Examiners
Michigan Supreme Court
925 West Ottawa
Lansing, MI 48913
Phone: (517) 373-4453
http://www.courts.michigan.gov/
    supremecourt/BdofLawExaminers/
    index.htm

MINNESOTA

**Minnesota State Board of Law
    Examiners**
380 Jackson Street, Suite 201
St. Paul, MN 55101
Phone: (651) 297-1857; for TTY: (800)
    627-3520, ask for (651) 297-1857
Fax: (651) 297-1196
http://www.ble.state.mn.us

MISSISSIPPI

Mississippi Board of Bar Admissions
P.O. Box 1449
Jackson, MS 39215
http://www.mssc.state.ms.us/
    BarAdmissions/default.asp

MISSOURI

Missouri Board of Law Examiners
407 Jefferson Street
Jefferson City, MO 65101
Phone: (573) 751-9814
Fax: (573) 751-5335
http://www.courts.mo.gov

MONTANA

Bar Admissions Administrator
State Bar of Montana
P.O. Box 577
Helena, MT 59624
Phone: (406) 442-7660
Fax: (406) 442-7763
http://www.montanabar.org

NEBRASKA

Nebraska State Bar Commission
635 South 14th Street, Suite 200
Lincoln, NE 68508
Mailing address:
P.O. Box 81809
Lincoln, NE 68508
Phone: (402) 475-7091 or (800) 927-0117
Fax: (402) 475-7098
http://www.nebar.com/nsbainfo/otherorgs/
    nsbc/index.htm

NEVADA

Admissions Department
State Bar of Nevada
600 East Charleston Boulevard
Las Vegas, NV 89104

Phone: (702) 382-2200
http://www.nvbar.org/admissions/
Admissions.htm

NEW HAMPSHIRE

Bar Admissions
Supreme Court
1 Noble Drive
Concord, NH 03301
http://www.courts.state.nh.us/nhbar/
index.htm

NEW JERSEY

New Jersey Board of Bar Examiners
P.O. Box 973
Trenton, NJ 08625
Phone: (609) 984-2111
http://www.njbarexams.org

NEW MEXICO

New Mexico Bar Examiners
9420 Indian School Road NE
Albuquerque, NM 87112
Phone: (505) 271-9706
Fax: (505) 271-9768
http://www.nmexam.org

NEW YORK

New York State Board of Law
Examiners
Corporate Plaza – Building 3
254 Washington Avenue Extension
Albany, NY 12203
Phone: (800) 342-3335 or (518) 452-8700
Fax: (518) 452-5729
http://www.nybarexam.org

NORTH CAROLINA

Board of Law Examiners
State of North Carolina
One Exchange Plaza, Suite 700
Raleigh, NC 27601
Mailing address:
P.O. Box 2946
Raleigh, NC 27602
Phone: (919) 828-4886
Fax: (919) 828-2251
http://www.ncble.org

NORTH DAKOTA

State Board of Law Examiners
Judicial Wing, First Floor

600 East Boulevard Avenue
Bismarck, ND 58505
Phone: (701) 328-4201
Fax: (701) 328-4480
http://www.court.state.nd.us/court/
committees/barbd/board.asp

COMMONWEALTH OF THE NORTHERN MARIANA ISLANDS

Bar Administrator
Supreme Court, Commonwealth of the
Northern Mariana Islands
P.O. Box 502165
Saipan, MP 96950
Phone: (670) 236-9800
Fax: (670) 236-9702
http://www.justice.gov.mp

OHIO

Office of Bar Admissions
Supreme Court of Ohio
65 South Front Street, 5th Floor
Columbus, OH 43215
Phone: (614) 387-3431
Fax: (614) 387-9349
http://www.sconet.state.oh.us/
Admissions

OKLAHOMA

Oklahoma Board of Bar Examiners
1901 North Lincoln Boulevard
P.O. Box 53036
Oklahoma City, OK 73152
Phone: (405) 416-7075
http://www.okbbe.com

OREGON

Oregon State Board of Bar Examiners
5200 SW Meadows Road
Lake Oswego, OR 97035
Phone: (503) 620-0222
http://www.osbar.org/admissions/
admissions.html

PENNSYLVANIA

Pennsylvania Board of Law
Examiners
5070A Ritter Road, Suite 300
Mechanicsburg, PA 17055
Phone: (717) 795-7270
http://www.pabarexam.org

PUERTO RICO

Board of Bar Examiners
Supreme Court of Puerto Rico
P.O. Box 902-2392
San Juan, PR 009022392
Phone: (787) 723-6033
http://www.tribunalpr.org

RHODE ISLAND

Rhode Island Board of Bar
Examiners
Clerk of the Supreme Court
250 Benefit Street
Providence, RI 02903
Phone: (401) 222-4233
Fax: (401) 222-3599
http://www.courts.state.ri.us/supreme/bar/
baradmission.htm

SOUTH CAROLINA

Office of Bar Admissions
Supreme Court of South Carolina
P.O. Box 11330
Columbia, SC 29211
Phone: (803) 734-1080
TTY: (803) 734-6365
Fax: (803) 734-0394
http://www.judicial.state.sc.us/bar

SOUTH DAKOTA

State Board of Bar Examiners
500 East Capitol
Pierre, SD 57501
Phone: (605) 773-4898
http://www.sdjudicial.com

TENNESSEE

Tennessee Board of Law Examiners
401 Church Street, Suite 2200
Nashville, TN 37243
Phone: (615) 741-3234
Fax: (615) 741-5867
http://www.state.tn.us/lawexaminers

TEXAS

Texas Board of Law Examiners
P.O. Box 13486
Austin, TX 78711
Phone: (512) 463-1621
Fax: (512) 463-5300
http://www.ble.state.tx.us

UTAH

Office of Bar Admissions
Utah State Bar
645 South 200 East
Salt Lake City, UT 84111
Phone: (801) 531-9077
http://www.utahbar.org/admissions

VERMONT

Board of Bar Examiners
2418 Airport Road, Suite 2
Barre, VT 05641
Phone: (802) 828-3281
Fax: (802) 828-1695
http://www.vermontjudiciary.org/bbe/
    bbelibrary/bbedefault.aspx

VIRGIN ISLANDS

**Virgin Islands Committee of Bar
    Examiners**
P.O. Box 70
St. Thomas, VI 00804
Phone: (340) 774-6680

Fax: (340) 777-8187
http://www.vid.uscourts.gov

VIRGINIA

Virginia Board of Bar Examiners
2201 West Broad Street, Suite 101
Richmond, VA 23220
Phone: (804) 367-0412
Fax: (804) 367-0416
http://www.vbbe.state.va.us

WASHINGTON

Admissions Department
Washington State Bar Association
1325 Fourth Avenue, Suite 600
Seattle, WA 98101
Phone: (800) 945-9722 or (206) 443-9722
http://www.wsba.org/lawyers/licensing/
    default1.htm

WEST VIRGINIA

West Virginia Board of Law Examiners
910 Quarrier Street

Suite 212, Davidson Building
Charleston, WV 25301
Phone: (304) 558-7815
Fax: (304) 558-0831
http://www.state.wv.us/wvsca

WISCONSIN

Board of Bar Examiners
110 East Main Street, Suite 715
Madison, WI 53703
Phone: (608) 266-9760
Fax: (608) 266-1196
http://www.courts.state.wi.us/bbe

WYOMING

Board of Law Examiners
500 Randall Avenue
P.O. Box 109
Cheyenne, WY 82003
Phone: (307) 632-9061
Fax: (307) 632-3737
http://www.wyomingbar.org/admissions/
    index.html

B. FEDERAL COURTS

In the federal court system, attorneys must be admitted into every federal court in which they wish to practice. Each federal court has its own admission procedures; entry generally requires meeting certain requirements.

**Administrative Office of the U.S.
    Courts**
Office of Public Affairs
Washington, DC 20544
Phone: (202) 502-2600
http://www.uscourts.gov
The U.S. Courts are made up of district courts, courts of appeals, and bankruptcy courts. (Links to many of these courts can be accessed at this office's Web site.)

U.S. Supreme Court
Admissions Office
Clerk, Supreme Court of the United States
One First Street NE
Washington, DC 20543-0001
Phone: (202) 479-3387
http://www.supremecourtus.gov/bar/
    baradmissions.html

**U.S. Court of Appeals for the Federal
    Circuit**
717 Madison Place NW

Washington, DC 20439
Phone: (202) 633-6550
http://www.fedcir.gov

U.S. Tax Court
Admissions Clerk
United States Tax Court
400 Second Street NW
Washington, DC 20217
http://www.ustaxcourt.gov

U.S. Court of International Trade
One Federal Plaza
New York, NY 10278
Phone: (212) 264-2800
http://www.cit.uscourts.gov

**U.S. Court of Appeals for Veterans
    Claims**
625 Indiana Avenue NW,
    Suite 900
Washington, DC 20004
http://www.vetapp.uscourts.gov

**U.S. Court of Appeals for the Armed
    Forces**
Clerk of the Court
450 E Street NW
Washington, DC 20442
http://www.armfor.uscourts.gov

U.S. Court of Federal Claims
Clerk's Office
717 Madison Place NW
Washington, DC 20005
Phone: (202) 357-6400
http://www.uscfc.uscourts.gov

APPENDIX IV
STATE BAR ASSOCIATIONS

Below is a list of attorney bar associations for the 50 states as well as for the District of Columbia and the territories of the United States. In some locations, membership in the state attorney bar is required in order to practice law in that state.

Note: All contact information and Web site addresses were current when the book was being written. If you come across a URL that no longer works, you may be able to find an organization's new Web site by entering its name in a search engine.

Alabama State Bar
415 Dexter Avenue
Montgomery, AL 36104
Phone: (334) 269-1515
Fax: (334) 261-6310
http://www.alabar.org

Alaska Bar Association
550 West 7th Avenue, Suite 1900
Anchorage, AK 99501
Phone: (907) 272-7469
Fax: (907) 272-2932
http://www.alaskabar.org

State Bar of Arizona
4201 North 24th Street, Suite 200
Phoenix, AZ 85016
Phone: (602) 252-4804
    or (866) 48-AZBAR
Fax: (602) 271-4930
http://www.azbar.org

Arkansas Bar Association
400 West Markham
Little Rock, AR 72201
Phone: (800) 609-5668
    or (501) 375-4606
Fax: (501) 375-4901
http://www.arkbar.com

State Bar of California
180 Howard Street
San Francisco, CA 94105
Phone: (415) 538-2000
http://www.calbar.org

Colorado Bar Association
1900 Grant Street, Suite 900
Denver, CO, 80203
Phone: (800) 332-6736
    or (303) 860-1115
Fax: (303) 894-0821
http://www.cobar.org

Connecticut Bar Association
30 Bank Street
P.O. Box 350
New Britain, CT 06050
Phone: (860) 223-4400
Fax: (860) 223-4488
http://www.ctbar.org

Delaware State Bar Association
301 North Market Street
Wilmington, DE 19801
Phone: (302) 658-5279 or (800) 292-7869
Fax: (302) 658-5212
http://www.dsba.org

The District of Columbia Bar
1250 H Street NW, Sixth Floor
Washington, DC 20005
Phone: (202) 737-4700
http://www.dcbar.org

The Florida Bar
651 East Jefferson Street
Tallahassee, FL 32399
Phone: (850) 561-5600
Fax: (850) 561-5826
http://www.floridabar.org

State Bar of Georgia
101 Marietta Street NW, Suite 100
Atlanta, GA 30303
Phone: (800) 334-6865 or
    (404) 527-8700
Fax: (404) 527-8717
http://www.gabar.org

Guam Bar Association
655 South Marine Corps Drive,
    Suite 202
Tamuning, Guam 96913
Phone: (671) 648-5050
Fax: (671) 646-9403
http://www.guambar.org

Hawaii State Bar Association
1132 Bishop Street, Suite 906
Honolulu, HI 96813
Phone: (808) 537-1868
Fax: (808) 521-7936
http://www.hsba.org

Idaho State Bar
525 West Jefferson
Boise, ID 83702
Phone: (208) 334-4500 or
Fax: (208) 334-4515 or (208) 334-2764
http://www2.state.id.us/isb

Illinois State Bar Association
Illinois Bar Center
424 South 2nd Street
Springfield, IL 62701
Phone: (217) 525-1760 or (800) 252-8908
http://www.illinoisbar.org

Indiana State Bar Association
One Indiana Square, Suite 530
Indianapolis, IN 46204
Phone: (800) 266-2581 or (317) 639-5465
Fax: (317) 266-2588
http://www.inbar.org

Iowa State Bar Association
521 East Locust
Des Moines, IA 50309
Phone: (515) 243-3179
http://www.iowabar.org

Kansas Bar Association
1200 SW Harrison Street
Topeka, KS 66612
Phone: (785) 234-5696
Fax: (785) 234-3813
http://www.ksbar.org

Kentucky Bar Association
514 West Main Street
Frankfort, KY 40601

Phone: (502) 564-3795
http://www.kybar.org

Louisiana State Bar Association
601 St. Charles Avenue
New Orleans, LA 70130
Phone: (800) 421-5722 or (504) 566-1600
http://www.lsba.org

Maine State Bar Association
124 State Street
Augusta, ME 04330
Phone: (207) 622-7523
Fax: (207) 623-0083
http://www.mainebar.org

Maryland State Bar Association
520 West Fayette Street
Baltimore, MD 21201
Phone: (800) 492-1964 or (410) 685-7878
Fax: (410) 685-1016
http://www.msba.org

Massachusetts Bar Association
20 West Street
Boston, MA 02111
Phone: (617) 338-0500
http://massbar.org

State Bar of Michigan
306 Townsend Street
Lansing, MI 48933
Phone: (800) 968-1442 or (517) 346-6300
Fax: (517) 482-6248
http://www.michbar.org

Minnesota State Bar Association
600 Nicollet Mall, #380
Minneapolis, MN 55402
Phone: (800) 882-6722 or (612) 333-1183
http://www.mnbar.org

The Mississippi Bar
P.O. Box 2168
643 North State Street
Jackson, MS 39225
Phone: (601) 948-4471
Fax: (601) 355-8635
http://www.msbar.org

The Missouri Bar
P.O. Box 119
Jefferson City, MO 65102
Phone: (573) 635-4128
Fax: (573) 635-2811
http://www.mobar.org

State Bar of Montana
P.O. Box 577

Helena, MT 59624
Phone: (406) 442-7660
Fax: (406) 442-7763
http://www.montanabar.org

Nebraska State Bar Association
635 South 14th Street
Lincoln, NE 68501
Phone: (402) 475-7091 or (800) 927-0117
Fax: (402) 475-7098
http://www.nebar.com

State Bar of Nevada
600 East Charleston Boulevard
Las Vegas, NV 89104
Phone: (702) 382-2200
Fax: (702) 385-2878
http://www.nvbar.org

New Hampshire Bar Association
2 Pillsbury Street, Suite 300
Concord, NH 03301
Phone: (603) 224-6942
Fax: (603) 224-2910
http://www.nhbar.org

New Jersey State Bar Association
New Jersey Law Center
One Constitution Square
New Brunswick, NJ 08901
Phone: (732) 249-5000
Fax: (732) 249-2815
http://www.njsba.com

State Bar of New Mexico
5121 Masthead Street NE
Albuquerque, NM 87109
Phone: (505) 797-6000
Fax: (505) 828-3765
http://www.nmbar.org

New York State Bar Association
1 Elk Street
Albany, NY 12207
Phone: (518) 463-3200
Fax: (518) 487-5517
http://www.nysba.org

North Carolina Bar Association
8000 Western Parkway
Cary, NC 27513
Phone: (919) 677-0561
http://www.ncbar.org

State Bar Association of North Dakota
504 North Washington Street
Bismarck, ND 58501
Phone: (701) 255-1404 or
    (800) 472-2685

Fax: (701) 224-1621
http://www.sband.org

**Commonwealth of the Northern
    Mariana Islands Bar Association**
P.O. Box 504539
Saipan, MP 96950
http://www.cnmibar.net

Ohio State Bar Association
1700 Lake Shore Drive
Columbus OH 43204
Phone: (800) 282-6556 or (614) 487-2050
Fax: (614) 487-1008
http://www.ohiobar.org

Oklahoma Bar Association
P.O. Box 53036
1901 North Lincoln Boulevard
Oklahoma City, OK 73152
Phone: (405) 416-7000
Fax: (405) 416-7001
http://www.okbar.org

Oregon State Bar
5200 SW Meadows Road
Lake Oswego, OR 97035
Phone: (800) 452-8260 or (503) 620-0222
http://www.osbar.org

Pennsylvania Bar Association
100 South Street
Harrisburg, PA 17101
Phone: (717) 238-6715 or
    (800) 932-0311
http://www.pabar.org

**Puerto Rico Bar Association (Colegio
    de Abogados de Puerto Rico)**
P.O. Box 9021900
San Juan, PR 00902-1900
Phone: (787) 721-3358
Fax: (787) 725-0330
http://www.capr.org

Rhode Island Bar Association
115 Cedar Street
Providence, RI 02903
Phone: (401) 421-5740
Fax: (401) 421-2703;
    TTY: (401) 421-1666
http://ribar.com

South Carolina Bar
950 Taylor Street
Columbia, SC 29202
Phone: (803) 799-6653
Fax: (803) 799-4118
http://www.scbar.org

State Bar of South Dakota
222 East Capitol Avenue
Pierre, SD 57501
Phone: (800) 952-2333 or (605) 224-7554
http://www.sdbar.org

Tennessee Bar Association
221 Fourth Avenue North, Suite 400
Nashville, TN 37219
Phone: (615) 383-7421
Fax: (615) 297-8058
http://www.tba.org

State Bar of Texas
1414 Colorado
Austin, TX 78701
Phone: (800) 204-2222
    or (512) 427-1463
Fax: (512) 427-4100
http://www.texasbar.com

Utah State Bar
645 South 200 East
Salt Lake City, UT 84111

Phone: (801) 531-9077
Fax: (801) 531-0660
http://www.utahbar.org

Vermont Bar Association
35-37 Court Street
Montpelier, VT 05601
Phone: (802) 223-2020
Fax: (802) 223-1573
http://www.vtbar.org

Virginia State Bar Association
707 East Main Street, Suite 1500
Richmond, VA 23219
Phone: (804) 775-0500
http://www.vsb.org

Washington State Bar Association
1325 Fourth Avenue, Suite 600
Seattle, WA 98101
Phone: (800) 945-9722
    or (206) 443-9722
Fax: (206) 727-8319
http://www.wsba.org

West Virginia State Bar
2006 Kanawha Boulevard East
Charleston, WV 25311
Phone: (304) 558-2456
Fax: (304) 558-2467 or (866) 989-8227
http://www.wvbar.org

State Bar of Wisconsin
5302 Eastpark Boulevard
Madison, WI 53718
Phone: (800) 728-7788
    or (608) 257-3838
Fax: (608) 257-5502
http://www.wisbar.org

Wyoming State Bar
500 Randall Avenue
P.O. Box 109
Cheyenne, WY 82003
Phone: (307) 632-9061
Fax: (307) 632-3737
http://www.wyomingbar.org

APPENDIX V
PROFESSIONAL UNIONS AND ASSOCIATIONS

You can contact the following organizations, or visit their Web sites, to learn more about careers, job opportunities, training programs, conferences, professional certification, and other topics. Many of these organizations have student chapters. Most have branch offices throughout the United States; contact an organization's headquarters to find out if a branch is in your area.

To learn about other local, state, regional, and national professional societies and unions, talk with local professionals.

Note: Web site addresses change from time to time. If you come across an address that no longer works, you may be able to find an organization's new URL by entering its name into a search engine.

ATTORNEYS

American Association for Justice
The Leonard M. Ring Law Center
1050 31st Street NW
Washington, DC 20007
Phone: (800) 424-2725
    or (202) 965-3500
http://www.atlanet.org

American Bar Association
321 North Clark Street
Chicago, IL 60610
Phone: (800) 285-2221 or
    (312) 988-5000
http://www.abanet.org

American Immigration Lawyers Association
918 F Street NW
Washington, DC 20004
Phone: (202) 216-2400
Fax: (202) 783-7853
http://www.aila.org

American Intellectual Property Law Association
241 18th Street South, Suite 700
Arlington, VA 22202
Phone: (703) 415-0780
Fax: (703) 415-0786
http://www.aipla.org

Association of Corporate Counsel
1025 Connecticut Ave NW, Suite 200
Washington, DC 20036
Phone: (202) 293-4103
http://www.acca.com

Association of Federal Defense Attorneys
http://www.afda.org

Federal Bar Association
2215 M Street NW
Washington, DC 20037
Phone: (202) 785-1614
Fax: (202) 785-1568
http://www.fedbar.org

International Municipal Lawyers Association
7910 Woodmont Avenue, Suite 1440
Bethesda, MD 20814
Phone: (202) 466-5424
Fax: (202) 758-0152
http://www.imla.org

Judge Advocates Association
8109 Overlake Court
Fairfax Station, VA 22039
http://www.jaa.org

Minority Corporate Counsel Association
1111 Pennsylvania Avenue NW
Washington, DC 20004
Phone: (202) 739-5901
Fax: (202) 739-5999
http://www.mcca.com

National Asian Pacific American Bar Association
910 17th Street NW, Suite 315
Washington, DC 20006
Phone: (202) 775-9555
Fax: (202) 775-9333
http://www.napaba.org

National Association of Criminal Defense Lawyers
1150 18th Street NW, Suite 950
Washington, DC 20036
Phone: (202) 872-8600
Fax: (202) 872-8690
http://www.nacdl.org

National Association of Women Lawyers
American Bar Center, MS 15.2
321 North Clark Street
Chicago, IL 60610
Fax: (312) 988-5491
http://www.nawl.org

National Bar Association
1225 11th Street NW
Washington, DC 20001
Phone: (202) 842-3900
Fax: (202) 289-6170
http://www.nationalbar.org

National Criminal Justice Association
720 7th Street NW, 3rd Floor
Washington, DC 20001
Phone: (202) 628-8550
Fax: (202) 628-0080
http://www.ncja.org

National District Attorneys Association
99 Canal Center Plaza, Suite 510
Alexandria, VA 22314
Phone: (703) 549-9222
Fax: (703) 836-3195
http://www.ndaa.org

National Employment Lawyers Association
44 Montgomery Street, Suite 2080
San Francisco, CA 94104

Phone: (415) 296-7629
Fax: (415) 677-9445
http://www.nela.org

National Lawyers Association
17201 East 40 Highway, Suite 207
Independence, MO 64055
Phone: (800) 471-2994
Fax: (816) 229-8425
http://www.nla.org

National Lawyers Guild
132 Nassau Street, Suite 922
New York, NY 10038
Phone: (212) 679-5100
Fax: (212) 679-2811
http://www.nlg.org

National Legal Aid and Defender
    Association
1140 Connecticut Avenue NW, Suite 900
Washington, DC 20036
Phone: (202) 452-0620
Fax: (202) 872-1031
http://www.nlada.org

PRACTICE AREAS

American Academy of Appellate
    Lawyers
15245 Shady Grove Road, Suite 130
Rockville, MD 20850
Phone: (301) 258-9210
Fax: (301) 990-9771
http://www.appellateacademy.org

American Association for Justice
The Leonard M. Ring Law Center
1050 31st Street NW
Washington, DC 20007
Phone: (800) 424-2725
    or (202) 965-3500
http://www.atlanet.org

American Association of Nurse
    Attorneys
P.O. Box 515
Columbus, OH 43216
Phone: (877) 538-2262
Fax: (614) 221-2335
http://www.taana.org

American Bar Association
321 North Clark Street
Chicago, IL 60610
Phone: (800) 285-2221
    or (312) 988-5000
http://www.abanet.org

American Bar Association—Health
    Law Section
http://www.abanet.org/health

American Bar Association—Section of
    Litigation
http://www.abanet.org/litigation

American Bar Association—Section of
    Taxation
http://www.abanet.org/tax

American College of Trust and Estate
    Counsel
3415 South Sepulveda Boulevard,
    Suite 330
Los Angeles, CA 90034
Phone: (310) 398-1888
Fax: (310) 572-7280
http://www.actec.org

American Health Lawyers Association
1025 Connecticut Avenue NW,
    Suite 600
Washington, DC 20036
Phone: (202) 833-1100
Fax: (202) 833-1105
http://www.healthlawyers.org

American Intellectual Property Law
    Association
241 18th Street South, Suite 700
Arlington, VA 22202
Phone: (703) 415-0780
Fax: (703) 415-0786
http://www.aipla.org

Association of Federal Defense
    Attorneys
http://www.afda.org

Copyright Society of the USA
352 7th Avenue, Suite 739
New York, NY 10001
Phone: (212) 354-6401
http://www.csusa.org

DRI
150 North Michigan Avenue, Suite 300
Chicago, IL 60601
Phone: (312) 795-1101
Fax: (312) 795-0747 or (3120 795-0749
http://www.dri.org

Federal Bar Association
2215 M Street NW
Washington, DC 20037
Phone: (202) 785-1614
Fax: (202) 785-1568
http://www.fedbar.org

International Trademark Association
655 3rd Avenue, 10th Floor
New York, NY 10017
Phone: (212) 642-1700
Fax: (212) 766-7796
http://www.inta.org

Institute for Professionals in Taxation
600 Northpark Town Center
1200 Abernathy Road NE, Suite L-2
Atlanta, GA 30328
Phone: (404) 240-2300
Fax: (404) 240-2315
http://www.ipt.org

Licensing Executives Society
1800 Diagonal Road, Suite 280
Alexandria, VA 22314
Phone: (703) 836-3106
Fax: (703) 836-3107
http://www.usa-canada.les.org

National Academy of Elder Law
    Attorneys
1604 North Country Club Road
Tucson, AZ 85716
Phone: (520) 881-4005
Fax: (520) 325-7925
http://www.naela.org

National Association of Criminal
    Defense Lawyers
1150 18th Street NW, Suite 950
Washington, DC 20036
Phone: (202) 872-8600
Fax: (202) 872-8690
http://www.nacdl.org

National Association of Patent
    Practitioners
4680-18i Monticello Avenue
PMB 101
Williamsburg, VA 23188
Phone: (800) 216-9588
Fax: (757) 220-2231
http://www.napp.org

National Association of Personal Injury
    Lawyers
23945 Calabasas Road, Suite 106
Calabasas, CA 91302
http://www.napil.com

National Association of Tax
    Professionals
720 Association Drive
P.O. Box 8002
Appleton, WI 54912
Phone: (800) 558-3402

Fax: (800) 747-0001
http://www.natptax.com

**National Association of Women
 Lawyers**
American Bar Center, MS 15.2
321 North Clark Street
Chicago, IL 60610
Fax: (312) 988-5491
http://www.nawl.org

**National District Attorneys
 Association**
99 Canal Center Plaza, Suite 510
Alexandria, VA 22314
Phone: (703) 549-9222
Fax: (703) 836-3195
http://www.ndaa.org

**National Employment Lawyers
 Association**
44 Montgomery Street, Suite 2080
San Francisco, CA 94104
Phone: (415) 296-7629
Fax: (415) 677-9445
http://www.nela.org

National Lawyers Association
17201 East 40 Highway, Suite 207
Independence, MO 64055
Phone: (800) 471-2994
Fax: (816) 229-8425
http://www.nla.org

National Lawyers Guild
132 Nassau Street, Suite 922
New York, NY 10038
Phone: (212) 679-5100
Fax: (212) 679-2811
http://www.nlg.org

**National Legal Aid and Defender
 Association**
1140 Connecticut Avenue NW, Suite 900
Washington, DC 20036
Phone: (202) 452-0620
Fax: (202) 872-1031
http://www.nlada.org

Tax Executives Institute
1200 G Street NW, Suite 300
Washington, DC 20005
http://www.tei.org

JUDGES

American Bankruptcy Institute
44 Canal Center Plaza, Suite 404
Alexandria, VA 22314

Phone: (703) 739-0800
Fax: (703) 739-1060
http://www.abiworld.org

American Bar Association
321 North Clark Street
Chicago, IL 60610
Phone: (800) 285-2221 or (312) 988-5000
http://www.abanet.org

**American Bar Association—Judicial
 Division**
http://www.abanet.org/jd

American Judges Association
300 Newport Avenue
Williamsburg, VA 23185
Phone: (757) 259-1841
Fax: (757) 259-1520
http://aja.ncsc.dni.us

American Judicature Society
The Opperman Center at Drake
 University
2700 University Avenue
Des Moines, IA 50311
Phone: (515) 271-2281
Fax: (515) 279-3090
http://www.ajs.org

**Association of Administrative Law
 Judges**
http://www.aalj.org

**Federal Administrative Law Judges
 Conference**
2020 Pennsylvania Avenue NW,
 Suite 260
Washington, DC 20006
http://www.faljc.org

Federal Bar Association
2215 M Street NW
Washington, DC 20037
Phone: (202) 785-1614
Fax: (202) 785-1568
http://www.fedbar.org

**National Association of Administrative
 Law Judges**
http://www.naalj.org

**National Conference of Bankruptcy
 Judges**
235 Secret Cove Drive
Lexington, SC 29072
Phone: (803) 957-6225
Fax: (803) 957-8890
http://www.ncbj.org

**National Conference of the
 Administrative Law Judiciary**
(part of the American Bar Association—
 Judicial Division)
http://www.abanet.org/jd/ncalj

**National Council of Juvenile and
 Family Court Judges**
P.O. Box 8970
Reno, NV 89507
Phone: (775) 784-6012
Fax: (775) 784-6628
http://www.ncjfcj.org

ALTERNATIVE
DISPUTE RESOLUTION
PRACTITIONERS

**Association of Family and Conciliation
 Courts**
6525 Grand Teton Plaza
Madison, WI 53719
Phone: (608) 664-3750
Fax: (608) 664-3751
http://www.afccnet.org

American Arbitration Association
335 Madison Avenue, Floor 10
New York, NY 10017
Phone: (800) 778-7879 or
 (212) 716-5800
Fax: (212) 716-5905
http://www.adr.org

**American Bar Association—Section of
 Dispute Resolution**
http://www.abanet.org/dispute

**American College of Civil Trial
 Mediators**
20 North Orange Avenue, Suite 600
Orlando, FL 32801
Phone: (407) 843-8878
Fax: (407) 425-7905
http://www.acctm.org

Association for Conflict Resolution
1015 18th Street NW, Suite 1150
Washington, DC 20036
Phone: (202) 464-9700
Fax: (202) 464-9720
http://www.acrnet.org

Association of Attorney-Mediators
P.O. Box 741955
Dallas, TX 75374
Phone: (800) 280-1368 or (972) 669-8101
Fax: (972) 669-8180
http://www.attorney-mediators.org

National Academy of Arbitrators
One North Main Street, Suite 412
Cortland, NY 13045
Phone: (607) 756-8363
Fax: (607) 756-8365
http://www.naarb.org

National Association for Community Mediation
1527 New Hampshire Avenue NW
Washington, DC 20036
Phone: (202) 667-9700
http://www.nafcm.org

LEGAL SUPPORT PROFESSIONALS

American Alliance of Paralegals
http://www.aapipara.org

American Bar Association
321 North Clark Street
Chicago, IL 60610
Phone: (800) 285-2221 or (312) 988-5000
http://www.abanet.org

American Bar Association—Standing Committee on Paralegals
http://www.abanet.org/legalservices/paralegals

American Marketing Association
311 South Wacker Drive, Suite 5800
Chicago, IL 60606
Phone: (800) AMA-1150
or (312) 542-9000
Fax: (312) 542-9001
http://www.marketingpower.com

Association for Computing Machinery
2 Penn Plaza, Suite 701
New York, NY 10121
Phone: (800) 342-6626
or (212) 869-7440
http://www.acm.org

Association of Legal Administrators
75 Tri-State International, Suite 222
Lincolnshire, IL 60069
Phone: (847) 267-1252
Fax: (847) 267-1329
http://www.alanet.org

Association of Support Professionals
122 Barnard Avenue
Watertown, MA 02472
Phone: (617) 924-3944
Fax: (617) 924-7288
http://www.asponline.com

International Association of Administrative Professionals
10502 NW Ambassador Drive
P.O. Box 20404
Kansas City, MO 64195
Phone: (816) 891-6600
Fax: (816) 891-9118
http://www.iaap-hq.org

International Legal Technology Association
9600 Escarpment, Suite 745
Austin, TX 78749
Phone: (512) 847-1940
Fax: (512) 847-1941
http://www.peertopeer.org

Legal Marketing Association
1926 Waukegan Road, Suite 1
Glenview, IL 60025
Phone: (847) 657-6717
Fax: (847) 657-6819
http://www.legalmarketing.org

Legal Secretaries International, Inc.
2302 Fannin Street, Suite 500
Houston, TX 77002
http://www.legalsecretaries.org

NALS
314 East 3rd Street, Suite 210
Tulsa, OK 74120
Phone: (918) 582-5188
Fax: (918) 582-5907
http://www.nals.org

National Association of Legal Assistants
1516 South Boston Avenue, Suite 200
Tulsa, OK 74119
Phone: (918) 587-6828
http://www.nala.org

National Association of Legal Search Consultants
1525 North Park Drive, Suite 102
Weston, FL 33326
Phone: (866) 902-6587
or (954) 349-8081
Fax: (954) 349-1979
http://www.nalsc.org

National Paralegal Association
Box 406
Solebury, PA 18963
Phone: (215) 297-8333
Fax: (215) 297-8358
http://www.nationalparalegal.org

Society for Human Resource Management
1800 Duke Street
Alexandria, VA 22314
Phone: (800) 283-SHRM
or (703) 548-3440
Fax: (703) 535-6490
http://www.shrm.org

Society for Information Management
401 North Michigan Avenue
Chicago, IL 60611
Phone: (312) 527-6734
http://www.simnet.org

LITIGATION SUPPORT PROFESSIONALS

American Guild of Court Videographers
1628 East 3rd Street
Casper, WY 82601
Phone: (800) 678-1990
Fax: (307) 472-5048
http://www.agcv.com

American Psychology-Law Society
http://www.ap-ls.org

American Society of Trial Consultants
1941 Greenspring Drive
Timonium, MD 21093
Phone: (410) 560-7949
Fax: (410) 560-2563
http://www.astcweb.org

Association of Medical Illustrators
P.O. Box 1897
Lawrence, KS 66044
Phone: (866) 393-4264
Fax: (785) 843-1274
http://www.ami.org

Council of International Investigators
2150 North 107th, Suite 205
Seattle, WA 98133
Phone: (888) 759-8884
or (206) 361-8889
Fax: (206) 367-8777
http://www.cii2.org

Demonstrative Evidence Specialists Association
http://www.desa.org

Evidence Photographers International Council
600 Main Street
Honesdale, PA 18431

Phone: (800) 356-3742
http://www.epic-photo.org

**International Process Servers
    Association**
2171 Monroe Avenue #206
Rochester, NY 14618
Phone: (585) 232-8590
Fax: (716) 546-3463
http://www.ipsaonline.com

**National Association of Investigative
    Specialists**
P.O. Box 82148
Austin, TX 78708
Phone: (512) 719-3595
Fax: (512) 719-3594
http://www.pimall.com/nais/nais.j.html

**National Association of Legal
    Investigators**
Phone: (800) 266-6254
http://www.nalionline.org

**National Association of Professional
    Process Servers**
P.O. Box 4547
Portland, OR 97208
Phone: (800) 477-8211 or (503) 222-4180
Fax: (503) 222-3950
http://www.napps.com

National Court Reporters Association
8224 Old Courthouse Road
Vienna, VA 22182
Phone: (800) 272-6272 or (703) 556-6272;
    for TTY: (703) 556-6289
Fax: (703) 556-6291
http://www.ncraonline.org

National Legal Video Association
80 Bloomfield Avenue, Suite 104
Montclair, NJ 07006
Phone: (973) 228-8772
Fax: (973) 228-6650
http://www.nlva.com

LITIGATION CONSULTANTS
AND EXPERT WITNESSES

Academy of Criminal Justice Sciences
7339 Hanover Parkway, Suite A
Greenbelt, MD 20770
Mailing address:
P.O. Box 960
Greenbelt, MD 20768
Phone: (800) 757-2257 or (301) 446-6300
Fax: (301) 446-2819
http://www.acjs.org

**American Academy of Forensic
    Psychology**
http://www.abfp.com/academy.asp

**American Association of Legal Nurse
    Consultants**
401 North Michigan Avenue
Chicago, IL 60611
Phone: (877) 402-2562
Fax: (847) 673-6655
http://www.aalnc.org

**American Institute of Certified Public
    Accountants**
1211 Avenue of the Americas
New York, NY 10036
Phone: (212) 596-6200
Fax: (212) 596-6213
http://www.aicpa.org

American Nurses Association
8515 Georgia Avenue, Suite 400
Silver Spring, MD 20910
Phone: (800) 274-4262
    or (301) 628-5000
Fax: (301) 628-5001
http://www.nursingworld.org

American Psychology-Law Society
http://www.ap-ls.org

American Society of Appraisers
555 Herndon Parkway, Suite 125
Herndon, VA 20170
Phone: (703) 478-2228
Fax: (703) 742-8471
http://www.appraisers.org

American Society of Criminology
1314 Kinnear Road, Suite 212
Columbus, OH 43212
Phone: (614) 292-9207
Fax: (614) 292-6767
http://www.asc41.com

**American Society of Farm Managers
    and Rural Appraisers**
950 South Cherry Street, Suite 508
Denver, CO 80246
Phone: (303) 758-3513
Fax: (303) 758-0190
http://www.asfmra.org

American Society of Safety Engineers
1800 East Oakton Street
Des Plaines, IL 60018
Phone: (847) 699-2929
Fax: (847) 768-3434
http://www.asse.org

American Sociological Association
1307 New York Avenue NW, Suite 700
Washington, DC 20005
Phone: (202) 383-9005
TDD: (202) 638-0981
Fax: (202) 638-0882
http://www.asanet.org

Appraisers Association of America, Inc.
386 Park Avenue South, Suite 2000
New York, NY 10016
Phone: (212) 889-5404
Fax: (212) 889-5503
http://www.appraisersassoc.org

**Association of Certified Fraud
    Examiners**
716 West Avenue
Austin, TX 78701
Phone: (800) 245-3321 or
    (512) 478-9000
Fax: (512) 478-9297
http://www.cfenet.com

**Association of Insolvency and
    Restructuring Advisors**
221 Stewart Avenue, Suite 207
Medford, OR 97501
Phone: (541) 858-1665
Fax: (541) 858-9187
http://www.airacira.org

**Forensic Accountants Society of North
    America**
4248 Park Glen Road
Minneapolis, MN 55416
Phone: (952) 928-4668
Fax: (952) 929-1318
http://www.fasna.org

Institute of Business Appraisers
P.O. Box 17410
Plantation, FL 33318
Phone: (954) 584-1144
Fax: (954) 584-1184
http://www.go-iba.org

**International Association of Accident
    Reconstruction Specialists**
P.O. Box 534
Grand Ledge, MI 48837
http://www.iaars.org

International Society of Appraisers
1131 SW 7th Street, Suite 105
Renton, WA 98057
Phone: (206) 241-0359
Fax: (206) 241-0436
http://www.isa-appraisers.org

**National Association of Certified
   Valuation Analysts**
1111 Brickyard Road, Suite 200
Salt Lake City, UT 84106
Phone: (801) 486-0600
Fax: (801) 486-7500
http://www.nacva.com

**National Association of Independent
   Fee Appraisers**
401 North Michigan Avenue, Suite 2200
Chicago, IL 60611
Phone: (312) 321-6830
Fax: (312) 673-6652
http://www.naifa.com

**National Association of Jewelry
   Appraisers**
P.O. Box 18
Rego Park, NY 11374
Phone: (718) 896-1536
Fax: (718) 997-9057
http://www.najaappraisers.com

**National Association of Master
   Appraisers**
303 West Cypress Street
San Antonio, TX 78212
Phone: (800) 229-6262
Fax: (210) 225-8450
http://www.masterappraisers.org

**National Association of Professional
   Accident Reconstruction Specialists**
P.O. Box 65
Brandywine, MD 20613
http://www.napars.org

**National Association of Traffic Accident
   Reconstructionists and Investigators**
P.O. Box 2588
West Chester, PA 19382
Phone: (610) 696-1919
http://www.natari.org

Society of Accident Reconstructionists
4891 Independence Street, Suite 140
Wheat Ridge, CO 80033
Phone: (303) 403-9045
Fax: (303) 403-9401
http://www.accidentreconstruction.com/
   SOAR

Western Society of Criminology
Criminology and Criminal Justice
   Division
Portland State University
P.O. Box 751
Portland, OR 97207

http://www.sonoma.edu/cja/wsc/
   wscpages/default.htm

COURT SUPPORT STAFF

American Bar Association
321 North Clark Street
Chicago, IL 60610
Phone: (800) 285-2221 or (312) 988-5000
http://www.abanet.org

American Deputy Sheriffs' Association
3001 Armand Street, Suite B
Monroe, LA 71201
Phone: (800) 937-7940
Fax: (318) 398-9980
http://www.deputysheriff.org

American Translators Association
225 Reinekers Lane, Suite 590
Alexandria, VA 22314
Phone: (703) 683-6100
Fax: (703) 683-6122
http://www.atanet.org

Federal Court Clerks Association
http://www.fcca.ws

Fraternal Order of Police
701 Marriott Drive
Nashville TN 37214
Phone: (615) 399-0900
Fax: (615) 399-0400
http://www.grandlodgefop.org

**International Association of
   Administrative Professionals**
10502 NW Ambassador Drive
P.O. Box 20404
Kansas City, MO 64195
Phone: (816) 891-6600
Fax: (816) 891-9118
http://www.iaap-hq.org

**International Association of Clerks,
   Recorders, Election Officials, and
   Treasurers**
http://www.iacreot.com

Legal Secretaries International, Inc.
2302 Fannin Street, Suite 500
Houston, TX 77002
http://www.legalsecretaries.org

NALS
314 East 3rd Street, Suite 210
Tulsa, OK 74120
Phone: (918) 582-5188
Fax: (918) 582-5907
http://www.nals.org

**National Association for Court
   Management**
300 Newport Avenue
Williamsburg, VA 23185
Phone: (800) 616-6165 or
   (757) 259-1841
Fax: (757) 259-1520
http://www.nacmnet.org

**National Association of Judiciary
   Interpreters and Translators**
603 Stewart Street, Suite 610
Seattle, WA 98101
Phone: (206) 267-2300
Fax: (206) 626-0392
http://www.najit.org

**National Court Reporters
   Association**
8224 Old Courthouse Road
Vienna, VA 22182-3808
Phone: (800) 272-6272 or (703) 556-
   6272 TTY; (703) 556-6289
Fax: (703) 556-6291
http://www.ncraonline.org

**The Translators and Interpreters
   Guild**
962 Wayne Avenue, Suite 500
Silver Spring, MD 20910
Phone: (800) 992-0367 or
   (301) 563-6450
Fax: (301) 563-6020
http://www.ttig.org

**United States Court Reporters
   Association**
4731 North Western Avenue
Chicago, IL 60625
Phone: (800) 628-2730
http://www.uscra.org

CRIMINAL JUSTICE
SUPPORT PROFESSIONALS

American Correctional Association
206 North Washington Street, Suite 200
Alexandria, VA 22314
Phone: (800) ACA-JOIN
http://www.aca.org

**American Deputy Sheriffs'
   Association**
3001 Armand Street, Suite B
Monroe, LA 71201
Phone: (800) 937-7940
Fax: (318) 398-9980
http://www.deputysheriff.org

American Humane Association
63 Inverness Drive East
Englewood, CO 80112
Phone: ((303) 792-9900
Fax: (303) 792-5333
http://www.americanhumane.org

American Probation and Parole Association
2760 Research Park Drive
Lexington, KY 40511
Phone: (859) 244-8203
Fax: (859) 244-8001
http://www.appa-net.org

American Professional Society on the Abuse of Children
P.O. Box 30669
Charleston, SC 29417
Tel: 843-764-2905
Phone: (877) 402-7722 or (843) 764-2905
Fax: (803) 753-9823
http://apsac.fmhi.usf.edu

Association of Traumatic Stress Specialists
P.O. Box 246
Phillips, ME 04966
Phone: (800) 991-2877
Fax: (207) 639-2434
http://www.atss.info

Federal Criminal Investigators Association
P.O. Box 23400
Washington, DC 20026
Phone: (800) 403-3374
Fax: (800) 528-3492
http://www.fedcia.org

Federal Law Enforcement Officers Association
P.O. Box 326
Lewisberry, PA 17339
Phone: (717) 938-2300
Fax: (717) 932-2262
http://www.fleoa.org

Fraternal Order of Police
701 Marriott Drive
Nashville, TN 37214
Phone: (615) 399-0900
Fax: (615) 399-0400
http://www.grandlodgefop.org

High Technology Crime Investigation Association
4021 Woodcreek Oaks Boulevard, Suite 156 #209
Roseville, CA 95747

Phone: (916) 408-1751
Fax: (916) 408-7543
http://www.htcia.org

International Association of Arson Investigators
12770 Boenker Road
Bridgeton, MO 63044
Phone: (314) 739-4224
Fax: (314) 739-4219
http://www.firearson.com

International Association of Asian Crime Investigators
P.O. Box 1327
Marina, CA 93933
Phone: (831) 901-4595
Fax: (831) 384-5321
http://www.iaaci.com

International Association of Crime Analysts
9218 Metcalf Avenue, Suite 364
Overland Park, KS 66212
Phone: (800) 609-3419
http://www.iaca.net

International Association of Women Police
http://www.iawp.org

International Homicide Investigators Association
10711 Spotsylvania Avenue
Fredricksburg, VA 22408
Phone: (877) 843-4442
Fax: (540) 898-5594
http://www.ihia.org

National Association of Pretrial Services Agencies
c/o Marilyn Walczak
Justice 2000, Inc.
2821 North 4th Street, Room 310B
Milwaukee, WI 53202
Phone: (414) 264-6635, extension 12
Fax: (414) 264-6640
http://www.napsa.org

National Association of Social Workers
750 1st Street NE, Suite 700
Washington, DC 20002
Phone: (202) 408-8600
http://www.naswdc.org

National Black Police Association
3251 Mt. Pleasant Street NW, 2nd Floor
Washington, DC 20010
Phone: (202) 986-2070

Fax: (202) 986-0410
http://www.blackpolice.org

National Court Appointed Special Advocate Association
100 West Harrison, North Tower
Suite 500
Seattle, WA 98119
Phone: (800) 628-3233
http://www.nationalcasa.org

National Organization for Victim Assistance
510 King Street, Suite 424
Alexandria, VA 22314
Phone: (800) 879-6682
or (703) 535-6682
Fax: (703) 535-5500
http://www.trynova.org

Professional Bail Agents of the United States
1301 Pennsylvania Avenue NW, Suite 925
Washington, DC 20004
Phone: (202) 783-4120
Fax: (202) 783-4125
http://www.pbus.com

EDUCATORS

American Association for Justice
The Leonard M. Ring Law Center
1050 31st Street NW
Washington, DC 20007
Phone: (800) 424-2725 or
(202) 965-3500
http://www.atlanet.org

American Association for Paralegal Education
19 Mantua Road
Mt. Royal, NJ 08061
Phone: (856) 423-2829
Fax: (856) 423-3420
http://www.aafpe.org

American Association of University Administrators
Roberts Hall 407
Rhode Island College
Providence, RI 02908
Phone: (401) 456-2808
Fax: (401) 456-8287
http://www.aaua.org

American Association of University Professors
1012 14th Street NW, Suite 500
Washington, DC 20005

Phone: (202) 737-5900
Fax: (202) 737-5526
http://www.aaup.org

American Bar Association
321 North Clark Street
Chicago, IL 60610
Phone: (800) 285-2221
   or (312) 988-5000
http://www.abanet.org

**American Bar Association—Section of
   Legal Education and Admissions to
   the Bar**
http://www.abanet.org/legaled/home.html

**American Bar Association—Standing
   Committee on Paralegals**
http://www.abanet.org/legalservices/
   paralegals/home.html

**American Conference of Academic
   Deans**
1818 R Street NW
Washington, DC 20009
Phone: (202) 884-7419
Fax: (202) 265-9532
http://www.acad-edu.org

American Counseling Association
5999 Stevenson Avenue
Alexandria, VA 22304
Phone: (800) 347-6647;
   TDD: (703) 823-6862
Fax: (800) 473-2329
http://www.counseling.org

Association of American Law Schools
1201 Connecticut Avenue NW,
   Suite 800
Washington, DC 20036
Phone: (202) 296-8851
Fax: (202) 296-8869
http://www.aals.org

Clinical Legal Education Association
http://www.cleaweb.org

Legal Writing Institute
http://www.lwionline.org

**National Asian Pacific American Bar
   Association**
910 17th Street NW, Suite 315
Washington, DC 20006
Phone: (202) 775-9555
Fax: (202) 775-9333
http://www.napaba.org

NALP
1025 Connecticut Avenue NW, Suite 1110
Washington, DC 20036
Phone: (202) 835-1001
Fax: (202) 835-1112
http://www.nalp.org

**National Association of State Judicial
   Educators**
http://nasje.org

**National Association of Women
   Lawyers**
American Bar Center, MS 15.2
321 North Clark Street
Chicago, IL 60610
Fax: (312) 988-5491
http://www.nawl.org

**National Career Development
   Association**
305 North Beech Circle
Broken Arrow, OK 74012
Phone: (866) FOR-NCDA
   or (918) 663-7060
Fax: (918) 663-7058
http://www.ncda.org

Society of American Law Teachers
http://www.saltlaw.org

LIBRARIANS

**American Association of Law
   Libraries**
53 West Jackson Boulevard, Suite 940
Chicago, IL 60604
Phone: (312) 939-4764
Fax: (312) 431-1097
http:/www.aallnet.org

American Library Association
50 East Huron Street
Chicago, IL 60611
Phone: (800) 545-2433;
   TDD: (888) 814-7692
http://www.ala.org

Association of Research Libraries
21 Dupont Circle, Suite 800
Washington, DC 20036
Phone: (202) 296-2296
Fax: (202) 872-0884
http://www.arl.org

Council on Library/Media Technicians
http://colt.ucr.edu

**Knowledge Management Professional
   Society**
P.O. Box 16444
Alexandria, VA 22302
Phone: (866) 315-6776
Fax: (757) 460-6672
http://kmpro.org

Special Libraries Association
331 South Patrick Street
Alexandria, VA 22314
Phone: (703) 647-4900
Fax: (703) 647-4901
http://www.sla.org

**Special Libraries Association—Legal
   Division**
http://www.slalegal.org

COMMUNICATIONS
PROFESSIONALS

**American Society of Journalists and
   Authors**
1501 Broadway, Suite 302
New York, NY 10036
Phone: (212) 997-0947
Fax: (212) 937-2315
http://www.asja.org

**Association for Continuing Legal
   Education**
8601 Ranch Road 2222, Building I,
Suite 220
Austin, TX 78730
Mailing address:
P.O. Box 4646
Austin, TX 78765
Phone: (512) 453-4340
Fax: (512) 451-2911
http://www.aclea.org

Criminal Justice Journalists
720 Seventh Street NW, Third Floor
Washington, DC 20001
Phone: (202) 448-1717
http://www.reporters.net/cjj

International Webmasters Association
119 East Union Street, Suite F
Pasadena, CA 91103
Phone: (626) 449-3709
Fax: (626) 449-8308
http://www.iwanet.org

Investigative Reporters and Editors
Missouri School of Journalism
138 Neff Annex
Columbia, MO 65211

Phone: (573) 882-2042
Fax: (573) 882-5431
http://www.ire.org

National Writers Union
113 University Place, 6th Floor
New York, NY 10003
Phone: (212) 254-0279
Fax: (212) 254-0673
http://www.nwu.org

Society for Technical Communication
901 North Stuart Street, Suite 904
Arlington, VA 22203
Phone: (703) 522-4114
Fax: (703) 522-2075
http://www.stc.org

Society of Professional Journalists
3909 N. Meridian Street
Indianapolis, IN 46208
Phone: (317) 927-8000
Fax: (317) 920-4789
http://www.spj.org

MANAGERS AND ADMINISTRATORS

Alliance for Nonprofit Management
1899 L Street NW, 6th Floor
Washington, DC 20036
Phone: (202) 955-8406
Fax: (202) 721-0086
http://www.allianceonline.org

American Association of Collegiate Registrars and Admissions Officers
One Dupont Circle NW, Suite 520
Washington, DC 20036
Phone: (202) 293-9161
Fax: (202) 82-8857
http://www.aacrao.org

American Association of University Administrators
Roberts Hall 407
Rhode Island College
Providence, RI 02908
Phone: (401) 456-2808
Fax: (401) 456-8287
http://www.aaua.org

American Bar Association
321 North Clark Street
Chicago, IL 60610
Phone: (800) 285-2221
     or (312) 988-5000
http://www.abanet.org

ASAE and The Center for Association Leadership
1575 I Street NW
Washington, DC 20005
or
The Ronald Reagan Building
1300 Pennsylvania Avenue NW
Washington, DC 20004
Phone: (888) 950-2723
     or (202) 626-2723
Fax: (202) 371-8315
http://www.asaecenter.org

Association of Legal Administrators
75 Tri-State International, Suite 222
Lincolnshire, IL 60069
Phone: (847) 267-1252
Fax: (847) 267-1329
http://www.alanet.org

Building Owners and Managers Association International
1201 New York Avenue NW, Suite 300
Washington, DC 20005
Phone: (202) 408-2662
Fax: (202) 326-6377
http://www.boma.org

Community Associations Institute
225 Reinekers Lane, Suite 300
Alexandria, VA 22314
Phone: (703) 548-8600
Fax: (703) 684-1581
http://www.caionline.org

Institute of Real Estate Management
430 North Michigan Avenue
Chicago, IL 60611
Phone: (800) 837-0706
Fax: (800) 338-4736
http://www.irem.org

Management Information Exchange
37 Temple Place, Suite 303
Boston, MA 02111
Phone: (617) 556-0288
Fax: (617) 507-7729
http://www.m-i-e.org

National Academy of Elder Law Attorneys
1604 North Country Club Road
Tucson, AZ 85716
Phone: (520) 881-4005
Fax: (520) 325-7925
http://www.naela.org

National Apartment Association
201 North Union Street, Suite 200

Alexandria, VA 22314
Phone: (703) 518-5141
Fax: (703) 518-6191
http://www.naahq.org

National Association of Residential Property Managers
184 Business Park Drive, Suite 200-P
Virginia Beach, VA 23462
Phone: (800) 782-3452
Fax: (866) 466-2776
http://www.narpm.org

National Employment Lawyers Association
44 Montgomery Street, Suite 2080
San Francisco, CA 94104
Phone: (415) 296-7629
Fax: (415) 677-9445
http://www.nela.org

National Legal Aid and Defender Association
1625 K Street NW, Suite 800
Washington, DC 20006-1604
Phone: (202) 452-0620
Fax: (202) 872-1031
http://www.nlada.org

ANALYSTS AND EXAMINERS

American Academy of Actuaries
1110 17th Street NW, 7th Floor
Washington, DC 20036
Phone: (202) 223-8196
Fax: (202) 872-1948
http://www.actuary.org

American Association for Affirmative Action
88 16th Street NW, Suite 800
Washington, D.C. 20006
Phone: (800) 252-8952 or (202) 349-9855
Fax: (202) 355-1399
http://www.affirmativeaction.org

American Land Title Association
1828 L Street NW, Suite 705
Washington, DC 20036-5104
Phone: (800) 787-ALTA
Fax: (888) FAX-ALTA
http://www.alta.org

American Society of Pension Professionals and Actuaries
4245 North Fairfax Drive, Suite 750
Arlington, VA 22203
http://www.aspa.org
Phone: (703) 516-9300
Fax: (703) 516-9308

Association of Legal Administrators
75 Tri-State International, Suite 222
Lincolnshire, IL 60069
Phone: (847) 267-1252
Fax: (847) 267-1329
http://www.alanet.org

Casualty Actuarial Society
4350 North Fairfax Drive, Suite 250
Arlington, VA 22203
Phone: (703) 276-3100
Fax: (703) 276-3108
http://www.casact.org

Conference of Consulting Actuaries
3880 Salem Lake Drive, Suite H
Long Grove, IL 60047
Phone: (847) 719-6500
Fax: (847) 719-6506
http://www.ccactuaries.com

Ethics and Compliance Officer Association
411 Waverley Oaks Road, Suite 324
Waltham, MA 02452
Phone: (781) 647-9333
http://www.theecoa.org

Health Care Compliance Association
6500 Barrie Road, Suite 250
Minneapolis, MN 55435
Phone: (888) 580-8373 or
(952) 988-0141
Fax: (952) 988-0146
http://www.hcca-info.org

Institute of Management Consultants USA
2025 M Street NW, Suite 800
Washington, DC 20036
Phone: (800) 221-2557 or (202) 367-1134
http://www.imcusa.org

International Claim Association
1155 15th Street NW, Suite 500
Washington, DC 20005
Phone: (202) 452-0143
Fax: (202) 530-0659
http://www.claim.org

Legal Marketing Association
1926 Waukegan Road, Suite 1
Glenview, IL 60026
Phone: (847) 657-6717
Fax: (847) 657-6819
http://www.legalmarketing.org

National Association of Enrolled Agents
1120 Connecticut Avenue NW, Suite 460
Washington, DC 20036
Phone: (202) 822-6232
Fax: (202) 822-6270
http://www.naea.org

National Association of Independent Insurance Adjusters
825 West State Street, Suite 117-C & B
Geneva, IL 60134
Phone: (630) 397-5012 or
(312) 315-2305
Fax: (630) 397-5013
http://www.naiia.com

National Association of Patent Practitioners
4680-18i Monticello Avenue
PMB 101
Williamsburg, VA 23188
Phone: (800) 216-9588
Fax: (757) 220-2231
http://www.napp.org

National Association of Tax Professionals
720 Association Drive
P.O. Box 8002
Appleton, WI 54912
Phone: (800) 558-3402
Fax: (800) 747-0001
http://www.natptax.com

National Contract Management Association
8260 Greensboro Drive, Suite 200
McLean, VA 22102
Phone: (800) 344-8096 or
(571) 382-0082
Fax: (703) 448-0939
http://www.ncmahq.org

National Eligibility Workers Association
P.O. Box 229
Cavalier, ND 58220
Phone: (888) 283-6392
Fax: (701) 265-4808
http://www.nationalnew.org

National Society of Compliance Professionals
22 Kent Road
Cornwall Bridge, CT 06754
Phone: (860) 672-0843

Fax: (860) 672-3005
http://www.nscp.org

Society for Human Resource Management
1800 Duke Street
Alexandria, VA 22314
Phone: (800) 283-SHRM
or (703) 548-3440
Fax: (703) 535-6490
http://www.shrm.org

Society of Actuaries
475 N. Martingdale Road, Suite 600
Schaumburg, IL 60173
Phone: (847) 706-3500
Fax: (847) 706-3599
http://www.soa.org

PROFESSIONS IN POLITICS

American Association of Political Consultants
600 Pennsylvania Avenue SE, Suite 330
Washington, DC 20003
Phone: (202) 544-9815
Fax: (202) 544-9816
http://www.theaapc.org

American League of Lobbyists
P.O. Box 30005
Alexandria, VA 22310
Phone: (703) 960-3011
Fax: (703) 960-4070
http://www.alldc.org

National Association of Counties
440 First Street NW
Washington, DC 20001
Phone: (202) 393-6226
http://www.naco.org

National League of Cities
1301 Pennsylvania Avenue NW,
Suite 550
Washington, DC 20004
Phone: (202) 626-3000
Fax: (202) 626-3043
http://www.nlc.org

Women in Government Relations
801 North Fairfax Street, Suite 211
Alexandria, VA 22314-1757
Phone: (703) 299-8546
Fax: (703) 299-9233
http://www.wgr.org

APPENDIX VI
RESOURCES ON THE WORLD WIDE WEB

Listed in this appendix are some Web sites that can help you learn more about many of the professions that are discussed in this book. You will also find some resources that offer career and job search information.

Note: All Web site addresses were current when this book was being written. If a URL no longer works, try this: Enter the name of the organization or the Web page title into a search engine to find the new address.

GENERAL INFORMATION

Global Legal Information Network
http://www.glin.gov

HG.org
Worldwide Legal Directories
http://www.hg.org

Internet Legal Research Group
http://www.ilrg.com

The 'Lectric Law Library
http://www.lectlaw.com

LLRX: Law Library Resource Xchange
http://www.llrx.com

Occupational Employment Statistics
(U.S. Bureau of Labor Statistics)
http://www.bls.gov/oes

Wikipedia
http://www.wikipedia.com

CAREER AND JOB INFORMATION

American Bar Association Career Counsel
http://www.abanet.org/careercounsel/home.html

America's Job Bank
http://www.ajb.org

Career Prospects in Virginia
http://www.ccps.virginia.edu/career_prospects

JobStar: Job Search Guide
http://jobstar.org

ISEEK
http://www.iseek.org

Lawjobs.com
http://www.lawjobs.com

Legal Career Center Network
http://www.thelccn.com

Monster
http://www.monster.com

Occupational Outlook Handbook
(U.S. Bureau of Labor Statistics)
http://www.bls.gov/oco

O*NET OnLine
http://online.onetcenter.org

USA Jobs
(U.S. Office of Personnel Management)
http://www.usajobs.opm.gov

WetFeet.com
http://www.wetfeet.com

PRE-LAW INFORMATION

Online Pre-Law Toolkit for School Counselors
(American Bar Association Career Resource Center)
http://www.abanet.org/careercounsel/prelaw

Law School Admission Council
http://www.lsac.org

Law School Admissions
(Jurist Intelligence)
http://jurist.law.pitt.edu/admissions.htm

Law School Admissions
http://www.law-school-admissions.com

Pre-Law Student Services
(Internet Legal Research Group)
http://www.ilrg.com/pre-law.html

ACADEMIC LAW LIBRARIAN

Education for a Career in Law Librarianship
(American Association of Law Libraries)
http://www.aallnet.org/committee/tfedu/education.html

International Association of Law Libraries
http://www.iall.org

Law Library of Congress
http://www.loc.gov/law/public/law.html

ACTUARY

The Actuarial Foundation
http://www.actuarialfoundation.org

Resources
(American Academy of Actuaries)
http://www.actuary.org/resources.asp

ADMINISTRATIVE LAW JUDGE

Links
(National Association of Administrative Law Judges)
http://www.naalj.org/links.html

Links
(National Conference of the Administrative Law Judiciary)
http://www.abanet.org/jd/ncalj/links.html

APPELLATE ATTORNEY

The Appellate Law Webpage
(Law Office of Bruce Adelstein)
http://www.appellatelaw.net

Appellate Practice
(American Bar Association—Section of
    Litigation)
http://www.abanet.org/litigation/
    committees/appellate

APPELLATE JUDGE

**Appellate Court: Structure,
    Jurisdiction, and Process State Links**
http://www.ncsconline.org/WC/
    Publications/StateLinks/
    AppCtsStateLinks.htm

Federal Appellate Courts
(Journalist's Guide to the Federal Courts)
http://www.uscourts.gov/journalistguide/
    appellate.html

The Federal Courts Law Review
http://www.fclr.org

Supreme Court of the United States
http://www.supremecourtus.gov

APPRAISER

Appraisal Associations
http://www.appraisaltoday.com/apprassn.
    htm

Appraisal Institute
http://www.appraisalinstitute.org

appraisersportal.com
http://appraisersportal.com

ARBITRATOR

Arbitration Forums, Inc.
http://www.arbfile.org/webapp

National Arbitration Forum
http://www.arb-forum.com

ASSOCIATION EXECUTIVE

Associations on the Net
(Internet Public Library)
http://www.ipl.org/div/aon

CEO Update
http://www.associationjobs.com

ATTORNEY

Counsel.Net
http://counsel.net

FindLaw for Legal Professionals
http://library.lp.findlaw.com

Law.Com
http://www.law.com

The Law Forum
http://www.lawforum.net

Megalaw.com
http://www.megalaw.com

National Conference of Bar Examiners
http://www.ncbex.org

The Professional Development Center
(FindLaw.com and the Center for
    Professional Development)
http://profdev.lp.findlaw.com

BAIL BOND AGENT

American Bail Coalition
http://www.americanbailcoalition.com

Bail Enforcement Agents
(Hi Tek's Investigator Database)
http://www.hitekinfo.com/links/Bail_
    Enforcement_Agents

Bail Yes, Inc.
http://www.bailyes.com/default.htm

California Bail Agents Association
http://www.cbaa.com

BAILIFF

Court Security
(National Center for State Courts)
http://www.ncsconline.org/WC/
    Education/CtSecuGuide.htm

**Ohio Bailiffs and Court Officers
    Association**
http://www.ohiobailiffs.com

BANKRUPTCY JUDGE

BankruptcyData.com
http://www.bankruptcydata.com

BankruptcyLawFirms.com
http://www.bankruptcylawfirms.com

Bankruptcy Information
(Bankruptcy Court for the Western
    District of Wisconsin)
http://www.wiw.uscourts.gov/bankruptcy/
    Bankruptcy_Info.htm

BOOK EDITOR

A Legal Publishers List
(Committee on Relations with
    Information Vendors)
http://www.aallnet.org/committee/criv/
    resources/tools/list

Publishing-Industry Network
http://publishing-industry.net

Association of American Publishers
http://www.publishers.org

BUSINESS APPRAISER

American Business Appraisers
http://www.businessval.com

Valuation Resources.com
http://valuationresources.com

CAMPAIGN MANAGER

Campaign Guide
http://www.completecampaigns.com/
    CampaignGuide.asp

Election Law @ Moritz
http://moritzlaw.osu.edu/electionlaw

Federal Election Commission
http://www.fec.gov

Political Resources On-Line
http://politicalresources.com

Project Vote Smart
http://www.vote-smart.org

CHILD PROTECTIVE
SERVICES CASEWORKER

Child Abuse Prevention Network
http://child-abuse.com

Child Welfare League of America
http://www.cwla.org

**Child Welfare Information
    Gateway**
http://www.childwelfare.gov

COMPLIANCE SPECIALIST

ComplianceResources.org
http://www.complianceresources.org

Seton Compliance Resource Center
http://www.setonresourcecenter.com

CONTRACT ADMINISTRATOR

Corporate Counsel Center: Business Contracts
http://contracts.corporate.findlaw.com

U.S. Business Contracts
(Carter McNamara)
http://www.managementhelp.org/legal/
    bs_cntrct/bs_cntrct.htm

CORPORATE COUNSEL

Corporate Counsel Center
http://corporate.findlaw.com

Corporate Law Resources
(Law and Policy Institutions Guide)
http://www.lpig.org/corporate.html

COURT ADMINISTRATOR

Conference of State Court Administrators
http://cosca.ncsc.dni.us

Institute for Court Management
(National Center for State Courts)
http://www.ncsconline.org/D_ICM/
    icmindex.html

COURT ANALYST

Bureau of Justice Statistics
U.S. Department of Justice
http://www.ojp.usdoj.gov/bjs

Federal Judicial Center
http://www.fjc.gov

COURT CLERK

Court Clerk Job Descriptions
(National Center for State Courts)
http://www.ncsconline.org/D_KIS/
    jobdeda/Jobs_Clerks(8).htm

i-courthouse
http://www.i-courthouse.com

COURT INTERPRETER

Court Interpretation
(National Center for State Courts)
http://www.ncsconline.org/D_Research/
    Courtinterp.html

Court Interpreters
(California Courts)
http://www.courtinfo.ca.gov/programs/
    courtinterpreters

COURT MEDIATOR

ADR in Appellate Courts
(National Center for State Courts)
http://www.ncsconline.org/WC/Events/
    ADRAppView.htm

COURT REPORTER

About Court Reporting
(Atkinson-Baker, Inc.)
http://www.depo.com/abtcrng.htm

Machine Shorthand Information Site
http://www.machineshorthand.com

OfficialCourtReporter.com
http://www.officialcourtreporter.com

COURT STAFF ATTORNEY

The Federal Judiciary
http://www.uscourts.gov

National Center for State Courts
http://www.ncsconline.org

COURT SUPPORT STAFF

Job Description Database
(National Center for State Courts)
http://www.ncsconline.org/D_KIS/
    jobdeda/main.htm

CRASH RECONSTRUCTION CONSULTANT

Accreditation Commission for Traffic Accident Reconstruction
http://www.actar.org

National Academy of Forensic Engineers
http://www.nafe.org

TARO: The Traffic Accident Reconstruction Origin
http://www.tarorigin.com

CRIMINAL INVESTIGATOR

Computer Crime and Intellectual Property Section
(U.S. Department of Justice)
www.cybercrime.gov

CopSeek.com
http://www.copseek.com

Federal Bureau of Investigation
http://www.fbi.gov

Prentice Hall's Cybrary
http://talkjustice.com/cybrary.asp

CRIMINAL LAWYER

American Bar Association, Section of Criminal Justice
http://www.abanet.org/crimjust/home.html

Criminal Defense Lawyer.com
http://www.criminaldefenselawyer.com

CRIMINOLOGIST

Academy of Criminal Justice Sciences
http://www.acjs.org

Criminal Justice Links
(by Cecil Greek, College of Criminology and Criminal Justice, Florida State University, Tallahassee, Florida)
http://www.criminology.fsu.edu/cjlinks

National Criminal Justice Reference Service
http://www.ncjrs.org

DEMONSTRATIVE EVIDENCE SPECIALIST

Demonstrative Evidence Expert Witnesses
(JurisPro Expert Witness Directory)
http://www.jurispro.com/subcategory.
    asp?category=16

Expert Witness Demonstrative Evidence
(Hieros Gamos Worldwide Legal Directories)
http://www.hg.org/experts/Experts-
    Demonstrative-Evidence.html

DIRECTOR OF ADMISSIONS

American Bar Association—Section of Legal Education and Admissions to the Bar
http://www.abanet.org/legaled

Pacific American Association of College Registrars and Admission Officers
http://www.pacrao.org

ELDER LAW ATTORNEY

American Bar Association Commission on Law and Aging
http://www.abanet.org/aging

American College of Trust and Estate Counsel
http://www.actec.org

Elder Care Network
http://www.keln.org

National Senior Citizens Law Center
http://www.nsclc.org

ELECTRONIC RESOURCES LIBRARIAN

Digital Librarian: Law Resources
http://www.digital-librarian.com/law.html

Digital Library Federation
http://www.diglib.org

ELIGIBILITY WORKER

Social Work Resources on the Web
http://www.library.csustan.edu/lboyer/socwork/resources.htm

United States Department of Health and Human Services
http://www.dhhs.gov

EMPLOYMENT LAWYER

ABA—Section of Labor and Employment Law
http://www.abanet.org/labor/home.html

My Employment Lawyer
http://www.myemploymentlawyer.com

National Employment Law Institute
http://www.neli.org

National Employment Law Project
http://www.nelp.org

ENROLLED AGENT

Tax Resource Center: Links to Associations and Organizations
http://accountant.intuit.com/practice_resources/tax/links/assoc_orgs.aspx

Tax Resources on the Web
(Alan Kalman)
http://taxtopics.net

ENVIRONMENTAL LAWYER

Environmental Law Net
http://lawvianet.com

Environmental Law Institute
http://www.eli.org

National Resource Defense Council
http://www.nrdc.org

U.S. Environmental Protection Agency
http://www.epa.gov

EQUAL OPPORTUNITY OFFICER

Americans with Disabilities Act
(U.S. Department of Justice)
http://www.ada.gov

ETHICS OFFICER

Business Ethics
(Sharon Stoerger)
http://www.web-miner.com/busethics.htm

Corporate-Ethics.US
http://www.corporate-ethics.us

Ethics Resource Center
http://www.ethics.org

U.S. Office of Government Ethics
http://www.usoge.gov

FAMILY COURT JUDGE

American Bar Association—Section of Family Law
http://www.abanet.org/family/home.html

Family Court Information Center
(New York City Family Courts)
http://www.courts.state.ny.us/kiosk/kiosk.htm

FAMILY LAW MEDIATOR

Divorce Source
http://www.divorcesource.com

Family Law Source
http://www.familylawsource.com

FORENSIC ACCOUNTANT

Forensic Accounting Demystified
(Alan Zysman)
http://www.forensicaccountant.com

National Association of Forensic Accountants
http://www.nafanet.com

FORENSIC PSYCHOLOGIST

Forensic Psychiatry and Psychology
(Carpenter's Forensic Science Resources)
http://www.tncrimlaw.com/forensic/f_psych.html

Forensic Psychiatry Resource Page
(Dr. James Hooper)
http://bama.ua.edu/~jhooper

Institute for Forensic Psychology
http://www.ifp-testing.com/index.html

Psychology and Law Resources for Students
(American Psychology-Law Society)
http://www.ap-ls.org/students/careersindex.html

GOVERNMENT LAWYER

American Bar Association— Government and Public Sector Lawyers Division
http://www.abanet.org/govpub

Executive Office for United States Attorneys
U.S. Department of Justice
http://www.usdoj.gov/usao/eousa

National Association of Attorneys General
http://www.naag.org

Office of Attorney Recruitment and Management
U.S. Department of Justice
http://www.usdoj.gov/oarm

Office of the Solicitor General
http://www.usdoj.gov/osg

U.S. Attorneys Office
U.S. Department of Justice
http://www.usdoj.gov/usao

GUARDIAN AD LITEM

Guardians Ad Litem
(CASAnet Resources)
http://www.casanet.org/library/guardian-
ad-litem/gal-e-index.htm

Florida Guardian ad Litem Program
http://www.guardianadlitem.org

HEALTH LAWYER

**American Society of Law, Medicine,
and Ethics**
http://www.aslme.org

**Center for Law and the Public's
Health**
http://www.publichealthlaw.net

Health Law
(Hieros Gamos Worldwide Legal
Directories)
http://www.hg.org/health.html

HUMAN RESOURCES MANAGER

Employment Law Resource Center
(Alexander Hamilton Institute)
http://www.ahipubs.com

HR Internet Guide
http://www.hr-guide.com

INDIAN LAW ATTORNEY

Indian Law Resource Center
http://www.indianlaw.org

**National Native American Law
Students Association**
http://www.nationalnalsa.org

Tribal Court Clearinghouse
http://www.tribal-institute.org

U.S. Bureau of Indian Affairs
http://www.doi.gov/bureau-indian-affairs.
html

INFORMATION TECHNOLOGY PROFESSIONAL

IT Toolbox Network
http://www.ittoolbox.com

Teknoids
http://www.teknoids.net

INSURANCE CLAIMS PROFESSIONAL

Claims-Portal.com
http://www.claims-portal.com

**Insurance Claims Investigation
Resource Center**
http://www.pimall.com/nais/insrec.html

INTELLECTUAL PROPERTY ATTORNEY

**American Bar Association Section of
Intellectual Property Law**
http://www.abanet.org/intelprop

Intellectual Property Law
(Hieros Gamos Worldwide Legal
Directories)
http://www.hg.org/intell.html

The Intellectual Property Law Server
(by George A. Wowk)
http://www.intelproplaw.com

JUDGE ADVOCATE

Links
Judge Advocates Association
http://www.jaa.org/Links.htm

JUDICIAL ASSISTANT

**Association of Bankruptcy Judicial
Assistants**
http://www.abja.org

JUDICIAL BRANCH EDUCATOR

Institute for Court Management
(National Center for State Courts)
http://www.ncsconline.org/D_ICM/
icmindex.html

**Rozier E. Sanchez Judicial Education
Center of New Mexico**
http://jec.unm.edu

JUDICIAL LAW CLERK

Judicial Clerkships
(Boston University School of Law)
http://www.bu.edu/law/contacts/careers/
clerkships/index.html

**Law Clerks and Clerking at the U.S.
Supreme Court**
http://jurist.law.pitt.edu/clerk.htm

Law Clerk Job Descriptions
http://www.ncsconline.org/D_KIS/
jobdeda/Jobs_LawClerks(16).htm

JUVENILE COUNSELOR

**Center on Juvenile and Criminal
Justice**
http://www.cjcj.org

The Children's Defense Fund
http://www.childrensdefense.org

National Juvenile Detention Association
http://www.njda.com

KNOWLEDGE MANAGER

**Information and Knowledge
Management Society**
http://www.ikms.org/aboutus/index.html

Intranets/Knowledge Management
(LLRX.com Resource Center)
http://www.llrx.com/intranets_and_
knowledge_management.html

LawLibTech
http://www.lawlibtech.com

LAW FIRM LIBRARIAN

**Choosing Law Librarianship:
Thoughts for People Contemplating
a Career Move**
(Mary Whisner)
http://www.llrx.com/features/librarian.
htm

**The Future of Librarians in the
Workforce**
http://www.libraryworkforce.org/tiki-
index.php

Law Librarian Blog
http://lawprofessors.typepad.com/law_
librarian_blog

LAW LIBRARY TECHNICIAN

Library Support Staff Resource Center
http://www.ala.org/ala/hrdr/
librarysupportstaff/Library_Support_
Staff_Resource_Center.htm

LibrarySupportStaff.com
http://www.librarysupportstaff.com

LAW PROFESSOR

Chronicle of Higher Education: Career Network
http://chronicle.com/jobs

Institute for Law School Teaching
(Gonzaga University School of Law, Spokane, Washington)
http://law.gonzaga.edu/ilst

Law Professor Blogs Network
http://lawprofessors.typepad.com

Teachlaw: Resources for Lawyers Who Want to be Law Professors
http://www.law.arizona.edu/depts/chin/
teachlaw/index.html

LAW SCHOOL CAREER COUNSELOR

VocationalPsychology.com
http://vocationalpsychology.com

LAW SCHOOL DEAN

Council on Law in Higher Education
http://www.clhe.org

Law School Buzz
(Jurist Legal News and Research)
http://jurist.law.pitt.edu/lawschoolnews

New Deans' Institute
http://www.aacte.org/Events/dean_
institute.aspx

LEGAL ADMINISTRATOR

American Bar Association Law Practice Management Section
http://www.abanet.org/lpm

Law Department Management Blog
(Rees Morrison CMC)
http://lawdepartmentmanagement.
typepad.com

LEGAL MANAGEMENT CONSULTANT

Law Biz Blog
(Ed Poll)
http://www.lawbizblog.com

The Law Practice Management Page
(John P. Weil & Company)
http://weilandco.com/manage.html

Legal Management Resource Center
(Olmstead and Associates)
http://www.olmsteadassoc.com/
Resource

LEGAL NURSE CONSULTANT

Vickie Milazzo Institute
http://www.legalnurse.com

Legal Nurse Consultants, Nursing Entrepreneurs
http://www.legalnursingconsultant.org

LEGAL RECEPTIONIST

National Receptionists Day
http://www.nationalreceptionists.com

Receptionist Jobs
http://receptionist.jobs.jobsearchsite.
com

LEGAL REPORTER

Ask a Reporter Archive
(The New York Times on the Web Learning Network/Student Connections)
http://www.nytimes.com/learning/
students/ask_reporters/archives.
html#faq

The Center for Public Integrity
http://www.publicintegrity.org

Jobs Page: Your Link to Newspaper Careers
(Detroit Free Press)
http://www.freep.com/legacy/jobspage

Law Reporting
(Jurist Intelligence)
http://jurist.law.pitt.edu/lawreporting

LEGAL SEARCH CONSULTANT

JurisResources.com
http://www.jurisresources.com

Recruiters Network
http://www.recruitersnetwork.com

Resources
http://www.searchconsultants.com/
resources

LEGAL SECRETARY

Legal Secretaries, Incorporated
http://www.lsi.org

Links of Interest
(NALS)
http://www.nals.org/links/index.html

LEGAL SERVICES MANAGER

Legal Services Corporation
http://www.lsc.gov

Sargent Shriver National Center on Poverty Law
http://www.povertylaw.org

LEGAL SUPPORT PROFESSIONAL

Deskdemon
http://us.deskdemon.com

International Association of Administrative Professionals
http://www.iaap-hq.org

LEGAL TECHNOLOGY CONSULTANT

Lawyer Lounge
http://www.lawyerlounge.com

Legal Technology Resources
NetTech, Inc.
http://www.nettechinc.com/lawtech.htm

LEGAL VIDEOGRAPHER

Attorney Guide to Legal Videography
http://www.laattorneyvideo.com/attorney-
guide

CLVS Community of Interest
(National Court Reporters Association)
http://clvs.ncraonline.org

LEGAL WORD PROCESSOR

Legal Word Processor Jobs
http://legal.word.processor.jobs.com

LEGAL WRITING INSTRUCTOR

Association of Legal Writing Directors
http://www.alwd.org

Barger on Legal Writing
http://www.ualr.edu/cmbarger/resources.htm

Legal Research and Writing
(Jurist Intelligence)
http://jurist.law.pitt.edu/sg_resch.htm

LEGISLATIVE ASSISTANT

FirstGov
(The U.S. Government's Official Web Portal)
http://www.firstgov.gov

Your Congress.com
http://www.yourcongress.com

LEGISLATOR, STATE OR FEDERAL

National Conference of State Legislatures
http://www.ncsl.org

Thomas
(Legislative Information on the Internet)
http://thomas.loc.gov

United States Association of Former Members of Congress
http://www.usafmc.org

LITIGATION ATTORNEY

Litigation Law
(Hieros Gamos Worldwide Legal Directories)
http://www.hg.org/litg.html

National Institute for Trial Advocacy
http://www.nita.org

Trial Lawyers for Public Justice
http://www.tlpj.org

LITIGATION CONSULTANT

American Academy of Forensic Sciences
http://www.aafs.org

Association of Certified Fraud Examiners
http://www.acfe.com

ExpertLaw
http://www.expertlaw.com

ExpertPages.com
http://www.expertpages.com

Expert Witness Network
http://www.witness.net

LOBBYIST

Influence: The Business of Lobbying
http://www.influence.biz

Lobbying Database
(The Center for Responsive Politics)
http://www.opensecrets.org/lobbyists/index.asp

Lobbying Resources
http://www.heartsandminds.org/links/lobbylinks.htm

LOCAL ELECTED OFFICIAL

State and Local Government on the Net
http://www.statelocalgov.net

Municipal Research and Services Center of Washington
http://www.mrsc.org

MARKETING MANAGER

Law Firm Marketing
http://www.lawyermarketing.com

The Law Marketing Portal
http://www.lawmarketing.com

The Legal Marketing Blog.com
(Tom Kane)
http://www.legalmarketingblog.com

MUNICIPAL JUDGE

Municipal Courts Resource Guide
(National center for State Courts)
http://www.ncsconline.org/WC/Education/MuniCtGuide.htm

Resources for Municipal Judges
(Rozier E. Sanchez Judicial Education Center of New Mexico)
http://jec.unm.edu/resources/judges-training-guides/municipal-resource-guide.htm

NEUTRAL

American Bar Association Section of Dispute Resolution
http://www.abanet.org/dispute

ADR Resources
(by Stephen R. Marsh)
http://adrr.com

Federal Mediation and Conciliation Service
http://www.fmcs.gov

NONPROFIT ORGANIZATION DIRECTOR

National Council of Nonprofit Associations
http://www.ncna.org

Nonprofit Career Network
http://www.nonprofitcareer.com

The Nonprofit FAQ
(Idealist.org)
http://www.nonprofit-info.org

Non-Profit Nuts & Bolts
http://www.nutsbolts.com/np-home.htm

PARALEGAL

American Bar Association—Standing Committee on Paralegals
http://www.abanet.org/legalservices/paralegals

Paralegal Education on Squidoo
(Nancy Dowling)
http://www.squidoo.com/paralegaleducation

PARALEGAL EDUCATOR

American Association for Paralegal Education
http://www.aafpe.org

PATENT AGENT

Association of Patent Law Firms
http://www.aplf.org

Patent and Trademark Office Society
http://www.ptos.org

Patent Law Links.com
http://www.patentlawlinks.com

Patent of the Week
http://www.patentoftheweek.com

PERSONAL INJURY LAWYER

Injuryboard.com
http://www.injuryboard.com

PersonalInjuryLawyer.com
http://www.personalinjurylawyer.com

PRETRIAL SERVICES OFFICER

The Corrections Connection
http://www.corrections.com

National Association of Pretrial Services Agencies
http://www.napsa.org

National Criminal Justice Reference Service
http://www.ncjrs.gov

PRIVATE INVESTIGATOR

Global Investigators Network
http://www.ginetwork.com

The PI Portal
http://www.pimall.com/nais/piportal.html

PROCESS SERVER

ServeNow.com
http://www.serve-now.com

Service of Process Resource Center
http://www.pimall.com/nais/processr.html

PROPERTY MANAGER

Landlords and Property Management Resource Cener
(Nolo)
http://www.nolo.com/category/lt_home.html

Property Management
(National Association of Realtors)
http://www.realtor.org/rodesign.nsf/pages/PropMgmtHome?OpenDocument

PROSECUTOR

American Prosecutors Research Institute
http://www.ndaa.org/apri

International Association of Prosecutors
http://www.iap.nl.com

Prosecutor Info Website
http://www.prosecutor.info

PUBLIC DEFENDER

The Defender Association
Public Defense in Seattle–King County, Washington
http://www.defender.org

First Judicial Circuit Public Defender Corporation
http://publicdefender.com

Tribal Public Defender
(National Tribal Justice Resource Center)
http://www.tribalresourcecenter.org/personnel/details.asp?34

PUBLIC INTEREST ADVOCATE

Idealist.org: Action Without Borders
http://www.idealist.org

Advocacy Institute
(Washington, D.C.)
http://www.advocacy.org

Campaign Institute
http://www.campaigninstitute.org

PUBLIC INTEREST LAWYER

Office of Public Interest Advising
(Harvard Law School)
http://www.law.harvard.edu/students/opia

Public Interest Clearinghouse
http://www.pic.org

Public Interest Law
New Jersey Law Network
http://www.njlawnet.com/public.html

Public Interest Law Initiative
http://www.pili-law.org

REAL ESTATE LAW ATTORNEY

American College of Real Estate Lawyers
http://www.acrel.org

Real-Estate-Law.com
(Joshua Stein)
http://www.real-estate-law.com

SCOPIST

The Court Reporting Store
http://www.thecourtreportingstore.com

Scoping FAQs
http://www.mazco.org/ssg/faq.htm

TAX LAWYER

e-legality.org
http://www.e-legality.org

Taxation Law
(Hieros Gamos Worldwide Legal Directories)
http://www.hg.org/tax.html

TITLE EXAMINER

National Association of Land Title Examiners and Abstractors
http://www.naltea.org

Source of Title
http://www.sourceoftitle.com

TRIAL CONSULTANT

An Interesting Career in Psychology: Trial Consultant
(by Joy Stapp, Ph.D.)
http://www.apa.org/science/ic-stapp.html

Jury Consultants Guide
http://juryconsultants.info

Trial Behavior Consulting
http://www.trialbehavior.com

TRIAL JUDGE

American Bar Association Judicial Division
http://www.abanet.org/jd

The Federal Judiciary FAQ
http://www.uscourts.gov/faq.html

Federal Magistrate Judges Association
http://www.fedjudge.org

National Association of Women Judges
http://www.nawj.org

National Center for State Courts
http://www.ncsconline.org

U.S. PROBATION OFFICER

United States Parole Commission
(U.S. Department of Justice)
http://www.usdoj.gov/uspc

United States Probation and Pretrial Services
http://www.uscourts.gov/misc/propretrial.htm

United States Sentencing Commission
http://www.ussc.gov

VICTIM SERVICES SPECIALIST

Directory of Crime Victim Services
http://ovc.ncjrs.org/findvictimservices

The National Center for Victims of Crime
http://www.ncvc.org

Victim Assistance Online
A Comprehensive Resource Center
http://www.vaonline.org

WEB DESIGNER

HTML Help
(The Web Design Group)
http://www.htmlhelp.com

Webmonkey: The Web Developer's Resource
http://www.webmonkey.com

Web Page Design for Designers
http://www.wpdfd.com

WebReference.com
http://www.webreference.com

GLOSSARY

administrative   Relating to the daily management of an organization such as a law firm or law school.

administrative agency   A government agency that carries out and enforces a particular area of law; for example, the U.S. Environmental Protection Agency oversees the federal environmental laws.

administrative board   The group of people in a government agency who makes decisions on whether individuals or groups have violated the laws that their agency enforces.

administrative hearing   A legal proceeding held before a government agency regarding violations of the laws that the agency enforces.

advocate   A person, such as a lawyer, who speaks on behalf of another person.

affidavit   A written statement that one swears is true under oath.

agent   A person who has the power to act for another person.

alternative dispute resolution   A way to settle a dispute without going through a court trial.

appeal   A written request to a higher court to review and overturn a judgment made in a lower court.

appellate court   A court that has the power to review and overturn the decisions made in lower courts.

appraise   To make an estimate of how much something is worth.

arbitration   A form of alternative dispute resolution; a third party listens to the arguments between two opposing parties, then issues a decision that both parties agree to accept.

arraignment   A court proceeding in which a person pleads guilty or not guilty to a criminal charge that he or she is accused of committing.

associate   An attorney who is employed by a law firm.

bail   Money or bond that a criminal suspect promises to give the court in order to be released from jail while waiting for his or her court trial.

bar association   A professional body of attorneys, commonly known as a bar; in many states, these organizations regulate the licensing of lawyers.

bar examination   A test administered by a state bar association which individuals must pass to be admitted to the bar in order to practice law in that particular state.

bench trial   A court trial in which a judge, rather than a jury, decides the facts.

bill   A proposed law.

billable hours   The number of hours that lawyers charge their clients for performing work for them.

brief   A legal document that lawyers submit to a court of law which presents the facts, argument, and pertinent laws that support their client's case.

calendar   A list of cases that are scheduled to be heard in court.

case   A suit or action taken before a court of law.

chambers   A judge's office.

charge   A formal statement that accuses a person of having committed a crime

claim   The request for money, property, or other benefits from an organization or government agency.

client   A person or group that receives services from an attorney, consultant, or other professional.

clientele   A group of customers.

code   A system of laws and regulations that govern a particular activity such as traffic or taxation.

compliance   The act of agreeing to do something, such as following specific laws.

constituent   A person who lives in a legislator's district.

consultant   An expert in a particular field who charges a fee for his or her professional advice and services.

continuing legal education (CLE)   Additional courses that lawyers must complete to maintain their ability to practice law.

contract   A legal agreement between two or more parties that creates an obligation to do or not do something.

convict *(v.)*   To declare that a person is guilty of committing a crime; *(n.)* A person who is serving a prison sentence.

corporation   A company or group of people that the law recognizes as having the power to act as a single body.

counsel *(v.)*   To provide legal advice; *(n.)* A lawyer.

court   A government body that has the power to resolve legal disputes.

court proceeding   Any hearing or court appearance related to making a decision about a civil or criminal case.

crime   An activity that involves breaking a law.

crime scene   Where a crime takes place.

criminal   A person who has committed a crime.

criminal defendant   A person who is accused of committing a crime and defends himself or herself against criminal charges in a court of law.

damage   The compensation awarded by a court to a person who has suffered a loss or injury due to the unlawful act of another party.

decision   The judgment, or opinion, that is made at the end of trying a case in a court of law.

defend   To speak on behalf of a person or group accused of wrongdoing.

defendant   In a criminal trial, the person charged with committing a crime; in a civil trial, the person or group who is charged of having done something wrong against another party.

defense attorney   The lawyer who represents the defendant.

deposition   An oral statement made by a witness under oath in an authorized place outside of a courtroom.

dispute   A disagreement between two parties.

district court   The name of the main trial court in the federal court system as well as in some state court systems.

docket   A list of court cases that take place within a certain timeframe.

entry-level job   A job that individuals can get with little or no work experience.

ethical   Honest.

ethics   A system of principles that governs how individuals or groups should behave within an organization.

evidence   The testimony, documents, and other information presented in a court of law to prove one's case.

executive branch   The body of government that is responsible for executing and enforcing laws.

expert witness   An individual whom a court recognizes as having the required knowledge, education, expertise, and credentials to address specific issues in a court trial.

federal   Having to do with the U.S. government.

felony   A serious crime such as murder, arson, kidnapping, or drug dealing; a person convicted of a felony may be sentenced to prison for several years or to death.

forensic   The application of science to the examination of legal issues.

general jurisdiction court   A court that has the authority to hear any type of criminal and civil cases.

general practice   A law firm that offers a variety of services in a number of law areas.

grievance   A complaint that employees file against their employers about working conditions.

hearing   A formal proceeding before a judge, administrative agency, or legislature in which evidence and arguments are presented to resolve a dispute about issues of law or fact.

independent contractor   A self-employed individual who performs contractual work for a person or organization.

information technology (IT)   The software and hardware that is used to store, protect, process, transmit, and retrieve information.

internship   The period of work a trainee or a low-level assistant completes in order to gain experience.

issue   A point of disagreement between parties in a lawsuit.

judiciary   The judicial branch of government.

J.D.   Juris doctor; the law degree that individuals must earn to become lawyers.

jurisdiction   The power to interpret and apply the law; also the area in which a judge, attorney, or law enforcement officer has the authority to perform his or her job.

juror   A member of the jury who is sworn to give a verdict on a legal case.

jury   A group of people who have sworn to listen objectively to the facts and issues of a case and then to provide a verdict.

juvenile   An individual under the age of 18.

law   The system of rules and principles that a community recognizes as being enforceable by proper authorities.

law clerk   A law student or lawyer who provides legal research and analysis support to judges.

lawsuit   A legal action that one party (the plaintiff) has brought against another party (the defendant) in a court of law.

lawyering skills   The abilities, such as legal research and legal writing skills, that attorneys need to conduct their work.

legal aid   Legal services that are available to individuals or groups who are unable to afford them.

legislative   Having the authority to make laws.

legislature   The branch of government that has the power to make laws.

liaison   The contact person of a group who maintains communication with other groups.

licensing board   A state agency responsible for regulating the issuance of licenses to attorneys or another profession.

licensure   The act of issuing a professional license.

limited jurisdiction court   A court (such as a family court or bankruptcy court) that may hear only certain types of criminal and court cases.

litigant   A person who is involved in a lawsuit.

litigation   A lawsuit.

litigation consultant   A professional who offers his or her expert services to attorneys involved in lawsuits.

LL.M.   Master of law degree.

lobby   To try to persuade an elected official or another influential person to support a particular cause.

local   Within a certain geographical area.

mediation   A form of alternative dispute resolution in which a third party helps two opposing parties settle a dispute.

memorandum   An informal document that is usually written as a means of communication between staff members of an organization.

misdemeanor   A minor crime, such as vandalism or disorderly conduct; a person committed of a misdemeanor may be required to pay a fine and/or serve a short sentence in jail.

motion   A request to a judge or court to make an order or ruling in favor of the party that asks for such an action.

municipal   Relating to a city or town that has its own local government.

negligent   Habitually being neglectful.

negotiate   To reach an agreement through discussion and compromise.

networking   Making contacts with colleagues and other people who may be able to provide information about job openings.

nonprofit organization   An organization that offers services and products to individuals or groups, but does not have the objective to make money from what they do.

obligation   A duty one performs because of a legal agreement or a moral conviction.

offender   An individual who has committed a crime.

opinion   A formal statement that a judge writes about his or her decision on a court case.

paralegal   A legal assistant; a person with legal training who performs routine legal tasks under the supervision of an attorney.

parole   The conditions a prisoner must fulfill when released early from his or her prison sentence.

partner   A lawyer who is one of the owners of a law firm.

party   One of two sides in a lawsuit.

patron   A customer.

plaintiff   The party who begins a lawsuit against an individual or group.

plea   The official statement that a defendant makes regarding a criminal charge made against him or her.

practice   A lawyer's business.

practice area   The area of law (such as criminal law or employment law) in which a lawyer offers advice and legal services.

practitioner   A person who practices a specific profession, such as law.

probation   A court-supervised sentence that an offender must fulfill instead of a prison sentence.

pro bono   Done for the public good, without pay or other compensation.

professional association   An organization that serves the interests of a profession; its membership is made up of those particular professionals.

prosecute   To put an individual or group on trial.

prosecutor   An attorney who represents the government in a criminal or civil case; he or she is responsible for putting criminal or civil defendants on trial.

regulation   A rule that a government agency establishes in order to fulfill the requirements of a law.

roster   A list of people, such as employees.

ruling   An official decision made by a judge or a court of law.

self-management skills   The abilities a worker needs to perform his or her duties without constant supervision.

sentence   The punishment a judge orders that a person convicted of a crime must serve.

service of process   The delivering of summonses, writs, and other court documents to individuals.

settlement   An agreement made between two parties in a dispute.

solo practitioner   An attorney who practices law alone.

statute   A law created by a legislative body.

subordinate   A person who is lower in rank or status in a workplace.

summons   A court document that directs a person to appear in court to answer a civil complaint that has been made against him or her.

supreme court   The highest court in a court system.

suspect   A person who is believed to have committed a crime.

task   A duty or job that an employee must perform.

teamwork skills   The abilities an employee needs to work effectively as part of a group on a work project or in a work unit.

testify   To answer questions in a court of law.

testimony   A statement that a person makes and swears under oath to be true.

title   A legal document that shows who owns certain property.

tort   A wrongful act for which an injured party can seek damages; for example, an injured party in a car accident may seek compensation for their medical bills.

transcript   An official word for word record of what was said in a trial, hearing, or other legal proceeding.

trial   A formal examination of the facts and issues in a criminal or civil case before a court of law.

try   To conduct a legal case in a court of law.

vendor   A business that sells services and/or products.

verdict   The decision made by a judge or jury about a case.

warrant   A court order that authorizes law enforcement officers to make an arrest, search for evidence, or perform another specific act.

witness   A person who has direct knowledge about a suspect, crime, or crime scene

BIBLIOGRAPHY

A. PERIODICALS

Print and online publications are available for many of the various occupations described in this book. These include magazines, journals, newspapers, newsletters, webzines, and electronic news services. This appendix lists a few publications that serve the interests of attorneys, litigation consultants, legal support professionals, and others.

To learn about other periodicals, you might:

- Talk with librarians, educators, and professionals for recommendations.
- Check out professional and trade associations. Many of them publish journals, newsletters, magazines, and other publications.
- Visit an online bookstore, such as Amazon.com, to view the listings of magazines it has to offer for sale. Use such keywords as *law* or *legal technology* as well as keywords for specific disciplines. If the Web site does not have a particular search engine for magazines, be sure to add the word *magazines* to your keyword. (For example: *attorney magazines.*)

You can also find listings of relevant periodicals at these Web sites: Internet Legal Research Group, http://www.ilrg.com; and Hieros Gamos, http://www.hg.org.

The following are some periodicals that various professionals read. You may be able to find copies at a school, law, academic, or public library. These periodicals may come in print or electronic form, or in both versions.

You may be able to find some of the print publications at a public, school, or academic library. Many of the print magazines also allow limited free access to their articles on the Web. Some of the Web-based publications are free, whereas others require a subscription to access certain issues and other resources. Some publications offer free subscriptions to students or professionals.

Note: Web site addresses were current when this book was written. If a Web site address is no longer valid, you may be able to find its new address by entering the name of the publication into a search engine.

ATTORNEYS

ABA Journal
(American Bar Association)
Phone: (800) 285-2221
http://www.abanet.org/journal

The American Lawyer
Phone: (800) 755-2773
http://www.americanlawyer.com

Findlaw Legal News and Commentary
http://news.findlaw.com

IDEA—The Intellectual Property Law Review
Phone: (603) 228-1541
http://www.idea.fplc.edu

Inside Counsel
Phone: (312) 654-3500
http://www.insidecounsel.com

The Internet Lawyer
Phone: (800) 296-8181
http://www.mddailyrecord.com/newsletters/internetlawyer/pub

IP Law360
Phone: (212) 537-6331
Fax: (212) 537-6371
http://ip.law360.com

Law.com
http://www.law.com

Law Practice
(American Bar Association)
Phone: (800) 285-2221
http://www.abanet.org/lpm/magazine/home.shtml

Minority Law Journal
http://www.minoritylawjournal.com

The National Law Journal
Phone: (800) 274-2893
http://www.nlj.com

JUDGES

APBnews.com
http://www.apbnews.com

The Federal Courts Law Review
(Federal Magistrate Judge Association)
http://www.fclr.org

The Third Branch Newsletter
(Administrative Office of the U.S. Courts)
Phone: (202) 502-2600
http://www.uscourts.gov/ttb

ALTERNATIVE DISPUTE RESOLUTION PRACTITIONERS

ADR World.com
Phone: (202) 536-4113
http://www.adrworld.com

Dispute Resolution Magazine
(American Bar Association)
Phone: (800) 285-2221
http://www.abanet.org/dispute/magazine/home.html

LEGAL SUPPORT PROFESSIONALS

@Law
(NALS Resource Center)
Phone: (918) 582-5188
Fax: (918) 582-5907
http://www.nals.org/atlaw/index.html

Law Office Computing
(James Publishing, Inc.)
Phone: (800) 394-2626 or (714) 755-5450
http://www.lawofficecomputing.com

Legal Assistant Today
Phone: (800) 394-2626 or (714) 555-5450
http://www.legalassistanttoday.com

Legal Management
(Association of Legal Administrators)
http://www.alanet.org/publications/legalmgmt.html

National Paralegal Reporter
(National Federation of Paralegal Associations)
http://www.paralegals.org

LITIGATION SUPPORT PROFESSIONALS

The Legal Investigator
(National Association of Legal Investigators)
http://www.nalionline.org/nalipublications.html

P.I. Magazine
Phone: (800) 836-3088 or (732) 308-3800
http://www.pimagazine.com

LITIGATION CONSULTANTS AND EXPERT WITNESSES

Criminologist

Crime Times
(Wacker Foundations)
http://www.crime-times.org

Criminology: An Interdisciplinary Journal
(American Society of Criminology)
http://www.asc41.com/publications.html

Forensic Psychologist

Psychology, Public Policy, and Law
(American Psychological Association)
Phone: (202) 336-5600
Fax: (202) 336-5568
http://www.apa.org/journals/law

COURT SUPPORT STAFF

Court Technology Bulletin
(National Center for State Courts)
http://ncsconline.org/D_Tech/courttechbulletin

Journal of Court Reporting
(National Court Reporters Association)
http://ncraonline.org/NewsInfo/JCR

Proteus
(National Association of Judiciary Interpreters
    and Translators)
http://www.najit.org/proteus/proteus.html

EDUCATORS

The Chronicle of Higher Education
Phone: (800) 728-2803 or (815) 734-1216
http://chronicle.com

Jurist: Legal News and Research
http://jurist.law.pitt.edu

LIBRARIANS AND INFORMATION SPECIALISTS

Ex Libris
(Marylaine Block)
http://www.marylaine.com/exlibris

KM World Magazine
Phone: (207) 236-8524
http://www.kmworld.com

Law Library Journal
(American Association of Law Libraries)
Phone: (312) 939-4764
http://www.aallnet.org/products/pub_journal.asp

Legal Division Quarterly
(Special Libraries Association)
http://www.slalegal.org/Newsletter

COMMUNICATIONS PROFESSIONALS

Publisher's Weekly
Phone: (800) 278-2991 or (515) 247-2984
http://www.publishersweekly.com

Quill
(Society of Professional Journalists)
Phone: (317) 927-8000
http://www.spj.org/quill_list.asp

MANAGERS AND ADMINISTRATORS

Associations Now
(ASAE and The Center for Association Leadership)
Phone: (888) 950-2723 or (202) 371-0940
http://www.asaecenter.org

The Chronicle of Philanthropy
Phone: (202) 466-1200
http://www.philanthropy.com

MIE Journal
(Management Information Exchange Journal)
http://www.m-i-e.org/journal/journal.htm

The Non-Profit Times
http://www.nptimes.com

ANALYSTS AND EXAMINERS

Actuary

The Actuary Magazine
(Society of Actuaries)
Phone: (847) 706-3500
http://www.soa.org

Compliance Officer

Profiles in Diversity Journal
Phone: (800) 573-2867
http://www.diversityjournal.com

Contract Administrator

Contract Management
(National Contract Management Association)
Phone: (800) 344-8096
http://www.ncmahq.org

Insurance Claims Professional

Claims Magazine
(The National Underwriter Company)
Phone: (800) 543-0874
http://www.claimsmag.com

PROFESSIONS IN POLITICS

Roll Call
Phone: (202) 824-6800
http://www.rollcall.com

B. BOOKS

Listed below are some book titles that can help you learn more about legal and legal-related careers. To learn about other books that may be helpful, ask professionals—individuals and organizations—as well as librarians for suggestions.

CAREER INFORMATION

Arron, Deborah. *What Can You Do with a Law Degree?* 5th ed. Seattle, Wash.: Niche Press, 2003.

Camenson, Blythe. *Careers for Legal Eagles and Other Law-and-Order Types.* 2nd ed. New York: McGraw-Hill, 2005.

Camenson, Blythe. *Real People Working in Law.* Lincolnwood, Ill.: NTC/Contemporary Publishing Company, 1997.

Davis, Mary L. *Working in Law and Justice.* Minneapolis, Minn.: Lerner Publications Co., 1999.

Deaver, Jeff. *The Complete Law School Companion: How to Excel at America's Most Demanding Post-Graduate Curriculum.* 2nd ed. New York: John Wiley & Sons, 1992.

Echaore-McDavid, Susan. *Career Opportunities in Education and Related Services.* New York: Checkmark Books, Facts On File, Inc., 2006.

Echaore-McDavid, Susan. *Career Opportunities in Law Enforcement, Security, and Protective Services.* New York: Checkmark Books, Facts On File, Inc., 2006.

Fair, J. Michael, and Laurence Shatkin, eds. *The O*NET Dictionary of Occupational Titles.* 3rd ed. Indianapolis, Ind.: JIST Publishing, 2004.

Greenburg, Hindi. *The Lawyer's Career Change Handbook: More than 300 Things You Can Do With a Law Degree.* New York: Avon Book, Inc., 1998.

Krannich, Ronald L., and Caryl Rae Krannich. *The Complete Guide to Public Employment.* 3rd ed. Manassas Park, Va.: Impact Publications, 1993.

Strausser, Jeffrey. *Judgment Reversed: Alternative Careers for Lawyers.* Hauppauge, N.Y.: Barron's, 1997.

Turow, Scott. *One L: The Turbulent True Story of a First Year at Harvard Law School.* New York: Warner Books, 1997.

U.S. Bureau of Labor Statistics. *Career Guide to Industries, 2006–07 Edition.* Washington, D.C.: Bureau of Labor Statistics, 2006. Available on the Web. http://www.bls.gov/oco/cg.

U.S. Bureau of Labor Statistics. *Occupational Outlook Handbook 2006–07 Edition.* Washington, D.C.: Bureau of Labor Statistics, 2006. Available on the Web. http://www.bls.gov/oco.

U.S. Department of Labor Employment and Training Administration. *Dictionary of Occupational Titles, Vol. 1.* 4th ed. Washington, D.C.: U.S. Department of Labor Employment and Training Administration, 1991.

ARBITRATOR

Dunlop, John, and Arnold M. Zack. *Mediation and Arbitration of Employment Disputes.* San Francisco, Calif.: Jossey-Bass, 1997.

Goodman, Allan II. *Basic Skills for the New Arbitrator.* 2nd ed. Rockville, Md.: Solomon Publications, 2004.

ATTORNEY

Abrams, Lisa L. *The Official Guide to Legal Specialties.* Chicago, Ill.: The BarBri Group, 2000.

Feinman, Jay M. *Law 101: Everything You Need to Know About the American Legal System.* 2nd ed. New York: Oxford University Press, 2006.

Munneke, Gary. *Careers in Law.* 3rd ed. New York: McGraw-Hill, 2003.

Munneke, Gary. *Opportunities in Law Careers.* New York: McGraw-Hill, 2001.

BOOK EDITOR

Sharpe, Leslie T., and Irene Gunther. *Editing Fact and Fiction: A Concise Guide to Book Editing.* New York: Cambridge University Press, 1994.

BUSINESS APPRAISER

Miles, Michele G. *The Business Appraiser and Litigation Support.* New York: John Wiley, 2001.

CAMPAIGN MANAGER

Faucheux, Ronald A. *Winning Elections: Political Campaign Management, Strategy and Tactics.* New York: M. Evans and Company, Inc., 2003.

Shea, Daniel M., and Michael John Burton. *Campaign Craft: The Strategies, Tactics, and Art of Political Campaign Management.* Westport, Conn.: Praeger Publishers, 2001.

CHILD PROTECTIVE SERVICES CASEWORKER

Berg, Insoo Kim, and Susan Kelly. *Building Solutions in Child Protective Services.* New York: W. W. Norton & Company, 2000.

Dubowitz, Howard, and Diane DePanfilis, eds. *Handbook for Child Protection Practice.* Thousand Oaks, Calif.: Sage Publications, 2000.

COURT INTERPRETER

De Jongh, Elena M. *An Introduction to Court Interpreting: Theory and Practice.* Lanham, Md.: University Press of America, 1992.

COURT REPORTER

Knapp, Mary H., and Robert W. McCormick. *The Complete Court Reporter's Handbook.* 3rd ed. Upper Saddle River, N.J.: Prentice-Hall, 1999.

Fatooh, Audrey, and Barbara Mauk. *Style and Sense: For the Legal Profession: A Handbook for Court Reporters, Transcribers, Paralegals and Secretaries.* Rev. ed. Palm Springs, Calif.: ETC Publications, 1995.

Reily, John R. *'Read That Back, Please': Memoirs of a Court Reporter.* Santa Barbara, Calif.: Fithian Press, 1999.

Saari, David J. *The Court and Free-Lance Reporter Profession.* New York: Quorum Books, January 1988.

CRIMINAL LAWYER/PUBLIC DEFENDER

Bergman, Paul, and Sara J. Berman-Barrett. *The Criminal Law Handbook: Know Your Rights, Survive the System.* 7th ed. Berkeley, Calif.: Nolo Press, 2005.

Hewett, Joan. *Public Defender: Lawyer for the People.* New York: Lodestar Books, 1991.

Wormser, Richard. *Defending the Accused: Stories from the Courtroom.* New York: Franklin Watts, Inc., 2001.

CRIMINOLOGIST

Barlow, Hugh D., and David Kauzlarich. *Introduction to Criminology.* 8th ed. Upper Saddle River, N.J.: Prentice Hall, 2001.

Purpura, Philip. *Criminal Justice: An Introduction.* Boston, Mass.: Butterworth-Heinemann, 1997.

ELDER LAW ATTORNEY

Sabatino, Charles P., et al. *The American Bar Association Legal Guide for Older Americans: The Law Every American over Fifty Needs to Know.* New York: Times Books, 1998.

Strauss, Peter J., and Nancy M. Lederman. *The Elder Law Handbook: A Legal and Financial Survival Guide for Caregivers and Seniors.* 2nd ed. New York: Facts On File, 2003.

EMPLOYMENT LAWYER

Fick, Barbara J., and the American Bar Association. *The American Bar Association Guide to Workplace Law: Everything You Need to Know about Your Rights as an Employee or Employer.* New York: Times Books, 1997.

Steingold, Fred S., and Amy Delpo. *The Employer's Legal Handbook.* 7th ed. Berkeley, Calif.: Nolo Press, 2005.

ETHICS OFFICER

Ciulla, Joanne B. (editor). *Ethics, the Heart of Leadership.* 2nd ed. Westport, Conn.: Praeger Paperbacks, 2004.

Seglin, Jeffrey L., and Norman R. Augustine. *The Good, The Bad, and Your Business: Choosing the Right When Ethical Dilemmas Pull You Apart.* New York: John Wiley & Sons, 2000.

FORENSIC ACCOUNTANT

Manning, George A. *Financial Investigation and Forensic Accounting.* 2nd ed. Boca Raton, Fla.: CRC Press, 2005.

FORENSIC PSYCHOLOGIST

Deyoub, Paul L., and Gretchen V. K. Douthit. *A Practical Guide to Forensic Psychology.* Northvale, N.J.: Jason Aronson, 1996.

Wrightsman, Lawrence S. *Forensic Psychology.* Belmont, Calif.: Wadsworth Pub. Co., 2000.

INDIAN LAW ATTORNEY

Conference of Western Attorneys General. *American Indian Law Deskbook.* 3rd ed. Boulder, Colo.: University Press of Colorado, 2004.

INSURANCE CLAIMS PROFESSIONAL

Schrayer, Robert M. *Opportunities in Insurance Careers.* New York: McGraw-Hill, 1999.

INTELLECTUAL PROPERTY ATTORNEY

Pressman, David. *Patent It Yourself.* 11th ed. Berkeley, Calif.: Nolo Press, 2005.

U.S. Dept. of Commerce. *Patents and How to Get One: A Practical Handbook.* Mineloa, N.Y.: Dover Publications, 2000.

JUDGE

Guide to the Federal Courts: An Introduction to the Federal Courts and their Operation. Know Your Government series. Washington, D.C.: WANT Publishing Co., 1985.

Bianchi, Anne. *Everything You Need to Know about Family Court.* New York: Rosen Publishing Group, 2000.

Burns, Robert P. *A Theory of the Trial.* Princeton, N.J.: Princeton University Press, 1999.

Neubauer, David W., and Stephen S. Meinhold. *Judicial Process: Law, Courts, and Politics in the United States.* 4th ed. Belmont, Calif.: Wadsworth Publishing, 2006.

O'Brien, David M. (editor) *Judges on Judging: Views from the Bench.* 2nd ed. Washington, D.C.: CQ Press, 2003.

Satter, Robert. *Doing Justice, A Trial Judge At Work.* New York: American Lawyer Books, Simon & Schuster, 1990.

Tobin, Robert W. *Creating the Judicial Branch: The Unfinished Reform.* Williamsburg, Va.: National Center for State Courts, 1999.

JUVENILE COUNSELOR

Humes, Edward. *No Matter How Loud I Shout: A Year in the Life of Juvenile Court.* New York: Simon and Schuster, 1996.

LAW SCHOOL CAREER COUNSELOR

Figler, Howard, and Richard Nelson Bolles. *The Career Counselor's Handbook.* Berkeley, Calif.: Ten Speed Press, 1999.

LEGAL ADMINISTRATOR

Lynton, Jonathon, Terri Mick Lyndall, and Donna Masinter. *Law Office Management.* 2nd ed. Albany, N.Y.: Delmar Publishers, 1996.

Weisbord, Ellen, Bruce H. Charnov, and Jonathan Lindsey. *Managing People in Today's Law Firm: The Human Resources Approach to Surviving Change.* Westport, Conn.: Quorum Books, 1995.

LEGAL MANAGEMENT CONSULTANT

Biswas, Sugata, and Daryl Twitchell. *Management Consulting: A Complete Guide to the Industry.* 2nd ed. New York: John Wiley, 2001.

LEGAL NURSE CONSULTANT

Bogart, Julie Brewer (editor). *Legal Nurse Consulting: Principles and Practice.* 2nd ed. Boca Raton, Fla.: CRC Press, 2002.

LEGAL REPORTER

Alexander, S. L. *Covering the Courts: A Handbook for Journalists.* 2nd ed. Lanham, Md.: Rowman and Littlefield Publications, 2003.

Cappon, Rene J. *The Associated Press Guide to Newswriting.* Foster City, Calif.: IDG Books Worldwide, 2000.

Seidman, David. *Exploring Careers in Journalism.* New York: The Rosen Publishing Group, Inc., 2000.

LEGAL SEARCH CONSULTANT

Gurney, Darrell W. *Headhunters Revealed! Career Secrets for Choosing and Using Professional Recruiters.* Los Angeles, Calif.: Hunter Arts Publishing, 2000.

Jupina, Andrea A. *The Recruiter's Research Blue Book.* 2nd ed. Fitzwilliam, N.H.: Kennedy Information, 2000.

LEGAL SUPPORT PROFESSIONAL

Anderson, Austin G. (editor). *Merriam-Webster's Legal Secretaries Handbook.* 2nd ed. Springfield, Mass.: Merriam Webster, 1996.

De Vries, Mary Ann. *Legal Secretary's Complete Handbook,* 4th ed. Englewood Cliffs, N.J.: Prentice Hall Trade, 1992.

Gilmore, Diane M. *Legal Office: Document Processing.* Cincinnati, Ohio: South-Western Educational Publishing, 1997.

Morton, Joyce. *Legal Office Procedures.* 7th ed. Upper Saddle River, N.J.: Prentice Hall, 2006.

Roper, Brent D. *Using Computers in the Law Office,* 4th ed. Clifton Park, N.Y.: Thomson Delmar Learning, 2003.

LEGAL WRITING INSTRUCTOR

Garner Bryan A. *The Elements of Legal Style.* 2nd ed. New York: Oxford University Press, 2002.

LEGISLATOR

Davidson, Roger H., and Walter Oleszek. *Congress and Its Members.* 9th ed. Washington, D.C.: CQ Press, 2003.

Price, David Eugene. *The Congressional Experience.* 3rd ed. Boulder, Colo.: Westview Press, 2004.

McDonough, John E. *Experiencing Politics: A Legislator's Stories of Government and Health Care.* Berkeley, Calif.: University of California Press, 2000.

LITIGATION CONSULTANT

Feder, Harold A. *Succeeding as an Expert Witness: Increasing Your Impact and Income.* Glenwood Springs, Colo.: Tageh Press, 1993.

Poynter, Dan. *Expert Witness Handbook: Tips and Techniques for the Litigation Consultant.* 3rd ed. Santa Barbara, Calif.: Para Publishing, 2004.

LOBBYIST

Guyer, Robert L. *Guide to State Legislative Lobbying.* Rev. ed. Gainesville, Fla.: Engineering the Law, Inc., 2003.

Rosenthal, Alan. *The Third House: Lobbyists and Lobbying in the States.* 2nd ed. Washington, D.C.: CQ Press, 2001.

Wolpe, Bruce C., and Bertram J. Levine. *Lobbying Congress: How the System Works.* Washington, D.C.: Congressional Quarterly, 1996.

LOCAL ELECTED OFFICIAL

Cohen, Eleanor, and Len Wood, eds. *Elected Official's Little Handbook: A Portable Guide for Local Government Legislators.* Ranchos Palos Verdes, Calif.: Training Shoppe, 1994.

NEUTRAL

Goodman, Allan H. *Basic Skills for the New Mediator.* 2nd ed. Rockville, Md.: Solomon Publications, 2004.

Kolb, Deborah M. *When Talk Works: Profiles of Mediators.* San Francisco, Calif.: Jossey-Bass, 1997.

Nolan-Haley, Jacqueline M. *Alternative Dispute Resolution in a Nutshell.* 2nd ed. St. Paul, Minn.: West Information Publishing Group, 2001.

NONPROFIT ORGANIZATION DIRECTOR

Drucker, Peter. *Managing the Non-Profit Organization: Principles and Practices.* New York: HarperCollins, 1990.

Wolf, Thomas. *Managing a Nonprofit Organization in the Twenty-First Century.* 3rd ed. New York: Simon & Schuster, 1999.

PARALEGAL

Estrin, Chere B. *Everything You Need to Know About Being a Legal Assistant.* Albany, N.Y.: Delmar Publishers, 1995.

Fins, Alice. *Opportunities in Paralegal Careers.* Rev. ed. New York: McGraw-Hill, 2005.

Larbalestrier, Deborah E. *Paralegal Practice and Procedure: A Practical Guide for the Legal Assistant.* 3rd ed. Englewood Cliffs, N.J.: Prentice Hall Press, 1994.

Southard, Jo Lynn. *Paralegal Career Starter.* 2nd ed. New York: LearningExpress, 2002.

Statsky, William P. *Introduction to Paralegalism : Perspectives, Problems, and Skills.* 6th ed. Clifton, N.Y.: Thomson Delmar Learning, 2002.

Wagner, Andrea. *How to Land Your First Paralegal Job: An Insider's Guide to the Fastest Growing Profession of the New Millennium.* 4th ed. Upper Saddle River, N.J.: Pearson Prentice Hall, 2004.

PROPERTY MANAGER

Griswold, Robert S. *Property Management for Dummies.* New York: Hungry Minds, 2001.

PROSECUTOR

Baker, Mark. *D.A. Prosecutors in Their Own Words.* New York: Simon and Schuster, 1999.

SCOPIST

Sober, W. Charley, and Linda Knipes-Sober. *Scopistry.* 2nd ed. Humble, Tex.: Logical Resources, 2000.

WEB DESIGNER

Burleson, Janet. *Conducting the Web Designer Job Interview.* Kitrell, N.C.: Rampant Techpress, 2004.

Niederst Robbins, Jennifer. *Web Design in a Nutshell.* 2nd ed. Sebastopol, Calif.: O'Reilly Media, Inc., 2001.

INDEX

SENIOR HIGH SCHOOL LIBRARY
SUNNYSIDE, WASHINGTON